D1321082

The Anonymous Marie de France

The Anonymous
Marie de France

R. HOWARD BLOCH

The University of Chicago Press / Chicago and London

R. Howard Bloch is the Augustus R. Street Professor of French at Yale University. He is the author or editor of six books, most recently *Medievalism and the Modernist Temper* (1995) and *God's Plagiarist: Being an Account of the Fabulous Industry and Irregular Commerce of the Abbé Migne* (1994), the latter published by the University of Chicago Press.

The University of Chicago Press, Chicago 60637
The University of Chicago Press, Ltd., London
© 2003 by The University of Chicago
All rights reserved. Published 2003
Printed in the United States of America
12 11 10 09 08 07 06 05 04 03   1 2 3 4 5

ISBN: 0-226-05968-5 (cloth)

This book is published with the assistance of the Frederick W. Hilles Publication Fund of Yale University.

Library of Congress Cataloging-in-Publication Data

Bloch, R. Howard.
    The anonymous Marie de France / R. Howard Bloch.
        p.   cm.
    Includes bibliographical references and index.
    ISBN: 0-226-05968-5 (alk. paper)
    1. Marie, de France, 12th cent. — Criticism and interpretation.   I. Title.

PQ1495 .B53 2003
841'.1—DC21

                                                                2002014840

Contents

Acknowledgments

It is, of course, impossible to thank adequately those who have contributed to this book which has fermented slowly in various academic and archival vats over the course of the last few years. I would like to express my appreciation of my students at the University of California, Berkeley, where the section on Marie's *Lais* came into being; my students at Columbia University where the section on the *Fables* was hatched; and my students at Yale University who have been through Purgatory on my account. The participants in the NEH Seminar on Marie conducted at Columbia in the summer of 1996 deserve special praise for pushing me in the direction of a book focused equally on Marie's three works. Of those with whom dialogue about Marie has been particularly intense, I express my deep gratitude to Margaret Pappano of Columbia, Karen Jambeck of Western Connecticut State, Zrinka Stahulak of Boston University, and Chantal Marechal of Virginia Commonwealth University and the guardian angel of Marie studies in the United States. Were it not for Scott Hiley's merciless trimming of my prose, the present volume might be less compact than at present. For this he is to be thanked, along with Alan Thomas and Randy Petilos who, again, have made publishing with Chicago a privilege and a treat.

Parts of this book have appeared in other publications. Portions of chapter 1 appeared in "The Medieval Text—'Guigemar'—as a Provocation to the Discipline of Medieval Studies," *Romanic Review* 79 (1988): 63–73; reprinted by permission of *Romanic Review*. Other portions of chapter 1 and portions of chapter 2 appeared in "Das Altfranzösische Lai als Ort von Trauer und Gedächtnis," in *Gedächtnis als Raum*, ed. Renate Lachmann and

x

Anselm Haverkamp (Frankfurt: Suhrkamp, 1991), pp. 189–206; reprinted by permission of Suhrkamp Verlag. Other portions of chapter 2 appeared in "The Dead Nightingale: Orality in the Tomb of Old French Literature," *Culture and History* 3 (1988): 63–78; reprinted by permission of Taylor and Francis, http://www.tandf.co.uk. Portions of chapter 3 appeared in "New Philology and Old French," *Speculum* 65 (1990): 38–58; reprinted by permission of *Speculum*. Other portions of chapter 3 appeared in "The Lay and the Law: Sexual/Textual Transgression in the *Lais* of Marie de France," *Stanford French Review* 14 (1990): 181–210, published by Anma Libri; reprinted by permission of Anma Libri. Portions of chapter 4 appeared in "Other Worlds and Other Words in the Works of Marie de France," in *The World and Its Rival: Essays on Literary Imagination in Honor of Per Nykrog,* ed. Tom Conley and Kathryn Karczewska (Amsterdam: Rodopi, 1999), pp. 39–57; reprinted by permission of Rodopi BV.

Note on Texts

The edition of the *Lais* I have used is that of Alfred Ewert, introduced by Glyn Burgess (Bristol: Bristol Classical Press, 1995). This edition is based on *Die Lais der Marie de France,* ed. Karl Warnke (Halle: Niemeyer, 1885). As for the English translation, I have used the Glyn Burgess and Keith Busby *Lais of Marie de France* (London: Penguin, 1986), modified where appropriate. For the *Fables,* the edition and translation used for all citations is that of Harriet Spiegel (Toronto: Medieval Academy of America, 1987). Quotations and translations of the *Espurgatoire Seint Patriz,* unless otherwise indicated, are from the Michael J. Curley edition, which is taken from that of Warnke: *Saint Patrick's Purgatory* (Binghamton: Medieval and Renaissance Texts and Studies, 1993).

Introduction

The voice that broke the silence of the forest was the voice of Anon. Some one heard the song and remembered it for it was later written down, beautifully, on parchment. Thus the singer had his audience, but the audience was so little interested in his name that he never thought to give it. The audience was itself the singer; "Terly, terlow" they sang; and "By, by lullay" filling in the pauses, helping out with a chorus. Every body shared in the emotions of Anons song, and supplied the story. VIRGINIA WOOLF

Let us assume for the moment that Marie de France was a woman and that she was French. It's not that I have strong evidence to the contrary or that I want to unsettle you by suggesting that the person you have always thought to be France's first woman poet—the author of the *Lais,* the *Fables,* the *Espurgatoire Seint Patriz*—was neither. Rather, concrete knowledge about her is so meager as to render imprudent anything but the most militant skepticism about almost every aspect of her life: where she was born and to what rank, who her parents might have been, whether she was married or single, where she lived and might have traveled, whether she dwelled in a cloister or at court, whether in England or France, whom she might have known in either place, of whom she was thinking in the dedication of her works, what she might have heard in the oral culture of twelfth-century France and what she might have read in the increasingly learned culture of the same era, whether she knew, or even wrote, the anonymous Breton lais akin to those more certainly attributed to her, whether she had come into contact, and in what version, with the works of this first generation of romancers, among whom Marie de France, like Chrétien de Troyes, Béroul, Thomas, or Robert de Boron, remains primarily—that is to say, only—a name.

I

But a name is not a bad place to begin, and here Marie is more forth-coming than most. In the three works attributed to her she names herself three times: at the beginning of the *lai* "Guigemar" ("Hear, my lords, the words of Marie, who, when she has the chance, does not squander her talents," "Oëz, seignurs, ke dit Marie, Ki en sun tens pas ne s'oblie" [v. 3]); in the epilogue to the *Fables* ("To end these tales I've here narrated/And into Romance tongue translated,/I'll give my name, for memory:/I am from France, my name's Marie," "Al finement de cest escrit/que en romanz ai treité et dit,/me numerai pur remembrance:/Marie ai nun, si sui de France" [v. 1]); and at the end of the *Espurgatoire* ("I, Marie, have put/The Book of Purgatory into French," "Jo, Marie, ai mis en memoire/Le Livre de l'Es-purgatoire/en romanz" [v. 2297]).

What is in a name?

At once too little. And too much. But first and foremost, a history, and a troubled one at that. The troubled history of the name "Marie de France" began in 1581 with its first citation in Claude Fauchet's *Recueil de l'Ori-gine de la Langue et Poesie Françoise,* where we read under the title "CXXVII. poetes François viuans auant l'an M.":

> Marie de France. LXXXIIII. Marie de France ne porte ce surnom pour ce qu'elle fust du sang des Rois: mais pour ce qu'elle estoit natifue de France, car elle dit:
>
> > "Au finement de cet escrit,
> > Me nommerai par remembrance,
> > Marie ai nom, si sui de France."
>
> Elle a mis en vers François les fables d'Esope moralisees, qu'elle dit auoir translatees d'Anglois en François. Pour l'amour au Conte Guilleaume,
> > "Le plus vaillant de ce Roiaume."[1]

Fauchet's characterization was repeated by Renaissance humanists. At the end of the sixteenth century, we find Marie's name in the works of François Grudé, sieur de La Croix du Maine (1552–92):

> MARIE de FRANCE, damoiselle Françoise for bien versee en la poësie vsitee de son temps, sçavoir en l'an de salut 1260, ou enuiron. Elle a mis en vers François les Fables d'Esope Moralisees, lesquelles elle a traduites de langue Angloise, en la nostre Françoise, comme tesmoigne Claude Fauchet en son recueil des Poëtes,

as well as in those of Antoine Du Verdier (1544–1600).[2]

For a long time Marie de France was assumed to have written in the sec-

ond half of the thirteenth century and to have been the author only of
the *Fables*. The first, in fact, to consider Marie as having written both the
Fables and the *Lais* was the Chaucerian Thomas Tyrwhitt (1730–86), who
notes that "the chief, perhaps the only, collection of these *Lais* now extant,
was translated into French octosyllable verse by a Poetess, who calls herself
Marie; the same without doubt, who made the translation of *Esope*, . . . , in
the reign of St. Louis."[3] Tyrwhitt's assumption that the *Lais* are the work of
a single author, that this author is named Marie, and that this Marie is the
same as the author of the *Fables* will be repeated in the first great essay devoted exclusively to her, that of the Abbé La Rue, *Dissertation on the Life and
Writings of Mary, an Anglo-Norman Poetess of the 13th Century, by Mons. La
Rue,* published by the Society of Antiquaries of London in 1797.[4] Indeed,
they have been repeated ever since: in the first edition of Marie's works, issued between 1820 and 1832 under the title *Poésies de Marie de France, Poète
Anglo-Normand du XIIIe Siècle ou Recueil de Lais, Fables et Autres Productions
de cette Femme Célèbre,* by J.-B.-B. de Roquefort; in F.-J.-M. Raynouard's
review in the *Journal des Savants* of 1820;[5] in the works of the great medi-
evalists after the Franco-Prussian War, Gaston Paris and Joseph Bédier,
though here the corpus covered by the name "Marie" remains somewhat
unstable. Paris, for example, attributes the anonymous Breton lais "Tydorel," "Guingamor," and "Tyolet" to Marie without saying exactly why,
just as his father, Paulin Paris, had included the "Evangile des femmes"
among her works.[6]

Still, we have only a name. For Marie's self-identification is the only clue
to the person, and certainty ends there. The name, rather than providing
clarity, produces instead a desire for more information, yields in fact a myriad of attempts at fuller identification of the name with a historical person.
Marie de France has been identified alternately as Marie de Champagne, the
daughter of Aliénor d'Aquitaine and Louis VII (Winkler); as Marie de
Compiègne mentioned in "L'Evangile des femmes" (Chabaille, Mall); as a
nun named Marie who wrote a "Vie de sainte Audrée" (Södergard); as Marie
de Boulogne, daughter of Stephen of Blois and Matilda of Boulogne and
abbess of Romsey (Knapton); as the illegitimate daughter of Geoffrey of
Anjou, the half-sister of King Henry II and abbess of Shaftesbury from 1181
to 1216 (Bullock-Davis, Crosland, Fox); as the abbess of Reading, the place
where the manuscript H of the *Lais* might have been composed (Levi); as
the daughter of the Norman count Galeran de Meulan, the wife of Hugues
Talbot, baron of Cleuville (Holmes, Flum).[7]

The aristocratic particle of her name, the "de" which normally indicates noble genealogy, and the "France" which could at the time have referred only to what is the "Ile-de-France," are misleading. Since the lack of any other reference to a "Marie de France" suggests that she was not of royal blood, that is, not of the House of France, the "de France" has to serve as a geographic designation, a term of origin. And, as a term of origin, it means, as critics have assumed since the eighteenth century, that she probably did not live in France. The arguments mustered in favor, if not of an English origin, then at least of English residence, are so numerous and diverse as to be almost convincing. Some are based on impressionistic notions of na-tional character—the melancholy British. "The English muse seems to have inspired her," writes the Abbé La Rue, who insists on calling her "Mary"; "all her subjects are sad and melancholy; she appears to have designed to melt the hearts of her readers, either by the unfortunate situation of her hero, or by some truly afflicting catastrophe. Thus she always speaks to the soul, calls forth all its feelings, and very frequently throws it into the utmost consternation."[8] De Roquefort, whose edition is dedicated to Gervais de la Rue, follows in the same depressive vein: "Ces *Lais* composés suivant l'usage du temps, sont généralement remarquables par le récit de quelques sin-gulières catastrophes."[9] So too, Gaston Paris incorporates the notion of mis-fortune into his definition of the lai, which contains "quelque histoire d'amour et généralement de malheur."[10] In the generation just after Paris, Alfred Jeanroy emphasizes Marie's melancholic tone; and in the generation following Jeanroy, Ernest Hoepffner finds her "always grave and serious," hardly capable of mustering a "pale smile."[11] For Jean-Charles Payen Marie is a poet whose sense of the fragility of happiness and whose disaffection with the world are the signs of a "pessimisme assez radical." Milena Mikhaïlova calculates that the *Lais* contain "eleven fatalities, of which two are burned alive, the death of a bird, a false death, and many wounded."[12]

Others seek linguistic proof of domicile, beginning with her name and the fact that names that contain geographical indications—Picard, Lalle-mand, or Langlois, for example—indicate that the person is a foreigner. Marie de France, by such logic, is believed to have lived abroad, a hypothesis supported by topological arguments: the place-names contained in the *Lais* cover a wealth of English and French sites belonging to Great Britain and Wales as well as to the Armorican Peninsula and Normandy.[13] The ono-mastics of English place-names is further reinforced by the fact that the *Lais,* or at least the Harley manuscript held in the British Museum, show characteristics of a continental writer working at the Anglo-Norman court. They offer proof of Marie's knowledge of the English language as well as of Latin and Breton / Welsh.[14] Marie professes to have rendered the *Fables* from an English collection of beast tales. The bilingual titles of "Bisclav-ret," "Laüstic," and "Chevrefoil" as well as the translation of certain French, Welsh, or Celtic words into English add to the insular argument.

The attempt to locate Marie geographically, to root her in the soil of a particular place, may in fact have marginally improved the health of a few medieval scholars on both sides of the Channel by drawing them out of the library into the great outdoors. Constance Bullock-Davis claims to have found the historical locus of action of "Milun" on the basis of a present-day "natural breeding place for swans . . . stretching from the mouth of the Rhymney to Portskewitt" and of the average weight and age of young male swans in the region.[15] In one of the few examples of medieval scholarship that might have involved automobile travel, Glyn Burgess wonders if it were possible that the "straight road," the "dreit chemin," that Marie mentions as running between Caerwent and the castle in "Milun" corresponds to the "Roman Julia Strata, running from Chepstow to Newport, the modern A48?"[16] Similarly, Gustave Cohen, in an example of amateur anthropology, recounts the story of how, having located the site of the action of "Les Deus Amanz" on a military map of the Vexin, he was "so piqued by curiosity" that he gathered his students ("mes agrégatifs et agrégatives") for an excursion to Pitre, de la Seine et de Pont-de-l'Arche. "Imagine our surprise," Cohen ex-claims, "at finding ourselves actually before a hill looming over the right bank of the river." "I spotted a peasant and said to my disciples, 'Now you're going to see how one carries out an ethnological inquiry. When it comes to making a fool of oneself, a professor is as good as anyone else.' Standing in front of a little plaque reading 'La colline des Deux-Amants,' I asked him Why?" What came out of the mouth of the peasant, "in whom all literary influence is excluded just as it was for the drafters of the military map," were the "essential elements" of "Les Deus Amanz," which, having been pre-served in situ since the twelfth century, Cohen concludes, "he must have learned in his childhood or adolescence."[17]

For a long time it was felt that Marie's dedications might offer insight into her origin, yet they too remain a mystery. The *Lais* are dedicated to a "nobles reis," which scholars have associated with various kings by the name of Henry. We do not know, however, whether Marie's Henry was, as her earliest critics thought, Henry III (Mall, La Rue); Henry II, who reigned from 1154 to 1189 (more later); his son, Henry the Young King, who was crowned in 1173 but died in 1183 (Levi); or, as Roger Dragonetti maintains, no king at all.[18] As for the Guillaume to whom the *Fables* are dedicated, speculation has ranged from William Longsword, the natural son of Henry II and Rosamonde Clifford (Warnke), to William Marshal (Levi, Soudée), Count William of Gloucester, the grandson of Henri I (Ahlström), William of Mandeville (Painter), William of Warren, and Guillaume de Dampierre from Flanders.[19]

The question of dates is every bit as vexing as that of dedication.[20] For a long time, it was widely believed that Marie de France lived in the thirteenth century, though the dates now given coincide roughly with the last half of the twelfth. Some scholars hold that the so-called anonymous Breton lais— "Désiré," "Tydorel," "Guingamor," "Graelant," "Doon"—were written before those of Marie; others, after hers, Marie being the sole source.[21] Still others see a common source for Marie and these anonymous tales, some of which are not so anonymous, like the obscene "Lai d'Ignauré" probably written by Renaut de Beaujeu and the "Lai de l'Ombre" of Jean Renart. The narrative lai as a genre flourished approximately in the hundred years between the mid-twelfth and mid-thirteenth centuries, though the lyric lai survived much longer and indeed became one of the fixed forms of the later Middle Ages.

We do not know for sure what Marie de France might have read, though it is held generally that this founding author of the "Matière de Bretagne" knew the so-called classical novels, especially the *Roman d'Eneas,* of which one scholar claims unsoundly that she is the author.[22] The sources of the *Lais* are, again, almost a complete mystery despite the plethora of attempts to locate models in the oral Celtic tradition of Wales as well as in late Latin, in the indigenous Breton tradition of La Petite Bretagne or the Armorican Peninsula, and even, as has been suggested recently, in biblical material. The mysterious boats, fantastic beasts, metamorphosing birds, werewolves, and fairies contained in the *Lais* attract like a magnet the folklorists for whom every analogy, in a kind of scholarly magical thinking, becomes a potential source. In the end, we really cannot say with certainty whether Marie's sources were written or oral. Indeed, Marie may speak in the prologue to "Guigemar" of the "tales she knows to be true, of which the Bretons have made a lai"; she may speak, as at the beginning of "Eliduc," of "the tale and the reason of an ancient Breton lai" ("De un mut ancïen lai bretun/Le cunte e tute la reisun/Vus dirai, si cum jeo entent/La verité, mun escïent" [v. 1]). Yet we do not really know precisely to what the "ancïen lai bretun" refers, or even, for that matter, whether the "entent" of the following line itself refers to "hearing," in which case we might assume that Marie had heard the lai sung, or to "understanding," a reading that is supported by the following line, which refers to the truth of the tale, according to Marie's comprehension. On at least one occasion Marie avows both an oral and a written source, when, in "Chevrefoil," she affirms, "many people have recited it to me and I have also found it in a written form" ("Plusurs le me unt cunté et dit / E jeo l'ai trové en escrit" [vv. 5–6]). We are a little better informed about the *Fables* that Marie claims originate in Aesop, were translated from Greek to Latin and from Latin to the English book of King Alfred, from which she renders them into French. Even here, however, we have no trace of any book of Alfred, and the first forty of Marie's animal tales seem to have been taken directly from the Latin Romulus tradition, while the remaining sixty originate in an unidentifiable mixture of various Ysopets. It is only in the case of the *Espurgatoire* that we possess a definite, coherent, and integral source in H. de Saltrey's *Tractatus Sancti Patricii;* and yet we know so little about H., who like Marie is only a name—yea, less than a name, only an initial—that H.'s text is merely another tantalizing wall, like that surrounding the entrance to Purgatory, through which no pilgrim may pass.

Despite our relative certainty concerning dates, the questions of geographical location, sources, milieu, and dedication are all to a greater or lesser extent mysteries that add up to the brutal fact that we do not have a clue as to who Marie de France, "cette poétesse sur laquelle on ne sait à peu près rien" in the words of Jean-Charles Payen, may have been.[23] Marie remains only a name, a name as detached as one can imagine from any more specific reference to a supposedly real person living in a particular place within a particular social setting at a particular time. Indeed, and I am not the first to suggest it, Marie de France comes as close as one can imagine to being anonymous. In this she is hardly unique: the authors believed to have written in Old French in the twelfth century are, like the sources of the early epic, either completely anonymous and referred to by the titles assigned by modern editors to their works—the *Roland* poet or the *William* poet, for example—or, like Chrétien de Troyes, Béroul, Thomas, or Robert de Boron, are only names attached to a work or to a body of works, names that refer to a hypothetical real person about whom we know little else.

Now what is interesting about being anonymous is, first, that it does not preclude an identity, it does not prevent our forming an image, and sometimes a rather precise image, of the person designated by a name. If we open, for example, the *Dictionnaire des lettres françaises,* volume *Moyen Age,* we find several entries under the rubric "Anonyme"—the "Anonyme de

Bayeux" and the "Anonyme de Béthune." Under the first we discover that
the "Anonyme de Bayeux" is simply another way of referring to the author
of two texts from the fourteenth century, *L'Advocacie Notre-Dame* and *La
Chapelle de Bayeux,* whose attribution is dubious: "Il faut donc, semble-t-il,
attribuer ces textes à un (ou deux) Anonyme(s) de Bayeux," concludes the
author of this particular entry. Under the second entry we read that the "Anonyme de Béthune" was the author of two prose chronicles edited at the
beginning of the thirteenth century and that "L'Anonyme était un Artésien
entré au service de la maison de Béthune sans doute en qualité de ménéstrel.
Il suivit Robert VII de Béthune en Angleterre, lorsque celui-ci se rattacha au
parti de Jean sans Terre, et participa par la suite à de nombreux événements
qui devaient figurer plus tard dans ses chroniques."[24] In the early thirteenth
century, the "Anonyme de Béthune" may have been anonymous, but for us
he is someone: someone assumed to have a gender, someone endowed with
biography, a life story according to which he participated in the events contained in his chronicle, someone who, finally, left his mark on history.[25]

For the twelfth and thirteenth centuries anonymity means merely that
we are uncertain about attribution, about matching the name of a particular work of literature with the name of a particular person, that is to say,
with other works or documents considered not to be literary in nature that
are attached to the same name; and thus we cannot match the name with
the places, dates, and deeds of a life. Or it means that such extraliterary documentation does not exist, cannot be found, that we are left to speculate
about the particular anonymous in question.

A lack of evidence has never prevented such speculation. On the contrary, one might even conclude from the precision with which Marie as well
as the Henrys and Williams to whom she dedicated her works has been
associated with this or that historical figure, alongside the precision with
which the place-names in the *Lais* and the *Espurgatoire* have been located geographically in England and France, that scholars abhor nothing so much
as the vacuum of the anonymous. They are driven quickly, automatically,
impulsively to identify, that is, to name; they cannot resist, even in the face
of the most evident lack of evidence, ascribing an identity, a life, to the in-
tolerable emptiness behind the names that, for the anonymous of the High
Middle Ages, are a veil behind which one slips easily but surely into ignorance. The resistance to anonymity, the will to identify, shapes the medi-
evalist's desire and, as Marie maintains in the prologue, is no different from
the desire of any reader to understand. Nor, as we shall see in the chapters
to follow, can the desire to know who Marie was be separated from sexual

knowledge, the desire of the body to know another, expressed on the level of theme.

This is why it seems so often in dealing with medieval texts that the less we know about the person attached to a name, the more speculation such a name, unencumbered by details enracinated in history or in any discourse outside of the text, engenders. The case of Marie de France is no different from any other case of authorial attribution in which we simply do not possess sufficient documentation to allow conjecture to reach closure. In this respect Marie remains an open text, an open book. Second, and the point could not follow more closely upon the wild, hypothetical, broadness of the historical characters assimilated to Marie's name, the urge toward such identification was not a uniquely medieval problem. At least it was not a problem lived in quite the same way as that of authorial attribution after the French Revolution, and, where medieval studies are concerned, in the high age of edition, especially in the second half of the nineteenth century. Here we touch upon one of those liminal moments in the history of a discipline at which the givens around which it comes into being cannot be detached from the characteristics attributed to the object of study. It is a little-known but nonetheless fundamental fact of medieval studies, for example, that the various versions of the language written in twelfth-century France did not, in the era predating fixed spelling, exist in any way resembling the dialectical varieties—Picard, Anglo-Norman, Champenois—to be found in grammars of Old French. The latter were, as Bernard Cerquiglini and others have shown, the product of nineteenth-century regularizations of spelling rooted sometimes in general grammatical patterns and sometimes in the fantasy of regularization itself.[26] Then, too, the famous families of manuscripts, the "stemmata," established by the comparative philologists of the nineteenth century according to contemporary models for the evolution of biological species correspond only vaguely to the medieval concept of textual production. Despite the urge to establish hard and fast trees and branches of relation and descent (usually from a lost original), the analogy between variant physiological traits and manuscript variants works only to the degree that it is not taken for the reality of the medieval text.[27]

To say that Marie de France comes as close as possible to being anonymous—to existing for us primarily as a name—is not to say, according to certain assumptions about authorship in the age of copyright, that she remains unconscious, or even that she remains unconscious of the question of authorial identity. It is easy to presuppose that a poet of the twelfth century who does not identify him- or herself was simply unaware of the conditions that make literary life since the Enlightenment seem authentic, that is, attached to the believable experience of an individual (and preferably a suffering) subject, sophisticated and consciously self-reflexive or complex. The anonymous work is synonymous with the naive work, the work that is not the product of an individual consciousness, which consciousness since the romantic period has been the equivalent of genius. Paradoxically, it has been seen historically as belonging to no one, or to everyone; for the anonymous work is either an orphan or a prostitute, either no one's child or everyone's baby, even when the baby is conceived, as issuing, according to the early theories of the origin of epic—those of Wolff, Lachmann, Herder, the Schlegels and the Grimms (but also to some extent Gaston Paris)—from something so noble as the collective soul of the people.

The concept of individual authorship is by no means unknown in the great anonymous centuries of French literature. On the contrary, Alistair Minnis has shown in some detail that the Latin tradition possessed elaborate means to discuss the title, cause, intention, rhetorical circumstances, usefulness, order, authenticity, and genre or part of philosophy to which a work belongs.[28] What is interesting where Marie de France is concerned is, first, that discussions of authorship occur in prologues, and no one is more devoted to the prologue than she. Second, the prologue is the site for a particular kind of discussion of authorship oriented toward the question precisely of the gloss. Moreover, we know from the Latin prologues contemporaneous to Marie that discussions of authorship are not naive at all; they can be quite sophisticated, involving not only the Aristotelian questions of efficient, material, formal, and final causes but questions of performance along with subsequent interpretations of the work.[29]

Given that the concept of authorship exists in the twelfth century and that it exists on a level of sophistication prospectively reminiscent even of the formal analyses of today, we must assume that for Marie anonymity is not simply a matter of lack of attention to detail, to the question of authorial identification or intention, but a more conscious choice, something that is nowhere more apparent than in the prologue to the *Lais:*

> Custume fu as ancïens,
> Ceo tes[ti]moine Precïens,
> Es livres ke jadis feseient
> Assez oscurement diseient
> Pur ceus ki a venir esteient
> Et ki aprendre les deveient,

> K'i peüssent gloser la lettre
> Et de lur sen le surplus mettre. (Prologue, v. 9)

It was customary for the ancients, in the books that they wrote (Priscian testifies to this), to express themselves very obscurely so that those in later generations, who had to learn them, could provide a gloss for the text and put the finishing touches to their meaning.

No poet of her time is more aware, even what we might call "critically aware," of the effects of language upon meaning, which makes it seem, though the assertion is still a bit premature, that though Marie may not choose to be literally anonymous, given that she offers us her name, she nonetheless chooses to remain just a name, no more than a name, a name into which, as she is also aware, those who read her might also read themselves. It is as if she were saying that authorship lies in that which writers choose not to say as well in what they say, which means that her revelation of a name and nothing more stands as a conscious choice: Marie sets the limits of obscurity, calibrates the gap between what we know and what we do not know of her, negotiates the degree of her anonymity.

This is not to suggest that Marie suggests that the writer might control the uses made of her name. On the contrary, as she is aware, the question of reception implies a loss of control, a danger. Here, I hesitate between saying "may imply" and "implies," opting for the second, since the danger, as will become obvious in later chapters on the *Lais,* is unavoidable. The textual gaps that allow the reader to insert him- or herself into a text, to insert his or her own meanings, are, as Marie insists, dangerous not only because readers abhor a vacuum, but because a vacuum abhors goodwill. The desire of the reader of the writerly text always implies to some extent a desire to be the writer, to supplant the writer, to usurp the—paternal?—power connected, especially in the medieval thinking of such issues, to authorship. Which is another way of saying that the reader remains envious of the writer, envy being, as we shall see, one of the defining themes of the *Lais* and the *Fables.* The obscurities of the very type Marie exposes are a place in which the reader not only interjects his or her meaning, but, inevitably, indulges the fantasy of replacing, or of actually being, the source.

Which is another way of saying too that the writer who leaves him- or herself open to be read, to the desire of the reader, to the potential usurpations bound up in reading, can only remain anxious, an anxiety expressed throughout the *Lais,* an anxiety negotiated in the *Fables,* an anxiety resolved in the *Purgatoire Seint Patriz,* and an anxiety explicitly articulated in the prologues as a concern with reputation. I am not the first to notice that Marie de France is intensely concerned about her name, what beginning in the eighteenth century will be considered a literary reputation, and what for the twelfth remains simply a question of how her work, synonymous with her name, will be received. One might even posit that France's first woman writer expresses an anxiety about subsequent reading and misreading that is, again, in consonance with contemporary literary theory in so far as it emphasizes the question of reception over that of production (though Marie is also assiduous, as we shall see, about the question of source). Thus, the prologue to "Guigemar":

> Ki de bone mateire traite,
> Mult li peise si bien n'est faite.
> Oëz, seignurs, ke dit Marie,
> Ki en sun tens pas ne s'oblie.
> Celui deivent la genz loër
> Ki en bien fait de sei parler.
> Mais quant il a en un païs
> Hummë u femme de grant pris,
> Cil ki de sun bien unt envie
> Sovent en diënt vileinie;
> Sun pris li volent abeisser:
> Pur ceo commencent le mestier
> Del malveis chien coart felun,
> Ki mort la gent par traïsun. ("Guigemar," v. 1)

Whoever has good material for a story is grieved if the tale is not well told. Hear, my lords, the words of Marie, who, when she has the chance, does not squander her talents. Those who gain a good reputation should be commended, but when there exists in a country a man or woman of great renown, people who are envious of their abilities frequently speak insultingly of them in order to damage this reputation. Thus they start acting like a vicious, cowardly, treacherous dog that will bite others out of malice.

In a passage that reminds us of the extent to which medieval literary theory is bound up in practice, Marie delves directly, consciously, into the question of reception. What will they say about me?

And she does well to be concerned, for even at the time other poets were jealous of her. Denis Piramus, a contemporary lyric poet attached to the court of Henry II and Eleanor of Aquitaine, writes in his own prologue to the *Vie de seint Edmund le rei:*

> E dame Marie autresi,
> Ki en rime fist et basti
> E compassa les vers de lais
> Ke ne sunt pas del tut verais
> Et si en est ele mult loee
> E la rime par tut amee,
> Kar mult l'aiment, si l'unt mult cher
> Cunte, barun e chivaler.[30]

And so it is with Lady Marie who put into rhyme and assembled and composed the verses of lays, which are not at all true; and for this she is much praised, and her rhymes are admired by all, for counts and barons and knights love her and hold her dear.

Denis Piramus's prologue seems to respond to, indeed echoes uncannily, Marie's concern expressed in her own prologue and remains proof positive that jealousy begins at home, that envy is the inevitable result of writing, which by its nature is open to interpretation and misinterpretation. Writing is for Marie de France the equivalent of vulnerability taken in its most literal, etymological sense, of *vulnera,* "wounds" represented as gaps in language that come back potentially, inevitably, as she insists repeatedly in the *Lais,* to harm.

It is my assumption that the healing of such a wound resides in sympathetic reading, what Augustine prescribes as the essence of proper exegetical understanding or reading with charity, which begins with an understanding of the nature of the wound, what, in other words, Marie's readers have said about her. Given the great quantity of scholarly and critical material, which is astutely annotated in Glyn Burgess's bibliography and supplements, this might seem like an overwhelming task.[31] The good news, however, is that those who have spoken of Marie have for the most part said similar things. Writing as she did as a lone woman among what must have seemed like a male horde of court poets, of which the envious Denis Piramus was just one, proposing as she did individualized postures of resistance to institutionally defined dilemmas, Marie would, I think, have been amused at the extent to which those who in subsequent centuries wrote about her belong to a crowd, the extent to which they seem to echo each other.

And what do they say?

The critics tend to insist, first, that Marie de France is the most human of poets, and that her poetry humanizes. "What Marie seeks in her tales is less a marvelous adventure, an astonishing event, than the elaboration of a human problem," writes Ernest Hoepffner; the *Lais* are "vibrating with humanity," notes Leo Spitzer; "Marie de France introduces a human element within tales of marvels," repeats Edgard Sienaert.[32] "These narratives that are so profoundly human," writes Philippe Ménard in a volume that is an encyclopedia of clichés culled from Marie's critics, "were not written to show or demonstrate anything. They depict men and women who seek each other and who love. . . . They tell of broadly human adventures. This is enough for our pleasure and the glory of the author."[33] Paula Clifford concurs: "In view of the more realistic and humanized approach to love, it is not surprising to find that Marie is interested in a relationship between equals, and that her men do not grovel for favors."[34]

One can ask what it means to be human, but for Marie's critics it is clear that to be human means, first of all, to be emotional. Ménard speaks of an "esthetics of emotion and of pathos."[35] Glyn Burgess points to Marie's "emotional involvement with her characters."[36] Being human means, second, to be intuitive; and this from the start. De Roquefort, one of the earliest of Marie's critics, sees her as sensitive: "To a refined taste, to graceful forms, to pleasant thoughts, she brings a great sensitivity."[37] Ménard conceives of Marie as a poetess "of penetrating subtlety and intuition" who "reaches intuitively the profound truth of beings." She represents the "happy fruit of talent and of effort, the happy marriage of precise observation and delicate intuition."[38] If Marie is intuitive, she is also simple; and this too from the beginning, as de Roquefort remarks apropos of the *Fables,* which, "composed by a mind that penetrates the secrets of the human heart, distinguish themselves especially by a superior reason, a simple and naive spirit in the telling, and by a refined and delicate justness in their morality and their reflections."[39] Marie is naive. Lucien Foulet claimed at the beginning of the last century that "Marie . . . in all simplicity . . . recounts how things happen, we find her naive, and we appreciate her naïveté"; Hoepffner, writing between the two world wars, extols Marie's capacity to create "gracious and naive tales without second thoughts."[40] She is for her modern critics, whose modernity hardly can be confused with originality, the purveyor of a world of "simple and clear sentiments"; in Ménard's phrase, "we find ourselves before a literature in which the general dominates over the particular, the exemplary over the individual, the simple over the complicated."[41]

Marie's simplicity implies that she is also spontaneous. "Is there any need to insist upon the degree to which Marie's sympathy for lovers, which one feels to be sincere and spontaneous, adds to the charm of her poetry and the degree to which it adds a human dimension?" asks Hoepffner. "Complexity is troubling, but simplicity is reassuring," weighs in Ménard: "We feel no hesitation before the portraits she draws. We know how to react. Spontaneously, we identify with her good characters and we distance ourselves from the bad. Everything becomes perfectly clear."[42] Which is another way of saying, of course, that Marie is natural. "In the place of artificial procedures that are not hers, Marie, being a master of what is natural, proceeds naturally," Hoepffner observes; "Marie prefers simple and natural actions to those infused with artifice," Ménard repeats.[43]

Imagining Marie as human—intuitive, spontaneous, natural—is, of course, a way of bringing her down to scale, and critics have insistently associated her with a delicate nature, a natural modesty that is at once psychological and esthetic. "As far as poetic talent goes," writes Edmond Faral, "that of Marie is modest." "More modest in her proportions, less brilliant in her qualities of language and style, using a psychology that is less profound and less penetrating, Marie gives off a discrete and rare poetic charm that one hardly finds anywhere else," Hoepffner observes. "Like a miniaturist of the Middle Ages, Marie de France works at the level of that which is refined and delicate," writes Ménard. Marie is, above all, discreet, moderate, modest, full of degree: "a discreet poetry . . . no descriptions of the sexual act . . . Marie is neither prudish nor extravagant. She strikes a balance between the two."[44]

What's more, Marie's modesty, synonymous with the moral categories of sincerity and honesty, translates into literary style. Where her language is concerned, she is considered to be simple, measured, clear, delicate, graceful, original, and, again from the start, full of charm but "without art." Among her early commentators, de Roquefort observes that Marie unites her own graceful artlessness to the pristine artlessness of the French language in its infancy: "The purity, preciseness, and elegance of her style are well known. Marie wrote in French at a time when the language, still in its childhood, could only offer simple expressions without art; she joined to it pleasant turns of phrase, and a natural manner of writing without making her efforts apparent."[45] Those who continued the work of the Benedictine *Histoire littéraire de la France* urge that "it be noted that her style is clearer, more polished, is softer and has greater harmony than that of most of the writers among whom she lived in England."[46] Gaston Paris speaks of "les charmants récits de Marie de France." In the words of Paris's student Joseph Bédier (1891), the *Lais* contain "no splendor in their style, no passion in their narrative, nothing but the grace of a very weak emotion, lightly drawn. But also, no filler, no rhetoric: an agile and refined language whose gracefulness is not without charm. She stops on the threshold of art. She emits a delicate little fountain of poetry, limpid and slight like those fountains in which bathe the fairies of her tales."[47] Bédier's phrase will reappear in Hoepffner's claim that "no literary artifice disrupts the immediate effect produced by Marie's poems," and Hoepffner's characterization will not be lost upon Ménard, who contends that "the esthetics of Marie de France are simple and parsimonious. She is content with language that is sober and stripped down."[48]

Marie's fundamental honesty is manifest in a simple style. The *Lais,* in contrast with, say, Jean de Meun's portion of the *Roman de la rose,* are without artifice; they mean, according to S. Foster Damon, what they say.[49] They are, as Süheylâ Bayrav maintains in a book on medieval symbolism, concrete, singularly devoid of images or symbols.[50] Marie is without manner. "With an honest talent and self-confidence in her trade, she cuts the figure of a good worker in the field of versification," asserts Ménard. "The honesty of her art distances her from all that is rhetorical manner: forced antitheses, witty phrases, and precious images. Our author does not seek to surprise or to astonish."[51] Marie's lack of manner is, moreover, linked to specific rhetorical traits—brevity, economy, understatement, and a reticence akin to self-denial. William S. Woods claims that she "uses but does not abuse" diminutives; Emmanuel Mickel maintains that she relies heavily upon the figure of abbreviation.[52] "It is clear," states Ménard, "that one of the marked traits of Marie's art is the economy of her means. It is no accident that she uses understatement (litote), the figure par excellence of self-effacement and of modesty."[53]

Marie is, above all, reassuring, comforting: "We have the pleasure of witnessing her fresh and vivid beginnings, of seeing her unexpected moves, of observing the beautiful harmony of a world in which hearts vibrate in unison and where all one has to do is to declare one's love in order that it be returned. This happy reciprocity and the unbreakable bonds that lovers share have something reassuring about them."[54] If Marie is comforting, it is because she is, finally, a good Christian: "Nature herself appears to be the agent of a higher Power; and Marie establishes a context of Christian order in her *lais* which leads one to assume that for her, as well as for her audience, the superior power is the Christian God."[55]

This little portrait painted by scholars is an attempt to counter the anonymity behind which lies the brutal fact that we know, finally, so little about Marie, who remains after all these years still just a name. Further, and the reader must have remarked it long before now, the particular constellation of traits attributed to her—humanness, spontaneity, intuitiveness, naturalness, simplicity, delicacy, moderation, clarity, sincerity, Christian goodness, and the capacity for comfort—can be said to be characteristics aligned with the feminine. In the absence of any further information about Marie, in the face of her anonymity, the traits associated with her seem to emanate strikingly from our original assumption about the only fact to be taken for granted—that Marie de France was a woman. They are ways that she would have understood, moreover, of filling in the gaps, the obscurities of meaning, as part of the process of reading and understanding. They tell us, finally, more about nineteenth- and twentieth-century readers' notions of the feminine than about the twelfth century. Indeed, carried to its logical extreme, which would not have been wholly unrecognizable to the medieval theologizing of both language and the feminine, the little we know about Marie is easily conflated with the Freudian positing of woman as enigma. Carried beyond its logical extreme, Roger Dragonetti offers a final Lacanian twist in the assimilation of the unknown, *fin'Amor,* language itself, and Woman to the *Lais,* which represent a "homage rendered to the eternal feminine of the maternal language of song." Echoing Michelet's famous dictum that "in the twelfth century God changed sex," Dragonetti sees in Marie the distillation of an "enigmatic feminine essence."[56]

Walter Benjamin remarks in an essay on the nature of libraries that one writes the books that one writes because one cannot find them elsewhere, that one writes the books one wants to read.[57] This volume is no exception. For I confess from the start that after years of reading Marie de France I cannot find much in what the critics have said about her—oscillating as it does between asymptotes of the weighing of swans and the interrogation of peasants, on the one hand, and the eternal feminine, on the other—that corresponds to my understanding of the text itself.

What, then, is the book about Marie that I would like to read? The book that I would write?

It is, first, a book that takes into account all of her works. What has been written about Marie up until now has largely focused upon the *Lais.* Not only can one can find very little indeed about the *Fables* and the *Espurgatoire Seint Patriz,* but, with the exception of Sahar Amer's recent *Ésope au féminin,* those who have considered the *Fables* have tended to do so as one example of the inherited genre of the animal tale, that is, without the specificity that Marie's *Fables* merit: "The fables, strictly speaking, in the Middle Ages, have no literary value," writes Gaston Paris; "most are only mediocre translations from the Latin. The collection that Marie composed around 1180 is interesting, it is true, but only because it is the adaptation of an English grouping."[58] Those who have studied the *Espurgatoire* have either limited themselves to the question of the accuracy of Marie's translation or mined this startlingly self-conscious and innovative work for documentary evidence of everything from theological attitudes toward the afterlife in the High Middle Ages to the actual geographical disposition of the entrance to the Otherworld in twelfth-century Ireland. In neither case have Marie's "other" works been considered with the same focus that characterizes treatments of the *Lais*. This volume is, then, a redress of what has for two centuries been a critical imbalance that has favored one field of her work, and not even the first attributed to her, to the detriment of the other two. If anything, I accord proportionally greater attention and space to the *Fables* and the *Espurgatoire* than to the *Lais*, which are the object of a myriad of articles, notes, and monographs beginning just after the French Revolution and, in keeping with Marie's admonition that "those to whom God gives knowledge and the gift of words should speak" (prologue, v. 1), increasing geometrically in the period between the Franco-Prussian War and the present.

This is a book that seeks, second, to resolve the question of Marie's anonymity not through recourse to documents outside of her works, but through close consideration of the evidence contained in all three of her texts. The thesis here presented entails accepting the fact that we will never know Marie from the outside, we will never even be able to disprove what Richard Baum has recently argued with unconvincing rigor, that she is not the author of the three works historically attributed to her. We will never know who the "real Marie" was in the way that we know who Marguerite de Navarre, Jane Austen, Emily Brontë, George Sand, Virginia Woolf, or Marguerite Duras really was, that is to say, in a way that allows us to assign a biography to her with the fantasy, ultimately, of reducing her works to such an elusive category as the person. Marie remains anonymous. Which does not mean that we cannot know her, only that any attempt to deal with the question of her anonymity must proceed internally, from the texts themselves, via an interpretation of the works associated with her.[59] While such a strategy may carry its own burden of sadness, it also brings rewards: "Anonymity," in the phrase of Virginia Woolf, "was a great possession. It gave the early writing an impersonality, a generality. It gave us the ballads; it gave us the songs. It allowed us to know nothing of the writer: and so to concentrate upon his song."[60]

We begin, then, from the premise that the scholar, faced with a mystery so resistant as the identity of France's first woman poet, a mystery that she herself proclaims in the prologue, must renounce the kind of certainty demanded by the positivist philological method that has dominated medieval, if not literary, studies for almost two centuries. Every work of criticism involves some form of risk, a gamble that initial intuitions will be borne out by readings of a more sustained sort; and I am wagering that it is possible to prove from within not only the coherence of Marie's oeuvre but that, far from being the simple, naive, natural, spontaneous, delicate, modest, clear, sincere, comforting, Christian figure she has been portrayed to be, Marie is among the most self-conscious, sophisticated, complicated, obscure, tricky, and disturbing figures of her time—the Joyce of the twelfth century. This is another way of asserting the other half of our assumption at the outset: that Marie was not only a woman but that she was also a poet.

As a poet, Marie was both a disrupter of prevailing cultural values and a founder of new ones. The prologue to the *Lais* is one of those founding texts that appear at a liminal moment in the history of the West. C. S. Lewis claims that there have been very few real moments of historical mutation and that the twelfth century was one; Charles Homer Haskins speaks of the "Renaissance of the twelfth century"; Marc Bloch, of the end of the "first feudal age"; Georges Duby, situating the seismic cultural break a little earlier, proclaims the "watershed years" preceding 1100. All are forms of recognition that something major took place between, say, the First Crusade and the Lateran Council of 1215, something in which it is difficult to place written texts; for writing both reflects a larger cultural shift and is part of such a shift within an essentially oral lay culture that breaks rather suddenly into writing, writing being both the symptom of change and its catalyst.[61] Activities heretofore conducted without it suddenly come to depend upon the written forms that have such a necessary effect upon the perceptual world of those who in increasing numbers beginning around the middle of the 1100s come into contact with literary works composed via writing as opposed to oral performance. Marie de France was acutely aware not only of her role in the preservation of cultural memory but of the transforming effects of writing, and written poetry in particular, upon and within oral tradition. The implications of such a shift for our understanding of literature are developed in the chapters that follow.

Marie's intervention in her inherited culture lies in her awareness of the importance of the subject. The prologue contains, as we have seen, as clear a statement as imaginable of the role of the individual psyche in the

interpretation of his or her world, a subject obliged to fill in inherited obscurities with his or her own meaning. And such a shift is part and parcel of
what appears as a psychologizing of externalized social categories from the
third decade of the twelfth century on. This trend, which can be seen in the
more individualized images of twelfth-century portraiture and sculpture, in
personalized notions of sin and penance and of individualized legal responsibility, in the singular, wandering, sometimes even isolated heroes of romance, in the suffering voices of the love lyric, in the tricky figures of the
Roman de Renart and the fabliaux, will culminate in the full-blown, internalized psychological model of allegory—in Guillaume de Lorris's, and especially Jean de Meun's, portion of *Le Roman de la rose,* where it finds explicit articulation in the figure of Faux Semblant:

> Je sai bien mon habit changier.
> Prendre l'un et l'autre estrangier.
> Or sui chevalier, or sui moine,
> Or sui prelat, or sui chanoine,
> Or sui clerc et or sui prestre,
> Or sui desciple et or sui mestre,
> Or chastelain, or forestiers.
> Briement, je sui de touz mestiers.
> Or sui princes et or sui pages,
> Or sai parler tretouz langages.[62]

I am very good at changing my clothes, at donning one outfit and discard-
ing another. At one moment I am a knight, at another a monk, now a prelate,
now a canon, now a clerk, now a priest, now disciple, now master, now lord
of the manor, now forester; in short, I am of every calling. Again, I am prince
one moment, page the next, and I know all languages by heart.

For Faux Semblant the world is seeming, a question of outer garments and
of languages that do not correspond to the inner essence of the person.

The shift away from the early medieval sense of fixed meanings, the so-
called realism of the early Middle Ages, and toward a relativizing of meaning based upon a heightened consciousness of the role of language in the
making of meaning, is present from the start and in a conscious manner in
the works of Marie, which is not to suggest that they are just language. On
the contrary, it is my contention that the coherence of the works of Marie
de France lies in her constant concern with language, that this concern is expressed in three quite different ways in the three works attributed to her, and
that the critical issue for France's first woman poet is precisely the question

of how language might negotiate relations between individuals in a world that is less and less defined by military might and increasingly ruled by models of mediated social exchange.

Such a project represents a modification of my view of Marie expressed in a series of articles written in the 1980s, which emphasized the extent to which language functioned as a closed system with its own laws of desire, transgression, and creation.[63] My vision of her at the time was rooted in the will to demonstrate the linguistic richness of Marie's text, its resistance to easy readings, in a word, its specificity as literature; and these essays were based almost exclusively on the *Lais*. My claim at present, rooted in a fuller consideration of all of her works, is that Marie's obsession with language in the *Fables* and the *Espurgatoire Seint Patriz* is no less, but that this obsession is worked out in different—more socially engaged—ways. We can, moreover, see in the philosophy of language developed in each individual work both a synthesis of and an escape from the dilemma of language's closure upon the world. Thus, we shall trace in the *Lais* Marie's articulation of the fatal effects of language conceived to be independent of the world, a view associated with theological attitudes toward the relation of words to material reality characteristic of the early Middle Ages. Second, we shall follow the ways in which the fatal speech acts contained in the *Lais* become in the *Fables*, under the guise of the animal tale as an imperfect social means, a means nonetheless by which individuals might both control the instincts of their own body and might survive in a "dog-eat-dog" world. Finally, we shall see the extent to which the *Espurgatoire* represents a synthesis of Marie's two other works in its presentation not of a fatal but of a salvific view of language, or rather language as a means to salvation, in a vision that integrates both earlier theological and social postures before the question of language's efficacy in the wider world. The three texts associated with Marie's name do not simply contain three attitudes toward language. To the extent to which they represent a working out of what Fredric Jameson in the 1970s termed the "prisonhouse of language"—and what Marie in the *Espurgatoire* represents as a "shadowy charter" ("chartre tenebruse"), both a prison and a charter—they are precious documents for the historical transformation of the twelfth century; for they are, as will become increasingly evident, founding articulations of what was for the time a new mental and social landscape based upon civilized, that is to say, nonviolent forms of interpersonal exchange, an increasingly abstract notion of civil polity, and the principle of an internalized psychology.

When I say that Marie's prologue contains a founding articulation of the question of the subjectivity of meaning, and thus of the subject, I am, of course, running somewhat roughshod over a wide variety of texts from the first half or even two-thirds of the twelfth century. One could just as easily have located such an embryonic moment in, say, the debate between Roland and Oliver in the *Chanson de Roland;* in the trial of Ganelon, who at the end of the same epic is accused of "treason" and defends himself by claiming "vengeance" rather than betrayal, thus engaging a debate about whether or not a single event witnessed by all can be described by two different words and thus have two different meanings;[64] in the *Roman d'Eneas,* which may be contemporaneous with the works of Marie, and which sows the seeds of depth psychology via the inner monologue or love debate. Yet, the *Chanson de Roland,* which is in many respects the literary version of this earlier universe, presents a great communality not only of values but of perceptions on the part of a homogeneous, socially exclusive warrior aristocracy. By the very nature of its oral formulaic composition, formulae being a communal form of language that implies that the world is what it seems to all who perceive it, there is no attempt to look behind appearances to find a rival reality, the truth behind false seeming. The role of the subject in interpreting his world (and here I have purposely not said "his or her" world) is minimal. The *chanson de geste* presents a multiplicity of events from a single point of view, but at no point is point of view thrown into question. On the contrary, the earliest epic contains a universe of fixed moral categories ("Chrestiens unt dreit, et païens unt tort," "Christians are right, and pagans are wrong"), a universe of externalized and fixed psychological categories ("Roland est preu, et Olivers est sage," "Roland is brave, and Oliver is wise"). This is another way of saying that history moves in only one direction since, in the absence of anything like free will, the individual is merely the vehicle of objective forces outside of his control—in this instance Christian Providence. *Roland* proffers a universe, finally, oriented toward the past, precisely because the powers of interpretation attributed to an individual subject, and therefore his ability to understand a world of increasingly particular realities, are so faintly drawn and because history according to such a paradigm is perceived as a text written once and for all, whose meaning simply will become apparent through time. It is my purpose here to show, on the contrary, that Marie de France not only renders opaque the question of the subject, brings it to our attention as a question, but that the three works attributed to her represent a working out of the issue of the individual in the world in such a way as not only to provide convincing evidence of a unifying obsession, but as also to convince us of her role in the making of a perceptual world, mental structures fundamental to the shaping of social life.

The prologue to the *Lais* suggests a movement past a past-oriented paradigm toward a future-oriented one, for the potential of a subject to interpret his or her world comes to be increasingly synonymous with his or her mastery of it. The prologue opens in the direction of individual free will, and this is the era in which moral philosophy, ethics, even the notions of sin and penance in the discourse of theology and of guilt in that of the law, are, as we shall see in our concluding chapters on the *Espurgatoire,* increasingly subjectivized. Despite her awareness of legal procedure in "Lanval" and despite her concern with political exemplars throughout the *Fables,* it would be difficult to prove that Marie de France functioned as either a jurist or a political theorist alongside the literary jurisconsults she may have encountered in or around the Angevin court. I think it can be shown that her works represent not only expressive symptoms of social change but dynamic forces in the transformation in the High Middle Ages of the nature and practice of legal process, and, in the case of the *Espurgatoire,* a moralization of the social bond and a legalization of the afterlife that can be understood in the specific historical context of the conquest, pacification, and administration of Ireland in the final decades of the reign of Henry II.

The privileging of something on the order of free will opens the question of history as a function of individual agency as opposed to the determinism of an earlier epoch. This amounts to attributing to Marie—as well as to others, but especially to her since she is the most conscious of this freedom—the birth of literature, or what has come to be called the literary. Joseph Bédier sensed this development with respect to the *Lais* as early as 1891: "One can say . . . that with them literature, properly speaking, is born. *Roland* could be sung in a public gathering place, or amidst the tumult of a drinking hall; but not *Eliduc* or *Perceval:* they are made for reflective reading. The noisy jongleur of epic is replaced by the *latinier,* who, in the 'women's chambers' *[chambres des dames]* where stained glass casts a toned down light, reads Breton tales."[65] As we will see repeatedly in the pages that follow, Marie more explicitly than others of her generation—Chrétien, Robert de Boron, or the Tristan poets—initiates literature as the expression within a closed form of a desire residing in the space between a world sensed as individual, interior, and subjective, on the one hand, and the demands of a world sensed as objective and collective, on the other. For while the others present on the level of theme the split between the desire of the individual and the givens of his or her world, a conflict visible in a myriad of motifs from the rivalry of lovers in the lyric, to the lovesickness and quests of romance, no one was more aware than Marie that the thematic expression of this very tension is the stuff of literature as a closed form whose very closure both mediates the space of such a gap and, like all closed systems, itself becomes an object of desire.

Marie's consciousness of the ways literature negotiates between individual and community is, for reasons that will become increasingly clear, equivalent to an integration of the principle not only of difference between the subject and the world, but of difference per se, sexual difference, an integration of the feminine into the wholly masculine world of the epics of the "first feudal age." "Yes, this literature is feminine," writes Bédier, echoing Denis Piramus's assessment some eight centuries earlier:

> E si en aiment mult l'escrit
> E lire le funt, si unt delit,
> E si les funt sovent retreire.
> Les lais solent as dames pleire:
> De joie les oient e de gré,
> Qu'il sunt sulum lur volenté.[66]

And they [counts and barons and knights] greatly love her writing, they have it read aloud, they have them [lays] often told, and they take delight. For lays are used to pleasing ladies: they hear them willingly and in joy, for they suit their taste.

It is, finally, the distinction drawn by a contemporary between the *chanson de geste* and the fabliaux, which appeal to men, and the lais and romances, which appeal to women, that permits us to hold in abeyance the question with which we began. Or, rather, to continue to believe for the moment that Marie de France was a woman, not because anything outside of the text makes it so, but because she wrote the *Lais,* to which we turn in our first chapter.

The Word *Aventure* and the Adventure of Words

In the prologue to the *Lais,* which is as close to a vernacular *art poétique* as the High Middle Ages produced, Marie begins with the question of beginnings. She is anxious about origins, about the genesis and genealogy of the tales that she, at the nodal point between past and future, will preserve in memory for generations to come. Having considered the possibility of translating from a Latin, that is to say, a written, source, she thinks instead of "that which she has heard" among the tales told by those "who first sent them into the world":

> Des lais pensai, k'oï aveie;
> Ne dutai pas, bien le saveie,
> Ke pur remembrance les firent
> Des aventures k'il oïrent
> Cil ki primes les comencierent
> E ki avant les enveierent. (v. 33)

I thought of lais that I had heard and did not doubt, for I knew it full well, that they were composed, by those who first began them and put them into circulation, to perpetuate the memory of adventures they had heard.

As the point of entry to the world of literature, as what Stephen Nichols identifies as "the first explicit canon revision in European history," the prologue raises from the start issues that will dominate not only the *Lais* but the *Fables* and the *Espurgatoire Seint Patriz* as well—issues of memory and transmission; of orality versus writing; of the reception of a work in the mind of others; of the uses to which wisdom from the past will be put; and,

finally, of what lies behind the text, the "lais" that in Old French can connote "that which is left behind," here subsumed in the little word *aventure*.[1]

The word *aventure* is one of the richly plurivalent signifiers of the *Lais* and
constitutes a liminal key to the whole. Referring to the brute material out of
which the *Lais* are made, the word *aventure* designates that which exists before and beyond the text in the fantasy of an unrecounted, unremembered,
chaotic realm of unarticulated consciousness, the very opposite of the assemblage—the form and structure—that literature represents. This is why
so many of the tales are literally framed by the word *aventure,* which, appearing at either the beginning or the end or both, marks the bounds of
where literature begins and ends, sets in relief that which it contains. "Just
as it happened, I shall relate to you the story of another lai" ("L'aventure
d'un autre lai,/Cum ele avient, vus cunterai" [v. 1])—thus begins "Lanval,"
in what amounts to a mini-prologue to the lai, whose epilogue reminds the
reader that adventure ends when Marie has no more to say: "No one has
heard any more about him, nor can I relate any more" ("Nul humme n'en
oï plus parler,/Ne jeo n'en sai avant cunter" [v. 645]). "Deus Amanz" com-
mences with a "celebrated adventure" that "once took place in Normandy"
("Jadis avint en Normendie/Une aventure mut oïe" [v. 1]) and concludes
with attention drawn to the composition of the lai:

> Pur l'aventure des enfaunz
> Ad nun li munz des Deus Amanz.
> Issi avint cum dit vus ai.
> Li Bretun en firent un lai. (v. 241)

> Because of what happened to these two young people, the mountain is called
> the Mountain of the Two Lovers. The events took place just as I have told
> you, and the Bretons composed a lai about them.

"Now that I have begun to compose lais, I shall not cease my effort but shall
relate fully in rhyme the adventures that I know," Marie affirms at the beginning of "Yonec," which ends, like "Deus Amanz," with an explanation
of how the lai came into being: "Those who heard this story long afterward
composed a lai from it."[2] Finally, in what now seems like somewhat of a formula for beginnings, Marie launches "Laüstic" with the promise that "I
shall relate an adventure to you from which the Bretons composed a lai"

("Une aventure vus dirai,/Dunt li Bretun firent un lai" [v. 1]), and closes no less conventionally:

> Cele aventure fut cuntee,
> Ne pot estre lunges celee.
> Un lai en firent li Bretun:
> Le Laüstic l'apelent hum. (v. 157)

This adventure was related and could not long be concealed. The Bretons composed a lai about it that is called *Laüstic*.

As that which lies outside of the lai, but of which the lai is made, "aventure" refers to an event, an *eventure*, that supposedly happened, a lived experience rooted in the body, the fantasy of the body present to itself, at its outer limits, the imagined wholeness of voice and body joined. "Aventure" refers to the material of the tale, that which lies outside of its formal telling, and also carries the unmistakable resonance of orality. In the beginning of "Equitan" we learn that the Bretons made lais out of the "adventures that they had heard":

> li Bretun.
> Jadis suleient par prüesce,
> Par curteisie e par noblesce,
> Des aventures que oïeent,
> Ki a plusur gent aveneient,
> Fere les lais pur remembrance,
> Que [hum] nes meïst en ubliance. (v. 2)

In days gone by the valiant, courtly, and noble Bretons composed lais for posterity and thus preserved them from oblivion. These lais were based on adventures they had heard and which had befallen many a person.

Marie hints, moreover, that she has heard one such tale in a manner that leaves little doubt about the fact of oral transmission: "Un ent firent, ceo oi cunter,/Ki ne fet mie a ublïer" (vv. 9–10). "I am minded to recall a lai of which I have heard and shall recount what happened," she states in her own voice in the first line of "Chaitivel," thus revealing, if not an oral source, at least an oral means of transmission of the "aventure"—hearsay ("Un lai dunt jo oï parler") of an adventure to be passed on by means of speech ("L'aventure vus en dirai"). Here we arrive at a second meaning of the term, that is, the "story of an experience," a "tale of adventure," as in Chrétien de Troyes's prologue to *Erec* where he speaks of joining "contes d'aventure" into a "bele conjointure."[3] An "adventure" here constitutes one episode in a larger narrative whole with the specific resonance of orality, of an oral account of an adventure of the type told by Chrétien's itinerant oral poets—jongleurs—as opposed to his own written version that will last, he maintains, as "long as Christianity itself" ("aussi longtemps que la Chrétienté"), the very name "Chrétien" being associated with the permanent preservation of the more fluid, dispersed, oral aventures in written form.

"Aventure" not only refers to the source of a tale, to the past from which the tale comes, and to the tale itself in its present form; "aventure"—from the Latin *ad* + *venire*—also relates prospectively to that which will come or happen. It carries the valence of an advent. Within such a future-oriented semantic range, an "aventure" contains its own genealogy, its own expectation for a meaning that is prescribed, predetermined, predestined. It is the equivalent of destiny, as, for example, in the case of Yonec, whose dying father tells his mother of the fate that awaits their unborn son:

> Quant il serat creüz e grant
> E chevalier pruz e vaillant,
> A une feste u ele irra,
> Sun seigneur e lui amerra.
> En une abbeïe vendrunt;
> Par une tumbe k'il verrunt
> Orrunt renoveler sa mort
> E cum il fu ocis a tort.
> Ileoc li baillerat s'espeie.
> L'aventure li seit cuntee
> Cum il fu nez, ki le engendra;
> Asez verrunt k'il en fera. (v. 425)

When he will have grown up and become a worthy and valiant knight, he will go to a feast with her and her husband. They will come to an abbey, and at a tomb they will visit, they will again hear about his death and how he was unjustly killed. There she will give the sword to his son to whom the adventure will be told, how he was born and who his father was. Then they will see what he will do.

Finally, as Erich Koehler observed,[4] "aventure" connotes chance, fortune, risk, and here is where we encounter the other side of the semantic coin: "Beloved," Guigemar exclaims at the end of the tale that bears his name, "how fortunate that I have discovered you like this!" ("Bele," fet il, "queile aventure/Que jo vus ai issi trovee!"). The multiple meanings of "aventure," which on the one hand concretizes, fixes, immobilizes that which is imagined to be beyond language, experience, and the body, also serves as a reminder that no matter how much one tries to pin meaning down, it remains, even in fixed form, uncontrollable, risky, undisciplined, excessive—an intractable "surplus of sense" in Marie's own phrase. And nowhere more uncontrollable, it turns out, than where the word *lai* itself is concerned.

LAI

As in most etymologies, the absolute origin of the word *lai*—its "first roots" (*primogenia*), to use the term of the great medieval source of etymologies, Isidore of Seville—is covered so completely by the mists of time as to remind us that the history of a word never leads to the rooting of language in reality but to a series of attestations of its use, of which the first takes on the burden of an origin sometimes so dissimilar to the present term as to pose the delicate issue of recognition. Indeed, how do we recognize two words as being the same word at different points in time—and sometimes at intervals of several hundred years—if they do not resemble each other?

The first mention of that which is taken to be the word *lai* is from the ninth century (830–50), where it appears in the marginalia of a religious text from the county of Ulster:

> Domfarcai fidbaidae fal
> fomchain *loîd* lain luad nadcel
> huas mo lebran indlinech
> fomchain trîrech inna nhen.[5]

In this citation "loîd" designates the song of the blackbird, while "trîrech" refers to the song of birds in general. The early editor of medieval texts Achille d'Arbois de Jubainville affirms an Irish origin for *lai* (via *loîd* and *laîd*), positing that from "song" the word came to mean a poetic genre specifically associated with such songs.[6] D'Arbois de Jubainville adds in a note that that the Irish *laîd* derives in fact from the Latin *laudis* (praise), in contrast to P. A. Levesque de la Ravallière who over a century earlier (1742) had maintained that *lai* derived from the Latin *lessus* (lamentation) and for this reason was associated with the genre of the plaint or lament.[7] Jean Maillard, who has written extensively on the musical lai and who seeks to demonstrate that the French word originates in Latin popular poetry via Celtic bards, maintains that the word *lai* is a deformation of the late Latin term *leodus (leudus),* designating Latin metrical rhythms adapted to vernac-

ular tongues, *leodus* itself being a deformation of *laus-laudis*. Indeed, a ca-
pitulary of Charlemagne dated 23 March 789 enjoins nuns "ut nullatenus
ibi uuinileodos scribere vel mittere praesumant," the word *uuinileodos* here
representing a work song.[8]

Another entire etymological chain for the French *lai* provides for passage
from Latin not through Irish or Breton but through a variety of potential
Germanic terms.[9] According to such a thesis, *lai* derives from *leodos,* a lat-
inized Germanic term parallel to the word *lessus,* which in texts from the
fifth century designates the chants executed by young girls before the tent
of Attila.[10] Indeed, the range of Germanic analogues is rich, for we find a
Germanic *leich* from the Gothic *laikan,* which later gives Old High German
leichi, leicha which are the equivalent of the Latin *modos* or *carmina;*[11] Old
Norse *lek* and *leikin;* Anglo-Saxon *lacan, lêc, lâcen;* Middle High German *leichen, liechen, leichete,* which also have the resonance of "to play," "to
joke," or "to mock"; Swedish *leka, lekte;* Norwegian *lege, legede;* and Ice-
landic *leikari,* which is used to designate a "jongleur."

In spite of the etymological murkiness surrounding the origin of the
word *lai,* of this there can be no doubt: the lai is linked to sound, to music, to song, and to poetry, words with song. In an article on the lyric lai
among the troubadours, Richard Baum maintains that, though the word
lai after the fourteenth century is resolutely dedicated to "song," in Old
Provençal it covers a range running from the aural sensation of noise, to
language or discourse, though for the most part it is concentrated on the
concept of music and song. Thus, *lai* can be the equivalent simply of a
sound, such as the sound of a bell or of birds, or of language itself, words,
and even discourse.[12] But most of all the word *lai* in Old Provençal designates some equivalent of song, poetic genre, or performance: a melody or
a musical air, a melody played upon a string instrument and accompanied
by sung words, a sung melody, a type of lyric composition distinct from the
canso, descort, vers, dansa, or *sirventes.* According to Baum, the Provençal
lai covers "a lyric genre with irregular structure characterized by the frequent repetition of certain metrical and musical formulas," a "chant with
isomorphic strophes inspired by a pious or moral theme,"[13] a "lyrico-epic
composition," a "narrative poem in the vernacular," or simply "poetry,"
"poetic activity" in general.

If the etymology of the word *lai* is opaque, that is to say, if certainty concerning the Celtic, Latin, or Germanic origins of the term attached loosely
to a wide spectrum of meanings having to do with the voice, with song, and
with poetic performance remains elusive, in this it resembles the word *aven-*

ture, the supposed lived experience beyond articulation. Both etymologies attest to the impossibility of words, for words, to move beyond words to anything on the order of reality or presence. The closest we get in the case of *aventure* is to something like the body and in the case of *lai* to the voice. When, however, we close the etymological dictionary and open the Old French lexicon, the meaning of the term *lai* appears to be even further dispersed, its very opacity enabling a plethora of sense. Indeed, one would be hard-pressed to find any other single syllable that casts greater doubt upon the imagined possibility of reading Old French literature with the aid of dictionary definitions, and no single syllable whose "surplus of sense" in Marie's phrase is more plentiful. In volume 4, page 691 of Godefroy we find that the word *lai* and its variants *lay, laye, laie, laiz, laes, lais* can be used as an adjective to connote the secular realm, or as a substantive to designate a lay person. By extension, it can refer to anyone not belonging to the university community or, as a corollary, to someone considered ignorant.[14] The word *lai* and its homonyms *laid* and *lait* are used variously as a synonym for "staddle" (MF *baliveau*), for that which is ugly, or, as in the *Miracles de Notre Dame,* as the word for another Marie's milk.[15] The adjectival homonyms *lé, ley, lay, let, lait, leit, laé, le* summon the idea of lightness, happiness, joy (possibly from the Latin *laetus*), just as *las, lax, lais* are used to connote sadness, misery, misfortune (Latin *lassus*). Where the syllable *lai* becomes more interesting, however, is in its power to signify that which is left, an excess, or testament (*legs*), which suggests not only a connection between the notion of residue, mark, or trace and the *Lais* as the written traces of the preexisting Breton *lai,* but also a place or *locus* from which to speak, or from which poetry becomes possible. "*La, lai, lay,* adv. se dit d'un lieu qu'on désigne d'une manière précise," specifies Godefroy on p. 685 of the same volume. Nor in this vein would it be an exaggeration to link the *Lais* with the principle of poetic construction or binding subsumed under the rubric of the *laisse* and elaborated in Old Provençal as the process of linking verses (*lassar*). Finally, the word *lai* is used in its OF forms *loi, lei, ley, lo, lays* to designate custom, usage, justice, or the law.

The excess of meanings that the word *lai* summons attests to a loss of univocity, to a dispersion of meaning, to the process of meaning as one of necessary deflection. Indeed, another of the semantic possibilities attached to the syllable "lez" resonates with the notion of "side," the French *côté*. As the hero and his men escape by sea, the author of the *Roman d'Eneas,* which is roughly contemporaneous with the *Lais* of Marie, describes in some detail how their ship is struck on one of its sides—"an l'un des lez"—by a wave."[16] Then too, in "Yonec," the lady, despite her imprisonment, "lies next to her love": "La dame gist lez sun ami" (v. 191).

HISTORY, PHILOLOGY, AND THE QUEST FOR ORIGINS

The uncovering and exploration of and—yes, why not just say it?—the reveling in the semantic instability of a little word like *lai* is taken as a sign of modern, and even postmodern, sensibility, one deemed by some inappropriate to the study of the Middle Ages. And yet, writing over seven hundred years ago, Marie participates in what was already a long tradition of an abiding sense of simultaneous historical and philological decay. One of the differences between the ancient and the medieval world is that where in the former history was cast in terms of "short wave" regenerative cycles (which might even include "long years"), the medievals cast the fate of man in broader, linear, degenerative terms.[17] Beginning with Augustine's elaboration of Eusebius's *Chronographia,* Christian history was considered to represent a long-range course of decline, a process of continual erosion according to specific periods—the *articuli temporum sive aetatum*—prior to final redemption at the end of human time. Further, if men evolve through time away from God, language (which is *proper* to man and, indeed, for thinkers from Cicero to Aquinas, the condition of the possibility of human society) is conceived to devolve—through use, catastrophe, translation, poetry (especially pagan verse)—away from an original state of proper meaning. According to the early medieval sense of history, a primary instance of signification—the moment against which everything else as a dissemination of men and of sense will be measured—occurred in the Garden of Eden. Adam is said to be the first to speak and the inventor of names. Hebrew, the original language, is sacred because it is imagined to be as close as any tongue can be to the thoughts of God at the time of Creation, and, as Philo of Alexandria asserts, to the *matter* of Creation.[18] This belief in the integrity of a primeval language—an *Ursprache* not unlike the Indo-European of the nineteenth-century comparative philologist—lasted for as long as the model of universal history prevailed, that is, almost one thousand years. Dante's search for beginnings, for instance, leads him back through "the first form of speech created by God together with the first soul" to the first Hebrew word, and beyond words to the sound *El,* "which," he maintains, "is neither question nor answer."[19] Meaning everything and excluding nothing, the primal moment of signification is both divine presence and a potential mirror of the created world—an undifferentiated utterance, absolute vocative, whose subsequent division into syllables, words, parts of speech, languages, regional tongues, city dialects, and intramunicipal patois serves as a reminder that the degenerative history of language parallels that of humanity.

The prologue to the *Lais* defines perhaps better than any other work of medieval French literature the extent to which medieval writers in the vernacular also conceived of their task in simultaneously historical and philological terms. Not only is the relationship between past and present thought to involve a process of continual decay, but that decay is, as can be seen in Marie's sense of the loss of original meaning through time, linguistic as well:

> Custume fu as ancïens,
> Ceo tes[ti]moine Precïens,
> Es livres ke jadis feseient
> Assez oscurement diseient
> Pur ceus ki a venir esteient
> Et ki aprendre les deveient,
> K'i peüssent gloser la lettre
> Et de lur sen le surplus mettre
> Li philesophe le saveient
> E par eus memes entendeient,
> Cum plus trespasserunt le tens,
> Plus serreient sutil de sens
> Et plus se savreient garder
> De ceo k'i ert a trespasser. (Prologue, v. 9)

It was customary for the ancients, in the books that they wrote (Priscian testifies to this), to express themselves very obscurely so that those in later generations, who had to learn them, could provide a gloss for the text and put the finishing touches to their meaning. Men of learning were aware of this, and their experience had taught them that the more time they spent studying texts, the more subtle would be their understanding of them, and they would be better able to avoid future mistakes.

Though Marie claims, in keeping with another of the topoi of the age, that experience taught men that "the more time they spent studying texts, the more subtle would be their understanding," it is precisely the necessity of study and understanding that bears witness to a loss of original meaning that, God-given, required no interpretation.[20]

The prologue to the *Lais* can be situated alongside an emphasis upon the primacy of origins, which is an important—yea, the defining—characteristic of early medieval grammar, where it produced a problematics of loss, or a split between what writers and thinkers *knew* about human language as an essentially flawed, irrecuperable medium and what they *felt* as a deep nostalgia for beginnings accompanied by the desire to return. This split was expressed in a variety of discourses including those of theology, philosophy, and history in addition to that of poetry. We see it, for example, in Saint Jerome's fascination with the problem of translation and in his obsession with the mysticism of Hebrew proper names; in Augustine's formulation of an exegetical philology according to which the exegete, "armed with the science of languages," undertakes to restore the diminutions of sense implicit in biblical translation.[21] Such a project is also associated with Augustine's vision of history in which naming, reproduction, understanding, and preaching are bound within an essentially verbal epistemology based upon the mediatory power of signs. As the bishop of Hippo affirms, prophecy, promise, and progeny are all allied:

> Of this there can be no doubt, since these are real facts which cannot be divested of meaning [and these facts are intended to mean something], and since from the very beginning of the human race, God, in his prescience, graciously inscribed in his works that which would come to fruition in centuries hence; he wanted for these things, revealed and written down at the opportune time—whether by the succession of men, or by his Spirit, or by the ministry of angels—to bear witness to those who serve him of the promise of future events and of the knowledge of their completion. Names, as signs, bear prospectively the mark both of their meaning and of their historical effects. Understood through time, they fulfill the promise—complete the genealogy—that they contain.[22]

A corollary of the Augustinian nostalgia for origins lies in the realm of sacramental theology, where the goal of apotheosis—the transcendence of the world of the senses—is, finally, a journey through perception and cognition toward the *intellectio* that would reunite not only the Father with the Son but the Speaker with his Word. Augustine's ideal moment, which remains indistinguishable from the sacrament itself, is a convergence of the form of knowledge with its object, a recuperation of the names that are the "images of things." "Everyone," he affirms, "seeks a certain resemblance in his way of signifying such that signs themselves reproduce, to the extent to which it is possible, the thing signified."[23] Augustine's sacramental theology finds, of course, an analogue in the widespread medieval practice of etymology as a means of producing knowledge of the perceptible world. This strategy reaches its fullest expression in the seventh-century encyclopaedist Isidore of Seville's *Etymologies,* a work, as Curtius maintains, that served as the basis of five centuries of culture.

Marie's presentation of the obscurity of the ancients can be seen to contain a theological dimension. To the extent to which she recognizes language to be a flawed vehicle, a discontinuous medium filled with obscurities, gaps, or holes, a contingent instrument belonging finally to the material world, she participates in a long tradition stretching from at least Augustine to the fourteenth century. Augustine, who offers at once the founding and the fullest account of a theologized sign theory, denies that language could produce knowledge of truth in the first instance. Words can, he maintains, make us remember what we always already knew, they can point us in the direction of truth; but, as material signs, words cannot lead directly to a knowledge of the nonmaterial realm—that is to say, of God, who remains the unique signified to which all words refer, to whom words remain in approximate relation, to whom they can never attain.

I am not suggesting that Marie de France's views on language as presented in the prologue to the *Lais* are essentially different from those of Augustine to be found in the *De Doctrina christiana,* the *De Trinitate,* or the *De Genesi ad litteram,* where the question of the adequacy of words is concerned. Augustine's speculation about signs, verbal signs in particular, which lies at the core of speculation about the personal, the social, and the metaphysical world, and the Augustinian tradition according to which words are flawed and indeed proof of the contingent nature of man, are manifest throughout all that is attributed to the name Marie de France. Indeed, defining her coherence as an author, Marie's obsession with language is expressed on both a thematic and a formal level; it is expressed with unmistakable consciousness sometimes, and at other times seemingly without awareness.[24] It is a drama that infuses almost every aspect of her poetic persona—from a focusing upon certain words in her lexicon of privileged terms, to an overall framing and shaping of individual lais and fables as well as of the Otherworld journey. It is stated in theoretical terms in the prologue to the *Lais* and in that to "Guigemar." It is played out in the *Lais* within the general context of what might be thought of as a theology of language involving different aspects of a common set of concerns: a desire for wholeness, integration, fullness versus a constant awareness of the partial and contingent, fragmentary and fragmenting, nature of linguistic expression; a desire to recuperate the past via memory versus the knowledge of the morbid effects of fixing a living or even an imagined past; an obsession with the question of just how, and how effectively, words signify, and to what they refer; a pervasive agonizing oscillation between the attempt to master words and the recognition that words master us.

Marie de France is an existential writer; and where in the theologized philological tradition of Augustine words may not lead directly to truth, and silence, as in the scene of conversion contained in the *Confessions,* is a prerequisite to the inner perception of a transcendent truth beyond words, she believes in, is committed to, the attempt, despite the odds against it, to produce meaning as seen, first of all, in the obligation to speak:

> Ki Deus a duné escïence
> Et de parler bon' eloquence
> Ne s'en deit taisir ne celer,
> Ainz se deit volunters mustrer.
> Quant uns granz biens est mult oïz,
> Dunc a primes est il fluriz,
> E quant loëz est de plusurs,
> Dunc ad espandues ses flurs. (Prologue, v. 1)

Anyone who has received from God the gift of knowledge and true eloquence has a duty not to remain silent: rather should one be happy to reveal such talents. When a truly beneficial thing is heard by many people, it then enjoys its first blossom.

In resonance with the Old Testament "In the beginning God created the heaven and the earth" and with the New Testament John "In the beginning was the Word," the prologue to the *Lais* begins with creation and with words. This poetics opens with God's creation of the artist, divinely endowed with "speech" and "eloquence," and with a duty to words. In this Marie is not alone, but shares in one of the potent topoi of the High Middle Ages—the responsibility not to remain silent but to share possession of knowledge. Poets of the second half of the twelfth and the thirteenth centuries, poets who, after all, are beginning to speak at a moment of cultural reawakening, often begin by speaking about speaking.[25]

The metaphorics of flowering knowledge belongs, of course, to biblical tradition, and is also to be found among Latin thinkers both preceding and contemporaneous with Marie. Hugh of Saint-Victor draws upon the Parable of the Talents in his condemnation of those who are capable of learning but choose not to do so contained in the preface to the *Didascalicon:* "Many of this sort, caught up in the affairs and cares of this world beyond what is needful or given over to the vices and sensual indulgences of the body, bury the talent of God in earth, seeking from it neither the fruit of wisdom nor the profit of good work. These, assuredly, are completely detestable."[26] The obligation to teach and speak is writ large across a variety of vernacular genres, where it represents, as in the prologue to the *Lais,* a means of beginning. "He who is wise should not hide but should show his wisdom, for when he passes from this world, he will be remembered forever"—thus begins the classical *Roman de Thèbes* in a manner similar to Benoît de Sainte-Maure's *Roman de Troie:* "Solomon teaches us and says, and one can read it in his writings, that one must not hide his wisdom."[27]

Among the didactic genres the analogy between flowering and writing is found in the fables in the prologue to the *Isopet de Lyon:*

> Un petit jardin ai hantey,
> Flours et fruit porte a grant plantey;
> Li fruiz est bons, la flours novele,
> Delitauble, plaisanz et bele.
> Li flours est example de fauble,
> Li fruiz doctrine profitauble.
> Bone est la flour por delitier;
> Lou fruit cuil, se vuez profitier.[28]

I have frequented a little garden that bears flowers and fruit aplenty. The fruit is good, the flowers fresh, delightful, pleasing, and beautiful. The flower represents the fable, and the fruit wise doctrine. The flower is there for the sake of pleasure; but he who wants to gather the fruit will gain knowledge.

Nor is the topos of the obligation to teach in the cause of a flowering of knowledge unknown within the satirical forms of the High Middle Ages. In the prologue to the lady's response to Richard de Fournival's request for love contained in the *Bestiaire d'Amour suivi de la Réponse de la Dame,* she reminds him that "a man who possesses sense and discretion should not use them to cause harm to any man or woman; and the man who knows how to say or do things does a good deed and worthy work in helping others." In Renaut de Beaujeu's *Lai d'Ignauré,* the anticourtly tale of the lover of twelve wives, the negative lesson in the fatal consequences of spreading one's love too thin nonetheless begins with the necessity of a sharing of that knowledge: "One who loves must not keep to himself, but should spread the word so that others might learn."[29]

Among the courtly romancers of Marie's generation, Chrétien de Troyes is the most insistent concerning the obligation to speak and the adverse effects of a failure to do so:

> Li vilains dit an son respit
> que tel chose a l'an an despit
> qui molt valt mialz que l'an ne cuide;
> por ce fet bien qui son estuide
> atorne a bien quel que il l'ait;
> car qui son estuide antrelait,
> tost i puet tel chose teisir
> qui molt vandroit puis a pleisir.[30]

The peasant in his proverb says that one might find oneself holding in contempt something that is worth much more than one believes: therefore a man does well to make good use of his learning according to whatever understanding he has, for he who neglects his learning may easily keep silent something that would later give much pleasure.

With the opening of *Erec et Enide,* which some consider alongside the *Lais* to be the first romance, and which is certainly the first Arthurian romance, we are, as in the case of Marie, plunged into the world of literature, by which I mean a self-conscious focus upon the process of writing itself, an awareness of the question of what it means to make literary texts. More precisely, we enter from the start into literature's questions to itself about language: about the difference between ordinary and poetic language, about intention and reception, about esthetic value, about the social implications of esthetics, in short, the question of origins. Every work is in this sense an awakening, a coming into being of something, a specific thing. "Li vilains dit an son respit" stands, moreover, as a proverb about the proverbial—that is to say a popular status of language—which goes to the heart of the subject matter of poetry, "tel chose," and to the question of the poet's relation to both authorial agency and meaning. Before the literary "thing" one is faced, in the prologue to *Erec et Enide* as well in that to the *Lais,* with the dilemma of choosing between "leaving off," silence and hiding ("taisir ne celer") for Marie and "easily keeping silent" for Chrétien ("tost i puet tel chose teisir"); or pleasure for Chrétien ("qui molt vandroit puis a pleisir") and a "flowering" and praise for Marie. The rhetorical pressure is, of course, as both Chrétien and Marie acknowledge, on the side of attention: it is better to make something out of nothing, which is potentially the source of pleasure, than to leave nothing alone. As in the case of Pascal's bet, it is better to be safe and stay alert than to "neglect," "leave off," or "antrelait."

In the defense of writing, a *causa scribendi* voiced as the moral obligation to speak, lies one of the deeply obsessive components of Marie's conceptual universe, one that is expressed both personally and collectively, both as a drama of language and as theme: on the one hand, one must speak, and, on the other, one is aware of the perils and pitfalls that speech entails. Where writing is concerned, one must write, convinced that writing may somehow reverse history's degenerative drift, while also aware of writing's fragmenting effects, that writing, finally, might contribute to rather than contain the very loss it appears to restore. This is an opposition that runs throughout the *Lais* and that is manifest from the start in Marie's making of literature a philological project, a project of reclamation in which memory and writing are conceived as means of countering the corrosive consequences of temporal decline.

THE WILL TO REMEMBER

No one is more aware than Marie of the usurious effects of time: the nature of the historical process always involves a loss. Literature as Marie conceives it is a memorial to that loss, representing as it does the various ways in which loss is externalized, figured, mourned, as well as the ways in which it might be recuperated. Here is where *memory* comes into play. Marie is haunted throughout the *Lais*, the *Fables*, and the *Espurgatoire* by the threat of a loss of memory, by the necessity of not forgetting that which is potentially lost because it is literally not articulated, not related, not given via language some more enduring form:[31]

> Des lais pensai, k'oï aveie;
> Ne dutai pas, bien le saveie,
> Ke pur remembrance les firent
> Des aventures k'il oïrent
> Cil ki primes les comencierent
> E ki avant les enveierent.
> Plusurs en ai oï conter,
> Ne[s] voil laisser në oblïer. (v. 33)

I thought of lais that I had heard and did not doubt, for I knew it full well, that they were composed, by those who first began them and put them into circulation, to perpetuate the memory of adventures they had heard. I myself have heard a number of them and do not wish to overlook or neglect them.

This passage seems to refer to an oral event as memory and as being itself remembered, as being that which Marie has "heard tell" about the "adventures" that others have heard, remembered, and recited—"Ke pur remembrance les firent/Des aventures k'il oïrent"—just as she has heard, remembered, and written them down. That which she remembers is, in other words, the memory of a memory, which is not fully recuperated, not really remembered, until it is fixed in writing. The point is consistent with what we find elsewhere: in "Chevrefoil," for example, a lai that is about writing and about the relation of oral to written expression, we read that Tristan was already a writer whose project of remembering is not so different from that of Marie:

> Pur la joie qu'il ot eüe
> De s'amie qu'il ot veüe
> E pur ceo k'il aveit escrit,
> Si cum la reïne l'ot dit,
> Pur les paroles remembrer,
> Tristam, ki bien saveit harper,
> En aveit fet un nuvel lai;
>
> . . . .
>
> Dit vus en ai la verité
> Del lai que j'ai ici cunté. (vv. 107, 117)

On account of the joy he had experienced from the sight of his beloved and because of what he had written, Tristam, a skilful harpist, in order to record his words (as the queen had said he should), used them to create a new lai. . . . I have told you the truth of the lai I have related here.

The term "remembrance" means, of course, remembering in the modern sense of the term. But "remembrance" also holds a connotation in Old French that has been lost in modern French except in the French countryside, where farmers still use it to refer to the recombination of dispersed lands. "Remembrance" in Marie connotes a reassembling of that which has been scattered, a recuperation of that which has been fragmented and lost, an articulation or rearticulation.[32] And so the obligation to speak, given an ethical cast, is also an obligation to remember, to heal the wound of dismemberment and loss, as Marie herself assimilates moral duty and memory in the self-characterization at the beginning of "Guigemar"—"Marie/ Ki en sun tens pas ne s'oblie," which means "Marie who does not neglect her duty or does not forget," but can be stretched to "Marie who is not forgotten in her time." For remembering is also prospective: s/he who forgets risks being forgotten. So too, alongside the obligation to speak, a case can be made for the relationship between memory and what we have seen to be Marie's fear that her work will be appropriated by others. As Mary Carruthers argues in her monumental book on memory in the Middle Ages, plagiarism can, in a tradition heavily dependent on the arts of memory, be conceived as a failure of memory.[33]

Memory for Marie is not simply a phenomenon of individual consciousness, a question of subjective moral agency, but a cultural mechanism as well: the memory of the individual is linked to a collective memory, to the commemoration implicit in the dedication contained in the general prologue:

> En l'honur de vus, nobles reis,
> Ki tant estes pruz e curteis,
> A ki tute joie se encline,
> E en ki quoer tuz biens racine,
> M'entremis de lais assembler,
> Par rime fere e reconter. (v. 43)

In your honor, noble king, you who are so worthy and courtly, you to whom all joy pays homage and in whose heart all true virtue has taken root, did I set myself to assemble lais, to compose and to relate them in rhyme.

Marie's passing on of her material is an act of remembering and literally of "assembling" that which has, in one possible reading, "been left behind— "M'entremis de lais assembler." It is a retelling in poetry or rhyme—"Par rime fere e reconter"—of that which has, as we learn in the prologue to "Guigemar," already been told: "Les contes ke jo sai verrais,/Dunt li Bretun unt fait les lais,/Vos conterai assez briefment" ("I shall relate briefly to you stories that I know to be true and from which the Bretons have composed their lais" [vv. 19–21]). In the recounting of that which has already been "counted," Marie inserts herself into a literary genealogy, a genesis of tales. Again, the obligation to speak, the study of the works of preceding generations, and the preservation of the record of the past establish a link, a genealogy, that serves to eradicate a sense of loss and to make whole—

that is, to give meaning to—the fragmentary and contingent nature of lived experience, the "adventure."

"GUIGEMAR"

The prologue to the *Lais* contains a virtual program for the writing and reading of medieval literature. France's first woman writer, at over six centuries' remove from Priscian, places herself in the same position to him as the author of the *Institutiones Grammaticae* stands in relation to the ancients; and, indeed, in a position analogous to ours in relation to her. So too Marie poses more generally the problem of the reader before any text; for the project in which she is engaged is not so much a philological as an epistemological undertaking, one that collapses the distinction between historical otherness and the otherness of writing, reading, and interpreting. Just as there can be no access to the past, there is no unmediated access to the text, any text, which, because of the degraded nature of verbal signs according to medieval sign theory, requires interpretation or gloss.

That which is desired, through gloss, is something like a proper signification or the full word, a place *(locus)* from which to speak because it is conceived to be ontologically grounded. "Locus," says Varro, in discussing the first element of speech, "is where something can be *locatum* 'placed.' Where anything comes to a standstill is a *locus* 'place.'"[34] The reader or interpreter desires access to the zone where, within such a verbal epistemology of return, all movement toward a source halts, where meaning is imagined to come to rest and to be immutable.

Words, figured to be ontologically grounded, become the objects of desire because they are imagined to be rooted, full, autonomous. Like Aquinas's proofs of God as the One who moves but is not moved, the One on whom others depend but who depends on nothing, the hypothetical full word is also without origin and contains its own value. Where poetry is concerned, it is the creator, the one who introduces obscurities, gaps, or holes in language (the trouvère) and who is most capable of attaining to the full word, who himself becomes the object of desire; and of jealousy, since *goloser* also means "to rival," "to be jealous of," jealousy causing, as we saw in the prologue to "Guigemar" (above, p. 12), others to act like a "vicious, cowardly, treacherous dog that will bite others out of malice." "Guigemar" is the story of an uninitiated knight's ill-fated hunt, journey to the Otherworld where he meets the imprisoned wife of a jealous old man, loves her for a year before being discovered, then returns—via a mysterious boat that

seems always to be waiting—to his original point of departure. The unhappily married woman eventually escapes to join him and undoes the knot
she has placed in his shirt as the sign of recognition.

Like the poet capable of the full word, Guigemar is at the outset an autonomous being—the one who, unspoiled, remains sexually undefined,
foreign to desire: "De tant i out mespris nature/Ke unc de nul amur n'out
cure" ("He had so scorned nature that he had no use for love" [v. 57]). And
yet he is at the same time, and precisely because of such a lack of definition,
the object of universal desire:

> Suz ciel n'out dame ne pucele
> Ki tant par fust noble ne bele,
> Së il de amer la requeïst,
> Ke volentiers nel retenist.
> Plusurs le requistrent suvent,
> Mais il n'aveit de ceo talent. (v. 59)

There was no lady or maiden on earth, however noble or beautiful, who
would not have been happy to accept him as her lover, if he had sought
her love. Women frequently made advances to him, but he was indifferent to them.

The hero participates in the fantasy of self-sufficiency, a being dependent on
no other, Being itself. Until, of course, he meets the same—the doe that is
also *hors de série,* unique because of its whiteness, but also because this doe
with antlers is as sexually undetermined as Guigemar:

> En l'espeise d'un grant buissun
> Vit une bise od un foün;
> Tute fu blanche cele beste,
> Perches de cerf out en la teste. (v. 89)

In the heart of a large bush he saw a hind with its fawn; the beast was completely white with the antlers of a stag on its head.

And until he shoots the arrow that signals directionality, the entrance of becoming and representation upon the narcissistic scene of Being, of the contingent upon the necessary, of history, time, and narrational kinesis upon
the hypostatized fantasy of plenitude: "Il tent sun arc, si trait a li,/En l'esclot
la feri devaunt" ("Guigemar stretched his bow, fired his arrow and struck the
animal in its forehead" [v. 94]). The shooting of the arrow that is drawn
to him—"trait a li"—is, in short, an inscription on the level of theme of
what narrative elaboration is all about and remains indistinguishable from

Marie's drawing of her own project: "Ki de bone matiere traite,/Mult li pese si bien n'est faite."

The semantic range of *traire* is rich indeed and presents another of those nodes of meaning that challenge the premise that reading classical or medieval texts is merely a matter of dictionary definitions. *Traire* defines the essence of Marie's own poetic project, her own desire. For *traire* (MF *tirer*) means "to shoot"; but it also means "to draw out," or, simply, "to draw," as suggested by the "traits" of the portrait of Venus painted on the wall of the lady's prison tower:

> La chaumbre ert peinte tut entur:
> Venus, la deuesse d'amur,
> Fu tres bien [mise] en la peinture,
> Les traiz mustrez e la nature
> Coment hom deit amur tenir. (v. 233)

> The walls of the chamber were covered in paintings in which Venus, the goddess of love, was skillfully depicted together with nature and obligations of love.

Then too, *traire* also signifies "to translate," "to transmit," or "to transform" and is the term for that which any author does in extruding or drawing one text from another: "De aukune bone estoire faire/Et de latin en romaunz traire."[35] As translation, *traire* implies the transformation of the same into the other; and if it means "to shoot," "to distance," or "to introduce difference," it is because such terms of alienation are homonyms of "to deceive." Indeed, given the fact that Old French, even though written, was intended for the ear (to be either recited or read aloud), there can be no difference between the words *traire* and *trahir*. "To draw or shoot" and "to betray" stand as proof of the treacherousness of a homophonic lack of difference in the sound of a word that can also mean "to differ."

The arrow that is drawn also betrays, is deflected, returns to the self that shoots, wounding the archer in exactly the same place as the impotent Fisher King of Grail tradition: the thigh. Guigemar's wound, the "plaie en la quisse," is a dismemberment, a gap or *faille* in the body, which, in seeking to be filled, provokes the quest for health that is a thematic version of the narrative quest for meaning. As Guigemar is found by his lady and her maid, the former places her hand upon his breast: "Chaut le senti e le quor sein" ("She discovered it was warm and his heart sound" [v. 300]), which can also be rendered, "She feels it warm, and his body bleeds," or "She feels it warm and his body signifies." "En la quisse m'ad si nafré,/Jamés ne quide es-tre sané!" ("I am so wounded in the thigh that I despair of ever being healed" [v. 319]) or "I despair of ever being signified." For the homophonic pair "sené"/"sané" can mean "sign," "sense" (as in Marie's original "surplus de sens"), and "health," as in the common designation of the "forcené" as the one who is both "outside of signs" and "out of his mind [senses]" or "un-healthy."

Such an assertion suggests that the hero's wanderings and attempt to overcome or reverse his own dismemberment are, on the level of plot, as-similable to the trouvère's avowed project of memory or "remembrement"; neither of which can be detached from the lacks—the *trous*—of the letter seeking a surplus of sense. Guigemar's displacements—to the Otherworld and back—represent an attempt to heal the wound opened by the deflected arrow: "Començat sei a purpenser/En quel tere purrat aler/Pur sa plaie faire guarir" ("He wondered where he could go to find a cure for his wound" [v. 125]). Displacements, of course, without the consciousness that the de-sire for bodily wholeness cannot be detached from the desire for plenitude of meaning and that this desire is, ultimately, the desire for desire (as well as the desire for gloss). For the boat in which the knight drifts carries him to the land of jealousy and desire with the understanding that it is in the wound that desire originates and that "love is a wound within the body": "Amur est plai[e de]denz cors" (v. 482).

Thus, despite her project of reassemblage, of "remembrement," of re-covering a past and passing it to the future via a process of cultural recuper-ation, Marie is deviled by the linguistic duplicity of words—that is to say, by the fact that words, no matter how finely they are assembled, are un-faithful, they betray. This is not simply a matter of one word meaning sev-eral and even multiple things, as in the case of *traire, sané,* or the word *lai* itself, not simply a matter of two words meaning the same thing, though one of the traits of Marie's style is a doubling of adjectives, nouns, adverbs, and verbs alongside of the double naming in her imposition of titles, but a doubling implicit in the process that also haunts her—that of translation. It is a matter of words having a life of their own. Regardless of the attempt to govern their meaning, words escape human intention to which they re-main indifferent. This is in my view the profound truth of the *Lais* and one aspect of Marie's poetic persona: an awareness perhaps greater than that of any other author of her time of the extent to which language escapes the at-tempt to master it, to contain it, and, at the same time, an equally great awareness of the necessity of the struggle for control. For her (as for me, which is perhaps why we get along so well), the essence of the human condition is an effort to impose meaning upon a diffident world.

This is another way of saying that we are getting to know Marie de France, that anonymous person who must remain so when viewed from the outside, but who begins to reveal this side of herself only from within where we detect a certain philosophical anguish before what is lived as a principle of linguistic loss. As we have seen, she emphasizes from the beginning of the prologue to the *Lais* a certain impossibility written into all communication, a gap between speaker and hearer, between writer and reader, that defines the parameters of authorial agency—and that makes out of reading an act of interpretation. The letter, once written, circulates: that is, finds its meaning in him or her who understands. Meaning in such a process of circulation becomes a function of an active subject, a participatory reader of a writerly text in the sense that Roland Barthes intended for our own era. As we shall see too, meaning, uncontrollable by the individual agent that produces it, entails a loss, a loss of control over a text sent out like a bottle thrown into the sea. Indeed, Marie sees the "first ones" to make such stories—"Cil ki primes les comencierent/E ki avant les enveierent" (Prologue, v. 37)—in just such terms: those who "begin" and who "send out," launchers in a word. The supposed sources of the *Lais* are no different from any other writer whose work is read, that is to say, potentially appropriated, by those to whom it is—or is not—addressed.

Such appropriation or misappropriation is unavoidable, first, because the sense added by the reader is never quite adequate to, never quite fits, that intended by the writer. Something always falls short of or exceeds authorial intention, even assuming that that intention is consciously known to the writer, if only because something always spills over the edges, is inappropriate, does not match up between two consciousnesses, two subjectivities, which, no how much they may think they may understand each other, remain radically different. That two individuals never manage fully to understand each other is neither an original nor a profound idea; nothing is more banal. The interest of such an idea for Marie, and indeed for us—not only for our critical selves, but for our everyday lives—lies in the analysis of where a text or the words of another do, or do not, fit, where the misunderstandings lie, the very word *lie* serving to designate both location and untruthful intent. For in the subjective contours of our own misinterpretations, either as readers or as lovers, we can detect not only the presence, but the specific shape, of our *desire*.

The excesses of meaning interjected by the reader—Marie's "surplus"—are, as she knows, never arbitrary, but always motivated.[36] *Gloser* means "to gloss" or "to interpret," which in medieval poetics is also always eroticized. "To gloss the letter" is "to desire" or *golozer* (from Lat. *glutio*) the letter, as in the Patristic association of letters with the corporeal. Then too, the "surplus of sense" that gloss produces sustains such a gloss on gloss. For *sens* can mean in Old French "sign," "sense," but also "seed" or semen (from Lat. *semino*); and the word *surplus* as "excess" and a spilling of seed equivalent to the much-abused French *jouissance* is regularly used in Old French, as it is in "Guigemar," to indicate the sexual act, pleasure that exceeds language—"Ensemble gisent et parolent/Et sovent baisent e acolent;/Bien lur coviegne del surplus,/De ceo que li autre unt en us!" ("They lay together and talked, kissing and embracing. May the final act, which others are accustomed to enjoy, give them pleasure" [v. 531]).

Marie, and she is not alone, makes a persuasive case for the analogy between sexual jealousy and the desire for the word. Thus the husband's dread of losing his young wife—"Gelus esteit a desmesure" ("He was excessively jealous" [v. 213])—is analogous to Marie's own anxiety at the thought of misappropriation, as the fear of having one's wife turned away from prison becomes equivalent to the fear of misprision: "Si gangleür u losengier/Le me volent a mal turner;/Ceo est lur dreit de mesparler" ("But just because spiteful tittle-tattlers attempt to find fault with me, I do not intend to give up. They have a right to make slanderous remarks" [v. 16]). Nor should it be thought that desire originates in anything like nature, the body, or a naturalism of the body that is so often mistakenly associated with medieval literature as preliterary or natural. On the contrary, the walled tower that is supposed to contain the woman and constrain her desire is, as we have seen, lined with pictures—and a book:

> Le livre Ovide, ou il enseine
> Comment chascun s'amur estreine,
> En un fu ardent le gettout
> Et tuz iceus escumengout
> Ki ja mais cel livre lirreient
> Ne sun enseignement fereient.
> La fu la dame enclose e mise. (v. 239)

In the painting Venus was shown as casting into a blazing fire the book in which Ovid teaches the art of controlling love and as excommunicating all those who read this book or adopted its teachings.

Guigemar's voyage, in other words, takes him to the Otherworld, but the Otherworld is a book, or the very letters and pictures that are the source of desire envisaged, as in the Paolo and Francesca episode of the *Inferno,* as an infinite regress toward other books, the very works from which the present catalyst to sexual longing has been drawn or "trahi." A book, furthermore, that contains its own formula of mandatory misreading in the promise to excommunicate all who read and follow its command. The book is the embodiment of a literary law—or *lei*—that prescribes its own transgression, signifies plurally and even in contradiction to itself, as opposed to the judicial law, which a society agrees to allow to signify univocally.

All of which poses the questions, To what does the letter, do letters, refer? Does the letter bear us to a sense outside of the text? To an Otherworld? Or does it refer, as the example suggests, only to other letters? Does the letter take us back to a place in the Varronian sense? To a nature? Toward the body? What is the relation of the letter to Guigemar's trajectory? What determines his course? Why is he necessarily drawn to the place of desire? Why does he return to the original point of departure? Are the voyages of the mysterious boat without pilot in some sense programmed or prescribed (see vv. 629, 678)? Is the question of the boat, finally, the same as the question of understanding, as whether or not sense returns to a place? If so, is there then a place, a code, a set of criteria or a doctrine outside the text from which to interpret its perambulations? Does the letter hit the mark, or, like Guigemar's arrow, only ricochet back to open a difference within the body, a difference from itself?

A reading of misreading that would return the letter to itself, turn it upon itself, is implicit in Guigemar's wound; for the "plaie" that bleeds and signifies is a "plait," or plea, the equivalent of speech itself. "Fair lady, let us put an end to this discussion" ("Bele dame, finum cest plait!" [v. 526]), says the frustrated lover, urging that they pass from speech to the lovemaking that Marie situates as a surplus beyond letters. Nor can the attentive reader avoid the identity of the wound that is a plea with the pleat or knot that, according to the traditional love ordeal, Guigemar and his lady alone can untie as the guarantee of reading each other. The shirttail that in the beginning stanches the wound ("De sa chemise estreitement/Sa plaie bende fermement," "He bound his wound firmly and tightly with his shirt" [v. 139]) is also a tangle of meaning, an undoable surplus of sense. The "plait" that is a pleat or a fold serves, in other words, and this according to Marie's own thesis concerning obscurity, as a reminder not only that the letter, as in the ordeal of the series of ladies who try to undo Guigemar's knot, remains closed ("Unc ne la purent despleier," "They never were successful" [v. 654]), but, once again, that desire is a function of the pleat's closedness: "Amur est plai[e de]denz cors" (v. 482). Which comes to be read, finally, as "Desire is a wound, knot, pleat, or plea in the body, or in the (textual) corpus." Rather, since the reader remains incapable of positing priority for a reading that would privilege either "pleat" or "plea," desire can be identified with the folds of a text, its pleats, its pleas, its resisting obscurities that, as Marie insists from the start, form the undoable knot of fiction. For the undoing of the shirttail—thematized at the end of "Guigemar" as an untying without cutting—merely gives way to the unfolding of another tale:

> A ses costez li met ses meins,
> Si ad trovee la ceinture.
> "Bele," fet il, "queile aventure
> Que jo vus ai issi trovee!
> Ki vus ad [i]ci amenee?"
> Ele li cunte la dolur,
> Les peines granz e la tristur
> De la prisun u ele fu,
> E coment li est avenu:
> Coment ele [s'en] eschapa;
> Neer se volt, la neif trova,
> Dedeinz entra, a cel port vient. (v. 820)

He placed his hands on her hips and found the belt. "Beloved," he said, "how fortunate that I have discovered you like this! Who brought you here?" She related to him the grief, the great suffering, and the dreariness of the prison in which she had been, and how things had turned out, how she escaped with the intention of drowning herself, but had found the ship, gone on board and arrived at this port.

Guigemar's circuit—from home to the fantasy-filled world of the book and back—is, at bottom, the closed cycle of fiction. This is where the discovery of the lovers, a supposed laying of hands upon the body and capture of the truth of adultery in flagrante delicto, comes into central focus: "Cel jur furent aparceü,/Descovert, trové, et veü" ("That day they were perceived, discovered, found, and seen" [v. 577]). It is the fact of being found—"trahit," compromised, and invented, "trové"—that sends Guigemar home and leaves the reader with the understanding that "to find," "invent," or "compose" ("contract," "negotiate") represents a despoiling, uncovering, unfolding of the pleat that betrays. Herein lies the text's link to the ideology of so-called courtly or secret adulterous love. For the poet, in composing, does to the lovers exactly what the jealous husband does to his wife and her lover: s/he betrays by revealing, and thus destroys at the very moment s/he creates. Such a premise justifies, I think, a reading at the level of the letter— "selunc la lettre et l'escriture" (v. 23)—which also pleases. It is, according to Marie, a pleasure to deplete the tale of sense: "Mult est bele, ki la depleie" (v. 160).

CHAPTER TWO

If Words Could Kill: The *Lais* and Fatal Speech

We have seen by way of introduction the extent to which a drama of language is played out in the works of Marie de France with particular reference to the general prologue to the *Lais* and to "Guigemar." Defined as globally as possible, this drama involves a deep desire on Marie's part for control over meaning, over intention—over words, in a word—versus a heightened consciousness of the unmasterability of language, of the resistance of literary language in particular to any attempt to control its unpredictable effects. It can be seen on the one hand in her insistence upon the obligation to speak, to share one's knowledge, or to teach, and in the wish for wholeness captured in the project of "remembrement," both a remembering, an act of cultural reclamation, and a reassembling, and on the other hand in her awareness of the contingent, fragmentary, and fragmenting nature of linguistic expression, the tendency of words, once assembled, to move in unforeseen directions, to take on a life of their own. Such is, finally, the meaning of "Guigemar," the tale of the arrow that returns to wound the one who launches it like a literary work, and of the hero whose quest for bodily wholeness takes him to the land of fiction and of love before returning in the end to the point of departure, and, finally, to conjugal union; the whole summed up in the knot to be undone without cutting.

Marie's language theater, which not only uses language as a poetic vehicle but makes of it an object of plotted scrutiny, places it on view in all its complicated opaqueness and infuses almost every aspect of her works on both a formal and a thematic level. The impulse toward wholeness manifests itself, in fact, in terms of a desire for structure in the most literal and concrete sense. Marie tends to frame her tales. In the *Lais* we find formal passages of entry and exit even when there is no independent prologue or epilogue; almost none are without markers of origin and of transmission, a showing of "how the lai was made," even when such points involve merely a vague allusion to source or a drawing of attention to the imposition of a name, a title, at beginning or end. Then too, as critics have noted for some time, the *Lais* tend to attract one another in pairs or in groups that can sometimes be defined even in terms of gender pairings—Lanval's feminine fairy benefactor, for instance, set against the dreams of rescue on the part of the imprisoned wives of "Yonec" and "Guigemar."[1] Unlike, say, the romances of Chrétien or the *Tristan* poets, unlike even the *Fables,* where much attention is paid to government and community, or the *Espurgatoire,* where Marie insists upon the spiritual fellowship of the saved and the damned, the couple is the operative social unit within the *Lais,* where the desire for wholeness is expressed in terms of love as a longing for union, a coupling, an appropriate—that is to say, equitable, decent, voluntary—love, which may even involve marriage.

Marriage, however, fails to satisfy the desire for wholeness on the part of a number of Marie's inevitably suffering heroes and heroines around the outer edges of these case studies in longing. At an extreme lurk those who, like Guigemar in the beginning, desire nothing more than to be beyond desire—autonomous, self-sufficient, entire unto themselves—or those who, as we shall see, confuse wholeness with abundance: Eliduc, who maintains two wives, and the lady of "Chaitivel," who, when it comes to suitors, prefers not to choose and wants to keep them all.

Here we arrive at one of the defining dilemmas of the *Lais* and the subject of this chapter: that is, the constant tension between the recurrent desire to "have it all" and the necessity of choice, which amounts to an analogy between the material of the story, its *aventure,* and the making of narrative. Marie's *Lais* seem, where language is concerned, to perform that which they recount, to expose the architectonics of their own creation in a way that permits us to erect as a trait of her style, indeed as a productive principle, the fact that almost anything that can be said about the themes of the *Lais,* whether on the level of economics, erotics, or social institutions, can also be said about her conscious concretization of language itself. This is not a question of interpretation, but, I think, a matter of authorial intent. To repeat, words for Marie are not merely a vehicle, a transparent medium through which we glimpse the portrait of a world that is narratively reclaimed and contained, but a theme—perhaps the theme—of the *Lais* as well as the *Fables* and *Espurgatoire.* For no matter how a particular tale is resolved, whether it ends happily as in the case of "Guigemar," "Lanval," and "Le Fresne," or unhappily, as in "Laüstic," "Deus Amanz," "Chaitivel," or "Equitan," or in a mixed manner as in "Yonec" and "Milun," or doesn't end at all as in "Chevrefoil," the tension between a desire for wholeness and a sense of loss both experienced by the characters and thematized in terms of language itself is the inescapable hub around which everything turns. Language is a character, perhaps the main character, capable of eliciting all the emotions connected to the various figures depicted in the *Lais*—trust, love, fear, jealousy, betrayal. For there is no separating Marie's *contes* from their form; rather, there is no separating the themes they contain in language from the thematic performance of language as a constant threat to the wholeness that is the object of all human longing, and, as we shall see in the pages that follow, from language as fatal.

From the beginning Marie's readers have sensed something melancholic in the *Lais* that, as far back as the eighteenth century, conjures geographic associations. The Abbé La Rue, it will be remembered, claims that "the English muse seems to have inspired her. All her subjects are sad and melancholy; she appears to have designed to melt the hearts of her readers, either by the unfortunate situation of her hero, or by some truly afflicting catastrophe."[2] And while there is no reason to believe that the English were any more gloomy in the twelfth or thirteenth century than the French or Anglo-Normans, the pioneering Abbé did sense something operative within Marie's text—that is, the extent to which the geographic sites of the *Lais* are infused with a sadness that seems often to be set in the soil, a sorrow out of which characters and situations seem to grow as if adapting to the depressive ecology of a dolorous natural habitat. The action of "Le Fresne" takes place in the land of "Dol" ("A Dol aveit un bon seignur" [v. 243, see also v. 362]), just as that of "Yonec" is situated on the river "Düelas" ("La cité siet sur Düelas" [v. 15]), both names carrying a sense of sadness, of "deuil" (from Latin *dolus*). The region of "Yonec," of which the old, jealous man is the lord, is called, further, "Carwent" (or "Carüent" in other transcriptions) ("En Bretain[e] maneit jadis/Un riches hum viel e antis;/De Carwent fu avouez" [v. 11]), as if the realm itself, from the Latin *careo, carere*, signified "to be cut off from," "to lack." The lord of the region of "lack" is wanting. The couple lacks progeny ("Unques entre eus n'eurent enfanz" [v. 38]). Most of all, the lady of "Carwent" lacks: she is deprived of the outside world ("Ne fors de cele tur n'eissi,/Ne pur parent ne pur ami," "She did not leave the tower for either family or friend" [v. 39]); of male company ("N'i ot chamberlenc ne huisser/Ki en la chambre osast entrer," "There was neither

chamberlain nor doorkeeper who would have dared enter the chamber"
[v. 43]); of speech ("Mes ja la dame n'i parlast,/Si la vielle ne comandast,"
"The lady would never have spoken without the old woman's permission"
[v. 35]); finally, she is robbed of her beauty because she lacks desire:

> Mut ert la dame en grant tristur;
> Od lermes, od suspir e plur
> Sa beuté pert en teu mesure
> Cume cele qui n'en ad cure. (v. 45)

The lady was in great distress, and she wept and sighed so much that she lost
her beauty, like one who no longer cares.

"Lanval" takes place in the city of "Kardoel" (and in some transcriptions
"Cardoel"), an allomorph of both *careokarere* and *duelldol*, just as "Laüstic"
is situated "En Seint Mallo," which resonates with the *malumhnal* that is its
theme. The action of "Les Deus Amanz" occurs in "Neustrie," which, Marie
tells is, "we call Normandy" ("Que nus apelum Normendie" [v. 8]); more
precisely:

> Une cité fist faire uns reis
> Quë esteit sir des Pistreis;
> Des Pistreins la fist [il] numer
> E Pistre la fist apeler.
> Tuz jurs ad puis duré li nuns;
> Uncore i ad vile e maisuns.
> Nus savum bien de la cuntree,
> Li vals de Pistre est nomee. (v. 13)

A king had a city built which he named after the inhabitants and called
Pitres. The name has survived to this day and there is still a town and houses
there. We know the area well, for it is called the Valley of Pitres.

The site of the fatal love test of this particular lai is the "vals de Pistre,"
or the "valley of pity," an unavoidable semantic association with the Old
French *pite* meaning "who has pity" or "worthy of pity" and *piteer,* "to have
pity," "to pity." Then too, the valley that is in the moral geography of Old
French literature linked to sadness is the place to which Lanval, despite the
appearance of rescue, repairs at the end of the lai that bears his name—
"Avalun," "in the direction of the little valley," "downhill."[3]

Indeed, the *Lais* often take us downhill, infuse in the reader a sense of
loss and decline. The ways in which loss manifests itself do, of course, vary.

We find, for example, a pattern of loss and recovery in "Lanval," where the hero is swept off to Avalon by the fairy queen, in "Guigemar," where, as we have seen, the lovers reunite in the end, in "Milun," where the son joins his parents in marriage, and in "Le Fresne," the lai with both the happiest and perhaps the most carefully plotted ending, in which true love triumphs, the malicious mother repents, and the parents who have consented to allow the archbishop to annul the marriage of their other daughter displaced by Fresne find her a rich husband in their own land. In each of these an initial state of fulfillment is interrupted by a temporary separation prior to recovery in the end, though sometimes, as in "Lanval," the recovery is somewhat incredible and only in the nick of time; or, as in "Le Fresne," somewhat accidental and, between the wedding ceremony and consummation of the marriage, none too soon; or, finally, as in "Milun," where the death of the lady's husband allows the son to give his mother to his father—"Lur fiz amdeus les assembla,/La mere a sun pere dona" (v. 529)—suspiciously well timed. Only "Guigemar," the first lai in the disposition of Harley 978, seems to enjoy a happy ending prepared narratively from the start or from somewhere around the middle, and not brought about by a sudden and factitious arrival of a rescuing fairy ("Lanval"), the accidental discovery of a piece of cloth dispensed with some twenty years earlier ("Le Fresne"), or the news of a liberating widowhood ("Milun"). After the first lai, it is, I am afraid, all downhill.[4]

From loss and recovery Marie quickly slides into a pattern of suffering and withdrawal from the world, as in "Eliduc," or suffering and revenge. "Equitan," "Bisclavret," and "Yonec" make it clear that there are certain losses that remain irrecuperable and that, when deliverance is no longer possible, getting even restores some sense of balance in the end. Even here, however, there are degrees. For the wronged husband of "Equitan" the death of his wife and her royal lover ("Issi mururent amb[e]dui" [v. 305]) is justified by a sense of distributive justice not unlike that meted out in the fabliaux—"[Anyone willing to listen] can take an example here: Evil can easily rebound on him who seeks another's misfortune" ("Ici purreit ensample prendre:/Tel purcace le mal d'autrui/Dunt le mals [tut] revert sur lui" [v. 308]). For the betrayed husband of "Bisclavret," cutting off his wife's nose is sufficient revenge for her misdeed, but it does not prevent her from remarrying and producing a lineage of women, some of whom, Marie specifies, are "born without noses and live noseless" ("senz nes sunt nees /E si viveient esnasees" [v. 313]). Yonec's revenge is, however, more enduring:

having heard the story of his father's death from his mother, who dies from the telling, he slays his father's killer, his mother's husband, on the site of his father's grave.

Where loss is not recuperated by withdrawal or revenge, it is pure, and nothing characterizes the *Lais* more than the irreversible sense of forfeiture and bereavement in "Chaitivel," whose other name is "Quatre Dols," "Deus Amanz," the story of the fatal love ordeal, and "Laüstic," where the death of the nightingale is synonymous with the death of love and, one assumes, the perpetual grief of lovers taken to be as good as dead. These are lais inscribed in the mood of loss, a mood hypostatized in "Chevrefoil," the least resolved of the lais, in which the ash tree dies without the honeysuckle that surrounds it:

> Ensemble poënt bien durer;
> Mes ki puis les volt desevrer,
> Li codres muert hastivement
> E li chevrefoil ensement. (v. 73)

The two can survive together; but if anyone should then attempt to separate them, the hazel quickly dies, as does the honeysuckle.

In "Chevrefoil" a lack of completion is both formal and thematic: a narrative fragment mirrors a state of suspended suffering without other resolution, as we know from other fragments, than love-death.

There is in the *Lais* a sense that love is tragic. Tragic not only for wives, but, it must be said, also for husbands, whose own sense of lack is more often than not expressed in terms of jealousy. We have already encountered the jealous old husband of "Guigemar," who meets his match in "Yonec": "Because she was so fair and noble, he took good care to watch over her and locked her in his tower" ("De ceo kë ele ert bele et gente,/En li garder mist mut s'entente:/Dedenz sa tur l'ad enserree" [v. 25]). In "Milun," we learn of the jealousy of the husband from the wife's point of view:

> "Mes jeo ne sui mie delivre,
> Ainz ai asez sur mei gardeins
> Veuz e jeofnes, mes chamberleins,
> Que tuz jurs heent bone amur.
> E se delitent en tristur." (v. 144)

I am not free. I have my chamberlain and many guards, young and old, who hate to see a just love and who delight in sadness.

Nor are fathers immune from a version of jealousy that in "Les Deus Amanz" has all the earmarks of a sexual scenario according to which the daughter has merely replaced the dead mother in the psychic economy of the patriarch, who considers "how he could prevent anyone seeking his daughter's hand": "Cumença sei a purpenser/Cument s'en purrat delivrer/Que nul sa fille ne quesist" (v. 29). Alongside of the jealous old men, however, we find the merely suspicious mates of the *Lais:* the husband in "Laüstic," who, "irritated," asks why his wife gets up so often at night ("Que ses sires s'en curuça/E meintefeiz li demanda/Pur quei levot e u ala" [v. 80]); the persistent wife of "Bisclavret," whose curiosity about her husband's unexplained absences finally gets the better of her; the uncomprehending wife of "Eliduc," who does not understand her husband's odd behavior (more later); the inquisitive Queen Guinevere of "Lanval," who pushes for an explanation for the spurning of her advances.

Nor is jealously strictly sexual. As we saw by way of introduction, Marie accounts for the wicked behavior of her detractors in terms of a form of envy of her good works that is thoroughly analogous to the jealousy of lovers. So too, the *Lais* are filled with knights envious of the prowess of their peers, of lords envious of their vassals, of wives envious of one another, as if such envy were a negative navel from which narrative is born. Thus, the knights of "Lanval" are envious of the hero's valor, generosity, beauty, and prowess ("Pur sa valur, pur sa largesce,/Pur sa beauté, pur sa prüesce,/L'envioënt tut li plusur" [v. 21]), as are those of "Milun": "He was widely known in Ireland, Norway, Gotland, England, and Scotland. Many people envied him" ("Mut fu coneüz en Irlande,/En Norweië e en Guhtlande;/En Loengrë e en Albanie/Eurent plusurs de li envie" [v. 15]). Eliduc's lord, who originally retains him for his courage ("Pur sa prüesce le retint./Pur tant de meuz mut li avint" [v. 35]), eventually becomes envious of his good deeds and chases him from the realm. Finally, Marie seems to suggest that if the gossipy wife of "Le Fresne" speaks ill of her neighbor's wife, it is because she is filled with an envy that, as we shall see, comes to haunt her: "Kar ele ert feinte e orguilluse,/E mesdisante e envïuse" ("For she was deceitful and arrogant, prone to slander and envy" [v. 27]).

MARIE *MAL MARIÉE*

The *Lais* in one respect represent a fantasy literature, a literature of evasion, a voyage to another land. In the case of "Guigemar," to the land of the

idyllic woman imprisoned in a tower lined with the fiction of a book of love
waiting for the perfect lover—who turns out also to be a virgin—to arrive
via a boat; in "Yonec," to another tower where another woman waits for the
ideal mate to slip in through the window; in the case of "Lanval," to a fantasy land of women whose beauty is beyond comparison with even that of
Queen Guinevere and who are the source of incomparable riches. This
is a world of dream, of the marvelous—of rescuing fairies, magic animals,
message-bearing swans, mysterious boats, curative weasels, enchanted chap-
els and swords, men metamorphosed into werewolves and hawks, not to
mention the Otherworld of Avalon—even when the manifestations of "le
merveilleux païen" are masked behind Christian trappings.

And yet a harsher reality lurks beneath the surface of the fantasy in the
form of unhappy women. So prevalent is the theme of the unhappy wife
that Marie is sometimes portrayed as the poetess of the "mal mariée," and,
given the license with which she plays with names, one is even tempted to
play upon her name—the Marie in whose work the husbands or "maris" are
the source of a virtual class of "mal mariées."

The women of the *Lais* are unhappy, first of all, because they are imprisoned. Sometimes imprisonment takes the form merely of close surveillance, as in "Laüstic," where the husband, who keeps a close watch on his
wife when he is present, has her watched equally closely when he is away
from home (v. 49). We have seen that the wife in "Milun" laments the extent to which she is under surveillance before, and the implication is also after, her marriage. So too, the husband of "Guigemar" has placed his wife in
a maximum security prison de luxe:

> Il ne la guardat mie a gas.
> En un vergier, suz le dongun,
> La out un clos tut envirun;
> De vert marbre fu li muralz,
> Mult par esteit espés e halz;
> N'i out fors une sule entree,
> Cele fu noit e jur guardee.
> De l'altre part fu clos de mer:
> Nuls ne pout eissir në entrer. (v. 218)

He did not take lightly the task of guarding her. In a garden at the foot of the
keep was an enclosure, with a thick, high wall made of green marble. There
was only a single point of entry, guarded day and night. The sea enclosed it
on the other side, so it was impossible to get in or out.

The husband of "Yonec" seeks to contain his wife behind the castle walls:

> Dedans sa tur l'ad enserree,
> En une grant chambre pavee.
> Il ot une sue serur,
> Viellë et vedve, sanz seignur;
> Ensemble od la dame l'ad mise,
> Pur li tenir meuz en justise. (v. 27)

He locked her in his tower in a large paved chamber. He had a sister, old and widowed, without a husband, and he placed her with the lady to keep her from going astray.

The imprisoned wife, the lady in a tower, is a leitmotif of the *Lais* that cannot be separated from the marital practices of France's nobility at the end of the first feudal age, or from the conflict between lay aristocratic and ecclesiastical models of marriage, or from what I have described elsewhere as a "biopolitics" of lineage.[5] The genealogical family implied, first of all, the exercise of a certain discipline with respect to marriage, the restriction of unions to the minimum necessary to assure the continuity of the family line. As Georges Duby and others have demonstrated for the regions of Mâcon and the northwest, noble families permitted the establishment of only one or two new households per generation, the rest of the unmarried sons being housed in monasteries and chapters, or simply remaining unattached and disenfranchised.[6] The noble family husbanded its reproductive resources so as to produce sufficient progeny to insure dynastic continuity without a surplus to deplete its wealth through the fragmentation of a patrimony divided among too many sons.

The constant tension between the drive toward consolidation and the tendency toward fragmentation of lands is one of the levels on which we can understand Marie's concern with wholeness and dispersion, the term *remembrement* surviving in modern French uniquely as a term referring to the realignment of scattered lands. Marie is concerned in an even more literal sense, however, with the question of inheritance, the production of heirs, proof positive of the proverb still current in French—"tout mariage est un héritage." Thus, Gurun in "Le Fresne" is motivated to marry out of his men's concern over succession: "They would be happier if he had an heir to inherit his land" ("Lié serei[en]t s'il eüst heir,/Quë aprés lui puïst aveir/ Sa terë e sun heritage" [v. 319]). In "Eliduc" the Lord of Exeter seeks to marry his only daughter because he is old and has no male heir: "Vieuz hum e auntïen esteit./Karnel heir madle nen aveit" (v. 93). The Lord of Carwent ("Yonec"), which I have identified with lack, is also old and lacks nothing so much as a successor:

> Mut fu trespassez en eage.
> Pur ceo k'il ot bon heritage,
> Femme prist pur enfanz aveir,
> Quë aprés lui fuissent si heir. (v. 17)

This man was very old and, because his inheritance would be large, he took a wife in order to have children, who would be his heirs.

Thus, if, as we have seen, Marie is concerned about cultural inheritance, about passing on a past that, unarticulated, is lost, the imprisoning old men in her works are themselves anxious about preserving a family line, passing on their property to a male heir. We see in Marie as good a representation of the feudal, aristocratic model of marriage as can be found in Old French literature.

And yet the rule of primogeniture alone—the concern for a "heir madle"—could not have insured the integrity of lineage if it had not been accompanied by a model of marriage appropriate to the unilateral transmission of the fief and to the organization of feudal society as a series of alliances between landholders with mutual obligations. Marriage represented in essence a treaty *(pactum conjugale)* to be negotiated between families. Such a complex web of kinship between the lineages of the postfeudal era depended, moreover, upon the careful surveillance of marital ties. In particular, it assumed a matrimonial system—possibly from Germanic tradition—involving early betrothal (often at age seven or ten), early marriage (often at puberty), and, above all, the choice of partners to be made by the family or feudal lord. A marriage was, under normal circumstances, concluded by the head of household *(caput mansi)* or the elders *(seniores)* of the lineage; in their absence, by the relatives *(amis charnels),* mother, brother, sister, or uncle; and when the potential spouse was an orphan, by the lord who exercised the right of wardship.[7] Under this "lay aristocratic model of marriage" (Duby), the consent of parties mattered minimally, while that of parents and guardians was the sine qua non of a legal union. The decision of who may marry whom was based upon a certain respect for canonical impediments and upon a careful husbanding of the paternal fief in accordance with an interlocking series of military, political, and social ties. The will of partners counted very little.

There is ample evidence of such practice in twelfth-century hagiography

and romance, where it constitutes from the start a pervasive theme. Alexis's
father in "La Vie de St. Alexis" chooses his son's bride; and it is his gaze upon
her in the nuptial chamber that pushes him toward sainthood. Iseult's first
thought, upon awakening from the effects of the love philter, which I have
maintained elsewhere is the equivalent of an awakening of social conscience, is that she should live in society "in order to give ladies away to
noble knights."[8] It is in the *Lais,* however, that we find the most developed
display of feudal marital practice, and the composite picture of marriage
that emerges is surprisingly similar to that of the historians whose conclusions supposedly derive from extraliterary accounts. The choice of partners
may vary from one lai to the next, but it is rarely that of the partners themselves. Indeed, only in "Guigemar," "Milun," and "Eliduc" do lovers actually marry, the first example being a case of rapt, the second a case of well-
timed widowhood (a "vidua ex machina"), and the third the result of a
generous first wife's willing retreat from the world. It is true that "Chaitivel"
offers the example of the dilemma caused by marital choice on the part of
those involved. But in all other instances, the right to marry is exercised by
the parents, the lord, or the vassals of those destined by others to be wed. In
contrast to the numerous saints' lives in which parents try to force children
to marry rather than to remain single or to enter holy orders, "Les Deus
Amanz" is a tale that turns around a jealous father's refusal to allow his
daughter to marry the man she loves or to marry at all:

> Li reis ot une fille bele
> [E] mut curteise dameisele.
> Fiz ne fille fors li nauoit;[9]
> Forment lamoit e chierissoit.
> De riches hommes fu requise
> Qui volentiers leussent prise
> Mes li rois ne la uolt donner,
> Car ne sem pooit consirer. (v. 21)

The king had a beautiful daughter, a most courtly damsel. He had no other
son or daughter except her whom he loved dearly and cherished. Her hand
in marriage was requested by rich men who willingly would have had her,
but the king did not want to give her away since he could not do without her.

The greater part of "Milun" is predicated upon the imposition of a father's
unhappy marital choice:

> Sis peres li duna barun,
> Un mut riche humme del païs.

. . . .
Al terme ke el fu donee,
Sis sires l'en ad amenee. (vv. 126, 151)

Her father betrothed her to a nobleman, a very wealthy man from the region. . . . When the time came for her to be given in marriage, her husband took her away.

The suffering of the young wife of "Yonec" is, as she laments, the result of the marriage arranged by her relatives:

Malëeit seient mi parent
E li autre communalment
Ki a cest gelus me donerent
E a sun cors me marïerent! (v. 81)

Cursed be my parents and all those who gave me to this jealous man and married me to his person!

The people of "Equitan" put pressure upon their king to marry against his desire to remain single in order to carry on an adulterous affair with his seneschal's wife ("He did not wish to marry. . . . The courtiers thought ill of him for this," "Il ne voleit nule espuser. . . . La gent le tindrent mut a mal" [vv. 199, 201]). Finally, in "Le Fresne," as in the Tristan legend, it is the barons who pressure their lord to marry a woman of his own class and to cast off the woman they consider inappropriate, a concubine ("suinant"):

Lungement ot od lui esté,
Tant que li chevaler fiufé
A mut grant mal li aturnerent:
Soventefeiz a lui parlerent
Que une gentil femme espusast
Et de cele se delivrast. (v. 313)

After she had been with Gurun for some time, the landed knights reproached him for it severely, and they often spoke to him saying that he should take a noble wife and free himself from Le Fresne.

The King Arthur of "Lanval" distributes not only the booty of war but "women and lands" ("Femmes e tere departi" [v. 17]).

To the extent to which the lay aristocratic marriages of the *Lais* were arranged, they were unhappy. Thus the theme, practically synonymous with the name of Marie, of the "mal mariée"—the woman constrained or literally imprisoned and thus the structural gap between marriage and love, between the inclination of lovers and the constraints of the community, whether it is represented by fathers, family, vassals, or lord. Which is another way of saying that to the extent to which love remains in courtly tradition outside of marriage, it is against or outside of the law. That is why there are so many lovers as outlaws (Tristan and Iseult, Lancelot and Guinevere); for, as Eliduc recognizes in the lai that bears his name: "If I were to marry my beloved, the Christian religion would not accept it" "S'a m'amie esteie espusez,/Nel suff[e]reit crestïentez" [v. 601]). In the series of lais in which marriage is imposed from the outside against the will of partners, Marie seems to offer a casebook of medieval marital practice according to Andreas Capellanus, who lays out the laws of love in opposition to both secular and ecclesiastical authorities. Andreas claims that only the rich, the beautiful, the elegant, the generous, the eloquent, the clean, the courageous, and the young may love (under sixty for a man, fifty for a woman, but not before fourteen for a man and twelve for a woman). He describes the stages of love in terms of sight, hope, a kiss, and finally the *commixtio sexuum*. But most of all, he prescribes in the ruling of the countess of Champagne, who has, it will be remembered, been identified, among others, as the real Marie, that love is by definition adulterous:

> We declare and we hold as firmly established that love cannot exert its powers between two people who are married to each other. For lovers give each other everything freely, under no compulsion of necessity, but married people are in duty bound to give in to each other's desires and deny themselves to each other in nothing. . . . Rightly, therefore, Love cannot acknowledge any rights of his between husband and wife. But there is still another argument that seems to stand in the way of this, which is that between them there can be no true jealousy, and without it true love may not exist, according to the rule of Love himself, which says, "He who is not jealous cannot love."[10]

To the extent that marriages are arranged, love is extramarital, against the law—"Kar n'est pas bien në avenant/De deus espuses meintenir,/Ne la lei nel deit cunsentir" ("For it was neither right nor proper to keep two wives, nor should the law allow it" [v. 1128]), says Eliduc. Yet, if the law (the "lei") does not allow it, the lai certainly does; for no theme runs more rampant throughout Marie's tales than that of adultery; coursing as it does from the adulterous couples in "Guigemar," "Bisclavret," "Equitan," "Laüstic," "Yonec," "Milun," and "Chevrefoil," to Eliduc, the man with two wives, and the adulterous queen of "Lanval." Moreover, to the extent to which love is adulterous, it is hidden. Thus the theme of discretion that we have already encountered in "Guigemar." "Love, when discovered, cannot last long"; "Thou shalt not be a revealer of love affairs," warns Andreas Capellanus in passages that might serve as a watchword of the *Lais*. Eliduc, for example, is not only a courteous man, but, as Guilliadun's messenger reports, a hidden one, his discretion being a surplus of character that confirms her willingness to speak of love: "I consider him courtly and wise, and he knows well how to conceal his feelings" ("Jeol tienc a curteis e a sage,/Que bien seit celer sun curage" [v. 423]). Then too, the secret lovers of "Guigemar" and "Yonec" are hidden in the towers that, intended to sequester the wives of jealous old men, ironically also serve to hide the very adultery they are meant to prevent. Thus, in "Yonec," when the old woman who is supposed to guard the young wife locks her away for the night, she unknowingly also seals in her lover:

> Li chapeleins s'en est alez,
> E la vielle ad les us fermez.
> La dame gist lez sun ami,
> Unke si bel cuple ne vi. (v. 189)

The chaplain left and the old woman closed the doors. The lady lay next to her beloved: I never saw so fair a couple.

"Lanval" is in some extended sense about nothing other than keeping love hidden, the discretion imposed by the fairy lady echoing as it does Andreas's prescription against revealing secret love affairs:

> "Ne vus descovrez a nul humme!
> De ceo vus dirai ja la summe:
> A tuz jurs m'avrïez perdue,
> Se ceste amur esteit seüe;
> Jamés ne me purriez veeir
> Ne de mun cors seisine aveir." (v. 145)

"Do not reveal this secret to anyone! I shall tell you the long and the short of it: you would lose me forever if this love were to become known. You would never be able to see me or possess me."

Tristan, who tries to pass unseen in "Chevrefoil," moves about alone and under the cover of night: "To avoid being seen he took to the forest all alone, only emerging after dark" ("En la forest tut sul se mist,/Ne voleit pas que hum le veïst;/En la vespree s'en eisseit" [v. 29]). Gurun and his lady ("Milun") are closely watched, yet they manage to meet several times, Marie tells

us, in the course of a twenty-year love affair carried on for the most part via
correspondence:

> Ensemble viendrent plusurs feiz.
> Nul ne pot estre si destreiz
> Ne si tenuz estreitement
> Quë il ne truisse liu sovent. (v. 287)

They came together on a number of occasions. No one can be so imprisoned
or so tightly guarded that he cannot find a way out from time to time.

And, of course, secretiveness is understood to be part of the adulterous love
depicted in "Equitan," "Laüstic," and, implicitly, "Bisclavret."

Now what is interesting about hidden love in the *Lais* is that it is always
sooner or later revealed.[11] Or, to hone the syllogism of love just a bit: if, to
the extent to which marriages are arranged, love is adulterous; and if, to the
extent to which love is adulterous, it is against the law; and if to the extent
to which it is against the law, it remains secret; then to the extent to which
it remains secret, it is disclosed. So consistent is the exposure of secret affairs
that such exposure can be posited as inevitable. Love in the *Lais* is, despite
the necessity of discretion, always revealed, lovers uncovered. Nor are they
unaware of the inevitability of betrayal. They know, or at least they suspect.
Thus the lady to Guigemar, "My fair, sweet friend, my heart tells me I am
about to lose you: we are going to be discovered" ("Beus duz amis,/Mis
quors me dit que jeo vus perc:/Seü serum e descovert" [v. 546]), before they
are "perceived, discovered, found, and seen" ("aparceü,/Descovert, trové et
veü" [v. 577]). Similarly, the bird lover of "Yonec" is singularly nervous in
responding to his lady's pleas to visit her often:

> "Dame," fet il, "quant vus plerra,
> Ja l'ure ne trespassera.
> Mes tele mesure esgardez
> Que nus ne seium encumbrez;
> Ceste vielle nus traïra,
> [E] nuit e jur nus gaitera.
> Ele parcevra nostre amur,
> Sil cuntera a sun seignur.
> Si ceo avi[e]nt cum jeo vus di,
> [E] nus serum issi trahi,
> Ne m'en puis mie departir,
> Que mei n'en estuce murir." (v. 199)

"Lady," he said, "whenever it pleases you, I shall be with you within the hour, but observe moderation so that we are not discomfited. This old woman will betray us and keep watch over us night and day. When she notices our love, she will tell her lord about it. If this should happen as I say and we are betrayed in this way, I shall have no way of preventing my death."

Which is, of course, exactly what happens. And happens in "Yonec" in a way that seems at once insidiously fated and exemplary.

Secret love in "Yonec" reveals itself. For if the effects of imprisonment upon the body of the wife are a loss of beauty ("Sa beuté pert en teu mesure/Cume cele qui n'en ad cure" [v. 45]), then love produces an equal and opposite change upon her aspect so as to reveal that which is to be kept secret:

> Pur la grant joie u ele fu,
> Que ot suvent pur veer sun dru,
> Esteit tut sun semblanz changez.
> Sis sires esteit mut veiz[ï]ez:
> En sun curage s'aperceit
> Que autrement est k'i[l] ne suleit. (v. 225)

The great joy she often experienced on seeing her lover caused her appearance to alter. Her husband was very cunning and noticed that she was different from her usual self.

The lovers are watched, a deadly formula as Marie remarks in an aside: "Alas! how ill-served were they on whom he wanted to spy in order to betray and trap them" ("Allas! cum ierent malbailli/Cil ki l'un veut si agaitier/Pur eus traïr e enginner!" [v. 254]). For the deadly combination of the changed appearance of a happy lover who is also observed leads to a sighting—"This one [the old woman] saw and took note of how he came and went" ("Cele le vit, si l'esgarda,/Coment il vient e il ala" [v. 275])—and the entrapment of yet another bird.

The entrapment of the lovers of "Yonec," like that of "Guigemar," is paradigmatic and allows us, finally, to complete the syllogism. For if, to the extent to which marriages are arranged, love is adulterous; and if, to the extent to which love is adulterous, it is against the law; and if, to the extent to which it is against the law, it remains secret; and if, to the extent to which it remains secret, it is disclosed; then, to the extent to which love is disclosed, it is tragic. To be more precise, with the exception of "Le Fresne" and perhaps "Milun," a certain morbidity hovers in and around the love theme of the

Lais. Love is conceived not only to involve suffering, to be a "wound in the body" ("Guigemar," v. 483), but to be fatal. And to be fatal in the literal sense of the term—to be fated. To love in the *Lais* is to die or to risk death so inevitably as to suggest a link between adulterous love as a theme and some more deeply defining generic law that allows us to glimpse one of those moments in Old French literature where theory—a theory of literature—inheres in practice, and practice, like the lady's bearing in "Yonec," discloses a wider rule of its own production and meaning.

What "Yonec" reveals about the revelation of secret love is that there is nothing the lovers can do to prevent discovery, since the very effects that love makes manifest in the body reveal its existence and therefore make it fatal; thus, the morbidity of the tale is, again as we saw in "Guigemar," linked to the question of representation—a "semblance which kills," as the fantasy lover acknowledges:

> "Ma duce amie,
> Pur vostre amur perc jeo la vie;
> Bien le vus dis qu'en avendreit:
> Vostre semblant nus ocireit." (v. 319)

"My sweet beloved, for love of you I am losing my life. I told you what would come if it: your appearance would slay us."

Indeed, if love is by definition to be hidden, and if, at the same time, it shows itself inevitably on the body of the lover as a semblance or symptom, is there not something fatalistic not only about love, but, at least in the *Lais*, about the very act of representation? I have asserted in relation to "Guigemar" that the poet, in speaking of secret or courtly love, reveals that which is, by definition, to be hidden, and that in composing, s/he does to the lovers exactly what the jealous husband does to his wife and her lover: s/he betrays by revealing, and thus destroys at the very moment s/he creates.

The morbidity that hangs over, lies at the core of, the *Lais* works, of course, in different ways, but of this there can be no doubt: that love is seen as fatal and that such fatalism is inextricably bound to the ways in which language, and poetic language in particular, is conceived to work to expose that which is abolished by becoming manifest. This is what occurs in "Guigemar" and in "Yonec," and what is erected to the level of a law of exposure in "Lanval" and "Laüstic."

"LANVAL" AND "LAÜSTIC"

"Lanval" is the story of a knight of Arthur's court who, though he possesses all the qualities of the courtly lover and though he participates in the royal campaign against the Picts and the Scots, is forgotten when the time comes to distribute the booty of war.

> Asez i duna riches duns:
> E as cuntes e as baruns,
> A ceus de la table r[o]ünde—
> N'ot tant de teus en tut le munde—
> Femmes et tere departi,
> Par tut, fors a un ki l'ot servi:
> Ceo fu Lanval, ne l'en sovient,
> Ne nul de[s] soens bien ne li tient. (v. 13)

The king gave many rich gifts to counts and barons and to those of the Round Table: there was no such company in the whole world. He apportioned wives and lands to all, save to one who had served him: this was Lanval, whom he did not remember, and for whom no one put in a good word.

Given the economic theme, which is of a piece with that of the rivalry of Arthur's vassals for his attention ("Because of his valor, generosity, beauty, and prowess, many were envious of him," "Pur sa valur, pur sa largesce,/Pur sa beauté, pur sa prüesce,/L'envioënt tut li plusur" [v. 21]), "Lanval" seems to summon its own historical/social context: The neglected knight, who also happens to be far from home ("He was the son of a king of noble birth, but far from his inheritance," "Fiz a rei fu de haut parage,/Mes luin ert de sun heritage" [v. 27]), is, in fact, about as pure an expression as can be found in Old French of the personal alienation of individual knights ("Now he was in a plight, very sad and forlorn," "Ore est Lanval mut entrepris,/Mut est dolent e mut pensis" [v. 33]), which Erich Koehler identifies with the alienation of an entire class—the twelfth-century lower nobility or squirarchy consisting in part of younger, unmarried sons.[12] Within the general crisis of aristocracy, menaced from above by the reconstitution of monarchy and from below by the rise of an urban bourgeoisie, the *bacheliers* or *jeunes* found themselves either without land or obliged to sell their holdings, and thus increasingly indebted to the caste of powerful feudal princes still possessed of the means (land, castle, and private armies) to rule. Lanval is impoverished not only because he has been neglected but because he has spent all he has: "Tut sun aveir ad despendu" (v. 30). Indeed, his situation can be understood as a projection of the material condition of both a class and a generation, whose dispossession, as Georges Duby has elaborated in a series of articles and books, is also the result of a matrimonial model that, as we have seen, works against the interests of women and younger sons. Under the rule of primogeniture, assuming that the first son survived to the age of marriage and reproduction, the younger branches were, in effect, left to wander far from home, were, like Lanval, "neglected."[13]

Thus seen within the context of the material condition of the lower nobility and within that of twelfth-century feudal marriage, Lanval's wandering off into the countryside and his encounter with the fairy lady represent a dream of possession. The lady has all that Lanval lacks. Where he is an exile at court, she leaves her own country to find him. Where he is neglected by Arthur, she prefers him to all other knights. Where Lanval is impoverished, she is so rich that "Queen Semiramis and the Emperor Octavian himself together could not buy the right panel of her tent" ("La reïne Semiramis,/Quant ele ot unkes plus aveir/E plus pussaunce e plus saveir,/Ne l'emperere Octaviën/N'esligasent le destre pan" [v. 82]). In the antithesis of Lanval's situation, and indeed in what could be read almost as a parody of the rescue of the damsel in distress by the valiant knight, the fairy lady promises eternal fidelity (in contrast to Arthur's neglect) and—more important—as much wealth as his heart desires:

> Ore est Lanval en dreite veie!
> Un dun li ad duné aprés:
> Ja cele rien ne vudra mes
> Quë il nen ait a sun talent;
> Doinst e despende largement,
> Ele li troverat asez.
> Mut est Lanval bien herbergez:
> Cum plus despendra richement,
> [E] plus avrat or e argent! (v. 134)

Now Lanval was on the right path! She gave him a boon, that henceforth he could wish for nothing that he would not have, and however generously he gave or spent, she would still find enough for him. Lanval was very well lodged, for the more he spent, the more gold and silver he would have.

The fairy lady is the literary incarnation of a fantasized solution to the material problems of the class of unmarried, unendowed, and wandering younger knights, an heiress who is a source of unlimited riches—under one condition that we have already seen: that Lanval not reveal her existence. Even this prohibition can, again, be understood in the context of the reality of the aristocratic matrimonial model. For, as C. S. Lewis pointed out as early as the 1930s, to the extent that marriage is a matter of convenience and does not depend upon the choice of partners, there will be a gap between love and marriage, between desire and the law. Love is in this respect a legal necessity and not an elective affinity, which leads logically to the cardinal courtly rule of discretion.[14]

Here we are the witnesses to a happy marriage indeed! The Marxian fairytale of the fairy lady as the idealized solution to the material disenfranchisement of lower nobility, joined to the Cambridge Catholic's protopuritanical relegation of love to the secret dirty realm of adulterous passion. Neither, however, explains the one essential element of the rescuing woman's stipulation, which "Lanval" shares with a number of *lais:* that the revelation of love follows just as logically from the vow of discretion as discretion can be said to follow from love. The oath is taken to be transgressed. We know, in fact, that it will be violated the moment it is spoken.[15]

Like the stark world of repeatedly entwined broken promises of "La Chatelaine de Vergi," the universe of "Lanval" is one of necessity in which characters seem drawn along by an inescapable logic of articulation according to which each narrative element entails the next as part of a causal chain that can only partially be accounted for by any extratextual or historical explanation.[16] The first element is based upon the assumption, only later confirmed by events, that the reason for Arthur's original neglect is not so much the rivalry between his knights as his own jealousy of the Queen's interest in Lanval; which neglect inspires the daydream and the promise not to tell; which promise is kept only until Guinevere's interest becomes manifest and she requests Lanval's love; which request, rebuffed, produces the charge of homosexuality, the denial of which provokes the famous boast of loving someone whose humblest attendant is more beautiful than the Queen; which boast leads not only to Lanval's realization that he has lost his love ("Il s'est[eit] bien aparceüz/Qu'il aveit perdue s'amie:/Descovert ot la druërie!" [v. 334]), but, in yet another medieval rendering of the Potiphar's wife motif, to the denunciation before Arthur, who, like the Duke of "La Chatelaine de Vergi," puts the wronged knight in a position of either proving the truth of his boast—which, as boast, prevents its own proof—or being punished.[17]

If "Lanval" seems to turn fatalistically around a certain logic of the promise made to be broken and of the boast that denies the possibility of substantiation, it is because both speech acts are so thoroughly enmeshed in the poetics of the lai as to make the transgression rendered in terms of self-canceling vows and conceits mere thematizations of a broader paradox, which is that of fiction itself. Lanval, after all, not only uses his newfound wealth to dress jongleurs but is the very figure of the poet. He is depicted as the loner, a dreamer. The Queen's charge of homosexuality carried, as we know from Marie's contemporary Alain de Lille, an association with rhetoric.[18] But most of all, Lanval's dilemma is that of the poet who transgresses the unwritten rule of the courtly relation subsumed in the dictum "If you say it, you lose it," who violates, in other words, what is imagined to be the integrity of an orality present to itself—and the fairy lady is just one version of such a fantasy of plenitude—every time she speaks. Put in other terms, the voice associated with the presence of the body, or even of bodies, is transgressed by the lai, which is merely its trace, by the very act of articulation, transcription being merely the limit of such transgression.

There is no better example of the fatalistic mutual implication of articulation and betrayal than "Laüstic," the story of two knights who are neighbors, one of whom, another "bacheler," is loved by the other's wife. It is unclear within the short narrative whether or not their love is consummated, whether or not, in other words, the body ever attains to a presence. Nonetheless, the lovers communicate by looking at each other from the windows of their respective homes. Asked by her suspicious husband why she gets up so often at night, the wife replies: "Lord, anyone who does not hear the song of the nightingale knows none of the joys of this world. This is why I come and stand here" ("Il nen ad joië en cest mund,/Ki n'ot le laüstic chanter./Pur ceo me vois ici ester" [v. 84]). And, as in "Lanval," the lady has betrayed herself in the act of speaking. For the lie intended to cover her delight, to keep love secret, reveals that which it is supposed to hide in the very moment that it is pronounced. In fact, the fatality of the lie can be traced, I think, further back than the lady's fatal speech act to the husband's question—"E meintefeiz li demanda/Pur quei levot e u ala" (v. 81)—which is rooted, as in the love written on the altered face of the lady of "Yonec," in the lover's bodily gestures at the window where she sits and looks when the lovers "were denied anything more" (v. 77). Despite the fact of hiding, love reveals itself. First in the body, which somatizes love's effects, and then in the language that speaks inevitably of that which is prohibited: in the moment that she speaks, the speaker destroys her own object of delight. Nor is Marie immune from the process of despoiling exposure she describes. The lai exposes that which is by definition intended to remain hidden: "This adventure was related and could not long be concealed. The Bretons composed a lai about it that is called *Laüstic*" ("Cele aventure fu

cuntee,/Ne pot estre lunges celee./Un lai en firent li Bretun:/Le Laüstic
l'apelë hum" [v. 157]).

The drama of language of "Lanval" is repeated in "Laüstic," where the
husband, jealous of his wife's pleasure, captures the nightingale by fashion-
ing a "laz"—"There was no hazel tree or chestnut tree on which they did not
place a snare or birdlime, until they had captured and retained it" ("N'i ot
codre ne chastainier/U il ne mettent laz u glu,/Tant que pris l'unt e retenu"
[v. 98])—as if, and the reference could not be more explicit, the nightingale
as voice were caught in Marie's own trap, which is the "laz/lai." For the dead
bird, thrown at the wife ("Sur la dame le cors geta,/Si que sun chainse en-
sanglanta/Un poi desur le piz devant" [v. 117]), makes a mark. The nightingale's body, the voice betrayed, is a form of writing upon the woman's body
and a message to be read. Indeed, the lady sends it to her lover like a letter
to inform him of betrayal:

> "Le laüstic li trametrai
> L'aventure li manderai."
> En une piece de samit,
> A or brusdé et tut escrit,
> Ad l'oiselet envolupé.
> Un sun vaslet ad apelé,
> Sun message li ad chargié,
> A sun ami l'ad enveié. (v. 133)

"I shall send him the nightingale and let him know what has happened." She
wrapped the little bird in a piece of samite, embroidered in gold, with writing all around. She called one of her servants, entrusted him with her message, and sent it to her beloved.

The lover, in turn, has the dead bird enshrined in a reliquary, which he
carries with him as long as he lives, as we realize that "Laüstic," which is
alternately spelled "L'Aüstic," resonates uncannily with audible sound—
the acoustic, modern French *écouter* from the Latin *auscultare*, meaning "to
hear," "to give attention to."[19]

We find in "Laüstic," as in "Lanval," the fantasy of a utopic plenitude or
presence, here however explicitly identified with pleasurable orality.[20] For
the supposed communication that the proximity of houses makes possible
is equated with pleasure: "They took delight in seeing each other, since they
were denied anything more" ("Delit aveient al veer,/Quant plus ne poeient
aveir" [v. 77]. Here it is worth stopping a moment at the word "delit," since
it is a key to the utopic presence associated with the body. The text *says* de-

light, but, one may ask, delight at what? Certainly not presence, since Marie is categorical: "They took delight in seeing each other, since they were denied anything more." The imagined pleasure of the body is a substitute for presence, a supplement, which is also synonymous with *délit* in the sense of the flagrante delicto in which the lovers are captured. For nowhere in the lai is the presence of a voice anything but a substitute for something else. The lovers are never present to each other, and the nightingale never sings to the lovers. It is itself nothing more than the sign of a ruse or lie told to calm the jealous husband's suspicions, an invention synonymous with the lai itself. In turn, the dead bird, encased—literally "embroidered and written" ("A or brusdé et tut escrit")—is sent like a poetic "envoi" to the lover once consummation or the presence of bodies is no longer even imaginable. Nor was it ever; for such presence in the lai is always deferred.

There is no language of presence either in "Laüstic" or anywhere else to represent the coupling of bodies, such coupling being, as we have seen in "Guigemar," a surplus that never enters language. An excess that cannot be said, the presence of the body is excluded from the text. Which is not to imply that poets do not try all the time to capture the body or that such attempts do not constitute the very essence of the poetic instance. On the contrary, Marie makes this clear in the general prologue, an *art poétique* that prescribes the making of texts as a series of rewritings, which, no matter how perfect, always leave a "surplus of meaning."

What I am suggesting is that in the *Lais* Marie's understanding of the body (and the voice) is ultimately always deferred by the text that supplants it, transgresses it in a sense analogous to Lanval's betrayal of the fictional fairy and the self-betrayal of the lady of "Laüstic." For the theme of betrayal dominates not only "Lanval" and "Laüstic" but a great many other so-called courtly work as well. In the *chanson de geste* betrayal takes the form of broken oaths, apostasy, and treason, whereas in the courtly text it is to be found—from Béroul's *Tristan* and Chrétien's *Lancelot,* to the prose romances of the thirteenth century—in the theme of capture of the bodies of lovers in flagrante delicto. Betrayal is a structuring principle of the courtly lyric, whose stock of characters includes the *losengers,* liars, false speakers, and flatters, but also denouncers of adulterers. So widespread, in fact, is the theme of betrayal that the indiscretions of Lanval and the lady of "Laüstic" seem fated. The fatalism of the boast—whether of the most beautiful woman or of the greatest joy in the world—underscores the extent to which in medieval texts the poetic and erotic are embedded in each other. Even the word *traire,* like the word *lai,* is one of those polysemic markers that, in their semantic richness, transgress the premise of an assumed plenitude inherent to verbal signs, for the ear can never hear as much, make as many distinctions, as the eye can see.

"EQUITAN" AND "LE FRESNE"

If words come back to haunt and even to destroy those who speak in "Lanval" and "Laüstic," their deadly effects seem even to precede speech in "Equitan," where the King, who has never seen the wife of his seneschal, falls in love with her by hearsay:

> Li reis l'oï sovent loër.
> Soventefez la salua,
> De ses aveirs li enveia;
> Sans veüe la coveita. (v. 38)

The king, having often heard her praised, frequently sent her greetings and gifts. They had never met, but he conceived a desire for her.

Hearsay engenders the desire to speak directly with her: "E, cum ainz pot a li parla" (v. 42). In this the King is not alone. The lady of "Laüstic" falls in love with her neighbor because of "the good things she has heard about him": "Et tant par ot en lui grant bien/Qu'ele l'ama sur tute rien,/Tant pur le bien qüe ele oï" (v. 25). Gurun falls in love with Fresne because of what has been said: "De la pucele oï parler;/Si la comença a amer" ("Le Fresne," v. 247). Milun benefits similarly from the news of his reputation, which reaches the ears of the unnamed lady of Southwales: "Ele ot oï Milun nomer;/Mut le començat a amer" (v. 25). So too, Guilliadun falls in love with Eliduc because of that which is said about him: "La fille al rei l'oï numer/E les biens de lui recunter" (v. 273). And if the lady of Guigemar is a "mal mariée" in a tower, the lady of Eliduc is a "mal fiancée" whose father at first imprisons her in a tower to keep her away from the enemy who wants to marry her and then, upon Eliduc's arrival, sings his praises, thus inciting her desire (v. 496).

One of the great themes of Old French romance, love by hearsay takes on a special meaning in the *Lais,* where it functions as a precursor to, or alongside of, the dangerous speech acts that so define the linguistic universe of Marie. Indeed, as the example from "Eliduc" makes clear, the "good things that are told *(recunter)* about him" represent a form of narrative thoroughly analogous to the telling of the lai itself; and Marie often uses the verb *cunter* or *recunter*—"Dit vus en ai la verité/Del lai que j'ai ici cunté" ("Chevrefoil," v. 117), "Plus n'en oï, ne plus n'en sai,/Ne plus ne vus en cunterai" ("Chaitivel," v. 239), "Al recunter mut me delit" ("Milun," v. 536)[21]—in order to describe the art of storytelling. Which inscribes a certain fatality into the relation of the body to its deeds, or rather into the relation between one's deeds, one's character, or one's beauty and what is said about them. The vicious cycle of reputation is such that the greater the prowess of a knight, as in the case of the neighbor in "Laüstic," "Milun," and "Eliduc," or the greater the beauty of the lady, as in the case of the seneschal's wife of "Equitan," the more appealing the words that are "recounted"; the more appealing the words that are "recounted," the more fated the attraction; and the more fated the attraction, the more fatal the seduction. The motif of love by hearsay represents an inscription within, and an embryonic form of, the art of storytelling itself. Once more, in the act of narration Marie spreads the word, creates the conditions of hearsay in her hearers, in a fashion thoroughly analogous to that which she describes as happening to the protagonists of the *Lais*. If language as an explicit theme of the *Lais* seems dangerous and often even fatal, it is because Marie performs in the very act of recounting that which she knows to be the impossible position of the poet who destroys by exposure.

"Equitan" is often represented as being more of a fabliau than a tale of love, and there is something uncourtly about the king who loves beneath his station, something comic about this bedroom farce that turns around the act of bleeding in order to keep love hidden, something farcical about the denouement in the bath tubs that belongs more properly to the tradition of the comic tale. Then too, to the extent to which the fabliaux can be considered to be didactic or to function according to a certain logic of distributive justice according to which "what A does to B, B will do to A, or what A does to B, C will do to A," "Equitan" can be considered to belong to the mode or the schema of the trickster tricked. Equitan is a king, Marie insists, whose role is to provide justice ("Sires des Nauns, jostis e reis" [v. 12]), and his very name is synonymous with equity. "Equitan" is in many respects about equity, as is obvious in the seneschal's wife's initial response that love is not worthy if it is not among equals—"Amur n'est pruz se n'est egals" (v. 137).

Where "Equitan" parts company with the fabliaux, however, is in the fatality of the ending, which is more cruel than most, and, more important, in the way in which the deaths of Equitan and of the seneschal's wife are inscribed in the language of love itself. Once engaged, speech in "Equitan," as in "Lanval," snowballs uncontrollably. Indeed, from the start, hearsay, speech in praise of the seneschal's wife's beauty, that which is said about her, leads to a desire to speak to her:

> Pur sei deduire e cunforter
> La fist venir a li parler.
> Sun curage li descovri,
> Saver li fet qu'il meort pur li;
> Del tut li peot faire cunfort
> E bien li peot doner [l]a mort. (v. 111)

To please and comfort him the King had her come and speak with him, whereupon he disclosed his feelings to her, letting her know that he was dying because of her and that she was well able to bring comfort to him or to cause his death.

The desire to speak to the seneschal's wife for whom "he is dying" is automatically, almost syllogistically, connected to the desire for the seneschal's death. "Accept this as the truth and believe me," King Equitan promises his beloved to calm her fear of being deceived, "if your husband were dead, I should make you my queen and my lady. I should not be deterred from this for anyone's sake" ("Sacez de veir, e si creez:/Si vostre sire fust finez,/Reïne e dame vus fereie;/Ja pur [nul] humme nel lerreie" [v. 225]). This is a promise that comes to haunt him. For the words, once spoken, turn back upon the speaker and, like Guigemar's arrow, Lanval's promise, or the white lie of the lady of "Laüstic," rebound uncannily. The death planned for the seneschal is, in fact, reserved for Equitan—"His evil plan had rebounded on him, whereas the seneschal was safe and sound" ("Sur lui est le mal revertiz,/E cil en est sauf e gariz" [v. 299]). The dispenser of justice and king ("jostis e reis") ironically insures equity by his own death, as the lai in the end assumes its name.

"Le Fresne" differs from "Equitan" in the happily resolved quality of its ending. Indeed, it is in many ways the most carefully resolved of all the lais in that Fresne marries the man she loves, Gurun; and Fresne's sister Codre is given away richly in the parents' country: "Mut richement en lur cuntree/Fu puis la meschine donee" (v. 513). "Le Fresne" resembles "Equitan," then, in the justness of its ending, and in one other important aspect, that is, the extent to which it turns around an almost fatal speech act: the mother's derogatory remark about the neighbor's wife who delivers twins. Fresne's mother is, in a portrait in which character is captured as a mouth, "bad-mouthed and envious":

Kar ele ert feinte e orguilluse
E mesdisante e envïuse.
Ele parlat mut folement
E dist, oant tute sa gent:
"Si m'aït Deus, jo m'esmerveil
U cest produm prist cest conseil
Que il ad mandé a mun seignur
Sa huntë e sun deshonur,
Que sa femme ad eü deus fiz.
E il e ele en sunt hunis.
Nus savum bien qu'il i afiert:
Unques ne fu ne ja nen iert
Ne n'avendrat cel' aventure
Que a une sule porteüre
Quë une femme deuz fiz eit,
Si deus hummes ne li unt feit." (v. 27)

She was deceitful and arrogant, prone to slander and envy. She spoke foolishly and said in front of the whole household: "So help me God, I am astonished that this worthy man decided to inform my husband of his shame
and dishonor, that his wife has had two sons. They have both incurred shame
because of it, for we know what is at issue here: it has never occurred that a
woman gave birth to two sons at once, nor ever will, unless two men are the
cause of it."

Nor does it take long for her judgment of her neighbor, which becomes notorious ("These words that were repeated became widely known throughout all Brittany" ["Asez fu dite e coneüe,/Per tute Bretaine seüe" (v. 50)]), to
recoil upon herself:

La dame que si mesparla
En l'an meïsmes enceinta,
De deus enfanz est enceintie;
Ore est la veisine vengie. (v. 65)

The same year the slanderer herself conceived twins, and now her neighbor
was avenged.

Marie may here hint that it is the husband's infidelity that has caused the
neighbor to conceive twins, that in talking about another the wife is, in reality, speaking the truth about herself. There are only two possibilities: either the wife speaks the truth in slandering her neighbor, in which case she
articulates unconsciously the possibility of her husband's unfaithfulness; or

the slander is false, given the biological reality of her own pregnancy and birth. In either case, Marie insists upon the power of words to turn against those who pronounce them, as the gossipy wife of "Le Fresne," in a phrase that resembles the return of the ill-intentioned speech act of "Equitan" ("Sur lui est le mal revertiz"), recognizes the danger of speaking ill of others: "Now I am paying the price. Whoever slanders and lies about others does not know what retribution awaits him" ("Sur mei en est turné le pis./Ki sur autrui mesdit e ment/Ne seit mie qu'a l'oil li pent" [v. 86]).

The mother's slander of her neighbor is, however, only the first of two speech acts that rebound against her. For the wife who decides to cast one of her daughters out unknowingly encounters her again when she seeks to remove Fresne from the home of the man to whom she intends to marry Codre, the daughter she has retained: "She planned to cast her out of her own house and advise her son-in-law to marry her to a worthy man" ("De sa meisun la getera,/A sun gendre cunseilera/Quë a un produme la marit" [v. 369]). In the end it is Codre who leaves Gurun and is married to another.

The dangerous speech acts of both "Le Fresne" and "Equitan" seem to illustrate Marie's warning about language in the prologue to "Guigemar." That is, words, like stories, once spoken, are "launched," sent out to find a meaning that not only is beyond the control of the storyteller or speaker but can also return to produce unforeseen effects. Indeed, Marie's drama of language, which pits the attempt to master meaning, to assemble, remember, and contain it, against an inherent unruly, entropic tendency for the meaning of words, once spoken, to escape, replicate, and to scatter, is nowhere more apparent than in the two names of the sisters of "Le Fresne." Codre, the sister who stays home and is raised under the parental roof, embodies the principle of union or "remembrement" in that her name is a homonym for *coudre,* "to sew."[22] "Fresne" (alternatively spelled "Freisne" or "Fraisne"), on the other hand, and this irrespective of the meanings that may in medieval folklore have been attached to the hazelnut and the ash tree, resonates with the Old French *fraindre* from the Latin *frango, frangere, fractum,* "to break, break in pieces, dash, break in two." Nor is it any accident that the sister who is cast out is accompanied by a signifying cloth, like the message-bearing samite of "Laüstic" or the message written on a stick of "Chevrefoil":

> A une pice de sun laz
> Un gros anel li lie al braz.
> De fin or i aveit un' unce;

> El chestun out une jagunce;
> La verge entur esteit lettree. (v. 127)

With a piece of ribbon, the lady attached to the child's arm a large ring made from an ounce of pure gold, with a ruby set in it and lettering on the band.

In the names of the sisters inheres the meaning of "Le Fresne," which is about breaking apart and coming together, about a speech act that rebounds and comes to haunt, about a child who is cast out and returns, about a sister who is retained and later displaced.

"BISCLAVRET"

"Bisclavret," which begins with a problem of language and of naming ("*Bisclavret* is its name in Breton, while the Normans call it *Garwaf*," "Bisclavret ad nun en bretan,/Garwaf l'apelent li Norman" [v. 3]), is often classified and considered apart as deriving its material and interest from the world of folklore. Yet it is every bit as much a part of the problematics of dangerous language as any of the lais that we have seen thus far.[23] Speech is from the start characterized as worthy of caution when a wife expresses the same fear concerning a spouse's absence that is hinted at in "Le Fresne" and that is the source of disaster in "Lanval":

> "Sire," fait el, "beau duz amis,
> Une chose vus demandasse
> Mut volenters, si jeo osasse;
> Mais jeo creim tant vostre curuz,
> Que nule rien tant ne redut." (v. 32)

"Lord," she said, "my dear, sweet love, I would gladly ask you something, if only I dared; but there is nothing I fear more than your anger."

If the rest of the lais are in some deep sense about language as a flawed, uncontrollable, and sometimes fatal medium, "Bisclavret" takes us even deeper into the morass. For this tale is about the irresistibility of the question, that is, about the wife's tenacious curiosity, despite her fear of articulation, concerning that which she knows will harm her. A curiosity that comes in stages: first the question, met with a warning:

> "Dame," fet il, "pur Deu, merci!
> Mal m'en vendra si jol vus di,
> Kar de m'amur vus partirai
> E mei meïmes en perdrai." (v. 53)

"Lady," he said, "in God's name, have mercy on me! If I tell you this, great harm will come to me, for as a result I shall lose your love and destroy myself."

Despite the warning, the wife's insistence elicits a confession:

> Suventefeiz li demanda;
> Tant le blandi e losenga
> Que s'aventure li cunta;
> Nule chose ne li cela.
> "Dame, jeo devienc bisclavret:
> En cele grant forest me met,
> Al plus espés de la gaudine,
> S'i vif de preie et de ravine." (v. 59)

She questioned him repeatedly and coaxed him so persuasively that he told her his story, keeping nothing secret. "Lady, I become a werewolf: I enter the vast forest and live in the deepest part of the wood where I feed off the prey I can capture."

And, as if confession weren't enough, the lady presses for details concerning the clothes which, similar to the rich swaddling cloth of "Le Fresne" or the inscribed samite of "Laüstic," are fetishized as the unmistakable signs—like the *objets trouvés* of cubist and Dadaist collages (a matchbook, a cut of newspaper or musical score, a scrap of chair caning)—that the man's story, like Fresne's origin, escapes fiction. (Which is a good trick, for it guarantees, like Lanval's sudden departure at the end, that fiction itself is true.) In any case, the exchange between husband and wife has something fated about it: the minute she asks, he resists; and the minute he resists, she presses; in fact, the more she presses, the more he resists, until, finally, the logic of the question can yield nothing but an answer: "She tormented and harried him so much that he could not do otherwise but tell her" ("Tant l'anguissa, tant le suzprist,/Ne pout el faire, si li dist" [v. 87]). Language that irresistibly, inevitably, reveals that which should be kept secret has effects analogous to those provoked by the lady's lie in "Laüstic" or by Lanval's indiscretion. With, however, this essential difference: where the revelation of a secret love results in its loss ("Say it and you lose it"), revelation of a secret identity in "Bisclavret" results in condemnation to it ("Say it and you will become it forever").

Bisclavret's wife's question is at bottom like Guigemar's arrow, which turns back upon the one who shoots, like the lady of "Laüstic's" treacherous lie or the wife's slander in "Le Fresne," in that language betrays the one who uses it. Indeed, the reason that Bisclavret's wife is so insistent is that she suspects that her husband's regular disappearance means that he has a mistress. And what could be worse than her husband's infidelity? Few things. But one of those is surely the fact that her husband is not just unfaithful to her, not just amorously double, but unfaithful to his species. And here there can be no doubt. The curious lady—a sister of Eliduc's wife—might very well have settled for learning that her husband were merely adulterous. But she learns that he is perverse in the most literal medieval sense of the term. He is a "bestourné," a bestial, the truth of which, once disclosed, kills her love, once said, once revealed, prevents the continuance of their relation, their lying next to each other:

> La dame oï cele merveille
> De poür fu tute vermeille;
> De l'aventure s'efrea.
> E[n] maint endreit se purpensa
> Cum ele s'en puïst partir;
> Ne voleit mes lez lui gisir. (v. 97)

The lady heard this remarkable revelation and her face became flushed with fear. She was greatly alarmed by the story, and began to consider various means of parting from him, as she no longer wished to lie at his side.

Thus the species-traitor's worst fear in the beginning—that he will lose his wife's love ("Kar de m'amur vus partirai" [v. 55])—becomes true, as if saying it, once again, made it so. So too with the wife's fear of her husband's infidelity, which is no sooner said than it causes her to become unfaithful, to marry the man who has sought her love even before her husband's disappearance ("La dame ad cil dunc espusee,/Que lungement aveit amee," "Then the knight married the lady he had loved for so long" [v. 133]), as if her desire (for the knight) from the beginning were to discover her husband's secret so that she might more fully live a secret of her own. It is as if the question, once posed, leads inevitably to disaster, as with the husband's question in "Laüstic," or, as if the origin of the wife's persistence resided in the ardent questions of her persistent suitor: "a knight who lived in the region and who had loved her for a long time, wooed her ardently, and served her generously" ("Un chevaler de la cuntree,/Que lungement l'aveit amee/ Et mut preié' et mut requise/E mut duné en sun servise" [v. 103]).

There is much to be said about the signifying werewolf of "Bisclavret," the way in which the King, like Guigemar's boat, or the swan of "Milun," seems mysteriously drawn to it, as the werewolf seems drawn to the King,[24] and about the way, finally, a message passes between the two; but "Bisclavret" is also in some profound sense about the question of noses, which defines the ending of this curious lai about curiosity. The werewolf venges himself by relieving his treacherous wife of her nose: "He tore the nose right off her face" ("Le neis li asracha del vis" [v. 235]). Nor do things stop there, for the wife's dismorphism becomes hereditary: "Plusurs [des] femmes del lignage,/C'est verité, senz nes sunt nees/Et si viveient esnasee" (v. 312). On one level, of course, we could read these lines as "Many of the women in the family, I tell you truly, were born without noses and lived noseless." But a quick look at the Old French dictionary shows how tricky the nose is. For *nes,* also spelled *neis, neys, neiz, naes, nees, nes, nis, nois, neies, nedes,* is an adverb meaning *même, pas même, pas du tout*—"even," "not even," "not at all." The nose is, in other words, the equivalent of "noes," and "Bisclavret," seen from this perspective, can be understood as the tale of a man who just can't say "no," or whose failure to say "no" to his wife's curiosity, a strange reenactment of the Fall, leads in effect to his wife's loss of her nose, exile, or expulsion ("[The King] banished the woman from the country, exiling her from the region," "La femme ad del païs ostee/E chacie hors de la cuntree" [v. 305]), and heritability of the lack of noes/nose. (I wouldn't presume to know which way to spell it.) The name "Bisclavret" again offers a key to Marie's fascination with tricky language and has not passed unnoticed by philologists. Joseph Loth claims that it derives from the Breton *bisc,* meaning "short," and *lavret,* "wearing breeches or short trousers." Heinrich Zimmer relates it to the Breton term *bleiz lavaret,* "speaking wolf." Th. Chotzen derives it from *bleidd Ilafar,* "the dear little speaking wolf" or *le bon loup fatidique.* H. W. Bailey explains the form *bisclavret* as *bleiz laveret,* "rational wolf." Finally, William Sayers proposes *bleiz claffet,* "wolf-sick, afflicted with lycanthropy," as the term "claff" is associated with leprosy.[25] However, if we were to take the name apart, "Bisclavret" can be divided into *bis,* "again," and *clavret,* which according to the dictionary is a "nail," a *clavreur* from the Latin *clavus,* or, alternatively, a *clavreüre,* a "key," from the Latin *clavis,* yielding, if we want to keep meaning open, or "supply surpluses of sense," as Marie suggests, either "again a nail," or "again a key." What I think I am saying is that we have again found the key to reading some of the most complex stuff the French Middle Ages produced, and it is not at all the simple, naive, spontaneous, artless creation it has been taken to be.

CHAPTER THREE

The Voice in the Tomb of the *Lais*

The fatality attached to language in the *Lais* seems to function in a number of tales according to what I have defined as a law of fated exposure, which takes a variety of forms—a promise made to be broken in "Lanval," a lie told to become true in "Laüstic," a suggestion of murder that kills the one who suggests it in "Equitan," an act of malicious gossip that comes to haunt the one who spreads it in "Le Fresne," an indiscretion with fatal effects in "Bisclavret." In each of these lais of revelation language works as an agent of despoiling disclosure. Further, as we have also seen, the overt speech act, whether a promise, a lie, a rumor, or an indiscretion, can be seen to be less the primary source of the morbidity connected to language in the *Lais* than its culmination. Above and beyond, below and before the individual acts of exposure that are dramatized lies a pervasive sense that language is dangerous and that a process of loss is engaged the moment one opens one's mouth. The disastrous effects of language lie hidden in the realm of hearsay, of innocent or justified questions, of articulated premonitions—all analogous, as we have also seen, to the deadly uncovering of the narrative itself. In Marie's theater of words she is both playwright and actor.

"ELIDUC"

The modes of linguistic disaster in the *Lais* are diverse. While a despoiling exposure functions in "Yonec," "Lanval," "Laüstic," and "Bisclavret," or dangerously ricocheting speech in "Equitan" and "Le Fresne," the lai of "Eliduc" takes us in a different direction altogether. This is not to deny that the mode of exposure is absent. On the contrary, love in this last lai of

Harley 978 is as secretive as elsewhere, for, as Eliduc recognizes, "The Christian religion does not permit me to take my love in marriage" ("S'a m'amie esteie espusez,/Nel suff[e]reit crestïentez" [v. 601]). Here too, the revelation of love is fatal. First, for the sailor who, in the storm that arises while the adulterous couple is crossing the Channel, blurts out the truth of Eliduc's conjugal situation:[1]

> "Femme leale espuse avez
> E sur celë autre en menez
> Cuntre Deu et cuntre la lei,
> Cuntre dreiture et cuntre fei." (v. 835)

"You have a loyal wife and now with this other woman you offend God and his law, righteousness and the faith."

The sailor's indiscretion offers another example of a despoiling exposure that rebounds to harm the speaker, who in this instance wants to throw Eliduc's mistress overboard to exorcise the forces of nature ("Lessez la nus geter en mer,/Si poüm sempres ariver" [v. 839]), and is himself tossed into the sea: "Then with his foot he [Eliduc] pushed him overboard and the waves bore the body away" ("Par le pié l'en ad jeté fors;/Les undes emportent le cors" [v. 863]). The disclosure of Eliduc's marriage also produces an effect of pseudo-death in the mistress who first swoons and then is left in the chapel for dead:

> Mes entre ses bras la teneit
> E confortout ceo qu'il poeit
> Del mal quë ele aveit en mer
> E de ceo que el oï numer
> Que femme espuse ot sis amis
> Autre ke li en sun païs.
> Desur sun vis cheï paumee,
> Tute pale, desculuree.
> En la paumeisun demurra
> Que el ne revient ne suspira. (v. 847)

But he held her in his arms and comforted her as best he could against her seasickness and because she had heard that he had a wife in his own country. She fell face down, quite pale and wan, in a swoon in which she remained, for she did not come round or breathe.

Words in "Eliduc" thus either kill or create the impression of death.

Fatality hangs over "Eliduc" as it does over other lais because of the poet's uncovering of what is the impossible equation that we have identified with courtly love poetry, which constantly transgresses Andreas's prohibition of exposure. "You must reveal what you must not reveal," the rule reads. And just as desire, exposed, disappears, presence, an imagined plenitude in language, once spoken, is betrayed. This is another way of saying that the lai is a liar, a deceiver, and that such deception cannot be divorced from the theme of adultery itself.

There is no better example of the doubleness of love and of language than "Eliduc," a tale of adultery and of divided political loyalties, both of which are enmeshed in the divided nature of names and of words. The lai of two women, Marie specifies, has two names—"From these two the lay of Guildelüec and Guilliadun takes its name. It was first called Eliduc, but now the name has been changed" ("D'eles deus ad li lais a nun / Guildelüec ha Gualadun. / Elidus fu primes nomez, / Mes ore est li nuns remuez" [vv. 21–24])—and is about the man who serves two masters, who is the vassal of two lords.[2] The initial drama of "Eliduc," like that of "Lanval," is political and involves the jealousy and neglect of one's lord. Eliduc is ejected by the "Reis de Bretaine la Meinur" because of the false accusations of those who are envious of the good that is his:

> Pur l'envie del bien de lui,
> Si cum avient sovent d'autrui,
> Esteit a sun seignur medlez,
> [E] empeirez e encusez,
> Que de la curt le cungea
> Sanz ceo qu'il nel areisuna. (v. 41)

The envy of his good fortune, which often possesses others, caused him to be embroiled with his lord, to be slandered and accused, so that he was banished from court without formal accusation.

Rejected without explanation ("Eliducs ne saveit pur quei" [v. 47]), Eliduc crosses the Channel, landing in Excestre; and the name, like so many of the names in the *Lais,* could not be more appropriate. For "Excestre" (modern Exeter) breaks down into *ex* + *cestre* and is the homonym of "et cetera," "and the others," which is exactly what "Eliduc" is all about—other lords, other lands, other women, other names. Once in Excestre, Eliduc finds another lord who endows him with other lands ("La fiance de lui en prist; / De sa tere gardein en fist" [v. 269]); and being without male heir ("Karnel heir madle nen aveit" [v. 94]), gives him the dowry third of his inheritance: "Del suen li ad offert asez, / La terce part de s'herité" (v. 628). Until, of course, the original lord, having in the meantime ejected Eliduc's accusers, recalls him when he needs his aid in his own wars. The "Reis de Bretaine la Meinur" is living proof, as Marie insists, of the peasant proverb "Amur de seignur n'est pas fiez" (v. 63), which means, of course, "The love of lords is not trustworthy," but which can also be understood, in the context of all we know about wordplay in the *Lais* and about the plasticity with which Marie elicits "surpluses of sense," as "the love of signifiers is not trustworthy," especially when one is dealing with a "Reis de Bretaine la Meinur," which in turn means, of course, "King of Lesser Brittany," but also "King of Brittany the Misleader" (MF *meneur*). This play of words occurs elsewhere in Old French in, for example, Rutebuef's "De Frere Denise," where the "freres meneurs" are brothers belonging to minor orders and "misleading brothers" or "misleaders," an interpretation that takes on special significance, as we shall see, in the context of Eliduc's own name.

Eliduc, the man of two lords, is also a man between two women, Guildelüec, the wife, and Guilliadun, the mistress. For if the love of lords is not trustworthy, that of Eliduc is even less so. He assures Guildelüec of his loyalty upon departure ("Mes il l'aseürat de sei / Qu'il li porterat bone fei" [v. 83]), and there is little reason to doubt his good intentions: "He had promised his wife, before leaving his own country, that he would love only her" ("Kar a sa femme aveit premis, / Ainz qu'il turnast de sun païs, / Quë il n'amereit si li nun" [v. 463]). Except, of course, for the fact that Eliduc, in keeping the promise to his wife, makes a similar promise to his mistress:

> "Lëaument vus jur e plevis:
> Si cungé me volez doner
> E respit mettre e jur nomer,
> Si vus volez que jeo revienge,
> N'est rien al mund que me retienge."
>
> . . . .
>
> Cele ot de lui grant amur;
> Terme li dune e nume jur
> De venir e pur li mener. (vv. 690, 697)

"Loyally I swear and pledge to you that, if you give me leave, grant me a postponement, and set a day by which you wish me to return, nothing on earth will prevent me from doing so. . . ." She had great love for him and set a period and fixed the day on which he was to return and take her away.

To the extent to which Eliduc has made the same promise to two women, he is a bigamist; and his bigamy is synonymous with ambiguity, the am-

bivalence of each woman's relation to him being contained in the only partial perception of the existence of the other: Guilliadun "did not know that
he had a wife" ("Ne saveit pas que femme eüst" [v. 584]); and Guildelüec,
unaware of Guilliadun, wonders why her husband, upon his return, seems
so withdrawn:

> Mut se cuntient sutivement.
> Sa femme en ot le queor dolent,
> Ne sot mie que ceo deveit;
> A sei meïsmes se pleigneit. (v. 717)

He behaved most secretively and his wife was sad in her heart because of this,
not knowing what it meant. She lamented to herself.

For the two women the bigamist is ambiguity. For Eliduc, however, the two
women are, when it comes to his loyalty, almost synonymous, their equiva-
lence captured in the partial homophony of their names "Guildelüec" and
"Guilliadun." There are few readers of "Eliduc," in fact, who do not have
difficulty keeping straight the name of the wife and that of the mistress, who
do not, in other words, experience some element of the confusion attributed to Eliduc.

Given the common first syllable of their names, the "Guil-" that denotes
"guile," Eliduc's two women are separated primarily by the final two syllables attached to such a tricky prefix: "-delüec" and "-liadun." Thus, Marie
poses the question of resemblance and dissimilarity, or that of translation,
which is, in some profound sense, what "Eliduc" is all about. Eliduc is the
hero who passes, like perhaps Marie herself, from one side of the Channel
to the other, from "Bretaine la Meinur" to England and back, not once but
twice. He is the hero who, loved by two women, is a mediating term between their similarity and difference. He is, in short, the one who poses the
question of what might be carried from one side of the geographic and linguistic divide to the other, of what might pass not only between disparate
lands but from one language to another. "Eliduc" has, as Marie specifies, un-
dergone a change of name, and Eliduc's own name offers a key to his function as a translator. On some deep level the crossing of the Channel and the
merging of names are, consciously or not, about the amalgamation of two
kingdoms and of two tongues. "Eliduc" is, finally, about the formation of
the Anglo-Norman realm and of the Anglo-Norman language.

I am convinced too that the name "Eliduc" conjures, in what is indu-
bitably a historical subtext for Marie, the name of Eleanor of Aquitaine, the
woman who passed across the Channel between two men and between two

lands, the woman whose ancestral history at the abbey of Fontevrault provides a resonant parallel with that of the lai; the notorious affair between Eleanor's paternal grandfather, Guillaume IX, and her maternal grandmother, Dangereuse, was the apparent cause of Guillaume's second wife Philippa's retiring to Fontevrault, where she joined his first wife, Ermengarde, who was then abbess.[3] Then too, "Eli-duc" summons the concept of *alius* + *ducere,* or *alio* [an old adverbial dative form of *alius*] + *ducere,* "to lead elsewhere." As the ambiguous bigamist, the master of the half-truths, the adulterous vassal of two lords, Eliduc is a "misleader," and never more so, it turns out, than when he claims to be telling the truth—"For I don't want," he claims, "to transgress my faith" ("Kar ne voil ma fei trespasser" [v. 739]). Eliduc incarnates the paradox of the liar: "When I tell you I'm telling the truth, I lie; and when I tell you I lie, I am telling the truth." Which is no different, at bottom, from what the lai does when it denounces the very ambiguity it sanctions—"Kar n'est pas bien në avenant/De deus espuses meintenir,/Ne la *lei* nel deit cunsentir" (v. 1128), which can be read: "the *law* does not permit bigamy"; "the *lai* does not permit bigamy"; "the *law* does not permit ambiguity"; "the *lai* does not permit ambiguity." Or, "When the *lai* tells you it does not permit double meaning, it means double."

As translator, Eliduc introduces another kind of sadness into what we have defined until now as the fatality of disclosure, an abiding sense that something is always lost when one passes from one language to another. Marie is obsessed, of course, by translation. Not only does she tell us that she has "drawn" the *Lais* from the Breton, the *Fables* from the English, and the *Espurgatoire* from the Latin, but she insists often at the beginning of several lais on giving names in several tongues: "Bisclavret ad nun en bretan,/Garwaf l'apelent li Norman" ("Bisclavret," v. 3); "Gotelef l'apelent en engleis,/Chevrefoil le nument Franceis" ("Chevrefoil," v. 115); "Laüstic ad nun, céo m'est vis,/Si l'apelent en lur païs;/Ceo est russignol en franceis/E nihtegale en dreit engleis (*"Laüstic* is its name, I believe, and that is what [the Bretons] call it in their land. In French the title is *Rossignol,* and Nightingale is the correct English word" ["Laustic," v. 3]). In offering a plethora of names in different languages, Marie becomes the fellow traveler of Eliduc, the man who wants to retain two lords and two wives, the one who wants to have it all, to bring it all back from one land, that is to say one language, to another; and yet who recognizes in the end that choice is necessary, that some things do not cross over from one place to another without sacrifice, in the case of "Eliduc" the withdrawal of one woman from the world in order to let the other pass, that some things do not transfer from one language to the next. On the contrary, something is always lost in translation; and if Marie uses the word *traire* to designate translation as an extrusion or pulling from one language to another, she also understands, as we have seen in connection to the arrow that turns upon Guigemar, that every such extraction involves a betrayal captured in the homonym *trahir*.

The *Lais* are laden with betrayal, the betrayal of lovers and of lords to be sure; but they also display, indeed are subtended by, a more global sadness connected to words—the betrayal of a plurivalent, multiple, undefined, amorphous, and universal state of presence and being, which can exist only outside of language, by the imposition of particular and univocal meaning, a reduction of the universal to the particular, a fragmentation, a cutting, a severing of something whole into its distinctive and thereby contingent parts. Marie is haunted by the betrayal of a certain plenitude in language that occurs whenever one chooses one tongue over another, one title over another, one term within a single language over another, whenever language is submitted to the reductive, partial, necessarily fragmentary nature of any particular expression. The dilemma of excluding and of fixing, even by the choice of one word over another, is captured in the theme of Eliduc's choice between two wives, but it also characterizes a series of lais shaped by the fatality of foreclosure, among which "Les Deus Amanz" and "Chaitivel" form a natural pair.

"LES DEUS AMANZ" AND "CHAITIVEL"

"Les Deus Amanz" is a tale of aborted choice, or the consequences of a refusal to choose, or more precisely, to allow the selection of a mate. For, we learn, the Lord of Pisteis, which we have equated with Pity, having lost his wife, does all he can to prevent his daughter from marrying. More precisely, in requiring that the man who marries his daughter must carry her up the hill outside of town without pausing ("Entre ses braz la portereit,/ Si que ne se reposereit" [v. 37]), he insures that no man will "ask for" her: "Lung tens remist cele a doner,/ Que nul ne la volt demander" (v. 47). The Lord of Pity is without pity, issuing as he does a challenge that appears to preserve the potential plethora of all suitors by entertaining the challenge of none. Until, of course, a suitor commits the speech act—the request—that narrows the field to one. "He knew full well that her father loved her so much that, if he asked for her, she would not be given" ("S'a sun pere le demandot,/ Il saveit bien que tant l'amot/Que pas ne li vodreit doner" [v. 79]), thinks the lover; "Ask my father for me" ("A mun pere me requerrez" [v. 108]), specifies his beloved; "He went and asked the king for his daughter" ("Al rei alat sa fille quere,/Qu'il li donast" [v. 146])—thus the coveted daughter's suitor accepts the ordeal in the course of which he dies.

"Les Deus Amanz" contains in some deep sense a conflict of genres and of genders within the context of an impossible choice of *gendre* (MF "son-in-law"). To the masculinist, epic world of unmediated brute force, in which a challenge passes from father to would-be son-in-law, is opposed another way of being in the world. Before undertaking the challenge the daughter sends her suitor to Salerno with a letter for her aunt who is "knowledgeable in remedies":

> En Salerne ai une parente,
> Riche femme, mut ad grant rente;
> Plus de trente anz i ad esté.
> L'art de phisike ad tant usé
> Que mut est saives de mescines. (v. 95)

I have a relative in Salerno, a rich woman with a large income, who has been there for more than thirty years and who has practiced the art of physic so much that she is well versed in medicines.

Here Marie plays on the word *mescine,* which means both "remedy" or "medicine" and "young girl." The man who, armed with letters ("E mes lettres od vus porter" [v. 102]), passes from niece to aunt, finds in Salerno a feminine way of knowing that involves a supplement to masculine force, a brew that reinforces. "She will give you such electuaries and such potions as will revive you and increase your strength" ("Teus lettuaires vus durat/Et teus beivres vus baillerat/Que tut vus reconforterunt/E bone vertu vus durrunt" [v. 105]), promises the beloved; and her choice of words could not be more fortuitous. For the phrase "teus lettuaires," which in some editions is transcribed as "teus lectuaires," resonates with reading, a *lectio,* and might seem to mean "such a remedy," the Old French *lectuaire* being translated into modern French *électuaire,* or pharmaceutical preparation. But *électuaire* also resonates with the Latin *electus* meaning "excellent" or "choice," and in this way incarnates the essence of the meaning of this lai about choice. "The aunt will give you medicine, and that medicine is choice," the lai seems to say.

Indeed, the lover has a choice: as he makes his way up the hill, the lady urges him to drink "in order that he might regain lost strength" ("'Amis,' fet ele, 'kar bevez!/Jeo sai bien que vus [a]lassez:/Si recuvrez vostre vertu!'" [v. 185]), yet he chooses not to:

"Ne m'arestereie a nul fuer
Si lungement que jeo beüsse,
Pur quei treis pas aler peüsse.
Cest gens nus escrïereient,
De lur noise m'esturdireient;
Tost me purreient desturber.
Jo ne vol pas ci arester." (v. 190)

"Providing I can still walk three paces, on no account shall I stop, not even long enough to take a drink. These people would shout at us and deafen me with their noise, and they could easily distract me. I shall not stop here."

The lover participates in an anxiety that has, as we have seen, plagued Marie from the start—the fear of what others will say or think. Indeed, he is convinced that an instant's hesitation in the exertion of physical force will allow commentary, will invite envy of the sort that has been the downfall of both Lanval and Eliduc. The suitor refuses the "mescine" that is synonymous with both medicine and the girl; he refuses the "lectuaire" that is the equivalent of choice. In this he does not so much counter the father as resemble him, for both refuse to choose in this existentialist lai that rejects, finally, the choice not to choose.

The dilemma of choice is reproduced in "Chaitivel," the story of a lady who has four suitors, three of whom are killed in a tournament and the fourth wounded in his genitals. "Chaitivel," like other lais, is a story which, like the love of Eliduc, has come by hearsay: "Talent me prist de remembrer / Un lai dunt jo oï parler" (v. 1). And a story about the fatality of choice, that is, about a reductive process of elimination in love mirrored by an equally tragic linguistic reduction.

The geographic situation of this lai is, here as elsewhere, significant. "Chaitivel" takes place in Nantes: "L'aventure vus en dirai / E la cité vus numerai. . . . En Bretaine a Nantes, maneit / Une dame que mut valeit" (vv. 3, 9). "Nantes"—*namp, nampt, nans*—in Old French means "gage," "caution," *nantissement.* And as such it takes a verbal form *(nantir)* which in modern French means "to be in" or "to take possession of." In this sense the only name pronounced in "Chaitivel" says it all: the lady wants to possess it all and will not opt for a proper name, she will not opt for property, for that which is specific, unique, single. She will not enter into possession of the one, so intent is she on keeping them all. Indeed, the lucky lady of "Chaitivel" is in the beginning overcome by a surplus of "sens"—"La dame fu de mut grant sens" (v. 49)—which can be understood to mean that, being the object of the suit of four knights, she has more "sens" in the sense of seed or *semence* than she can use, but also that she has a lot of meaning, a lot of sense, a lot of good sense in not choosing. Indeed, her good sense consists precisely in understanding what she loses in choosing one: "They all had such great merit that she was unable to choose the best, yet she did not wish to lose all three in order to retain just one" ("Tant furent tuz de grant valur,/Ne pot eslire le meillur./Ne volt les treis perdre pur l'un" [v. 53]).

The dilemma of the lady of "Chaitivel" looks like simply an erotic choice, a choice of love object, a choice of bodies. Yet it is in some deep sense also about names. The lady refuses in simplest terms to pronounce, to pronounce one name and leave off the others. Unlike the lady, however, for whom a "surplus of sens" is the equivalent of a surplus of men's names ("so many men, so little time"!), the men are all too willing to pronounce. For they are fetishists in the strictest sense of the term. Wearing a piece of the lady's dress, a part taken for the whole, they make a semiological display of the love object: "They all regarded her as their beloved, wore her love token, a ring, sleeve, or pennant, and used her name as a rallying cry" ("Tuz la teneient pur amie,/Tuz portouent sa drüerie,/Anel u mance u gunfanun" [v. 63]). Crying her name out loud, they dare to do in public what she refuses, that is, to proclaim, to articulate a choice.

In this the four knights, like Lanval or the lady of "Laüstic," make a fatal mistake. For there is something fated about the tournament: in "crying her name," that is to say in pronouncing, it is their death that is pronounced, as the tournament is literally "cried" or announced:

> E chescun escriot sun nun.
> Tuz quatre les ama e tient,
> Tant que aprés une paske vient,
> Que devant Nantes la cité
> Ot un turneiement crïé. (v. 70)

Each used her name as a rallying cry. She loved and retained all four, until one year, after Easter, a tournament was proclaimed before the city of Nantes.

As surely as the tournament is "cried," the semiological display of their love, the objects of their fetishism, are recognized: "Their opponents recognized them by their ensigns and shields" ("Cil defors les unt coneüz/As enseignes e as escuz" [v. 89]). And as surely as they are recognized, three of the four are killed, and the fourth is wounded. And wounded not just any old place, but in the same place as Guigemar and the Fisher King of Grail tradition—in the thigh: "Par mi la quisse e einz el cors / Si que la lance parut fors" (v. 123). The fourth knight's wound, and here there can be little doubt, is a castration, for even when he recovers and should theoretically have also recovered the lady's love, he complains of being unable to "experience the joy of a kiss or an embrace or of any pleasure other than conversation" ("Si n'en puis nulle joie aveir / Ne de baisier, ne d'acoler, / Ne d'autre bien fors de parler" [v. 219]). Here we are faced with a cruel irony: if the lady's failure to pronounce implies a surplus of sense—a surplus both of meaning or of names and of semen—the knights' anxiousness to pronounce ends in a complete absence of seed and of sexual desire.

In the medieval thinking of the link between words and the world, one can find the assimilation of the relation of universal categories to the particular, and in particular to their expression in language, to an act of castration.[4] The prime example is, of course, that of Jean de Meun, who participates along with his traditional sources (Hesiod through Ovid, Claudian, Macrobius) in the myth of a prelapsarian era before the existence of desire, private property, social difference, or the linguistic difference brought about by Reason's imposition of names on things. Jean's version of the fall from an original unity, a state of undefined plenitude and grace analogous to the period in which the lady of "Chaitivel" held four men and four names in abeyance, into multiplicity involves a family drama emphasizing the connection of semiological and physical dismemberment.[5] Both involve a loss—bodily, linguistic, ontological—caused by naming and by a detachment of language from the fantasized possibility of univocal meaning. One loses all in taking one ("Ne voil tuz perdre pour l'un prendre" [v. 156]), and one is left with only words: "Ne d'autre bien, fors de parler."

In "Chaitivel" the drama of constricting choice proliferates as a theme and as an eponymic framework for the poem. Not only does the lady, who is never herself named, not want to pick one name over the others because of the fatal consequences of such a choice, but Marie herself, in the position of the lady, admits that "there lived in Brittany four men whose names I do not know" ("En Bretaine ot quatre baruns, / Mes jeo ne sai numer lur nuns" [vv. 33]). Marie does not know how to name the lai in the beginning:

> L'aventure vus en dirai
> E la cité vus numerai
> U il fu nez e cum ot nun:

> Le Chaitivel l'apelat hum
> E si [i] ad plusurs de ceus
> Ki l'apelent Les Quatre Duels. (v. 3)

I shall recount what happened, name the city where it was composed, and
tell you its title. It is generally called "Le Chaitivel" (The Unhappy One), but
many people call it "Les Quatre Duels" (The Four Sorrows).

Her initial hesitation over the title emanates from the dispute, revealed only
at the end, over what to call the story we have just read. In seeking to remember those for whose dismemberment she is responsible, the lady proposes to make a lai:

> "Pur coe que tant vus ai amez,
> Voil que mis doels seit remembrez:
> De vus quatre ferai un lai
> E Quatre Dols vus numerai." (v. 201)

Because of my great love for you all, I want my grief to be remembered. I
shall compose a lay about the four of you and entitle it "The Four Sorrows."

We could find no better example of the tension in the *Lais* between dispersion and recuperation, between dismemberment and remembrance, or of
the nostalgic effects of choice. For the remaining knight, his potency di-
minished, insists upon a name change from "Quatre Dols" to a diminutive
that reduces four to one—"Chaitivel," from the Latin diminutive *captivu-
lus*, "dear little captive," rather than *captivus*—and also recognizes what one
loses when one chooses:

> Li chevaliers li respundi
> Hastivement, quant il l'oï:
> "Dame, fetes le lei novel,
> Si l'apelez Le Chaitivel!" (v. 205)

When he heard these words, the knight replied quickly: "My lady, compose
the new lay, but call it 'The Unhappy One!'"

In fact, Marie concludes, both names of the lai were preserved, and though
"some of those who put it into circulation call it 'The Four Sorrows,' . . . it
is commonly known as 'Chaitivel.'"[6] Both names fit, for the matter of the
tale "requires it": "Chescun des nuns bien i afiert,/ Kar la matire le requiert"
(v. 234). It is hard to imagine a better fit between substance and form, for
the tale about the resistance to naming a love object also resists naming itself. Marie, like the lady, knows that one loses many in choosing one.

"Chaitivel" is framed at beginning and end by the question of naming the lai. Rather, the hesitation of the beginning is resolved in the end by a re-naming not unlike that which takes place in "Eliduc": "Elidus fu primes nomez,/Mes ore est li nuns remüez" (v. 22). This may seem like a minor point, but it is indicative of a wider process of cultural transfer that is linked to the forging of a culture as a process of renaming, more precisely, as I have suggested above, the making of Anglo-Normandy. It is no accident, I think, that Marie specifically states at the beginning of "Les Deus Amanz" that the action took place in "Neustrie" that we now call "Normandy" ("Verité est kë en Neustrie,/Que nus apelum Normendie" [v. 7]), for such linguistic transformation is a wider principle within the *Lais*. No framing motif is more common than Marie's reminder that the story she will tell or has just told comes from material—an "aventure"—that the Bretons made into a lai. And, as she insists in the prologue, she has translated the Breton lais that she has heard (or read) into Old French. Marie has, in other words, changed the names in what is a more general process not unlike the change of a name or a title at the end of "Chaitivel" and "Eliduc." The process of cultural transformation that she works via translation is so enmeshed in the drama of names and of renaming found in "Chaitivel" that it is impossible to sep-arate the story from its title. Nor is it possible to separate either from the lan-guage drama defined earlier in terms of a desire for unity expressed in terms of a "remembrement" and the uncontrollable tendency of language to scat-ter into particularity and difference. Marie's urge to preserve all the names and her proffering of the multiple names in several tongues holds, at bot-tom, an urge to have them all; and, given the knowledge that this is impos-sible, to bring back in a relation of compilatory, compensatory juxtaposi-tion as many meanings as possible.

Thus, the logic of betrayal works on many levels in the *Lais,* both the-matic and linguistic. We have seen that Guigemar is betrayed by the arrow that returns to wound him in the thigh, that the lady of "Le Fresne" is be-trayed by her own malicious gossip, the lovers of "Equitan" by criminal sug-gestion, the husband of "Bisclavret" by indiscretion, the wife of "Laüstic" by a lie, Lanval by a boast. The surviving lover of "Chaitivel" is betrayed, first by the lady's refusal to choose, then by the loss implied in such a choice. Thus, betrayal seems in the *Lais* to be wrapped up more in the speech acts of court than in the martial acts of the battlefield. It emanates from a sense of what one loses when one passes from one language to another, but, more generally, of what one loses when one enters into language, whenever one chooses one word over another, whenever one enters into narrative and strings together a series of single words taken from a larger paradigm. It will be remembered too that the word *traire,* which means "to extrude," "to draw," "to draw out," "to translate," as well as "to betray," is also a synonym of *trover,* "to invent" in the sense of poetic *inventio,* and "to discover" as in the betrayal of lovers. To write or treat *(traire)* is to betray *(trahir);* or, to carry this idea further, to write, to choose one word over another, is to betray an imagined immanence, whether that immanence is figured as the body or the voice, or, as Roger Dragonetti has suggested, "the memory of the musical origin of the lai itself."[7] It is, as in the case of the nightingale, to ensnare and contain it in a trap, a "laz" ("Laüstic"), to kill it; and, ultimately, to entomb the living voice in the dead letter of a text, to silence it.[8]

This is why there are so many tombs in Marie's works. The lady of "Chaitivel," having killed three and maimed one by her commitment not to commit, makes it up to them with convalescent and perpetual care:

> "Les morz ferai ensevelir,
> E si le nafrez poet garir,
> Volenters m'en entremetrai,
> E bons mires li baillerai."
> En ses chambres le fet porter;
> Puis fist les autres cunreer,
> A grant amur e noblement
> Les aturnat e richement.
> En une mut riche abeïe
> Fist grant offrendre et grant partie
> La u il furent enfuï. (v. 161)

"I shall bury the dead, and if the injured knight can be healed, I shall gladly take care of him and provide him with a good doctor." She had him carried into her chamber and then arranged for the others to be laid out for burial, lovingly, nobly, and lavishly arrayed. She gave large offerings to a rich abbey where they were buried.

The lady of "Laüstic" encloses the body of the dead bird in a reliquary that functions as a memory device, a memorial.[9] Yonec's father's tomb becomes the site of his mother's remembrance and of the transfer of the tale of birth (v. 495). The lovers of "Les Deus Amanz" are interred in a marble tomb ("Sarcu de marbre firent quere, / Les deus enfanz unt mis dedenz" [v. 236]). More important, their burial is preceded by a desperate attempt to revive the lover by an infusion of the potion that signifies "medicine" and "the girl" or femininity ("Sun beivre li voleit doner" [207]) and that spills on the ground with marvelous ecological effect. The "mescine" also designated by the term "lectuaire," which resonates with *lectio* or reading, is spilled on the ground such that "many good plants were found there which took root" ("Meinte bone herbe i unt trovee / Ki del beivrë orent racine" [v. 218]). In a passage that recalls the honeysuckle entwined around the hazel tree in "Chevrefoil," we find ourselves before the image of writing planted in the ground, which image points again to Marie's original invocation in the prologue not to remain silent, but to "spread one's flowers." "Les Deus Amanz" is significant in yet another respect: for the "mescine" / "lectuaire" that are buried on the hill become the hill, endow it with its name that is inseparable from the lovers' bodies that are buried there as well as from the lai itself:

> Pur l'aventure des enfaunz
> Ad nun li munz des Deus Amanz.
> Issi avint cum dit vus ai;
> Li Bretun en firent un lai. (v. 241

Because of what happened to these two young people, the mountain is called the Mountain of the Two Lovers. The events took place just as I have told you, and the Bretons composed a lay about them.

In the memorial it constructs, "Les Deus Amanz" buries the body and the voice of adventure in the tomb of writing.

What this suggests is that the *lai,* as a vestige or *legs,* is the tomb of the voice, a site of remembrance, and a monument to desire or to the pain that attends it. Thus, in "Eliduc" the moment of the woman's burial and the hero's withdrawal from the world to the abbey is the moment he becomes a lyric poet:

> "Le jur que jeo vus enfuirai
> Ordre de moigne recevrai;
> Sur vostre tumbe chescun jur
> Ferai refreindre ma dolur." (v. 947)

"The day that I bury you I shall take holy orders. On your tomb every day I shall make my grief resound" [or "I will refrain my sadness"].

Again, the *lai* functions as a legacy, the site of mourning and of loss, more precisely, of a loss of imagined plenitude.[10]

To summarize just a bit, we find in the *Lais* three modes of fatalistic despoliation: exposure, translation or crossing over, and foreclosure. We have seen the extent to which those who speak in the *Lais* risk death, with the understanding that it is the poetess who at bottom breaks the prohibition of disclosure by uncovering secret love affairs. So too does she betray by the "pulling" or "extrusion" of one language from another, which implies an act of killing or excision, a leaving behind of that which does not pass, an elimination of one cultural system in opting for another, and, when the same thing is signified by two words in two different tongues, an exclusion of one in opting for the other. At bottom, the process of choosing languages is the problem *of* language: the choice of one word when there are many. The poetess is the one who violates the fantasy of plenitude by choosing and who thus places the presence of the voice in the tomb of writing. Like the cautious lady of "Chaitivel," she always loses something in "taking one."

We are describing, of course, not only a process of cultural and linguistic transfer from Breton to Old French, but, within Anglo-Norman culture, the transformation of an oral culture into a written one. I realize the complication of using such crude terms as "oral" and "written culture," for oral cultures have texts, and orality is always a form of writing taken in the largest sense. I would not be tempted to do so were it not for the insistence of Marie, who in the *Lais* constantly draws attention to the ways in which orality is drawn into writing.

"MILUN" AND "CHEVREFOIL"

Two lais seem to dramatize writing explicitly. The first, "Milun," contains many elements we have seen thus far: love by hearsay, the imposition of a father's unhappy marital choice, the lady confined to a castle, the hiding of an illicit passion, in this instance for a period of some twenty years. But with a difference. The son born out of wedlock to Milun and his lady is, as in "Le Fresne," hidden, and the relation of the parents is maintained via an exchange of letters tucked under the wing of a swan, letters that not only are the vehicle for both the expression and the hiding of feelings, but come to substitute for them. Indeed, once the lovers no longer have access to each other, they enter, like Abelard and Heloise, into written communication:

> Milun se prist a purpenser
> Coment il li purat mander,
> Si qu'il ne seit aparceüz,
> Qu'il est al païs [re]venuz.
> Ses lettres fist, sis seela.
> Un cisne aveit k'il mut ama,
> Le brief li ad al col lïé
> E dedenz la plume muscié. (v. 159)

Milun started to work out how he could inform her, without being detected, that he had come back home. He wrote a letter, sealed it, and tied the letter around the neck of a swan that he loved dearly and concealed it amongst its feathers.

The swan is carried to the imprisoned lady, who feels the writing under its feathers and trembles: "Le col li manie e le chief,/Desuz la plume sent le brief,/Le sanc li remut e fremi" (v. 219). As in the case of Iseult in "Chevre-foil," the lady recognizes her lover's name ("De sun ami cunut le nun" [v.230]), and, starving the bird ("Le cigne ot laissié jeüner" [v. 259]), "she contrives to obtain ink and parchment" ("Tant quist par art e par engin/Kë ele ot enke e parchemin" [v. 255]), then writes a letter "according to her plea-sure, sealing it with a ring": "Un brief escrit tel cum li plot,/Od un anel l'enseelot" (v. 257).

The swan or "cisne" via which letters are passed is the homonym of the sign or *signe*, its wing, as in the original missive sent by Milun, the seal that hides. The swan, like the knotted shirttail of "Guigemar," the rich cloth of "Le Fresne," the "lectuaire" of "Les Deus Amanz," the "bastun" or carved stick of "Chevrefoil," the reliquary of "Laüstic," is one of those images that not only encapsulate, in the sense of Eliot's objective correlative, an entire lai, but also contain within them the idea of writing as theme. For the swan that is the vehicle of communication between lovers, that seals or hides their passion, works via the feather that hides the letter: "Le brief li ad al col lïé/ E dedenz la plume muscié" (v. 165), which can be read "he tied the letter to the neck and hid it in the feather." Alternatively, Milun hides his message "in the quill or pen," "under the feathers or under the pen." How could one imagine a clearer statement than this—"that the secret message is hidden under or by the pen." The feather or quill that hides is, moreover, located under the throat, as if Marie were again positing the possibility of the dis-placement of the voice by writing.

Read and understood, the hidden message provokes:

> El le receit mut bonement;
> Le col li manie e le chief,
> Desuz la plume sent le brief.
> Le sanc li remut e fremi:
> Bien sot qu'il vient de sun ami. (v. 218)

She received [the swan] fittingly. She stroked its neck and head and felt the letter beneath its feathers. Her blood ran cold, for she realized it was from her beloved.

Now what is most astonishing about this curious passage about reception is that it can also be taken to be about the act of writing itself, the phrase "Desuz la plume sent le brief" referring to Marie's own writing—"under the pen she feels the letter." In this case the pleasure or the affective power that writing contains, its capacity to make blood run cold ("Le sanc li remut e fremi"), makes of it an escape. Like the appearance of the bird lover of "Yonec," the arrival of the swan connotes the arrival of writing, or writing as rescue or deliverance from the prison of an arranged marriage.[11]

It is, of course, somewhat of a leap, but it is more than reasonable to conclude that in the motif of hidden letters, the "cisne" that signifies and the material activity of writing in "Milun," we come as close as one could imagine to a confession on Marie's part, a revelation, if not of her own situation, at least of the situation of the woman writer, or rather of the woman who, constrained by a stifling marriage, resorts to writing as an escape, turns like Lanval to the liberating fairy of fiction. Such an explanation accounts too for the starving of the bird—"Le cigne ot laissié jeüner" (v. 259)—which figures the starving of the lovers who are satisfied only by writing. For it is the case that the lovers of "Milun," like those of "Laüstic," do not enjoy the presence of the body, the "surplus" that is the equivalent of sexual joining. On the contrary, Marie specifies that they actually met in person only "a number" of times over a period of two decades:

> Vint anz menerent cele vie
> Milun entre lui e s'amie.
> Del cigne firent messager,
> N'i aveient autre enparler,
> E sil feseient jeüner
> Ainz qu'il le lessassent aler;
> Cil a ki le oiseus veneit,
> Ceo sachez, quë il le peisseit.
> Ensemble viendrent plusurs feiz. (v. 279)

Milun and his beloved maintained this way of life for twenty years. The swan acted as messenger. They had no other intermediary and they starved it before releasing it. Whoever received the swan fed it, of course. They came together on a number of occasions.

What could be clearer than the hierarchy established in terms of bodily pleasure and speech, on the one hand, and writing, on the other? For if the lovers of "Laüstic" "took delight in seeing each other, since they were denied anything more" (v. 77), the lovers of "Milun" take delight in writing to each other when they can have no more, letters being a substitute for presence. Writing defers presence, it serves both to excite desire and, as substitute, to defer it: "He sent her a sealed letter by means of the swan assuredly. Now she would send back word of her feelings" ("Brief a seel li envea/Par le cigne, mun escïent,/Or li remandast sun talent" [v. 364]), the last line of which can be read "then she sent back [word] of his desire" or "then she deferred [sent back] her desire."

"Milun" is in some deep sense about writing as deferral. Indeed, the son conceived out of wedlock is sent away with a letter attached to his own neck and is a kind of letter sent by his mother, as per her instructions intended for Milun, to her sister:

> "Si li manderai par escrit
> E par paroles e par dit
> Que c'est l'enfant [a] sa serur,
> Si'n ad suffert meinte dolur;
>
> . . . .
>
> Vostre anel al col li pendrai,
> E un brief li enveierai:
> Escrit i ert le nun sun pere
> E l'aventure de sa mere." (vv. 71, 77)

"You will inform her in writing and by word of mouth that this is her sister's child that has already caused her much suffering. . . . I shall hang your ring round its neck and send her a letter. In it will be its father's name, and the story of its mother's misfortune."

A letter to be read or understood, moreover, at some later date:

> "Quant il serat grant e creüz
> E en tel eage venuz
> Quë il sache reisun entendre,
> Le brief e l'anel li deit rendre;
> Si li cumant tant a garder
> Que sun pere puisse trover." (v. 81)

"When it is fully grown and has reached the age of reason, she should give the child the letter and the ring. Let her command the child to keep them until it has been able to find its father."

To complete our conjecture concerning Marie or the woman writer of the High Middle Ages just a bit, one can see in Milun and the lady's son and the letter around his neck an analogy between writing and progeny. Writing creates its own inheritance, it is its own legacy or *legs,* it is the illegitimate child—the "Sanz Per" (v. 342), the "Peerless One" who is also "Without Father," as he is named—of the woman constrained by her material condition and who escapes via fiction.

The fantasy of evasion in "Milun" is that of the letter launched finding its proper destination, of the swan that always manages to return with its letters to its address and of the reunion of the father with the son/letter. Which is exactly what happens at the end when Milun recounts the story of love deferred via writing:

> Milun ad a sun fiz cunté
> De sa mere cum il l'ama
> E cum sis peres la duna
> A un barun de sa cuntre[e],
> E cument il l'ad puis amee,
> E ele lui de bon curage,
> E cum del cigne fist message,
> Ses lettres li feseit porter,
> Ne se osot en nului fier. (v. 490)

Milun told his son about his love for his mother and how her father had given her to a nobleman from the region and how he had continued to love her and she him wholeheartedly. He also told how the swan became his messenger and took his letters, because he dared not trust anyone.

The tale recounted to his son is, in fact, that of "Milun," an inscription of the lai within the lai, which, to complete the fantasy of plenitude and the restoration of the presence of bodies, is synonymous with the son's desire, rejoined to his father, to join his parents in marriage ("Par fei, bel pere./Assemblerai vus e ma mere" [v. 499]), which desire is fulfilled by a messenger, a "mescine" carrying a remedy in the form of another letter:

> Si cum il eirent le chemin,
> Si encuntrerent un meschin:
> De l'amie Milun veneit,
> En Bretaigne passer voleit;
> Ele l'i aveit enveié.
> Ore ad sun travail acurcié.
> Un brief li baille enseelé;
> Par parole li ad cunté
> Que s'en venist, ne demurast;
> Morz est sis sires, or s'en hastast! (v. 509)

As they made their way, they encountered a servant: he came from Milun's beloved and was intending to cross over to Brittany. She had sent him there, but now his task was shortened. He gave Milun a sealed letter and told him verbally that he should come without delay. Her husband was dead, he must now make haste!

The convenient death of the mother's husband signals an end to deferral— "Que s'en venist, ne demurast"—in this fictive world where wishing, or rather writing, makes it so.

Another lai that explicitly dramatizes writing is, of course, "Chevrefoil," which illustrates all that we have seen thus far where the question of meaning is concerned. For if each lai, as I have maintained throughout, has a navel, an internal point of origin, a place from which the tale can be said to have been generated as a tale (an internally coherent and closed narrative structure as opposed to the potential external source of the story), a center of gravity if you like, then we find in "Chevrefoil," which is in many ways the least closed and coherent of all the *Lais,* an inscription of the poet. Tristan, one of the actors in the story, is said to have composed the lai that we have just read: "Pur les paroles remembrer,/Tristam, ki bien saveit harper,/En aveit fet un nuvel lai" (vv. 112–14). One notices immediately how closely Tristan's intention as a poet resembles Marie's own intention from the beginning, her project of "remembrance," a preserving of some supposedly more labile (oral?) form of "aventure." There was in the twelfth and thirteenth centuries a tradition that portrayed Tristan not only as a lover and as a hunter (a master of crafts, among which was living in the forest), but as a maker of lais—a "maitre ès lais amoureux." "Chevrefoil" was known by the middle of the twelfth century, as seen in the *chanson de geste Garin li Loherains:*

> et font feste moult grant
> Harpes et gigues, et jougléors chantant
> En lor chançons vont les lais viëlant
> Que en Bretagne firent ja les amants
> Del Chievrefoil vont les sonet disant
> Que Tristans fist que Iseut ama tant.[12]

Gerbert de Montreuil's *Perceval* (1220–25) contains a curious poem entitled "Tristan ménestral," in which the hero is disguised as a jongleur at Marc's court. So too, several anonymous Arthurian lais are attributed to heroes of legend. Tristan, for example, is said to have composed five lais—the "Lai de plour," "Lai du Boivre plesant," "Lai du Déduit d'Amour," "Lai mortel,"

"Lai Recort de Victoire"—as well as two letters that resemble lais, "A vous Roi qui bien estes Rois" (to King Arthur) and "A vos amis qui de bontez" (to Lancelot), and one strophe of a lai, "Grant tens a que je ne vi cele." The Chansonnier of Berne attributes to Tristan the famous "Lai du Chèvrefeuille," a specious attribution, given the fact that Marie's narrative lai is earlier.[13]

Marie's inscription of Tristan differentiates it from the rest of the *Lais*. Elsewhere the assumption is that the lai itself is a written transcription of some oral state of the story, an "aventure." Marie is rather explicit on this point. Here, however, she is just as explicit concerning the fact that Tristan is working from a written source:

> Pur la joie qu'il ot eüe
> De s'amie qu'il ot veüe
> E pur ceo k'il aveit escrit,
> Si cum la reïne l'ot dit,
> Pur les paroles remembrer,
> Tristram, ki bien saveit harper,
> En aveit fet un nuvel lai. (v. 107)

On account of the joy he had experienced from the sight of his beloved and because of what he had written, Tristram, a skillful harpist, in order to record his words (as the Queen had said he should), used them to create a new lay.

Marie identifies her source from the beginning not only with a pleasure akin to that of Tristan, but, exceptionally, with a written one alongside of an oral one. She has read it and heard it ("Plusurs le me unt cunté e dit/E jeo l'ai trové en escrit" [v. 5]), a double access that in fact duplicates some of the interpretive questions of the tale itself.

But what is Tristan's written source?

One, evidently, that he has himself produced, for we learn in the tale that Tristan is a writer. And, what's more, joy is not the only source of inspiration: having learned the Queen is about to pass alongside the road, Tristan can hardly contain his impulses, which are not so much erotic as they are scribal:[14]

> E Tristram est al bois venuz
> Sur le chemin quë il saveit
> Que la rute passer deveit,
> Une codre trencha par mi,
> Tute quarreie la fendi.
> Quant il ad paré le bastun,

> De sun cutel escrit sun nun.
> Se la reïne s'aperceit,
> Qui mut grant garde en perneit—
> Autre feiz li fu avenu
> Que si l'aveit aparceü—
> De sun ami bien conustra
> Le bastun quant el le verra.
> Ceo fu la summe de l'escrit
> Qu'il li aveit mandé e dit. (v. 49)

Tristram entered the wood along the road he knew the procession would have to take. He cut a hazel branch in half and squared it. When he had whittled the stock he wrote his name on it with his knife. If the Queen, who would be on the lookout, spotted it (on an earlier occasion she had successfully observed it in this way), she would recognize her beloved's stick when she saw it. This was all he wrote, because he had sent her word.

No passage has caused more difficulty for scholars of Old French literature than this one, beginning with the question of what literally Tristan wrote on the stick.[15] Some maintain that he wrote his name and nothing else. "Quant li ad paré le bastun,/De sun cutel escrit sun nun." In that case, the question remains, To what does the famous "summe de l'escrit" refer? At least one scholar sees in the "nun" not a name but a message, a *nuntium*.[16] Some maintain that Tristan inscribes the entire encapsulated story of their love (vv. 63–78) on the stick. Indeed, this interpretation is sustained by the later reference to Iseult's recognition of "all the letters": "Le bastun vit, bien l'aparceut,/Tutes les lettres i conut" (v. 81). Among those who maintain that an abridged form of their story is on the squared stick, there are those who claim that the impossibility of putting that much writing on a piece of wood is solved by Tristan's use of code on the *codrier*—the famous Ogamic writing of Irish tradition.[17] Which leads to the further possibility that the entire lai is written on the stick. Some argue that Tristan has written on the four sides of the hazel stick only the four distichs of the message contained in lines 77–78: "Bele amie, si est de nus:/Ne vus sanz mei, ne mei sanz vus!" Others that what has happened, in fact, is that Tristan has sent a message previously to the Queen, and that this message contained the "summe de l'escrit/Qu'il li aveit mandé et dit." Still others claim that the key word here is "summe" and that, despite the fact that Tristan has quite literally only written his name, the Queen understands the entire story from the sight of it, as the relation between Tristan's name and the lover's story is assimilated to the relation of the letter and the spirit. The "summe de l'escrit" is a summa, a *somme,* an interpretation, one of the key medieval metaphors for the process of producing meaning being precisely that of the bark or covering *(integumentum)* and the wood.

The question of the writing on the hazel stick is the question of writing in general, one of those representations of representation which in Marie reverts to the question of linguistic surplus—the "surplus of sense," the ways in which words do not fit but constantly overflow our attempts to contain their meaning. There are simply too many possible interpretations, none of which prevails in any absolute, motivated, ontologically grounded sense.[18] Indeed, so tangled is the problem of interpretation here that one is even tempted to see an intentional obscurity on Marie's part of the type she accuses the ancients of introducing into their writing so that those who come after and who are obliged to understand will be obliged to supply their "surplus of sense."

Where the question of meaning is concerned, "Chevrefoil" resists resolutely all attempts to reduce it to univocal sense even on the most literal level of what we are to understand as being written on the page. Hence the question at the end of naming the lai that Tristan has made:

> Asez briefment le numerai:
> Gotelef l'apelent en engleis,
> Chevrefoil le nument Franceis.
> Dit vus en ai la verité
> Del lai que j'ai ici cunté. (v. 114)

I shall very briefly name it: the English call it "Gotelef" and the French "Chevrefoil." I have told you the truth of the lay I have related here.

One of the surpluses that the "lai" leaves, and we must not forget that one of the meanings of the word *lai* is *restes* or "lees," that which is left, is the polysemy of meaning in this particular case and the monogamy of the couple Tristan and Iseult. For whatever is written on the stick one thing is clear: the stick or wood and that which surrounds it, the "integumentum," expressed in terms of the hazel stick entwined by honeysuckle, is, like the pleated shirttail at the end of "Guigemar," an inextricable knot:

> D'euls deus fu il [tut] autresi
> Cume del chevrefoil esteit
> Ki a la codre se perneit:
> Quant il s'i est laciez e pris
> E tut entur le fust s'est mis,
> Ensemble poënt bien durer;

Mes ki puis les volt desevrer,
Li codres muert hastivement
E li chevrefoil ensement.
"Bele amie, si est de nus:
Ne vus sanz mei, ne mei sanz vus!" (v. 68)

The two of them resembled the honeysuckle that clings to the hazel branch:
when it has wound itself round and attached itself to the hazel, the two can
survive together; but if anyone should then attempt to separate them, the
hazel quickly dies, as does the honeysuckle. "Sweet love, so it is with us: without me you cannot survive, nor I without you."

So too, "Chevrefoil" evokes the ending of "Les Deus Amanz," in which inseparable lovers die and are buried together on the hill that flowers because
of the herbal brew that is spread there. With one important difference:
among all the lais "Chevrefoil" is the least resolved, the most fragmentary,
and for this reason the lai in which Marie not only creates internally the
knot most resistant to understanding even of the most literal sort, but in
which she manages to leave as open as possible the plurivalent possibilities
of meaning, in which, to invoke the vocabulary of "Chaitivel" as well as
"Les Deus Amanz," she chooses not to choose.[19] The consequences for the
lovers are hardly less tragic in this tale determined by the legend surrounding its beginning and end, and "Chevrefoil" is no less a drama of language
than the other lais in that the only thing Marie cannot choose is to remain
silent, despite the fact that speech in her theology of words is also fatal. In
the instant she chooses to write of Tristan's writing, the lovers, like the love-
birds of "Laüstic" and "Lanval," are dead. The "tragedy of words" that hangs
over "Chevrefoil" is captured, as Roger Dragonetti notes in a remark that
seems especially appropriate to the tale of a writing stick, in the name "Tristram" decomposed into the Old French elements *triste* + *rame* (MF *rameau*)
or "sad branch."[20]

The existential drama of doomed choices that we have been tracing is all
the more entrapping given Marie's initial prohibition of silence and imposition of the obligation to speak set forth so radically in the prologue. Faced
with the choice to remain silent or speak, the poet is obliged to speak; yet in
speaking s/he courts death. Like Lanval or the lady of "Laüstic," she cannot
express secret love without revealing it, cannot transcribe the presence of the
voice without betraying it. This is why speech acts in the *Lais* appear to be
so dangerous, to come back to haunt or kill the one who speaks. For the
situations in which the heroes and heroines, or even the minor figures like

the sailor in "Eliduc," find themselves are thoroughly analogous to that of
the poetess who in writing kills the living voice, places it in the tomb of

"YONEC"

The burying of the voice in the necropolis of the lai is nowhere more manifest than in "Yonec," which we have discussed in terms of the despoiling
revelation and self-revelation of the woman whose happiness is written on
her face. "Yonec" offers yet another example of a bird, a body, and the symbol of a voice. Trapped, cut, the bird bleeds, and its blood, like that on the
lady's blouse in "Laüstic," becomes a form of writing, first upon the sheet
("Devant la dame al lit descent,/Que tut li drap furent sanglent" [v. 315])
and then upon the ground:

> A la trace del sanc s'est mise,
> Qui del chevaler [de]curot
> Sur le chemin u ele alot.
> Icel senti[e]r errat e tient. (v. 342)

She followed the trail of blood that flowed from the knight onto the path she
was taking and to which she kept.

The trail of blood leads, ultimately, to another bed, a deathbed and the
scene of pre-scription, a prewriting of the rest of the tale, as the bird now
mutated back into a man prophesies the birth of a son who will avenge him.
And avenge him not just anywhere but at yet another burial site—"At a
tomb they would visit they would again hear about his death and how he
was unjustly killed" ("Par une tumbe k'il verrunt/Orrunt renoveler sa
mort/E cum il fu ocis a tort" [v. 430]). The entombed bird of "Yonec"
stands as an unmistakable representation of the captured voice with all the
sense of loss that such capture, associated with the conversion of the voice
into writing, carries with it. For the written lai, a dead letter, the tomb of the
living voice, becomes, again as in "Eliduc," a site of mourning; and mourning becomes the locus of the theme dear to Marie of "remembrement"—
a remembering of the truth of a paternity based upon love and not the
legal convention of marriage, and a reassembling of the family as the son
before the true father's grave slays his slayer. Moreover, the site of mourning
and of the recognition of true paternity is also the site of literature, the navel
of the lai, that place in the tale where its own origin becomes manifest—a

retelling of the tale prior to its transfer, its going public, its "sending out,"
in Marie's phrase:

> Oianz tuz, li ad coneü
> Que l'engendrat e sis fiz fu,
> Cum il suleit venir a li
> E cum sis sires le trahi;
> La verité li ad cuntee.
> Sur la tumbe cheï pasmee;
> En la paumeisun devia;
> Unc puis a humme ne parla. (v. 533)

For all to hear, she revealed to him that this was his father and he his son,
how he used to come to her and how her husband had betrayed him. She
told him the truth, fell into a faint on the tomb, and while unconscious,
died. She never spoke again.

A transfer that is mythologized in the end in keeping with the general genesis of such tales contained in the prologue:

> Cil que ceste aventure oïrent
> Lunc tens aprés un lai en firent,
> De la pité, de la dolur
> Que cil suffrirent pur amur. (v. 551)

Those who heard this story long afterward composed a lay from it, about the
sorrow and grief that they suffered for love.

Nor can we forget the location of the action of "Yonec," which takes place
on the river Duelas (v. 15), a name resonating with a sense of sadness, of
deuil. We have seen the importance of the name "Eliduc," the misleader in
love, whose name (*alio + ducere*, "to lead elsewhere") tells all. So too, one can
hardly miss the significance of "Yonec," a combination of the first person
pronoun *ego*, which by the twelfth century was written *ge, je,* or *jo,* and *neco*
or *necare—je tue.* Which is exactly what he does. And is exactly what the
poet or poetess does in uncovering secret love, killing it, betraying presence,
placing the voice in the tomb of writing. The *Lais* are a *legs,* a monument to
desire, a site of mourning, a site of remembrance, and a site of truth, as the
ultimate resting place of Yonec's father who was, after all, the essence of a
fiction, which originated in the lady's desire, but, once spoken, is dead. "I
kill," Marie confesses in "Yonec"—"Neco."

In the language theater of the *Lais,* the dramatization according to the

modes of exposure, crossing over, and foreclosure, we find an essentially theological view of language as tragic. To be within the realm of language is to
live within that of incarnation, to recognize the irreparable effects of the Fall
compounded by the irreconcilable differences between humans and the un-
translatable differences between languages after Babel. To be trapped within
language, to be constrained by its material, contingent nature, is no different for the Marie of the *Lais* than being trapped within the materialism of
the body and of all corporeal things.

CHAPTER FOUR

Beastly Talk: The *Fables*

The word *fable* designates both a discourse and a literary genre, the root referring, as in the fabliau "La Vieille Truande," to the raw matter of a story out
of which the poet makes a tale, matter conceived before literary treatment:

> Des fables fet on les fabliaus.
> Et des notes les sons noviaus.
> Et des materes les canchons,
> Et des draps, cauces et cauchons.[1]

Out of fables one makes fabliaux; out of notes, new sounds; out of material,
songs; and out of cloth, socks and shoes.

Functioning as the *aventure* does for the lai, the basic material of the fable,
having been transformed, gains the resonance of a didactic "tale" alongside
the *dit, beau dit, mots, beaux mots,* or *aventure,* which also carries, as we have
seen, the meaning "story." Because of the lesson that it is intended to teach,
the fable is closer to the "exemplum" than to other short forms, yet remains
distinct from the "miracle" as from the *dit moral.* For however much the
fable may exhibit elements of realism and of the new materialism of France's
and Anglo-Normandy's burgeoning courts and urban centers, about which
we will have more to say later, it cannot escape association with the opposite of the truth. In a semantic heritage reaching back to late antiquity, the
word *fable* is also synonymous with a lie, with ruse, or with fiction, its meaning doubling that of *truffe, risée, mensonge, merveille, fantosme, bourde,* or
gabet, a distinction that the poet of the epic *Aiol* invokes in generational and
generic terms:[2]

Cil novel jongleur en sont mal escarni:
Por les fables qu'il dient ont tout mis en oubli,
La plus veraie estoire ont laissiet et guerpi,
Je vos en dirai une qui bien fait a cierer.[3]

These new jongleurs are badly shamed. Because of the fables they recount they have squandered everything, and the most truthful story they have forgotten and abandoned. I will tell you one worthy of belief.

At once the opposite of the truth, a synonym of ruse, and a morality tale full of lessons, the fable is double. Indeed, unlike the didactic works that often seem like its religious analogue, the fable, like the fabliau, is often capped by a moral at the end; twice double, it is preceded by a title, which historically has served as an index to the ethical contents of the tale, and concluded with a moral or general truth that carries the particular tale to a more general, and in the case of animal fables, human plane. Then too, where the works of Marie de France are concerned, there is a sense in which the *Fables,* as explicit lessons sustained by a seemingly conscious set of moral precepts, serve to double the *Lais,* which are much more discreet in their didactic pressure, leading to the question: To what extent can the *Lais* and the *Fables*—should they, must they—be read together? In what ways do they resemble each other? To what extent can any such resemblance be taken as proof that they were written by the same anonymous Marie de France? To what degree do they, despite their radical generic difference, offer internal evidence of a single poetic persona?

THE *FABLES* AND THE *LAIS*

As seen repeatedly in previous chapters, Marie is obsessed by beginnings, and the *Fables* are no exception. On the contrary, read alongside the prologue to the *Lais,* the prologue to the *Fables* transforms the obsession with beginnings into a structural pattern, whose numerous and significant points of resemblance work, even were it not for the presence of the name Marie in both, to allay any doubt that they were written by the same person. Marie's way of beginning the *Fables* alongside the specific terms of that beginning—a recall of the duty to study with care, evocation of sources, emphasis on the importance of memory, recognition of the issues of translation and transmission, concern for reputation, and awareness of the pedagogical or moral effects of writing upon individual character—is part of the same bundle of framing anxieties seen in both the prologue to the *Lais* and the prologue to "Guigemar."

Marie's reminder in the *Lais* of the duty of those with talent to spread their knowledge is repeated in the *Fables* in terms so similar as to plunge the reader from the start into a universe that seems familiar: "Those persons, all, who are well-read,/Should study and pay careful heed" ("Cil ki seivent de lettruüre,/Devreient bien mettre cure" [v. 1]). Further, the object of care or study is philosophy: those who possess learning should pay attention "To fine accounts in worthy tomes,/To models and to axioms:/That which philosophers did find/And wrote about and kept in mind" ("Es bons livres e escriz/E as [es]samples e as diz/Ke li philosophe troverent/E escristrent e remembrerent" [v. 4]). More precisely, in a passage that resembles nothing so much as her reference to Priscian at the beginning of the prologue to the *Lais,* Marie maintains that we must remember the ancients who themselves studied those who went before: "Ceo firent li ancïen pere" (v. 11). Learning represents an infinite regress with which we are already acquainted: that is, the ancients or philosophers stand in relation to their sources as Marie stands in relation to them, and as we stand in relation to her. The pedagogical paradigm of the *Fables* is every bit as inscribed from the start in a project of memory and of cultural preservation as is that of the *Lais.*

The philosophers or the ancients, Priscian in the prologue to the *Lais,* have already remembered, an act that Marie reproduces in remembering them, memory being the equivalent of writing not only throughout the *Lais,* but in the series *troverent, escristrent,* and *remembrerent*—in the equation, even among the ancients, of invention, writing, memory, and conservation; in the role of speaking and writing as an antidote to dispersion. Marie is as obsessed by memory in the *Fables* as she is in the *Lais.* And not only by cultural memory, but by the urge to be remembered. Memory in the epilogue to the *Fables* is the occasion for naming herself ("Me numerai pur remembrance:/Marie ai num, si sui de France" [v. 3]) and is accompanied by a warning to those who might allow themselves to be forgotten ("E il fet que fol ki sei ublie!" [v. 8]) that, again, echoes uncannily a similar warning in the prologue to "Guigemar": "Oëz, seignurz, ke dit Marie,/Ki en sun tens pas ne s'oblie" (v. 3). In both the *Fables* and the *Lais* memory provides the impetus to invention among the writers who have preceded and whose company Marie joins via her own remembering of the lais she has heard: "Plusurs en ai oï conter,/Ne[s] voil laisser ne oblïer" (v. 39).

Marie is aware of linking herself via memory and writing to a tradition in whose transmission she, like the ancients or medieval intermediaries, will play a role. In the *Lais* she repeatedly evokes her source in the primarily oral material she preserves. In the *Fables* she identifies an ultimate source in Aesop who transmitted them in written form to "his master," who translated them from Greek to Latin:

> Esop[es] escrist a sun mestre,
> Que bien cunust lui e sun estre,
> Unes fables ke ot trovees,
> De griu en latin translatees. (v. 17)
>
> Thus Aesop to his master wrote;
> He knew his manner and his thought;
> From Greek to Latin were transposed
> Those fables found and those composed.

This suggestion is undermined, however, by the epilogue to the *Fables,* in which it is clearly Aesop himself who has translated the tales from the Greek to Latin—"This book's called Aesop for this reason:/He translated and had it written/In Latin from the Greek, to wit" ("Esope apel'um cest livre,/Qu'il translata e fist escrire,/Del griu en latin le turna" [v. 13])—which was in turn translated by King Alfred from Latin to English before Marie rendered them in French: "King Alfred, who was fond of it,/Translated it to English hence,/And I have rhymed it now in French" ("Li reis Alfrez, que mut l'ama,/Le translata puis en engleis,/E jeo l'ai rimee en franceis" [v. 16]). Marie is obsessed by the transmission of sources, by the process of translation, and by the cultural transformation that translation implies. Indeed, it can be no accident that she returns in the epilogue to the *Fables* to the same polyvalent expression for translation that, as we saw in the *Lais,* serves to define poetry itself—that is, the little word *traire,* meaning "to draw," "to treat," "to translate," "to betray." "Al finement de cest escrit,/Que en romanz ai treité e dit" (v. 1): thus Marie begins the epilogue in which she insists upon her "drawing" the French from the English ("M'entremis de cest livre feire/E de l'engleis en romanz treire" [v. 11]) in terms so similar to her description of the project of translation in the prologue to the *Lais* ("De aukune bone estoire faire/E de latin en romaunz traire" [v. 29]) that the reader, once again, cannot fail to be struck by her framing fixation upon the question of translation, which, as we shall see, is even more central to the *Espurgatoire.*[4]

In the passage from one language to another lies the possibility of self-transformation, as the project of rewriting, also captured in the prologue to the *Lais* under the rubric of glossing, carries a potential for self-improvement, a rewriting of the person. The purpose of knowledge in the *Lais* is an avoidance of vice ("Ki de vice se volt defendre / Estudïer deit e entendre" [v. 23]), which in the *Fables* is presented as self-correction, as if the self were a text subject to emendation:

> Par moralité escriveient
> Les bons proverbes qu'il oieient,
> Que cil amender se peüssent
> Ki lur entente en bien eüssent. (Prologue, v. 7)

> The sayings which they heard, they wrote,
> So that the morals we would note;
> Thus those who wish to mend their ways
> Can think about what wisdom says.

The knowledge and self-knowledge that concern Marie in the prologues to the *Lais* and the *Fables* are practically and prospectively oriented: in the one instance they are collective and cumulative (*Lais,* Prologue, v. 19); and in the other they are associated, as we shall see when discussing the psychological traits and social values implicit to the animal tale, with an awareness passed from father to son of the perils and pitfalls of living in a tricky world: "The emperor, named Romulus, / Wrote to his son, enunciating, / And through examples demonstrating, / How it behooved him to take care / That no one trick him unaware" ("Romulus, ki fu emperere, / A sun fiz escrit, si manda, / E par essample li mustra, / Cum il se deüst contreguater / Que hum nel p[e]üst enginner" [*Fables,* Prologue, v. 12]).

Where alertness is concerned no one is more attuned than Marie to what others will think about her. No one is more concerned by her reputation, a worry that invades both prologues around the issue of dedication. In the *Lais* she is anxious not to be thought excessive by the king to whom they are dedicated: "Do not consider me presumptuous if I make so bold as to offer you this gift" ("Ne me tenez a surquidie / Si vos os faire icest present" [v. 54]); and in the *Fables* she is worried that she might be thought to be crude or lowly for having followed the orders of the Count William whose name figures in the epilogue (v. 9): "Ki que m'en tienge pur vileine, / De fere mut pur sa preere" (v. 36). Most of all, Marie is alert to the envy of others, to the question of appropriation, to the potential in every literary beginning, or "sending out," for plagiarism and for criticism. It will be remembered that in the prologue to "Guigemar" Marie is obsessed by the "vicious, cowardly, treacherous" dogs who are envious and will speak ill of her, an obsession that is also present in the *Fables* in the form of a fear that clerics will claim her work as their own: "Put cel estre que clerc plusur/Prendreient sur eus mun labur" (Epilogue, v. 5). Marie is aware of the value of her labor, one might even venture that she is conscious of its proprietary nature, which is never very far from the theme with which she begins—the duty to write.[5]

The fear of plagiarism has, in fact, profound roots in the fable tradition. The prologue to the second part of the Greek collection attached to the name of Babrius, which later became known as "the Aesop," contains a comparison between the rapine of animals and that of poets whose only skill lies in imitation:

> Fable, son of King Alexander, is the invention of the Syrians of old, who lived in the days of Ninus and Belus. The first to tell fables to the sons of the Hellenes, they say, was Aesop the wise; and to the Libyans Cybisses also told fables. It remains for me to present them in a new and poetic dress, bridling the iambic verse of my fables, like a warhorse, with trappings of gold. I was the first to open this door; but when I had done so, others entered in who publish poems resembling the riddles of a more learned muse, skilled in nothing more than imitating my example. But I tell my fables in a transparent style. I do not sharpen the teeth of the iambs, but I test them and refine them as it were in the fire, and I am careful to soften their sting.[6]

Then too, there is something about the fable that makes it an ideal vehicle for misunderstanding. As the Latin poet Phaedrus, whose fables came to be known under the rubric "Romulus" (which may have inspired the Romulus of Marie's prologue), observes in the epilogue to Book III, the fable, by its very fictive nature, represents a form of resistance literature whose meaning contains a necessary element of subterfuge.[7]

Marie is afraid of being misunderstood, and, worse, misappropriated. Which is why, finally, I think she loves prologues and epilogues as much as she does; why she prefaces the *Lais* and the *Fables* as well as "Guigemar" with a preliminary expression of anxiety about how her work will be understood; why she ends the *Fables* with a parting wish to be correctly understood along with mention of her name. Indeed, the naming of the tale, which is such an obsessive motif in the *Lais,* the naming of individual lais, which serves like the general prologues and epilogue as an interpretative frame, participates in the same anxious urge to control reception, which is fulfilled in the *Fables* by the moral or general principle that is tacked to the end of each story and stands as a generic marker. Indeed, though Marie cannot be credited with having introduced the moral to the fable, it is still the case that the lesson to be learned after the narrative has ended, the guiding interpretation of the ending maxim, coincides with her preoccupation—in both the *Lais* and the *Fables*—with reception, with mastering meaning, and thus with the beginning of a critical tradition.

If the *Lais* and the *Fables* are linked by the defining substance of their prologues and epilogues, they are also closer thematically than one might assume. Though they seem generically unrelated, there are numerous and significant unsuspected points of resemblance between them, the first of which stems from Marie's use of animals in the *Lais*. Birds, fantastical or real, play a central role in "Laüstic," "Milun," and "Yonec." So too, the werewolf of "Bisclavret" can be considered to be an animal of sorts. The ending of "Eliduc" turns around the curative power of a weasel, which, in its exemplary attempt to revive its mate, its mourning and fetching of a medicinal flower, seems to participate more in the tradition of the bestiary than in that of either the lai or the fable. What remains significant, I think, is that the animals of the *Lais* remain so bound in Marie's eyes to the principle of communication. The nightingale of "Laüstic" is linked to the poetic voice; the swan of "Milun" passes messages between lovers under the feathers/pens of its throat. In several instances, too, Marie poses in the *Lais* the question that will dominate the *Fables:* that is, the place of the animal, or of the animal instincts, within the human world. The bird of "Yonec" represents a fantasized fulfillment of the imprisoned woman's repressed desire. The werewolf of "Bisclavret," which can be seen to represent the husband's beastly other self, is distinguished by its ability to communicate with the King in this proto-fable that not only raises the issue of the place of the animal within the human realm but develops the theme so widespread in the *Fables* of the relationship between the violent animal world of the forest and the gentler social space of court or town.

If some of the *Lais* feature animals, not all of the fables can be said to be animal tales. Many, in fact, depict an exclusively human world; and in this they are closer to the fabliaux than to the *Lais*.[8] "The Widow Who Hanged Her Husband" (no. 25), which recalls both the classical "Widow of Ephesus" and the fabliau "La Dolente qui fu fotue sur la tonbe," recounts the story of the knight who overcomes the interdiction against burying criminals by convincing a recent widow to disinter her husband and to hang him in the place of his relative, a thief, whom he has lowered from the gallows. "A Man, His Stomach, and Its Members" (no. 27) reproduces the political allegory of the interdependence of rulers and ruled also found in John of Salisbury's *Policraticus*.[9] "The Rich Man and the Two Serfs" (no. 41) con-

tains the simple tale of a lord's questioning of two servants who want to appear clever by pretending to carry on a conversation with each other. In
"The Doctor, the Rich Man, and His Daughter" (no. 42), a young woman
who, in the course of a medical analysis, has lost a sample of her sick father's
blood, for which she substitutes her own, is discovered to be pregnant. In
"The Surveyor" (no. 91), a plotter curses his measure, which replies in its
own defense. Finally, Marie's *Fables* are home to a virtual subgenre of tales
that, again like the fabliaux, depict the tricks of clever women played upon
unsuspecting husbands—"The Peasant Who Saw Another with His Wife"
(no. 44), "The Peasant Who Saw His Wife with Her Lover" (no. 45), "The
Peasant and His Contrary Wife" (no. 95), "The Peasant and His Cantankerous Wife" (no. 96).

Some of the *Fables* are mixed, that is, involve the interpenetration of
human and animal worlds, a mix that lies at the core of the interesting and
completely original way that the *Fables* figure the place of the instincts in a
new social order. Some involve interaction not between men and animals
but between men and the natural world, as in "The Blacksmith and the
Axe" (no. 49); or between animals and the natural world, as in "The Snake
and the Field" (no. 83). Then too, several fables resonate thematically with
a particular lai in an unobvious but nonetheless revealing way. "The Thief
and the Witch" (no. 48), for example, depicts a sleeping thief awakened by
a witch who encourages him to continue his trade and who promises to help
him wherever he is. He does, is caught, and is condemned to hang. Calling
out repeatedly for her help, even as they have placed the rope around his
neck, he emits one further cry. But:

> Ele respunt par faus sermun:
> "Puis cele hure te ai bien aidié—
> E meintenu e cunseillié.
> Mes ore te vei si demener,
> Que ne te sai cunseil duner.
> Purpense tei quei tu feras—
> Ja par mei cunseil n'avras!" (v. 32)

> With lying tongue, she answered thus:
> "Since then, I've been much help to you—
> supported and advised you, too.
> But when I see you act this way,
> I don't know what wise words to say.
> Decide yourself, what you should do—
> I'll no more be advising you!"

"The Thief and the Witch" can be seen as an anti-"Lanval," the story of a would-be rescuing female who, unlike the one in the lai, does not arrive in the nick of time to save the condemned man in the end. Similarly, a pair of fables involving the transgression of a prescription offer an analogue to Lanval's promise of discretion that is broken in the instant that it is made. In "The Dragon and the Peasant" (no. 52), a departing dragon entrusts a peasant with an egg under the proviso that if anything happens to it, the peasant will lose his powers ("Tost sereit mort, s'il fust brusez" [v. 15]). The man breaks it in order to seize the dragon's gold, just as in "The Hermit and the Peasant" (no. 54) the peasant defies the hermit's prohibition against lifting a bowl under which he has placed a mouse.

Another example of the thematic resonance between fable and lai, "The Bat" (no. 23), recapitulates the theme of a necessary choice. A lion summons all the four-footed animals to do battle against the birds, led by an eagle. The bat observes cautiously and decides, first, that since the lion is strongest, he will join the other rodents. However, when he sees the birds flying, he changes sides. Once among them, he tries to hide his feet but is discovered, as both the birds and the beasts complain about him to the goddess, who banishes him from daylight and plucks out his feathers. The moral of "The Bat" has to do with the necessity not only of loyalty but of choice; and in this it captures Marie's preoccupation with the paradigmatic issue of choice in "Chaitivel," where the woman's refusal to choose entails a banishment of sorts from the "daylight" of the love she might have had.

But the *Fables* and the *Lais* resemble each other on a far deeper level, a level that renders irrefutable the case for common authorship and indeed is proof of a coherent creative identity working through two different genres, in the shared obsession with language as difficult, opaque, and flawed. We have seen the extent to which each individual lai works out a drama of language conceived to be dangerous and sometimes even fatal. The *Fables* too are filled with problematic, dangerous, and fatal speech acts, of which the following represent only a partial catalogue of the panoply of linguistic abuse that, read in this light, becomes practically synonymous with the animal tale.

SPEECH ACTS IN THE *FABLES*

A number of fables involve accusations that for the most part are false. In "The Wolf and the Lamb" (no. 2), a wolf drinking upstream of a lamb accuses it of troubling its water; when reminded by the lamb that, given their relative positions, it is he whose water is contaminated, the wolf counters that the lamb's father did the same six months earlier. Reminded by the lamb that he was not yet born, the wolf accuses the lamb of impertinence and grabs him by the neck. "The Dog and the Ewe" (no. 4) presents another false assertion coupled with false oaths within a legal context, the courtroom providing one of the standard settings of the fables. A dog bringing a ewe before a judge accuses her of having borrowed a loaf of bread. The charges denied, the dog produces as witnesses a wolf and a kite, which swear to the truth of the allegation, forcing the ewe to sell her wool to repay the debt and leaving her to freeze to death as her accuser and the false witnesses devour her carcass. In one of the rare instances in which an accusation is success- fully denied, "The Sick Lion, the Deer, and the Fox" (no. 71), a deer is sum- moned to court by a lion who has been advised that only the heart of a deer might cure him of his illness. Refusing to come at first, the deer does appear but flees. Summoned a second and then a third time, the deer is killed by a fox who, accused by the other animals of having stolen the deer's heart, de- fends himself with the claim that the deer knowingly came to court where he knew he would be killed, thus offering prima facie evidence of the fact that he had no heart and that he—the fox—could not therefore have stolen it. "The Swallow and the Sparrows" (no. 84) offers a virtual exercise in the dynamics of true and false communication, an incredibly sophisticated tangle of accusations and lies. A flock of sparrows, hesitating to eat a farmer's grain, is encouraged by a swallow to enter the farmer's barn. When the swallow then observes the farmer plugging all the holes in the walls, she warns the sparrows to stay outside. The farmer's servant, observing the swal- low's warning to the sparrows, advises his master to lie deliberately in the swallow's hearing. The swallow, thus falling into the linguistic trap, is ac- cused by the dying sparrows of passing on false information ("Dunc ten- cerent a l'arundele,/Que ele lur ot dit male novele"), to which she responds by accusing the farmer of having lied: "'Cil me menti,/E jeo menti vus tut autresi'" (v. 39).

The accusations that run through the *Fables* are accompanied by a series of reproaches, complaints, and blame. "The Frogs Who Asked for a King" (no. 18) are so disappointed when they are sent a log that, having sworn fealty to it, they defecate upon it until it sinks, then complain to the God- dess, who sends them an adder which moves a little too much, bringing "death to the frogs he seized and ate" ("Que tuz les dovore e treit a mort" [v. 32]). In a companion piece, "The Peacock" (no. 31), a peacock complains to the Goddess that his voice is not commensurate with his beauty and that he is shamed by comparison with the lowly nightingale. And, finally, in what strikes the modern reader as the medieval equivalent of an existential complaint, "The Wolf and the Crow" (no. 59), a wolf, observing a crow sitting on the back of a ewe, laments that the other animals "would shout me down" were he to do the same (v. 10).

The reproaches found in the *Fables* are in some measure balanced by their opposite—boasts, praise, and self-praise. In "The City Mouse and the Country Mouse" (no. 9), each stresses the advantages of life in her own domain: the country mouse, the abundance of food in the forest; and her city cousin, the richness of her rooms, "and splendid pantries, cellars fine,/ Excellent drinks, and meals divine" (v. 21). A companion piece, "The Wolf and the Dog" (no. 26), contains a similar boast on the part of a dog about the ease of life in town. In "The Ass and the Lion" (no. 35), an ass brags that he is as powerful as the lion and seeks to prove it by braying at an assembly of animals. Seeing the animals flee, the ass considers himself to have triumphed, until the lion sets him straight. Similarly, in "The Wolf and the Beetle" (no. 65), a beetle that has crawled up the anus of a wolf boasts, upon emerging, that he is his victim's equal, just as in "The Fly and the Bee" (no. 86) each boasts of superior worth, a motif we'll return to when treating the relation of this particular series of fables to medieval debate.

The *Fables* are filled with promises, vows, and wishes. We have seen above the broken promise of the witch (no. 48) who pledges her assistance to a thief. In "The Wolf and the Crane" (no. 7), a wolf promises to reward a crane for removing a bone from its neck and then reneges, arguing that it is enough, being a wolf, not to have bitten the crane's head off. "The Wolf and the Sheep" (no. 50) is premised upon a wolf's vow not to eat meat during Lent, a vow broken as soon as the nominalist wolf finds himself alone with a sheep and declares it to be a salmon: "Jeol puis bien prendre pur un mutun,/ S'il mangerai pur un saumun" (v. 19). "The Dragon and the Peasant" (no. 52) and "The Hermit and the Peasant" (no. 53) represent, as we have seen, a pair of fables involving broken pledges. In "The Peasant and the Goblin" (no. 57), a wife, upon hearing that a goblin has granted her husband three wishes, uses the first to endow him with a beak in order to be able to extract marrow from a bone; the husband uses the second boon to return to normal in this fable reminiscent of the fabliau "Les Quatre Souhaiz Saint Martin." In "The Wolf and the Hedgehog" (no. 72), a wolf breaks a mutual defense pact by refusing to rescue the hedgehog from the hunter's dogs and is himself held at bay. Finally, "The Peasant and the Snake" (no. 73) is a fable of broken promises in which a snake aids a man to prosper in return for a bowl of milk. His wife, however, encourages him to kill the serpent; and when the peasant misses his axe blow, the serpent kills the couple's flock and child before both snake and peasant come to an agreement based upon external signs rather than upon their original oral understanding:

> "Ne sai cument te crerreie,
> Tant cum en ceste pere veie
> Le cop ke ta hache i feri.
> E jeo le sai tres bien de fi,
> Quant le berz verras devant tei,
> U tes enfes fu mort par mei,
> Que de mei t'estut remembrer.
> Tu ne me purras ublïer." (v. 91)

> "For how, indeed, can I trust you
> As long as on this rock I view
> The mark made on impact," asks the snake.
> "And this I know well for a fact:
> Whenever you the cradle see
> There where your child was killed by me,
> You'll have to think about me yet.
> You won't be able to forget."

The motif of the snake that kills the child belongs, of course, to European folklore; and there are several versions in Latin as well as the vernacular tongues.[10] Yet one still senses that for Marie the idea of memory sparked by the material mark on a stone or embodied in the empty cradle, as opposed to the oral accord, has a special appeal.

Just how special this particular nexus of memory and mark is, in fact, can be appreciated fully only by a comparison of Marie's version with other versions of the same motif. This is a tale included among Aesop's fables under the title "The Plowman and the Snake Who Had Killed His Son," where the snake reminds the man who has tried to kill him that "neither of us can pretend to any good feelings, neither I when I see the gouge you have made in the rock, nor you when you look at the tomb of your child."[11] Most medieval versions, however, belong to the tradition known as the "Anonyme de Nevelet" because of their inclusion in Isaac Nevelet's *Mythologia Aesopica* published in Frankfurt in 1610 under the title "Anonymi Fabulae Aesopeae," though Léopold Hervieux found in the Library of Vienna, MS lat. 303, a reference to "Waltarius" as the author of the collection, and, in a gloss to the edition of Lyon of 1480, "Galterus Anglicus fecit hunc librum sub nomine

Esopi."[12] Since then the *Isopet de Lyon,* the *Isopet I,* and the *Isopet III de Paris* have been grouped with the *Romulus* of Walter l'Anglais. The *Isopet de Lyon,* which dates from around 1300, makes no mention of marks but takes the offending object, the axe, as the sign of harm: "As long as you possess such a big axe, there will be no peace, in my view" ("Tant con tu portes si grant aiche/Ne sui je pais sur, que je saiche"), says the serpent to the peasant who has attacked him. The moral of the *Isopet de Lyon* has to do with the values of trust and false friendship: "Know that I can never be the friend of one who has once wronged me."[13] So too, the *Isopet I,* known as the *Avionnet,* concentrates upon the weapon and makes no mention of the sign, nor does the prose *Isopet III de Paris.*[14] In fact, the only version to link the axe blow with what we might think of as sign theory is Walter's original *Romulus,* which reads: "Anguis ait:/'Non ero securus dum sit tibi tanta securis,/Dum cutis haec metuit vulnera scripta sibi'" (vv. 7–8).[15] Indeed, not only does the text reproduced by Julia Bastin in her *Recueil général des Isopets* link the wound with writing, but the variants of verse 8 introduce the question of memory, as MS V, Paris, BN, lat. 15135, reads "haec memor est" in the place of "haec metuit" and contains the notation "memorat" in the margin; MS S, Paris, BN, lat. 14381, reads "memoret" for "metuit"; and MS L, Lyon, Bibliothèque de l'Académie, 57, reads "meminit."[16] All of which would be less significant if it were not for the fact that Walter l'Anglais was archbishop of Palermo and chaplain of Henry II of England and that the date of composition most plausibly ascribed to his fables is 1175, both of which place him in a time frame, and within the social orbit, of Marie de France. I am not suggesting, of course, that Marie knew Walter, which would be the purest speculation. Rather, that we find a curious concern on both Marie's and Walter's part with the question of the wound, memory, and with writing, a concern absent in the later works that we know to derive from Walter. Indeed, the explicitness and the elaborateness of Marie's version of "The Peasant and the Snake," compared even to that of Walter who may have been her contemporary, testifies to the specificity of her obsession with linguistic marks.

Pleas, requests, and prayers abound in the *Fables.* "The Pregnant Hound" (no. 8), for example, recounts the pleading of one dog to another to let her use her house in order to have her pups; once the pups have grown to a size to be able to move on, however, they eject the original owner from her house. In "The Crow and the Ewe" (no. 40), a ewe requests that a crow sitting on its back and plucking its wool remove itself and "go stay on the dog a spell" ("Seez une piece sur le chien" [v. 8]). In "The Peasant Who

Prayed for a Horse" (no. 54), a serf who already has one horse but who prays for a second one emerges from church only to discover that thieves have removed his first horse instead; and in a companion piece, "The Peasant Who Prayed for His Wife and Children" (no. 55), a selfish worshiper is cursed for praying only for his own kin. In "The Kite and the Jay" (no. 87), a sick kite requests that his mother ask a nearby jay to pray for him in his hour of need, which she refuses on the grounds that the kite has mistreated the jay in the past "and defecated on his birdies" ("E sur ses oiseus esmeulti" [v. 14]). "The Hare and the Deer" (no. 97), which might be paired with "The Peacock" (no. 31), contains an appeal to the Goddess on the part of a hare for antlers like a deer's. Finally, "The Rich Man Who Wished to Cross the Sea" (no. 100) contains simply a prayer for a safe journey.

The prayers and pleadings of the *Fables* are doubled in a number of tales by seductions and false flattery intended to seduce. And this practically from the start in "The Mouse and the Frog" (no. 3), which is a cruel version of the enticement to change habitat encountered in "The City Mouse and the Country Mouse" (no. 9) and "The Wolf and the Dog" (no. 26). A frog, anxious to devour a mouse, first adopts her mode of speech ("Demanda li, en sa reisun,/Si ele ert dame de la meisun" [v. 11]), before luring her, in terms that resemble those of a courtly lover, from her home in the mill to his natural dwelling in the swamp: "'Tant i averez joie e deduit,/Jamés n'avriez talent, ceo quit,/De repeirer a cest mulin'" ("'There you'll have such delight, such bliss/That I believe you'll have no wish/Ever to come back to this mill'" (v. 41). Indeed, in the outcome Marie emphasizes the power of words to seduce: "Such promises and crafty skill/And flattery went to her head./She trusted frog—but was misled" ("Tant li premet par sun engin/E la blandist par sa parole,/Que la creï, si fist ke fole" [v. 44]). A similar seduction occurs in "The Widow Who Hanged Her Husband" (no. 25) in the thief's verbally adept promise of affection: "Then cunningly he spoke to her./He said that comfort now was near./Love him, and she would soon find cheer" ("Cuintement ad a li parlé:/Dit li que ele se confortast./Mut sereit lez, se ele l'amast" [v. 20]). Yet not all seductions in the *Fables* have the earmarks of romance; many contain blandishments meant to satisfy other appetites. In "The Fox and the Dove" (no. 61), a seductive fox tries to convince a dove that the king has declared peace in the land and that she could come down from her inaccessible perch. The wary dove is not taken in, however, in this tale whose moral captures the need for alertness to the dangers of verbal enticement whenever one species addresses another, which expresses, in other words, a suspiciousness of language to which we shall return:

> Si vet des feluns veiz̈iez.
> Par eus sunt plusurs enginnez
> Par parole, par faus sermun,
> Cum li gupilz fist le colum. (v. 33)

> And so it goes with scoundrels sly.
> For many folks are hoodwinked by
> Their crafty words and lying talks
> Just as the dove was by the fox.

Finally, in a mock religious seduction, the voracious cat of "The Cat, the Vole, and the Mouse" (no. 102) pretends to be a bishop and to want to hear the confession of the mice who, like the wary dove, wisely distrust his words.

When seduction fails there are, of course, threats, taunts, and the warnings that are the very stuff of Marie's consciousness of the irresistible lure of certain speech acts. In "The Fox and the Bear" (no. 70), the former tries to seduce the latter who threatens to beat him "with her stave" before being chased and entangled in a bramble, where the fox, like Renart in pursuit of Isengrin's wife Hersent, has his will with her. Asked what he is doing, the fox mockingly transforms the bear's original threat into more than words. "The Boar and the Ass" (no. 76) contains the threats and jabs of a boar against an ass that refuses to move from the center of a road. In "The Snake and the Field" (no. 83), a field warns a snake not to take anything from it. Finally, in a series of pedagogical fables, parents warn their offspring against the dangers lurking in the outside world: "The Wolf and the Kid" (no. 90) turns around a mother goat's warning to her kid not to let anyone enter their home while she is gone; "The Doe and Her Fawn" (no. 92) similarly features a mother's warning against hunters, as does "The Crow Instructing His Child" (no. 93).

Of the myriad speech acts contained in the *Fables,* none is more central than the advice offered either on an individual basis or in a more formal juridical or political setting. In "The Sun Who Wished to Wed" (no. 6), the animals seek the advice of Destiny, who in turn asks their advice before deciding to forbid the sun to take a partner lest his strength should increase and overwhelm them. "The Sun Who Wished to Wed" finds a companion piece in "The Vole Who Sought a Wife" (no. 74), which is the fable of fables where advice is concerned. For here the "vainglorious" vole, intent upon marrying someone of higher lineage than his own, first consults the sun, who advises him to marry the daughter of a cloud, since clouds trump sun with their shade; he consults the cloud, who advises him to marry the daughter of the wind, since the wind trumps clouds when it blows; the wind in turn advises the vole to marry the daughter of the stone wall that resists even his strongest blows.

"The Eagle and the Crow" (no. 12) is a parable of bad advice, as the eagle who has managed to catch a whelk but cannot imagine how to open its shell is advised by a crow to let it fall from high onto a rock from which the crow retrieves and devours it. By way of contrast, "The Swallow and the Linseed" (no. 17) is a parable of good advice that goes unheeded. For when the swallow recognizes in the farmer's linseed the origin of flax, and in flax a potential source of ensnaring nets, "how flax might bring birds to their end" (v. 6), she gathers all the birds with the advice to eat the linseed before it germinates. The birds do not believe her and are caught, occasioning a moral about the importance of recognizing wisdom. In "The Blacksmith and the Axe" (no. 49), a blacksmith consults a council of trees as to the best type of wood out of which to fashion an axe handle. Having been advised to select the thornbush, which he does, the blacksmith proceeds to fell the very trees that offered good advice. Indeed, in this speech act that rebounds upon the speaker, we recognize something of the linguistic fatalism that rebounded to harm in the lais of "Guigemar," "Equitan," and "Le Fresne." "The Lion and the Fox" (no. 69) offers a similar message within a more public setting; for when the court of animals seeks the advice of the fox as to how a sick lion might be cured, the wolf seeks to profit from the fox's absence by advising that they might kill him as a lesson to his kin. When the fox does eventually arrive, he claims to have been in Salerno where the doctors prescribed flaying a wolf alive, collecting his blood within his skin, and rubbing it on the lion's chest. Thus, bad advice is repaid with even worse advice, as Marie concludes in a phrase that is the equivalent of a natural law of relations among the animal species, and thus among men: "Those who plan ill for other men / Will get the same thing back again" ("Tel purchace le mal d'autrui, / Que cel meme revient sur lui" [v. 57]).

The lie, of course, is a speech act for which Marie shows particular affection in the *Lais* as well as the *Fables* and indeed is a key to the fabulously complicated attitude toward language found in the animal tale. Marie neither wholly endorses nor wholly condemns the lie, whose effects and meaning are conditional and situationally determined. We have seen, for ex-

ample, in "The Swallow and the Sparrows" (no. 84) the destructiveness of
the farmer's intentional lie and the moral condemnation of habitual lying:
"Nul sage hum ne devreit creire/Parole, nule si ele ne fust veire./Tel creit
mençunge en sun curage,/Que il turne a grant damage" ("A wise man must
not trust forsooth/A single word that's not the truth./Who in his heart believes a lie/Will grievously be hurt thereby" [v. 47]). So too, Marie displays
a pair of fables built upon the lies of unfaithful wives who are in some deep
sense the bourgeois sisters of the imprisoned wives of the *Lais,* the ladies of
"Guigemar," "Yonec," and "Milun," and even the wife in "Laüstic," whose
lie, as we have seen, returns to haunt her. "The Peasant Who Saw Another
with His Wife" (no. 44), in which a wife in bed with a man other than her
husband convinces her husband that he has experienced a false perception
of the scene by showing him his reflection in a tub of water and pointing
out that he is not actually in the water with his clothes on, turns around the
question of truth and lies. "'You cling to lies as to verity,'" ("Tu ve[u]ls
mençoinge tenir a veire" [v. 13]), the clever wife maintains; to which the husband foolishly replies that he "can only trust what he sees" ("'Jel vit,' fet il,
'sil dei bien creire'" [v. 14]), in this triumph of wit over the senses and, in
startling contrast to the aristocratic fatalism of the *Lais,* even over social situation: "From this example comes this lore:/Good sense and shrewdness are
worth more   /And will, to many, more help give   /Than wealth or any
relative" ("Par ceste essample nus devise/Que meuz vaut sen e quointise—
/E plus aide a meinte gent—/Que sis aveirs ne si parent" [v. 33]). In a companion piece, "The Peasant Who Saw His Wife with Her Lover" (no. 45), a
man sees his wife entering the forest accompanied by another. Confronted
by this scene, she claims that someone also saw her mother and grandmother in similar fashion just before their death and proposes dividing their
property. He withdraws his original perception and accusation, which, he
maintains, must have been a lie ("'Mençunge fu quanque jeo vi!'" [v. 36]),
as the wife elicits an oath of obedience (v. 46). The moral of "The Peasant
Who Saw His Wife with Her Lover" resonates with the misogynistic morals
attached to several of the fabliaux: "And so, forewarned all men should
be/That women know good strategy./They've more art in their craft and
lies/Than all the devil can devise" ("Pur ceo dit hum en repruver/Que
femmes seivent enginner:/Les vezïez e li nunverrable/Unt un art plus ke
deable" [v. 53]).

The difference between the status of the lie in the *Lais* and in the *Fables*
offers a good measure of the contrast between the nature of language in the
two genres; indeed, the fable can be seen to contain the revenge of clever

wives for their condemned sisters, the "mal mariées," of the more courtly form. What's more, a number of fables center specifically upon the usefulness, and even virtue, of lies. In "The Wolf and the Sow" (no. 21), for example, a pregnant sow, confronted by a wolf anxious to devour her young, convinces him that it would be unseemly to give birth in the presence of a male. The moral tacked to this tale of justifiable feminine ruse addresses directly the contextual nature of the lie, which determines its moral valence: "All women ought to hear this tale / And should remember it as well: / Merely to avoid a lie, / They should not let their children die!" ("Ceste essample deivent oïr / Tutes femmes e retenir: / Que pur sulement mentir / Ne laissent lur enfanz perir!" [v. 21]).

In a pair of fables involving advice solicited by unjust rulers we see the usefulness of the lie in the public discourse of the political arena. Upon the withdrawal of the lion as their ruler, the animals of "The Wolf King" (no. 29) elect the wolf, who swears an oath not to "eat any meat, no matter what" ("ne mangast char, tant ne quant" [v. 34]). Shortly after his coronation, the wolf summons a roe deer and, making her swear to tell the truth, solicits her opinion about his breath. The roe deer, anxious to comply, says "it smelled so terrible / It was almost unbearable" ("que si pueit / Que a peine suffrir le poeit" [v. 47]), for which insult the wolf, aided by a compliant court, puts the roe deer to death. A second beast, summoned to answer the same question and having observed the consequences of telling the truth, "replied she knew no scent / So fragrant and so excellent" ("Dit li que plus süef odur / Ne senti mes, ne meillur" [v. 67]). With, of course, the result that the court condemns her to death for her lie. Finally, a monkey, summoned in the third instance, and having observed both the truth and the lie, proclaims that he "did not know," and is eventually eaten for hesitation. In its companion piece, "The Monkey King" (no. 34), two men who have lost their way in the forest come upon a monkey court and are asked by the king what he thinks of the royal family; to which the first replies honestly, "'You're monkey and she's monkeyess— / Ugly, wicked, hideous'" ("'Tu es singe, e ele singesse— / Leide, hiduse, e felunesse'" [v. 39]); and the second with a lie: "It seemed to him, this one averred, / A lovelier folk he'd never seen" ("E il lur dit ke li semblot / Que unc ne vit plus bele gent" [v. 46]). With the result, different from that of "The Wolf King," that the honest man is shamed and the liar is lauded.

A number of fables turn around the beneficial effects of lies; rather, they make abundantly clear not only that not all lies are condemned on principle but that there are certain occasions on which they are justified. "The Billy Goat and the Wolf" (no. 94) is one such case in which a billy goat, cornered by a wolf, asks to be allowed to say a prayer before death, and when the request is granted, profits from the occasion to call for help. Others, such as "The Peasant and His Horse" (no. 47), turn around the clever lie as a means of self-defense in an unjust world. Still others, such as "The Fox and the Wolf" (no. 88), contain even a logical disquisition on the nature of animals and the nature of lies. What emerges from even so brief a consideration of the status of the lie in the *Fables* is a systematically contextual vision of the nature of truth. As seen in "The Wolf King" (no. 29) and "The Monkey King" (no. 34), two parables of truth and lies, the truth of words is a source neither of condemnation nor of salvation, but is trumped by a higher truth of the body, which is the equivalent for Marie of the part of the animal in man. What emerges most forcefully from the *Fables* is a suspiciousness of speech, a sense not that words return to haunt or to harm, as in the *Lais,* but that they must be held to constant scrutiny in order to determine just what their meaning is, and therefore what their effects might be, in any given situation.

   Part of what the animal world of the *Fables* shares with a human social model has to do with the attempt—among animals, among animals and men, among men—to trick one another with words. So widespread is this defining motif, in fact, that it is practically coterminous with the genre as a whole; and a few examples will suffice. In "The Peasant and the Beetle" (no. 43), a doctor examining a man into whose anus has crawled a beetle declares him to be pregnant, a diagnosis that, in Marie's words, coincides with the mass of people's desire to believe. In "The Birds and the Cuckoo" (no. 46), the birds, called upon to elect a king, are impressed by the sound of a cuckoo. In order to test its mettle, this parlement of fowls sends a titmouse which, unimpressed by the look of the cuckoo, "jumped up to a higher limb/And defecated over him" ("Sur une branche en haut saili,/Sesur le dos li esmeulti" [v. 37]). When the cuckoo "did not say a word/And did not seem the least disturbed" ("Unc li cuccu mot ne dist/Ne peiur semblant ne l'en fist" [v. 39]), the titmouse concludes with the other birds that the cuckoo is not a fowl capable of backing up his words with actions. Indeed, Marie concludes, in an antirhetorical thrust that we have also seen in the frightening bray of the ass in "The Ass and the Lion" (no. 35), that political sovereignty is more than a verbal matter: "Although [a verbose leader] will talk and threaten harm,/He cannot stir up much alarm" ("E veut manacer

e parler, / Que mut petit fet a duter" [v. 75]). So too the moral of "The Peasant and the Goblin" (no. 57), the story, it will be remembered, of wasted
wishes: "And so with many it will be—/Those people lose out frequently/
Who trust too much in what they hear,/In speeches that beguile and blear"
("A plusurs est si avenuz—/Suventefez unt perduz/Ki trop creit autri parole,/Que tut les deceit e afole" [v. 27]). In a final example of the suspiciousness of speech motif, "The Wolf and the Kid" (no. 90), a kid, having
been warned by his mother who leaves him home alone, is not fooled by the
wolf who tries to imitate a goat's voice, but recognizes, in what is a virtually
independent motif in the *Fables,* the difference between voice and body:
"Que la voiz de sa mere oï,/Mes sun cors nent ne choisi" (v. 15).

This last example is significant, for the question may have occurred long
before now: Given that Marie works from an acknowledged source (even
though it is a lost one), and given that other examples of individual fables
also belong to the genre of the animal tale, what is there in her *Fables* that
allows us to attribute the obsession with problematic speech acts specifically
to Marie and not to some broader horizon of expectation?

A comparison between the "The Wolf and the Kid" as it appears in the
Isopet II de Paris (no. 40) and as it is rendered by Marie offers a clue to the
specificity of Marie's animal tales. Both turn around essentially the same
plot, yet in the *Isopet II de Paris,* which is dated approximately a century after the *Fables,* the wolf merely approaches the door and requests entry:

> Le Leu s'en vient a l'us.
> "Or sus, fait il, or sus!
> Oeuvre l'uis a ta mere!
> Je t'aport a mangier
> Trop mieus que ne fis hier:
> Mieus te fais que ton pere!"[17]

The wolf comes up to the door. "Get up," he says, "get up! Open the door
for your mother! I am bringing you things to eat even better than yesterday:
I treat you better than your father!"

The question of voice and of imitation does not figure in the *Isopet II de
Paris,* as it does in Marie's example. More important, the moral of the former stresses the importance of honoring one's mother and father,[18] while
that attached to Marie's fable, on the other hand, focuses specifically upon
the importance of discerning between true and false advice, upon the question, so prevalent in the *Fables,* of the relative worth of truth and lies; and
it is this emphasis upon the secondariness of speech, on language's capacity

to render truth as well as to deceive and seduce, on the role of words, in other words, in the making of moral value that distinguishes her fables from the rest.

AN ETHICS OF LANGUAGE

The speech acts of the *Fables*—the accusations, reproaches, complaints, blame, boasts, promises, vows, wishes, pleas, prayers, seduction, false flattery, threats, taunts, warnings, advice, and lies—serve to mark a fundamental difference between the vexed knot of language and reference in the *Lais* and in the animal tale. To be more precise, while the relation between language and being may be pertinent to—yea, may be the defining element of—the *Lais,* this relation is not so central to the *Fables,* where it is more appropriate to speak of a thematics of rapport between words and the world. Put another way, whereas language is thrown into question both formally and thematically in the *Lais,* it is merely a theme in the *Fables,* and that theme is conceived, above all, in social terms. By that I mean that the suspicion of words is contained, there is something beyond language to which language is beholden, by which it can be controlled. Every speech act is not so much metaphysical as it is existential, situational, a function of a particular agency in relation to other agencies and always within a particular context of power—that is to say, political as well as social ties.[19]

Marie's mistrust of words in the *Fables* can be situated, of course, within the context of a more general distrust of verbal and visual representations. Indeed, a number of tales turn specifically around the question of perspectival illusion in what amounts to a virtual subgenre involving the relationship between truth and point of view as well as the trustworthiness of the senses. In "The Dog and the Cheese" (no. 5), a greedy dog mistakes the reflection in the water of the cheese he holds in his mouth for the real thing and thereby loses both what he has and what he thinks he might have had, according to the moral having to do specifically with the relationship of desire to false belief: "Those who desire more than is just / Will be undone by their own lust. / They'll lose whatever they had before, / And get from others nothing more" ("Ki plus coveite que sun dreit, / Par sei memes se recreit; / Kar ceo qu'il ad pert sovent, / E de autrui n'a il nent" [v. 15]). One of the most popular animal fables of the Middle Ages,[20] "The Dog and the Cheese" is a version of "The Fox and the Moon" (no. 58), in which a fox mistakes the reflection of the moon on water for a piece of cheese and proceeds to drink until he bursts; and it recalls "The Peasant Who Saw Another with

His Wife" (no. 44), another tale of reflected illusion in which the deceitful wife before her husband's image in the tub convinces him that he cannot trust his senses. So too, "The Peasant Who Saw His Wife with Her Lover" (no. 45), in which another adulterous wife convinces her husband that he is not to believe what his eyes have seen.

Among the fables that point to just how tricky not only language but also visual images can be, none is more complex or powerful than "The Lion and the Peasant" (no. 37). A man and lion, discussing the relative worth of each, find themselves in front of a painting of a peasant killing a lion. The lion asks who painted it, using the man's response as a means of defining the difference between the human and animal world: "'It is a fact known everywhere:/A man can paint, sculpt pictures, too./These things a lion cannot do'" ("'Ceo est a tut puple coneü/Que hum seit entailler e purtrere,/Mes li leüns nel seit pas fere" [v. 18]). It is as if Marie were associating the universe of animals with action and that of men with representations—and, of course, with false images. Continuing their walk, the man and the lion happen upon a gladiator match in which a recreant baron is devoured by a lion, with the suggestion that in the end reality is stronger that any image. "The lion asked the peasant next/If all seemed as it was of yore" ("Li lïuns li ad dunc demandé/Si lui semblot cum einz ot fet" [v. 50]). And when the peasant responds, "Quite different from before" ("Dit li vileins, 'Autrement vet!'" [v. 52]), the lion asserts the primacy of deeds over their representation:

> "Ainz que fussums cumpainuns,
> Me mustrastes une peinture
> Sur une pere par avanture.
> Mes jeo te ai plus verrur mustree,
> A descuvert l'as esgardee." (v. 54)

> "Before our comradeship was fast,
> I was, by you, a painting shown,
> Which chanced to be upon a stone.
> But what I've shown is far more true:
> It's what you see in front of you."

"The Lion and the Peasant" is among the original fables of Aesop where, in an abbreviated form, the man brags in front of the image that "we are stronger than you," to which the lion replies: "If lions could make statues, you would see plenty of men under the paws of lions." Yet the moral of the original "Man and Lion Traveling Together" has nothing to do with the falsity of images: "Many people boast of how brave and fearless they are, but when put to the test are exposed as frauds."[21] Marie, however, uses the narrative core of the tale as the pretext for a general reflection upon images in this fable that denounces even the falsity of fables:

> Par essample nus veut aprendre
> Que nul ne deit nïent entendre
> A fable, ke est de mençuinge,
> Ne a peinture, que semble sunge.
> Ceo est a creire dunt hum veit l'ovre,
> Que la verité tut descovre. (v. 59)

> From this example we should know
> Not to accept that something's so
> From fables which are but false seeming
> Or paintings similar to dreaming.
> Believe only in what you see:
> The truth revealed openly.

A distrust of images and of words runs throughout the *Fables,* which depict a world in which meaning is often detached from intention, and in which neither the eyes nor the ears are to be trusted. Marie displays a series of tales in which the falsity of the voice is pitted against the truth of the body. This is the case, as we have seen, in "The Wolf and the Kid" (no. 90). So too, "The Preacher and the Wolf" (no. 82) poses radically the question of meaning versus intention, of the words of the voice versus the body. This tale, paradigmatic to the degree that the fables were used throughout the Middle Ages to teach the elements of rhetoric and grammar, turns around the efforts of a priest "to teach the wolf the alphabet." Having taught him the letters *A, B,* and *C,* the preacher asks the wolf to spell what he can ("'Di que te semble, si espel'" [v. 11]).[22] "The wolf replied to this, 'A lamb!'" (v. 12), which forces the teacher to recognize the truth of the appetite beneath the civilizing process. Marie's moral urges caution before the words that let slip one's truest intentions:

> Le plus dit hum sovent:
> Cel dunt il pensent durement
> E par lur buche est cuneü,
> Ainceis que seit d'autre sceü.
> La buche mustre le penser,
> Tut deive ele de el parler. (v. 15)

And thus, with many men you'll find
Whatever's topmost in their mind
The mouth lets slip, and first they say
What might come out some other way.
The mouth exposes what one thinks
Though it would speak of other things.

Nor is there anything inherently superior about words or the voice, as we see in "The Wolf and the Shepherd" (no. 30), another study in the dynamics of communication pitting one faculty of perception against another. This is the story of a wolf pursued by hunters and hidden by a shepherd, who with his mouth and hand gestures so as to pretend to hide the wolf while his eyes point elsewhere. The shepherd seems, on the one hand, to throw the hunters off the track; yet, suspicious of his protégé, the shepherd contradicts his words with his regard, a conflict not lost upon the clever wolf, who makes the distinction between the truth of the voice and arm versus that of the eyes:

> Li lus respundi cuintement,
> "Ta lange, tes meins vereiment
> Dei joe," fet il, "bon gré saveir.
> Mes une rien te di pur veir—
> S'il alast a ma volenté,
> Ti oil sereient ja crevé!
> Ta lange, tes meins me garirent;
> Ti oil pur poi me descovrirent." (v. 25)

> The wolf replied most cunningly,
> "Your tongue and your hands certainly
> Should have," he said, "my gratitude.
> But I'll say this with certitude—
> Were I to have it all my way,
> Your eyes would be smashed out for aye!
> Your tongue, your hands they rescued me;
> Your eyes put me in jeopardy!"

Once again, a comparison with other versions of the tale shows just how deeply emplotted Marie's consciousness of the conflict between the senses really is and indeed how essential it is to a new and dynamic model of the personality. In the original Aesopic version, a woodcutter deliberately denounces a fox, yet the hunter "took no notice of his gestures and simply took him at his word." Aesop's narrative as well as his lesson turns, in other words, around bad intentions and character: "One could apply this fable to men who make protestations of virtue but who actually behave like rascals." Babrius no. 50 portrays the woodsman as deliberately deceitful and the moral as a lesson from the gods: "The Divinity is wise and cannot be deceived. No one, though he may think his perjury will go unheeded, escapes the penalty for it."[23] The *Isopet II de Paris* depicts the herdsman's false look, which, again, is simply misunderstood by the hunters, and again elicits a charge of intentional betrayal.[24] The *Isopet de Chartres* makes a similar case for deliberate denunciation on the part of the herdsman accompanied by a missed cue on the part of the hunters and a general denunciation of traitors:

> Ne fet pas mout grand vasclage
> Hom qui est de double corage
> De trahir autri par derriere;
> Quant par guingner moustre la chose
> Que a la bouche dire n'ose,
> Sachiez c'est ribaude maniere.[25]

The man who has a deceitful heart is not very noble when he betrays another behind his back; you should know that when he indicates with a look the thing that the mouth dares not say, it is a churlish way of acting.

Thus, while other versions of "The Wolf and the Shepherd" emphasize wicked intentions, the will to betray, Marie's insists upon the situational dynamics implicit in the shepherd's alertness not only to the danger to the wolf from the hunters, but to the danger to himself from the wolf. Nor does her moral consist, as do the others, of a general homily on the treacherous motives of traitors; rather, it contains a relativizing of the position of each of the three characters in this drama of half-truths and shared suspicions. Such a relativizing of perspective constitutes an essential element of the existential thinking at the core of Marie's *Fables*.

In the place of an ontology of language characteristic of the *Lais,* a placing of language in direct relation to being, with the result that language, because of its necessarily contingent nature, is always lacking, always insufficient, and thus always dangerous, if not fatal, we find in the *Fables* an ethics of language[26]—a series of examples, a catalogue, a repertory of the possibilities of the good and bad uses, the propitious and noxious effects, of words; and in the social world to which words refer we glimpse the consequences of actions caused by words but also of actions that are words. The language of—more precisely, the representation of—speech acts in the *Fables* seems to contain an inside and an outside, yielding a sense that not all language is fatal. On the contrary, there are good and bad uses of words; truths and lies; true and false accusations, boasts, and reproaches; just and unjust pleas, vows, and threats; promises to be kept and to be broken; good and poor advice.

So conscious is Marie of the good and bad uses of language that it can be said without exaggeration that she includes even silence in the panoply of privileged speech acts of the *Fables*. Indeed, the series of tales that turn around the question of when and to speak and when not to constitute a sub-genre of discretion. "The Thief and the Dog" (no. 20) is the story of a thief who offers a loaf of bread to a watchdog guarding a flock of sheep. The dog first refuses, then, upon urging, reveals that he understands the thief's mo-tivation: "'For I can see, yes I've discerned/That you intend my mouth to stuff/So that I can't let out a woof'" ("Jeo sai tres bien a escïent/Que ma buche veus estuper/Que jeo ne puisse mot suner" [v. 14]). In "The Monkey and Her Baby" (no. 51), a mother brings her child before the lion king who, asked if it is beautiful, declares that "an uglier beast he'd yet to see" ("Une plus leide beste ne vit" [8]) and orders her to take it home. On the way, the monkey mother, filled with wounded pride, cannot resist speaking again; and despite the lion's admonition, asks the same question of a bear who de-clares the baby so beautiful that he would like to kiss it, which he does, de-vouring it on the spot. Marie's moral, which could just as well be tacked on to "Lanval," "Equitan," "Laüstic," "Bisclavret," "Le Fresne," or "Yonec," has to do with discretion: "Pur ceo ne devereit nul mustrer/Sa priveté ne sun penser" ("And for this reason you should not/Disclose your secret or your thought" [v. 25]). The rooster of "The Cock and the Fox" (no. 60), having been beguiled into closing his eyes to sing, finds himself in the mouth of the running fox, whom he convinces in turn to shout at the pursuing hunters. Thus losing his game for having opened his mouth at the wrong moment, "the fox began to curse his mouth/For speaking when it ought to hush" ("La buche cumence a maudire,/Ke parole quant devereit taire" [v. 30]); which curse is reciprocated by the rooster who condemns his eyes: "'Maudire l'oil, ki volt cluiner,/Quant il deit guarder e guaiter'" (v. 33). Together, the cock and the fox seem to be saying, "Keep your eyes open and your mouth closed," a message manifest in Marie's moral, which could not be a clearer statement of the ethics of silence and of speech: "And thus with fools, for they all will/Speak out when they their tongues should check/And check their tongues when they should speak" ("Coe funt li fol: tut li plusur/Paro-lent quant deivent taiser,/Teisent quant il deivent parler" [v. 36]). "The Wolf and the Boatman" (no. 79) offers a similar lesson in timing. To the request to be ferried across a river, a boatman requires a clever wolf to cite "three wise sayings." Agreeing, the wolf utters a first banality—"'He does well who does well, you know'" ("'Bien fet, ki bien fet, ceo savez'" [v. 19])— followed by a second: "'He does far worse, who'er does naught'" ("'Mut fet pis, ki ne feit'" [v. 24]). Pressed to produce the third, the wolf refuses until they reach the shore, at which time he claims to have been afraid to speak for fear of being ejected from the boat. Finally, "The Hawk and the Nightingale" (no. 67) stands as a companion piece to "The Cock and the Fox," in which the clever nightingale, invited to sing by a hawk, refuses to open its mouth until the distance between them is sufficiently great to insure her safety.

I maintained in the discussion of the *Lais* that Marie de France played an original and significant role in the recuperation of a culture and in the forging of a new sense of identity within the late feudal world; and this through the systematic and relentless depiction of this world as fatally flawed, its institutions (especially marriage) as doomed, indeed, as haunted by a death wish so inescapable that it is posited at the level of language itself. The aristocrats of the *Lais* need only speak for the world to crumble around them. The universe of the *Fables* is, however, much more open. Indeed, Marie's *Fables* are dominated by issues having to do with the dynamics of communication and the place of such communication in the constitution of a changing human community. In contrast to the linguistic fatalism that hovers over the *Lais,* the *Fables* constantly proffer the notion that words are powerful not so much because they kill (which they can), but because words are the instruments of relations between animals, and, of course, between men.

What Marie seems to be saying in the *Fables* is that actions have ethical consequences, which are different from the ontological consequences depicted in the *Lais,* that their effects have limits. The universe of the *Fables* is thus posited not as a tragic and inescapable state of being in the flesh, but as a series of recuperable moments along a continuum of the will. For often what is at stake has to do with assessing the relation between the intention, meaning, and consequences of actions, and thus the place of the will in defining relations between the human, as well as the animal, members of a perceptually altered world.

As in the *Lais,* Marie asserts in a number of fables the necessity of choice, of choice conceived, once again, in ethical rather than ontological terms. We have seen, for example, the extent to which "The Bat" (no. 23) illustrates the existential maxim concerning the freedom to choose anything but not to choose. A companion piece can be found in "The Badger and the Pigs" (no. 77), in which a badger, seeing pigs eat excess acorns, pretends to be one; but when he sees them being slaughtered, he denies it. The *Fables* seem to assert something like not only the efficacy but the freedom of volition, since language in the *Fables* does not seem to be condemned and to condemn, as in the *Lais;* rather, language is invested with intention, and a correct reading of the motives of others, along with a mastery of one's own, is the key to, I am tempted to say "surviving," but will resist, and say simply "being," in the world.

Many of the fables are about assessing the designs of the other in order to engage in appropriate action oneself. In "The Fox and the Dove" (no. 61), it will be remembered, a fox tries to induce a dove sitting on a signpost to come down and sit beside him, since the king has decreed peace among all the animals of the kingdom. When the dove then alerts him to the arrival of knights with their dogs, the fox flees, claiming that he doesn't know whether the dogs have heard yet of the proclamation. The drama here is clearly psychological, and it is such that one has the impression not so much that language is condemned as a feature of the inescapable condition of our existence in a degraded world, of which the inefficacy of signs is but one manifestation, but that language is endowed with intention and that intention is, if not entirely controllable, at least one arm in the struggle for survival. It is not that language is universally censured but that speech is portrayed to be often worthy of distrust, as Marie posits a certain agency of individual inclination within a world inhabited by those pictured increasingly as the masters and mistresses of an individualized fate.

I know it sounds corny, and such a concept is more complicated than it seems, but as subject as the figures of the *Lais* are to the winds and whims of the mysterious external forces of a world in which boats and swans lie waiting to carry their elected passengers and messages to preordained destinations, Marie seems to make the claim in the *Fables* that the fate of the individual is determined to some extent by the assessments and decisions that he or she makes in the course of a curiously more rationalized existence, which does not exclude, of course, the determining effects of chance or even of the body whose very nature, as we shall see in the chapter that follows, distinguishes the fate of individual members of larger species within the animal tale from the determined destinies of the heroes and heroines of the *Lais.*

CHAPTER FIVE

Changing Places: The *Fables* and Social Mobility at the Court of Henry II

Compared with the *Lais,* Marie's *Fables* are existential literature, a difference that, as we have begun to see in the previous chapter, may be explained in part by genre.[1] The repeated necessity of existential choice to some degree belongs to the fable tradition. Marie's "The Dog and the Cheese" (no. 5), for example, features a cheese, whereas other versions of the same tale, such as that contained in the *Isopet I—Avionnet,* turn around a piece of meat. The poet of "Du Chien qui passoit l'iaue et tenoit une piece de char" (no. 5) is in fact aware of the necessity of a narrative decision—"The dog passed by a pond of water, / In its mouth a soft cheese, / Though some say it was flesh" ("Le Chien passoit une yaue a no, / En sa geule un fromaige mo, / Autre dient que ce yere chars")[2]—which, again, can be seen to correspond to Marie's obsession with the choice of titles for individual lais, or, in "Chaitivel," with the choice of suitors. The moral of "Du Chien qui passoit l'iaue et tenoit une piece de char" has to do precisely with the obligation to choose, for "he who does two things at once," the narrator reminds us, "does not do them well" ("Qui fait deus choses tout ensemble, / Très bien ne les fait, ce me samble").[3] But whereas in the *Lais* there is no choice without tragic and even fatal consequences, as seen in the fear felt by the lady of "Chaitivel" of "choosing one and losing the rest," selection within the fable, linked to the question of intention, remains more optimistically open. To borrow another example from the *Isopet I—Avionnet,* "Du Prodomme et de la Mustele" (no. 38), a man catches a weasel ("Beloste") which asks to be spared. When the man asks why, a speech act inconceivable within the *Lais,* the weasel reminds his captor that it catches the man's mice. The man replies that if the weasel caught mice it was for its own good and not his. The moral of "Du Prodomme et de la Mustele" has to do, in fact, with the necessity of assessing intention: "La volentés le fait descueuvre:/La regardés, non pas a l'euvre" ("The truth of the act lies in the intent: look to it, not to the result").[4] From the point of view of the weasel, the question of intention is, of course, moot; and we will return to the reasons for such mootness, which lie in the body. Yet, the fable points to an essential characteristic of the genre, and something that is of prime interest to Marie—the assessment of intent as a means of understanding the world, and thus the relativizing of acts whose meaning and consequences are determined more by their "cause" than by their effect: "La cause nuit et si profite,/De la cause vient le merite."

Marie is obsessed in the *Fables* by the question of perspective and of interpretation as the determining element of value, and of value as a determinant of action. This is not to say that the question of perspective does not enter the *Lais*. Indeed, it does, in, say, "Eliduc," where the difference between what the wife and the mistress know independently of each other is crucial to a drama of half-truths that cannot be reconciled except by the withdrawal of one of the factors—the wife—from the equation. "Eliduc" is in some profound sense about the failure of binary opposites to find a third term, to find an equation in a universe in which no one, not even Eliduc, has other than a partial perception of a world whose very absolutism renders choice the equivalent of sacrifice. Denis de Rougemont remarked apropos of a similar absolutism attached to the Tristan myth, "Mr. and Mrs. Tristan, imagine that!" Similarly, one might say, "Mr. and Mrs. Eliduc, imagine that!" One could imagine it, of course, only as a lai transformed into a farce, into bourgeois drama, or, more realistically, into a fable in which the protagonists of the impossible love triangle manage to avoid death and withdrawal from the world via an "arrangement."

Again, this is because words in the *Fables* have an outside, which is crucial to an ethics as opposed to an ontology of language, for it implies the empty space of good and bad interpretation, decision, and action, the empty space of choice and will. Where the question of interpretation is concerned, there is no more instructive fable than "The Affectionate Ass" (no. 15), which is about nothing if not the necessity of a correct understanding of the signs of the world. For in this tale an ass, jealous of the affection bestowed by his master on a dog, imitates the dog by fawning all over the master with his hooves and ends up being beaten by the master's servants. The moral warns explicitly about the dangers of social climbing in this tale that turns around the difference between the same action performed by animals of different dimension, one of the fables which, understandably in the urban environment of which we speak, serves to establish and enforce the principle of measure.

The fable of fables where the relativity of perspective is concerned is "The Peasant and His Horse" (no. 47), in which a man who wants to sell his horse is dissatisfied with an offer of only twenty sous. Buyer and seller agree to let the first man they encounter at market set the price. However, when this man, who happens to be blind in one eye, sets a price at ten sous, the peasant refuses and is sued by the buyer for breach of contract. The seller's defense before the court is that since the man in the market saw the horse with only one eye, he saw only one-half of its worth: "Pur ceo l'aveit demi preisié,/Qu'il ne'en veeit fors la meité" (v. 42). The moral of this tale of competing perspectives and relative worth has to do with self-reliance, thinking on one's feet, cleverness in speaking before the law, the relativism of the truth and the making of believable lies (v. 51, see p. 189). That so many of the *Fables* should end in or involve judicial trials is significant and indicative, again, of the open relativizing effects of the will in finding a third term—a sentence—as opposed to the tragic closed absoluteness of the *Lais*. For the perspectival relativizing of "The Peasant and His Horse" implies, as Marie insists by way of conclusion, the possibility of escaping even the most difficult situation: "The wise man in a dreadful plight/Can often turn his wrong to right" ("Li sages hum en grant destreit/Turne suvent sun tort en dreit" [v. 61]). The world of the *Fables,* unlike, say, that of *La Chanson de Roland,* is one in which the meaning of signs is not given, but must be correctly read. The truth of the *Fables* lies not in the dispensation of truth, but in the exposition of an opposition between truth and lies, more and less credible illusion, to be translated into the good and the bad, and, finally, into appropriate and inappropriate action.

SCHOLASTICISM AND THE *FABLES*

It is neither an exaggeration nor a misnomer to speak of the scholasticism of the *Fables,* which show from the start a pedagogical thrust. Robert Falkowitz makes the case that old Babylonian fables and related forms were used in the first half of the second millennium B.C. as "part of the Old Babylonian school curricula for teaching the learned Sumerian language to students coming from a Semitic vernacular context."[5] Aristotle associates fables and oratory.[6] In the late fourth century B.C. the first collection of Aesopic fables in prose was published by the orator Demetrius of Phalerum as a handbook for the use of writers and speakers.[7] Fragments on papyri and wax tablets point to the fact that Babrius's collection of Aesopic fables in Greek iambic verse "was already a school-text in the third and fourth centuries A.D."[8] Aesop's Latin translator, Phaedrus, insists upon the corrective function of the fable: "That which is Aesopic in kind is confined to instructive examples; nor is anything else aimed at in fables than that the mistakes of mortals may be corrected, and that one may sharpen his wits by a close application to them."[9] Quintilian associates the oral indoctrination of fables with the first steps of learning, a prerequisite to a pupil's study of rhetoric: "Let them learn first to tell the fables orally in clear, unpretentious language, then to write them out with the same simplicity of style; first putting the verses into prose and translating the substance in different words, then paraphrasing it more freely, in the course of which they may abbreviate some things and elaborate others, so long as they preserve the poet's meaning."[10] Macrobius distinguishes between two kinds of fables, one for children and the other for more serious purpose.[11] Priscian specifies that "a fable is an oration fashioned so that it has a life-like form which manifests an image of truth. Thus the fable is the first thing that orators teach to children."[12] Fable collections were used throughout the Middle Ages as a basic element in the education of schoolboys and for the purpose of teaching rhetoric (as well as translation).[13] More than a hundred of the school manuals based upon the Latin translation of the Greek verses of Babrius have survived to the present day.[14] Beginning in the patristic period the exemplary status of fables was used in preaching, as can be seen in sermon books like the *Paris Promptuarium,* John of Bromyard's *Summa Praedicantium,* and Jacques de Vitry's *Exempla.*[15]

Marie's *Fables,* as Karen Jambeck has shown, are a mirror of princes whose importance for the formation of moral character cannot be overestimated: through the animal tale the pupil learns Latin and rhetoric at the same time that he ingests politics and the rules of social responsibility. Such a usage is not unique to the West: the old Indian *Pancatantra* is a tale told for the edification of the sons of princes in the art of survival.[16] The prose version of Phaedrus, known as the *Romulus,* takes its name from the dedicatory letter sent from a certain Romulus to his son Tiberius or Tiberinus.[17] So too, in Marie's prologue the Emperor Romulus addresses his son "through examples demonstrating,/ How it behooved him to take care/ That no one trick him unaware" (v. 14). The pedagogical model of the fables is essentially parental, didactic, and pragmatic. Of this there is no more telling example than that contained in the *Isopet de Lyon,* "Dou Pere qui chestoie son anfant" (no. 51), which exposes explicitly the fable's teaching on teaching.[18] A father who chastises his disobedient son without effect discovers that the only tactic that works is to beat one of his household servants instead.[19] He learns this method of teaching from a fable which the narrator proceeds to tell: a man wants to harness a young untamed ox to pull his plow, but the young animal balks, "because of the yoke which irritated him so" ("Dou jou qui tant li desplaisoit"). The man asks an older ox to teach his own son by example. And it works: "Thus the man through his wise ox cured the untamed one of his folly; without complaining he pulled his load and didn't seek to escape." The lesson of this fable within a fable has to do with the effectiveness of symbolic violence—"In order to remedy the lion's pride, have the dog beaten before his eyes"—in the maintenance of social order: "The great must teach wisely their learning whether by word or by example, the small must believe humbly."[20] "Dou Pere qui chestoie son anfant" provides a lesson in the effects of fiction, which are oblique and unconscious. The beatings and eatings of the animal tale comprise a chastisement of children that cannot be made more directly.

Where Marie's *Fables* are concerned, not only are the individual tales set within a didactic framework by the moral tacked to the end, but a group of tales involving parental instruction form a virtual subgenre. "The Doe and Her Fawn" (no. 92), for example, contains a lesson in the correct interpretation of signs. As the innocent fawn spots a hunter, the mother warns: "'Of him you should be most in dread;/Fear him with all your might,' she said" ("'C'est cil, dunt plus te deiz cremer;/E greinur poür puz aver'" [v. 13]). When the attentive fawn then perceives the hunter dismounting and hiding, he wrongly concludes, "We have no need to fear./I'm sure that he no harm intends" ("Nus n'estut pas," fet il, "duter./l ne nus veut fere nul mal" [v. 18]). "The Doe and Her Fawn" is a negative lesson, since the mother's correction of her son's false interpretation of the hunter's moves—"'Oh no, dear son, you're wrong,' said she" ("'Nenil, beu fiz, de ceu n'i ad nïent'" [v. 23])—is a lesson unheeded. Marie's own moral to this tale of a lesson twice unlearned has to do with the efficacy of lessons and of a prospective alertness that is, as we shall see, one of the most persistent conclusions to be drawn from the *Fables:* "For many men these words are apt:/Fools do not cry until they're trapped./When fools don't heed what wisdom says,/They're dupes of their own stupid ways" ("En reproche dit hum suvent,/Fous ne crent, dici qu'il p[r]ent./Quant fol ne vuet crere le sage,/Suvent i pert par sun utrage" (v. 33).

"The Doe and Her Fawn" finds a companion piece in "The Crow Instructing His Child" (no. 93), in which a crow instructs his young to flee when he sees something in a man's hand. However, in this case, when the young crow asks if he should flee if there is nothing in the man's hand, the older crow dismisses him, considering the lesson learned. The moral of "The Crow Instructing His Child" brings home the extent to which we stand in relation to Marie as the pupil to the instructor within the essentially pedagogical context of the *Fables:* "A lesson from my tale now hear," Marie prescribes, "When someone does an infant rear,/Then sees him grow up shrewd and smart,/He should be happy, glad of heart!" ("Par cest essample nus dit tant:/Quant hum ad nurri sun enfant,/Qu'il le veit sage e veizïé,/Le queor ad joius e lié!" [v. 17]). Finally, "The Knight and the Old Man" (no. 101) serves to situate the pedagogical relation of parent and child within a specifically scholastic setting in which the scholar poses a series of questions to the magister. "To what land should I go?" a knight asks. "To a land where people would love you," the old man replies. "What if I cannot find such a land?" the knight asks, to which the old man answers, "Go to a land where people are afraid of you." "And if I cannot find such a land?" "Then go to where they're not afraid of you." "And if I cannot get there?" "Then go to a land where you never see anyone and no one knows where you are." The speech act here dramatized resembles the scholastic *questio* whose enigmatic moral merely underscores the ludic qualities of the exchange: "And thus this lesson shows a way/To deal with what a fool will say:/More than he ought to, he inquires/He then hears more than he desires" ("Par cest essample nus veut sumundre/Que se deit hum a fol respundre,/Ki plus enquert kil ne devereit;/Si ot suvent que ne vodreit" [v. 23]).

At their outer limit Marie's pedagogical fables show the earmarks of a scholastic debate, whose topic, as in "The Doe and Her Fawn" or "The Crow Instructing His Child," is survival. "The Fox and the Cat" (no. 99), for example, begins, like "The Knight and the Old Man," with a question: "The cat then asked the fox to tell/In what way he'd defend himself/If he should meet adversity" ("Li chaz al gupil demanda,/Par quels se defendera/La u il erent entrepris" [v. 5]). To the fox's boast that he possesses a hundred tricks in order to survive, the cat claims to know only one: "'Kar jeo ne sai fors un engin'" (v. 15). The fox's hundred tricks do not work, however, when the dogs arrive and he finds himself obliged to seek the cat's help in this fable that transforms a succession of boasts into a debate. "The Fox and the Cat" is, of course, a violent version of "The Cricket and the Ant" (no. 39), in which a frivolous cricket seeks the assistance of a resourceful provident ant, who chastises and turns him away. So too, "The Wolf and the Dove" (no. 98), in which a wolf's criticism of the dove's house—"'You're labouring so hard, I see,/Gathering, massing wood,' said he;/'You can't improve your house this way'" ("'Mut te vci,' fet il, 'travaillcr,/Cuillir merin e purchacer;/Jeo ne vei meudre ta meisun'" [v. 5])—is returned:

> Dunc respundi li culum,
> "E jeo te vei tuz jurs berbiz cuillir,
> Aignel e mutuns retenir;
> E si n'en es meuz avancez
> Ne plus riches ne plus preisez." (v. 8)

> The dove responded right away,
> "And I see you collecting lambs,
> Gathering sheep, amassing rams;
> That's not made you superior
> Or more esteemed or wealthier."

Given that the hunters do not arrive, as in "The Fox and the Cat," nor does winter descend, as in "The Cricket and the Ant," there is an element of pure linguistic exchange in "The Wolf and the Dove," a gratuitousness reproduced in a number of fables structured, as in "The Wolf and the Boatman" (no. 79), along the lines of formal debate. "The Fly and the Bee" (no. 86) turns around the question of which insect is more noble, the former maintaining that he may go "where the bee dare not be seen" (v. 5) and that the fruits of the bee's labor are appropriated by man. The bee, however, maintains that the fly is loved by no one and "has no honor for his deeds" (v. 18), whereas he, bee, is loved and protected by all. Marie's moral denounces the man who boasts and exalts himself with words.

"The Peasant and His Contrary Wife" (no. 95) is a parable of contradiction in which the couple argues over a matter of words. For the argumentative wife contradicts her husband's seemingly innocent remark that, "He'd seen no meadow, all his life,/Cut with a scythe so evenly" (Que unc mes des oilz ne vit/Nul pré fauké si üelement" [v. 6]) with the assertion, "'Rather it was cut with shears'" ("'Ainz fu a uns forces trenchez'" [v. 9]). This seemingly meaningless quarrel, like the fabliau "De la Dame escolliée," is about conjugal power within the ménage: "'You take away whatever's mine;/And me, you vilely undermine'" ("'La meie veus fere remeindre;/Par engresté me vols ateindre'" [v. 17]), protests the enraged husband, who proceeds to cut out the tongue of the wife who continues the debate beyond her capacity for speech by using her fingers "to show/The meadow had been clipped by shears" (v. 25). It is no accident, I think, that "The Peasant and His Contrary Wife" (no. 95) is paired with "The Peasant and His Cantankerous Wife" (no. 96), in which, again as in "De la Dame escolliée," the husband, alert to his wife's contradictory nature, suggests that she do the opposite of what he in truth wants. When his workers, for example, seek beer and bread, he knows better than to ask directly but instructs them to ask his wife and to pretend that he opposes the idea. Upon discovery of the ruse, she flees, and, in the course of the chase that ensues, falls into the river. As the peasants spread out to look for her, the husband explains that his contradictory wife will not float downstream like everyone else, "but went against the water's flow—/ Behaving in her death, this wife,/ Exactly as she'd wished in life" ("Od reddur n'est mie turnee—/ En sa mort ne feïst ele mie/ Ceo que ne vot fere en sa vie" [v. 48]). The moral of "The Peasant and His Cantankerous Wife" denounces those who quarrel with their lord, who, when he realizes it, takes vengeance, as Marie thus reminds us that words are a form of action, and actions have ethical consequences (v. 51).

One senses not only an ethos of struggle between the species, but a socialized form of natural selection in the spirit of debate that animates the *Fables* and that serves to situate them—beyond the universalizing realm of animal riddles or of the flytings to be found in many early Indo-European societies—within the context of a return of Aristotelian thought in the West.[21] And though Marie never mentions Aristotle explicitly, she does not wander very far, I think it can be shown, from the generic horizon of the animal tale in which the relationship between narrative and the principles of formal reasoning are made explicit. The poet of the *Isopet I—Avionnet,* for example, insists at the strong point of the epilogue upon the mutual implication of fables and logic:

> Je vous afermë et creant,
> De ce ne mentiré neant,
> Que estudier en Ysopet
> N'est pas euvre de mignopet;
> Car l'en y treuve verité
> Combien que fable recité
> L'ait; ce n'est pas a merveillier:
> Qui en logique vuet veillier,
> Il trouvera que de premisses
> Fausses, ensamble bien assises,
> S'an suit vraie conclusion.
> Yceste est vraie opinion.[22]

I insist and promise, and in this there is no lie, that studying Ysopet is not a trifling thing; for one finds truth there regardless of how true a recited fable may be; and of this there is no wonder: for he who pays attention to logic knows that a true conclusion can be drawn from false premises that are well put together. This judgment is true.

The epilogue to the *Isopet de Chartres* claims Aristotle's influence in the leaving off of rhyme:

> Tout ce m'a mandé Aristote
> Que je ne fusse ydyote,
> Et que je lessasse a rimer.
> Dit m'a que j'aprenge sophie
> Et la soe philosophie
> Se je ne veil coudre ou limer.[23]

Aristotle taught me all this, that I should not be stupid but that I should leave off rhyming. He told me that I should learn logic and his philosophy if I don't want to sew or file[?].

The author of the *Isopet de Chartres* claims to have translated the "Avionet," or Walter l'Anglais's *Romulus,* and admits to having been sidetracked by Aristotle ("Més Aristote me detire") in what amounts to an attempt to place the traditionally fictional animal tale on the side of truth, or at least on the side of the Aristotelian *Ethics* which he invokes explicitly:

> Mès d'autre part de Dagoubert
> Songie, qui tenoit pour foubert
> Tel fablierre et tel causidique;
> Mès je respon: "La chose ocure
> Quiert tesmoing apert a grant cure,"
> Dit Aristote en veil Etthique.[24]

But, on the other hand, I thought of Dagobert, who held for a fool such a teller of tales and such a pleader; but I respond: "An obscure matter seeks a clear and careful explanation," as Aristotle says in the old Ethics.

Despite the equation of fable and fiction with which we began, there is a sense that fables produce philosophical truth—or a practical version of philosophical truth, practical wisdom—through the animal in the fable.

It is, of course, ironic that the animal tale, a supposedly popular genre, one of the simple forms, short pieces aimed at least in part at children, should turn out to be so complicated; that they should, for all their apparent naïveté, enter the complex orbit of the Aristotelian revival of the late twelfth and thirteenth centuries. And yet, even a cursory reading of Marie's *Fables* brings home the extent to which the sophistication of the *Lais* is continued—in a different mode, with reference to a different world—in her concern with the determining effects of language upon perception, in her stress upon interpretation and the relativizing of perspective, in her contextualizing of the meaning of words and deeds, in her emphasis upon intention in the formulation of ethical judgment and upon the will in the warrant of ethical action. Such an assertion is, of course, based upon a reading of the *Fables* in which no individual tale might sustain the entire claim, but according to which together they make the composite point. Thus the effort to buttress each and every segment of the argument we have been building with several examples; thus the uncovering of natural pairs of tales, which may be linked either thematically or even sequentially, and of which Marie, as others have noted with respect to the *Lais,* is especially fond; thus too the location of logical groupings within the whole.

Among representative fables none is more pertinent to Marie's interest in logic than "The Fox and the Wolf" (no. 89). In this tale of the two animals who bring their quarrel to court, the lion/judge rules that the wolf is in the wrong and the fox is right. However, since lies are more consonant with the wolf's nature and better suit his temperament than "truth does fox's disposition./Of neither could he bring conviction" ("'Sa mençunge est plus covenable/E meuz resemble chose estable/Que del gupil la veritez.'/Nul de eus ne deit estre jugez" [v. 15]). Neither, the lion concludes, will be punished. In the clash of the material facts of the case with the nature of each beast, the tale gives just a hint of the sophisticated moral reasoning that will come to characterize legal and penitential theory beginning in the twelfth, but especially in the thirteenth, century. For the tale turns around categories of good and bad, innocence and guilt, that are shown to be not immutable ideas or categories, but commingling qualities in a single being—a wolf lying more than a fox, a fox capable of the truth, two beasts, as the medievals might have put it, that are *bestornées,* acting equally against their nature.

The difference between external action and internal nature marks, moreover, an essential difference between the medieval bestiary, which works as a glossary of animal nature, and the ethical universe of Marie's *Fables* in which right and wrong are defined in relative rather than absolute terms and the question of innocence and guilt is situational. This is not to suggest that Marie is a moral relativist. On the contrary, she is as opposed here to the refusal to choose as she is in "The Bat" (no. 23), in "The Badger and the Pigs" (no. 77), or in "Chaitivel"; and the negative judgment passed upon the scholastic lion's failure to judge only reaffirms Marie's existential principles.[25] So too, the message of "The Rich Man, the Horse, and the Billy

Goat" (no. 64) in which an inflexible man wishes to sell both animals at the same price. When a merchant who wants only the horse begins to bargain, the seller refuses, thus losing both sales, with the moral that the ignorant man does not know how to discriminate between good and bad habits. At the threshold of an age whose intellectual life will be defined increasingly by the question of distinctions, Marie subtly undercuts the rigidity of even minor everyday absolutism in favor of a spirit of compromise in which not only good and bad but in this instance profit and loss can be imagined to be combined. Marie practices in the *Fables* the moral equivalent of double account bookkeeping in the commercial realm.

Though we know so little about her life and her person that almost nothing can be said about her with certainty, it seems nonetheless unlikely that Marie would have had direct contact with Aristotelian ethical thought, which would have had to consist of the Latin commentaries on the *Nicomachean Ethics* that began to appear in the twelfth century, well before the formal commentaries of Albert the Great, Siger de Brabant, or Thomas Aquinas.[26] Marie does not claim, as does the poet of the *Isopet de Chartres* approximately a hundred years later, to have "been instructed by Aristotle." And yet in reading the *Fables* one has the impression of a moral universe on the cusp of the Aristotelian turn.

ABELARDIAN ETHICS

It makes little sense to speak of what we think of as ethics or as moral philosophy among the theologians and canonists of the twelfth century. Though lots of attention is devoted to the question of original sin and, in the Augustinian mode, to the ontological status of evil, relatively little is accorded to what we think of as actual sin in any sense that would have meaning for the practical social and political situations alluded to directly or indirectly in the *Fables*. Ethics was not part of the seven liberal arts as they figure in the writings of Boethius, Cassiodorus, or Isidore. The twelfth-century teachers who considered ethics at all either place such a practical discipline at the end of the list of the seven arts (Honorius of Autun, Stephen of Tournai, Godfrey of Saint-Victor) or fit ethics between the language arts and theoretical philosophy, alongside practical philosophy, economics, and politics (Hugh of Saint-Victor, William of Conches).[27] In the chapter schools, the schools of the regular canons, and the monastery schools where the liberal arts figured in the twelfth-century curriculum, every effort was directed at reconciling, through the art of *moralisatio,* classical moral thinkers with the meaning of

Scripture and with Christian ideas of virtue; and this via the *florilegia* or collections culled from the writings of Virgil, Lucan, Ovid, Cicero, Juvenal, Horace, Statius, Seneca, and Macrobius, inter alia.[28]

If there is one exception to the general dearth of ethical thinking *strictu sensu* in the period under discussion, it is Abelard's *Ethics,* which, as some maintain, may have had only a limited influence upon twelfth-century doctrine,[29] but which stands nonetheless as a thesis, where the question of fault is concerned, by which the moral thought of the High Middle Ages can be measured. Again, it is unlikely that Marie had any direct contact with the works of Abelard. However, in reading the *Fables* one has the uncanny sense of having encountered Marie's existential ethical universe elsewhere—more precisely, in the relativism of the notion of sin contained in Abelard's writing on ethics. Indeed, in separating legal punishment from fault, Abelard offers examples that might be right out of Marie de France. Take, for example, the case of the mother so poor that she cannot buy clothes for her suckling baby, who unavoidably smothers "the one she clasps with the utmost love" and is punished as a lesson to others. Or the instance of false witness:

> Occasionally also it happens that someone is accused by his enemies before a judge, and that a certain imputation is made about him by which the judge knows he is innocent. However, because they insist and demand a hearing at a trial, they commence the suit on the appointed day, produce witnesses, albeit false ones, to convict him whom they accuse. Since the judge can in no way rebut these witnesses with plain reasons, he is compelled by law to recognize them and, having accepted their proof, he punishes the innocent man.[30]

We saw the theme of wrongful judgment in the *Fables* in "The Dog and the Ewe" (no. 4), whose moral might have illustrated the dichotomy between guilt and justice contained in the *Ethics:* "This example serves to tell / What's true for many men as well: / By lies and trickery, in short, / They force the poor to go to court. / False witnesses they'll often bring / And pay them with the poor folks' things" ("Par ceste essample nus meut mustrer: / E de meint hume le puis prover, / Ki par mentir e par tricher / Funt les povres suvent pleider. / Faus tesmoines sovent traient, / De l'aveir as povres les (a)paient" [v. 35]).

Abelard's death occurred within a decade, more or less, of what must have been the date of Marie's birth,[31] and there is little to connect them other than a shared interest in the moral dimension of the relation of cause and effect and in a relativizing of ethics based upon the separation of intention and act.[32] Abelard's ethics are characterized by the relative indifference of the act; and, like Marie, he resorts to exemplary stories in order to make this point. Indeed, the same act may be performed by two different men with different intentions, producing opposite ethical effects.[33] Conversely, two men may perform different acts with equal guilt. Abelard distinguishes, in fact, between the man "who sins openly and scandalizes many and corrupts by his example" and the other, who, "sinning secretly, harms only himself."[34] So relative is the Abelardian act, so refined is Abelard's notion of relativity, that not only might the same act performed by two different people have opposite meanings, not only might different acts performed with the same intent have the same meaning, but a good deed performed with bad intent can be bad, and a bad deed performed with good intent can be good; acts performed by the same person at different times yield divergent effects.[35]

Marie's *Fables* are filled with examples of good and bad advice, false and true accusations, harmful and even beneficial lies. Similarly, for Abelard, the moral meaning of any particular act is situationally defined, and the true intent behind the deed is sometimes the result of a secondary, and not always the apparent, cause:

> Moreover, if anyone held in prison wants to put his son there in his place so that he may seek his own ransom, surely we do not therefore simply concede that he wants to put his own son in prison—something which he is driven to endure with floods of tears and with many sighs? At any rate such a will which consists in great grief of mind is not, I would say, to be called will but rather suffering. . . . Thus the sick man is said to want a cauterization or an operation in order to be healed and martyrs to suffer in order to come to Christ or Christ himself in order that we may be saved by his suffering. Yet we are not therefore compelled to concede simply that they want this.[36]

One realizes just how relativistic Abelard is when he is compared, for example, to Anselm of Canterbury, whose ethics, which belong to a generation before the Parisian master, are infused with objectively defined Augustinian categories of evil and good.[37] As we see in the reply of the Teacher to the student in *The Fall of Satan,* justice and injustice are mutually exclusive and not relative terms:

> I think now that you know—since injustice is only the absence of justice and to be unjust is simply not to have justice—why it is that we call the absence of justice "injustice" only after justice is lost, and not before it is given; and you now know why we call not-having justice "being unjust," and regard

both injustice and being unjust as reprehensible. For the absence of justice is never disgraceful except in a case where it ought to be present.[38]

One seizes the enduring radicalness of Abelard's emphasis upon intent as opposed to act in comparing him with Aquinas who, a century and a quarter later, does contextualize acts, at least acts of evil, which may be evil for a variety of reasons. For an act to be good, however, it must be wholly good. Where morality is concerned, Aquinas remains a realist to the degree that the exterior act is seen as the expression of the intention behind it, one of the circumstances determining the meaning of the particular instance of the deed.[39]

APPETITE AND ENVY

If there is any area in which Abelard is not a relativist, it is that of self-preservation, the will to live—unless, of course, one is a martyr as in the example above:

> For consider: there is an innocent man whose cruel lord is so burning with rage against him that with a naked sword he chases him for his life. For long that man flees and as far as he can he avoids his own murder; in the end and unwillingly he is forced to kill him lest he be killed by him. Tell me, whoever you are, what bad will he had in doing this. If he wanted to escape death, he wanted to save his own life. But surely this was not a bad will?[40]

In the kill-or-be-killed confrontation of one violent will against another the relativizing perspective of both the *Ethics* and the *Fables* can be seen to stand in direct opposition to something on the order of instinct. In both instances ethical principle operates only insofar as it might mediate the natural urge on the part of every animal species, and of every individual member of a species, toward survival in the predatory context of a generalized state of warfare—Hobbes avant la lettre?—among the beasts.

Where the struggle for survival is concerned, Marie subscribes to something on the order of a marauding food chain in which each animal seeks to ingest those that find themselves below it while risking ingestion by those higher on the spoliative ladder. Thus, "The Mouse and the Frog" (no. 3), in which the frog, seeking to swallow a mouse, tries to drown it by attaching a string to its foot and plunging into deep water, until both are swept away by an observant kite that ignores the mouse and devours the frog instead. So too, "The Fox and the Eagle" (no. 10), in which an eagle swoops down and carries off one of the fox's young to her nest, in return for which the fox takes a burning brand and sets the eagle's nest on fire. The moral of the tale has to do with mistreatment and redress, or with a certain Realpolitik in the hierarchized humanized animal kingdom:

> Par ceste essample entendum nus
> Que si est del riche orguillus:
> Ja del povre n'avera merci
> Pur sa pleinte, ne pur sun cri.
> Mes si cil se pust dunc venger,
> Sil verreit l'um tost suppleer." (v. 17)

> This story has a lesson which
> Tells of a man haughty and rich:
> He shows the poor no charity
> No matter what their cry or plea.
> But if the poor can wreak vengeance,
> The rich will bow in deference.

The question of deference reappears in "The Ailing Lion" (no. 14), for the dying beast is quickly surrounded by those who would profit from his frailty, who would take his place. "Some came to see what they'd receive:/ What gifts the lion by will would leave" ("E teus i a i vunt pur dun / A la devise del leün" [v. 9]). Others come to strike a blow with impunity at the king of the beasts in whom they sense weakness, in this tale whose concluding epimythium teaches a cynical lesson that is part and parcel of the moral universe of Marie's *Fables*:

> Ki unc chiece en nunpoeir,
> Si piert sa force e sun saveir.
> Mut le tienent en grant vilte,
> Nis les plusurs qui l'unt amé. (v. 35)

> That he who sinks to impotence,
> Who's lost strength and intelligence,
> Will be regarded with great scorn,
> Even by those whose love was sworn.

We have seen a similar warning in "The Crow and the Ewe" (no. 40), which has to do with how people's own sense of what they can get away with determines their behavior: "A cat well knows which beard to lick!/ The sly are never at a loss/ To know whom they can walk across" ("Bien seit chaz ki

barbe il lecche!/Bien s'aparceit li vezïez/Les quels il peot aver suz piez"
[v. 20]). A similar lesson is to be found in "The Wolf King" (no. 29), where
the withdrawal of the lion leaves the wolf free to devour all the other animals, again despite his sworn oath "that he'd touch no beast anywhere." Finally, a number of tales like "The Bat" (no. 23) or "The Wolf and the Beetle"
(no. 65) recount the internecine wars between the species of the animal
kingdom, just as "The Eagle, the Hawk, and the Doves" (no. 62) contains
the tale of a hawk who is the eagle's seneschal and who menaces the doves
playing below him, with the understanding that the predatory instinct of
each bird species is merely held in check by the species immediately superior to it.

The case has been made that the state of perpetual warfare among the
beasts is predicated upon a specifically ornithological model. Jean Batany
maintains, for example, that the aggressive pecking order that we see in a tale
like "The Eagle, the Hawk, and the Doves," which reflects contemporaneous social reality, was originally articulated in terms of the world of birds.[41]
Whether or not the motif began with fowl, it was by the twelfth century
sufficiently generalized and sufficiently shared by other species as to render
the search for sources somewhat less urgent. Indeed, one of the ways that
contemporaneous human struggles for territory were figured was in terms
of the animal world; and this particularly in the Anglo-Normandy where
Marie de France, irrespective of which side of the Channel, resided. Henry
I is described as "a lion of justice." The chaos of the reign of his successor is
described by the chronicler of Battle Abbey, the Norman war memorial to
the victory at Hastings, as a bestial struggle: "Stephen became king but his
justice was little regarded and he who was strongest got most."[42] John of
Salisbury, who might have been Marie's contemporary and even might have
known her if she, like he, knew the court of Henry II, also uses animal im-
agery to describe Stephen's reign, though the serious tone, the violence of
the description, and the absence of any narrative thread make the bestially
defined descriptions of court life contained in John's *Entheticus* as far from
fable as one might imagine:

> To this man who ordered the customs and laws of the ancients to be torn
> away, arbitrariness counted as reason. He surpassed Midas in avarice, the lion
> in savagery, the cunning fox in deceits and tricks, he who oppressed the
> people, who despised law and equity, than whom every wolf and tiger was
> more gentle, dirty more than a pig, more butting than any he-goat, a seller
> of the church, strong by treachery, eager for human blood and a defender of
> wild beasts, he who was a public enemy with the title of king.[43]

So too, Thomas Becket rails against the "bestiae curiae"; and he is not alone.[44] Gerald of Wales, Richard Fitz Neal, Glanvill, Peter of Bois, Walter Map all describe the court of Henry II as a competitive terrain on which courtiers compete with each other, and artists compete with courtiers, for the recognition that is the equivalent of territory, a simultaneously social and ecological niche.[45]

Regardless of its origin, the predatory rule is generalized for Marie and operates not only among the birds but among all the species. Nor would it be so significant were it not for the fact that this model of belligerent nature finds an equivalent social model within the *Lais*. Indeed, Marie provides a paradigm of human behavior in the prologue to "Guigemar" that is not only based upon a metaphor from the animal world but completely consonant with the competitive, dog-eat-dog, kill-or-be-killed ethos of the *Fables:*

> Mais quant il a en un païs
> Hummë u femme de grant pris,
> Cil ki de sun bien unt envie
> Sovent en dïent vileinie;
> Sun pris li volent abeisser:
> Pur ceo commencent le mestier
> Del malveis chien coart felun,
> Ki mort la gent par traïsun. (v. 7)

But when there exists in a country a man or woman of great renown, people who are envious of their abilities frequently speak insultingly of them in order to damage this reputation. Thus they start acting like a vicious, cowardly, treacherous dog that will bite others out of malice.

Marie's portrayal of the courtier as a biting dog is not an original one. Boethius refers to the vicious courtiers at Theodoric's court—and the analogy has been made between the administratively centralized Ostrogothic court and that of Henry II—as "palatinae canes."[46] Though the genre of criticism of court life is less developed on the French side of the Channel than in England, Alain de Lille speaks of "henchmen of princes, the palace dogs."[47]

Given all that has been written about Marie de France, relatively little space has been accorded the theme of envy, which provides an essential link between the social world of the *Lais* and the natural world of the *Fables,* which furnishes a common model for human and animal behavior, and which is indeed one of the themes of the age.[48] Among the ills decried by the social critics of the court of Henry II, none occupies greater pride of place than envy. And not only do John of Salisbury, Walter Map, Nigel Wireker, Thomas Becket, and Gerald of Wales share with Marie a common obsession with the psychological causes and social effects of envy, but the terms they use are so similar as to seem traceable less to the spirit of the age, especially since the theme is less prevalent in France than in Anglo-Normandy, than to a shared social milieu. Walter Map offers in *De Nugis Curialium* a general theory of envy and an origin in the genealogy of the Gods. Linked to the fallen angel Lucifer, Envy's envy of those above her (and accompanying scorn of those below) is but the sign of the attempt "at regaining her old home." Envy, moreover, is limitless: "Every other vice seems to have some limits marked out to it; this one alone oversteps all bounds, repines at being shut within the world, has her pestilent abode in all that live in earth, sea, or air, so that even worm may be seen to envy worm."[49]

The envious worm—the worm of envy—is the lowliest of the creatures attached to the metaphorics of animal envy. Thomas Becket speaks of the "worm" as well as the "serpent" with its dangerous bite.[50] Walter Map draws upon the realm of the birds and the insects in his description of the justiciars of Henry II's court preying upon the weak as well as upon each other:

> There, too, are creatures of the night, the screech-owl, whose eyes love darkness and hate light. . . . [T]hough they place careful ambushes everywhere, their first concern is to follow up the odour of carrion. . . . This Court, too, sends out beings whom it calls justices, sheriffs, undersheriffs and beadles, to make strict inquisition. These leave nothing untouched or untried and, bee-like, sting the unoffending—yet their stomach escapes uninjured.[51]

John of Salisbury, like Marie, settles upon the comparison of envious courtiers, schoolmen, and monks to biting dogs:

> A happy lot is a stimulant to envy; and a wretched man alone is free from these, and he alone is without enemy. While consuming jealousy longs to harm others and fans the flames, it is most of all consumed by its own fire; and it is stabbed by its own spurs, it gnaws itself with its cruel teeth and utterly perishes from its own attack. No one is able to avoid the biting and the jaws of the dogs which the school, which the cloister, which the harmful court favors.[52]

Nor is there any question of how envy works—what excites it, what its object is, what sort of speech and acts it elicits. It will be remembered that Marie associates envy with accomplishment, as "when there exists in a country men or women of great renown." In a spectacular version of Marie's initial perception and indeed a further link between the two, Abelard ascribes his persecution by others to their envy of his intellectual prowess. Thus, "William [of Champeaux] was eaten up with jealousy and consumed with anger" at the defection of students to the Parisian master. Banished to Melun, Abelard, citing Ovid—"Envy seeks the heights, the wind sweeps the summits"—claims that "the more his jealousy pursued me, the more my reputation spread." A similar situation arises with Anselm of Laon, whose students, "began secretly to turn him against me, until their base insinuations succeeded in rousing his jealousy," in what amounts to a vicious cycle in which the envy of others serves for Abelard as proof of the essential rightness of his positions.[53] So too, John of Salisbury, in a cynical version of Marie's envy of merit, recognizes that in the life of the court the more one has, the more one is envied, "because by winning for yourself the favor of one, you excite the envy of all the rest. For they regard themselves as deprived to their own hurt of whatever is bestowed upon others."[54] Gerald of Wales, again like Marie, links envy to injured literary merit, defending his *Topography* against those whose enviousness of its evident qualities is expressed in both praise and scorn.[55] He too, in a phrase redolent of Marie's concern with reputation as well as with sending her message out so that those who envy her might begin to bite, links the viciousness of literary reception to the enduring quality of writing as opposed to the transitory nature of the voice, "since written works, once they have been published, do not pass away, they continue in being to the everlasting shame or renown of their author."[56]

The image of literary life at the court of Henry II is one of intense rivalry among courtier poets, as we see in Huc de Rotcland's attack upon Walter Map, which resembles Denis Piramus's attack upon Marie (see above, p. 13):

> El mund nen ad un sul si sage,
> Ki tuz jurs seit en un curage,
> Kar cist secles l'ad ore en sei:
> Nel metez mie tut sur mei!
> Sul ne sai pas de mentir l'art,
> Walter Map reset ben sa part;
> Nepurquant a la meie entente
> Ne quit pas, ke nul de vus mente.[57]

There is not a single man alive so wise that he can always be of the same mind, for he is of this world. Don't lay it all on me! I am not the only person

who knows the art of lying, Walter Map is very good at it too. Nevertheless,
I don't believe willingly that any of you tells lies.

What I am suggesting is not only that the dates of Hue de Roteland's literary activity (1174–91), like those of John of Salisbury and Walter Map, coincide with those of Marie, but that the coincidence of interest in the question of envy sets a context for our understanding of Marie's yoking of the
theme of envy in the *Lais* with that of animal appetite in the *Fables,* while
it also points to a closer link between Marie de France and the court of
Henry II than has heretofore been established. Here again, in the absence of
hard documentary evidence, the claim, which is not original, is still somewhat conjectural.[58] Nonetheless, this particular nexus of concern with the
omnipresence of envy as a psychological and social mechanism, the relative
absence of such an obsession among French as opposed to Anglo-Norman
writers, and the fascination with the metaphorics of animality lends cre-
dence to the claim that Marie lived and worked in and around the court of
Henry II, who, after all, moved freely and frequently between the two sides
of the Channel.[59]

    Within the human world, by which Marie here means the social world
of life at court, envy functions such that each individual remains on the
lookout for weakness in others, lies in wait to weaken those possessed of an
acknowledged strength, seeks to bite those perceived to be bitable.[60] The
theoretical model of social behavior found at the beginning of "Guigemar"
is reproduced elsewhere in the *Lais* among those who are envious of Lanval
and who conspire with King Arthur in his neglect, among the knights envious of the hero of "Eliduc," in the wife of "Le Fresne" envious of her pregnant neighbor. Yet, the model of the vicious, envious courtier anxious to
weaken those in whom he perceives strength and ready to pounce upon
those in a weakened state finds its most general expression in the paradigm
of the state of nature in the *Fables,* for example in "The Ailing Lion" (no.
14), where the animals assemble to assail the king of the beasts only when he
has been immobilized:

> Li bucs de ses cornes la but(ut)e.
> E li asnes, que pas nel dute,
> Od le pié le fiert sur le piz.
> De l'autre part vient li gupilz,
> As denz le mort par les oreilles. (v. 13)

> The goat used horns the lion to butt.
> And then the ass, who feared him not,

With hoof struck lion on the chest.
Fox, from another side, came next,
And with sharp teeth he bit each ear.[61]

It would be hard to imagine a more powerful representation of the imbrication of human and animal worlds than the analogy between the "vicious, cowardly, treacherous dogs" of the *Lais,* ready to bite those whose reputation they have attacked, and the butting goat, kicking ass, and biting fox of the *Fables,* which profit from the infirmity of the lion. The analogy offers further proof, moreover, of what we have identified as the situationally defined ethos of the *Fables,* of which the *Lais* offer only a hint: that is, the eagerness of each individual to take another's place, which leads, as we shall see, to a paradigm of social integration responsible for the fable's most radical social effects.

LOGIC AND THE BODY

All of this is a way of saying, of course, that envy as a socially motivating force within human society finds an equivalent in, indeed is underpinned by, the predatory power of the appetite of animals, which is predicated in the *Fables* at the level of nature and is a natural function of the body. The nature of the beast and, by analogy, of the human animal is to eat or be eaten. This much belongs in some extended sense to the horizon of expectation of the fable and, though interesting for the link that it builds with the *Lais,* would not serve to distinguish Marie from the other fablers ready, as she acknowledges, to take her place. What does separate Marie from the pack has to do with her interest in logic, also a characteristic of the genre; more precisely, with the juxtaposition evident through the *Fables* of logic and appetite, of reason and the body. For the question that Marie poses most persistently in the *Fables* is not whether man acts like an animal (this much is obvious), but whether that which makes him human, that is, his capacity for reason, might overcome his fundamentally predatory animal nature. This is why so many of the fables—and the issue is not unrelated to their humor—seem to stage a drama of logic and the body.

One senses the importance of the juxtaposition of the logical faculties and the flesh almost from the start in, say, "The Wolf versus the Lamb" (no. 2), in which the threatened lamb, accused of drinking upstream of the wolf, rightly points out that in reality "my water comes from you," and rightly responds to the accusation that his father did the same six months previously that he was not yet born; all of which serves only to provoke that moment of foreclosure, characteristic of a number of fables which are variants of "The Wolf versus the Lamb," in which logic cedes to violent attack, in which the body cuts short the possibility of any further exchange, in which language, in a word, cedes to appetite: "'So what?' the wolf responded next/. . . The wolf then grabbed the lamb so small,/Chomped through his neck, extinguished all" ("'E ke pur ceo?' li lus ad dit/. . . Dunc prist li lus l'aignel petit,/As denz l'estrangle, si l'ocit" [vv. 26, 29]). So too, "The Dog and the Ewe" (no. 4) with its false accusation or premise of the ewe's not having returned the bread that he did not borrow and whose logical consequences are also false. "'Why lie about such petty stuff?/Return it or the going's rough!'" ("'Menti en ot pur poi de pris/Ore li rendist, einz qu'il fust pis!'" [v. 23]), menaces the dog who waits, along with the kite and the wolf, for the death of the ewe who has sold his wool in order to pay the trumped up judicial costs, as the breakdown of logic again yields flesh:

> Li chiens i vient, sa leine en porte,
> E li escufles d'autre part,
> E puis li lus, trop est li tart
> Que la chars fust entre eus destreite,
> Kar de viande eurent suffreite. (v. 28)

> The dog was there, her fleece to strip.
> The kite came for his share of fleece;
> The wolf was anxious for his piece.
> They could not wait her flesh to eat,
> For they'd been hankering after meat.

The "hankering after meat" of "The Dog and the Ewe" finds a parallel in "The Lion, the Buffalo, and the Wolf" (no. 11A), another parable of logic versus appetite. For when the time comes to divide the spoils of the chase among the members of the hunting party, the lion claims that the deer, which has been divided into four parts, is entirely his. The first part, the lion argues, is his rightful portion as king; the second part comes to him as a member of the hunting party; the third portion is his "by right because he killed the deer"; and the fourth belongs to him, the lion threatens, "because anyone who took it would be his mortal enemy" ("E ki la quarte part prendreit,/Ses enemis morteus serreit" [v. 23]). "The Lion, the Sheep, and the Goat" (no. 11B) contains essentially the same tale with the variation that the third part goes to the lion because "he is the strongest" (v. 36) and an extended moral in which Marie acknowledges the relationship between social hierarchy and gain: "E si nul guain deivent partir,/Li riches vout tut retenir" (v. 47). In both "The Lion, the Buffalo, and the Wolf" and "The Lion, the Sheep, and the Goat," a certain logic, or false logic, is juxtaposed with force, force being the equivalent of animal appetite in a contest according to which the strongest prevails: "When they heard what the lion said," we read in no. 11B, "His friends left all the deer and fled" ("Tuit li cumpainun, quant l'oïrent,/Tut li laisserent, si fuïrent" [v. 39]).

The same is true, as we have seen, of "The Wolf and the Sheep" (no. 50), in which the wolf, having taken a vow not to eat meat, is unable to keep his vow and devours a sheep by declaring it to be a salmon. This is a tale that turns around the principle that appetite rules all; rather, that appetite trumps reason in the moment of bodily foreclosure, which in some extended materialistic sense is another version of the fatalism of the *Lais,* the medieval rendering of the body as destiny, without, of course, the lai's tragic effect. "The Preacher and the Wolf" (no. 82) represents a theoretical version of "The Wolf and the Sheep," as the aborted grammar lesson in which *A,* *B,* and *C* end up, in the mouth of the wolf, spelling "a lamb" brings home in speech the precedence of the body. Finally, in what is perhaps the most complicated rendering of Marie's obsession with logic versus appetite, "The Sick Lion, the Deer, and the Fox" (no. 71), the fox, whose urge to devour is such that he cannot wait even until the deer is flayed, manages to escape prosecution with the claim that the deer had no heart: otherwise he would not willingly have come a third time to court. Marie's conclusion introduces a twist into what elsewhere appears to be the law of the strongest, that is, the law of the strongest argument:

> Par memes ceste raisun,
> Quant fols prent sage a cumpainun,
> Si nul rien deivent partir,
> Li sages se set al meuz tenir,
> Par parole l'autre deceit;
> Sa mençunge pur verité creit. (v. 69)

> It's often like this in the end,
> Whene'er a fool has a wise friend.
> If something should be portioned, then
> The wise man has more acumen.
> His talk deceives the other, who
> Believes the smart man's lies are true.

"The Sick Lion, the Deer, and the Fox" represents a triumph of appetite over will and of false logic over appetite, in this tale, like "The Lion, the Buffalo, and the Wolf" and "The Lion, the Sheep, and the Goat," of the division of spoils.

This particular series of tales strikes to the core of a number of issues of concern to jurists as well as social critics at the court of Henry II. Indeed, John of Salisbury is outraged at the widespread corruption of judges and provincial governors[62] and equates the inequality of formal justice with the predatory nature of the animal realm:

> Wisdom says: "The wild ass in the desert is the prey of the lion, and so are the poor the food of the rich. And as humility is an abomination in the eyes of the haughty, so is the poor man abhorred by the rich. The rich man when in trouble will find strength in his friends; but when a humble man falls, he is driven away by those who know him. If the rich man is cozened he has many to aid him; he speaks proudly and they justify him. When the man of poor estate is cozened, he is only blamed therefor; he speaks wisely and no place is made for him. The rich man speaks, and all keep silence, and extol even to the clouds what he said; the poor man speaks, and they say, 'Who is this man?' and if he stumble, they destroy him."[63]

In a passage reminiscent of "The Dog and the Ewe" (no. 4), John traces in the *Entheticus* the "Consequences at the Bar" of judicial bribery:

> Under this king the poor wolf feared hanging, worthy of being set free if he could give a sheep: if he could give a sheep, stolen or snatched away by force, carried off from a widow, then was he without reproach; the wolf who could shear the flock and knew how to give wool, this wolf was innocent, this wolf was worthy of a sheep. It did not harm the fox to have deceived, if he was willing to share his gain with the shepherd.[64]

Walter Map too denounces the corruption of the royal justiciars, sheriffs, and sergeants who "swarm like bees everywhere sucking their honey."[65]

Alongside the dishonesty of judges, the great and not so great Angevin landholders were concerned by the legal, or seemingly legal, or sometimes legally justifiable, seizures of land that characterized Stephen's reign as well as that of Henry. Moreover, it was by no means obvious or according to custom that, in the phrase of W. L. Warren, "wrongs should be righted only by recourse to the courts." On the contrary: "A man, it was felt, should be prepared to fight for his rights, and have recourse to the courts only if self-help failed. Customary law, therefore, did not frown upon a man who forcibly deprived another—provided he had right, as well as might, on his side. It was only 'unjust disseisin' which was held to be wrong."[66] Under Henry II, however, the question of dispossession was given a legal cast with, first, the proclamation of an "assize" in 1166 by which dispossession made "unjustly and without judgment" came to constitute a wrong against the king's peace, and, after the chaos of 1176, what came to be known as the "assize of novel disseisin" according to which a "jury of recognition," led by a royal justiciar, was to answer the questions: (1) "had the plaintiff, as he alleged, been disseised of the freehold in question, unjustly and without judgement, within the time limit laid down?" (2) "did the person who was alleged by the plaintiff to have committed the disseisin in fact do so?" The losing party, judged "at the king's mercy," paid whatever monetary "penalty (amercement) was appropriate."[67] It is hard not to see in the question of forcible seizure of land, of war versus legal procedure, or, within the judicial process, of justifiable versus nonjustifiable expropriation according to the law of the strongest, a playing out of some version of the issue of violence versus reason that lies at the core of Marie's *Fables,* and that is expressed over and over again in the opposition between logic and the body.

CHANGING HABITAT

The question of reasoning—the scholastic cast of the *Fables* involving debate, logic, and false logic—versus appetite is for Marie essentially a pedagogical one, as she asks over and over again, What can be learned? What are the limits of the body? How and to what extent can the body be disciplined? What is the relationship of nature to nurture? For a number of tales, again a minigenre within the whole, involve animals that seek to change their status or function within the bestial hierarchy.

"The Ass Who Wanted to Play with His Master" (no. 15) is the story of an ass who observes a dog's actions and is envious of his rewards. Seeking to emulate the dog, he overpowers his master physically and is beaten, the moral of the tale having to do with the limits of physical characteristics and birth. Marie condemns "Those who to raise themselves aspire/And who into a higher place desire—/One that's not fitting to their girth/And most of all, not to their birth" ("Que tant se veulent eshaucer/e en tel liu aparagier—/Que ne avient pas a lur corsage,/Ensurketut a lur parage" [v. 45]). We find a similar message in "The Hawk and the Owl" (no. 80), in which a hawk hatches an owl's eggs and is outraged when the owl young foul her nest. The lesson, as the hawk recognizes, is that one can hatch an egg, yet one cannot change the nature of the hatched. "The Hawk and the Owl," which is about the limits of learning, is paired with "The Eagle, the Hawk, and the Crane" (no. 81), which extends the domestic situation to a public one. In this story of the war between an eagle and all the other birds against a hawk, the birds decide to send a crane, because of "her long neck," to flush the hawk from a hollow in an oak, with the result that, when the hawk grabs its beak, the frightened crane befouls the birds waiting anxiously below. Shamed and abandoned by her allies, the crane flees to another land, yet over the sea meets a seagull who asks if the crane still has the "implement of her shame"; and to the reply that she still has it with her, the seagull advises her to return home since "it may do worse things elsewhere" (v. 43). The moral of the tale is, again, that one can change location but not one's essential nature. Those fables depicting the difficulty and the limits of change illustrate the proverb "The leopard cannot change its spots," which Marie renders as "The wolf cannot change his skin." Indeed, "The Grey Wolf" (no. 66), the shortest of the fables, is another of the parables of pedagogy that, like "The Preacher and the Wolf" (no. 82), have to do with the bounds of learning:

> Par veille essample recunte ici
> Que tuit li lus sunt enveilli
> En cele pel, u il sunt né;
> La remainent tut lur eé.
> Ki sur le lu meist bon mestre,
> Quil doctrinast a estre prestre,
> Si sereit il tut dis gris lus,
> Fel e engrés, leiz e hidus. (v. 1)

> An ancient story here is told
> Of how all wolves grew very old
> Inside the skin they were born in,
> Spending their whole life in this skin.
> No matter who might be his teacher
> And tell him how to be a preacher,
> A grey wolf's what he'll be for aye,
> Mean and ugly, base and sly.

This is not to say that wolves do not try to change. On the contrary, in "The Two Wolves" (no. 88), one wolf, lamenting to another that men will not go near them, proposes that they do a good deed by helping men in a nearby

field to gather and bind their stalks. As soon as the animals approach, however, the men cry out and the wolves run, showing, again, the difficulty of
changing nature, or, rather, of changing the perception of one's nature.

Several tales turn, as we have seen, around the issue of nature and perception, or the inner essence of the beast versus the attempt to present itself
as other than it is, which is not unrelated to the nominalism we have identified with the wolf of "The Wolf and the Sheep" (no. 50) who pretends to
observe his vow not to eat meat by renaming a sheep a salmon. Thus, in
"The Bat" (no. 23), a bat sides first with the lion and then with the eagle
in the war between terrestrial animals and the birds, and in its companion,
"The Badger and the Pigs" (no. 77), a badger first pretends to be a pig, then
seeks to hide its feet. So too, the question of whether or not a wolf might
change its skin finds its analogue among the birds in the question of
whether a bird might switch feathers. In "The Peacock" (no. 31), a peacock
complains to Destiny that he cannot sing and would like a change of voice;
the crow of "The Crow in Peacock's Feathers" (no. 68) pulls out his own
feathers and "did in peacock feathers dress / To make his body beauteous"
("Des pennes al poün s'aürne. / Trestut sun cors bel aturne" [v. 9]). When
the peacocks recognize that he is not one of them, they mutilate him such
that he longs for his former body before "they beat him up; they killed the
crow" (v. 15). "The Crow in Peacock's Feathers" is thematically related to
"The Hare and the Deer" (no. 97) in which a hare, looking at a deer, asks
the Creator for horns, but once the boon is granted, he "could not carry
them around / And could not move with them, he found" ("Mes nes poeit
mie porter, / Kar ne saveit od tut aler" [v. 17]). The moral of "The Hare and
the Deer" is particularly interesting where the question of changing species,
and thus of social mobility, is concerned, encompassing as it does the theme
dear to Marie both in the *Fables* and the *Lais* of noxious envy:

> Par ceste essample veut mustrer:
> Le coveitus e le aver
> Veulent tuz jurz tant comencer
> E si se veulent eshaucer,
> Si enpernent par lur utrage,
> Que lur turne a damage. (v. 21)

> From this example you should see
> Folks covetous and miserly:
> They always start such projects as
> They think will raise their social class.

What they attempt through foolishness
Turns back on them, injurious.

Finally, it is no accident, I think, that Marie concludes her collection of animal tales with a fable of nature versus habit, as if neither nature nor nurture were to have the last word, which belongs by rights in the animal tale to the enduring conflict between the two. Thus, the woman in "The Woman and Her Hen" (no. 103), observing her barnyard fowl scratching for grain, offers to feed her. The hen, however, claims that to stop scratching would be against its nature—"Such is my nature and my way" (v. 20)—as nature and nurture seem to merge. Nor can it be an accident that the very habit of mind that cannot be changed has to do, as the moral shows, with unchecked appetite:

> Par ceste essample veut mustrer,
> Que plusurs gens poënt trover
> Aveir e ceo que unt mester;
> Mes ne poënt pas changier
> Lur nature ne lur usage,
> Tuz jurs coveitent en lur curage. (v. 21)

> And thus we see, from hen and grain,
> That many people can obtain
> Riches and everything they need;
> And yet they cannot change, indeed,
> Their nature or accustomed ways,
> They lust within, for all their days.

Appetite within the animal realm is for Marie the moral equivalent of envy within the social world, as the *Fables* end where the *Lais* began, with the envy of "vicious, cowardly, treacherous dogs."

The question of nature versus nurture is nowhere more present in the *Fables* than in the series of tales involving changing places, as if the possibility of shifting animal habitat were synonymous collectively with the pretensions of the individual to change his or her appearance or the appearance of his or her behavior. We have seen, for example, that "The Mouse and the Frog" (no. 3) represents a drama of seduction in which the frog tries to devour the mouse by removing it from its natural element. More important are the tales in which the animals themselves conceive the possibility of a move. In "The Hares and the Frogs" (no. 22), some of the hares decide that they would like to "leave their grove" in order to escape its dangers. The wise hares, however, counsel against such a move; and when their counsel is rejected, the hares come upon a pond where their presence frightens the frogs, leading them to conclude that "after foolishness we strove/When we abandoned our home grove" ("Que nus alum querant folie,/Que nostre grave avum guerpie" [v. 25]). As in "The Eagle, the Hawk, and the Crane" (no. 81), in which the crane learns that she still has the "implement of her shame" wherever she goes, or "The Knight and the Old Man" (no. 101), in which the knight, also anxious for safety, is advised to go to "a land where you never see anyone and no one knows where you are," the frogs head home, having learned, as we see in the moral, that the level of fear is everywhere the same: "No kingdom will they ever find/Anywhere known to humankind/Where everyone lives free of fear,/Where toil and sorrow disappear" ("Jamés regne ne troverunt/Ne en cele tere ne vendrunt/Que tut tens seient sanz poür,/U sanz travail u sanz dolur" [v. 37]).

The desire for a change of habitat is linked in Marie's thinking to the desire for a change of sovereignty, as is visible in "The Frogs in Search of a King" (no. 18), in which the frog community seeks to break with a long residential tradition, to move from water to land and to live under a new leader, to which Destiny accedes by sending a log. The log, which neither moves nor speaks, incurs the scorn of the frog community, which defecates on it until it sinks. When the frogs then appeal for a replacement, Destiny sends an adder that devastates the frogs, whose protests elicit the cynical reminder that they have only received the ruler they had asked for. "The Frogs in Search of a King" is paired with "The Doves and the Hawk" (no. 19), in which the doves, anxious for a protector, choose a hawk who ends up devouring them.

If the moral of the tales involving the individual's desire for a change of appearance is that "the leopard cannot change its spots" or "the wolf cannot change its skin," the moral of the desire for change of habitat is that "the grass always appears greener on the other side of the fence," which is precisely the point of "The Horse and the Hedge" (no. 63), in which a horse sees the grass in a meadow but not the thorns in the hedge, which prick him as he jumps in. A similar lesson is to be learned from "The Beetle" (no. 75), in which a beetle, filled with envy observing an eagle ("Enz en sun quor fu mut envïus" [v. 8]), seeks to leave his dunghill and fly with the birds. The beetle, like the bat of no. 23 or the badger of no. 77, discovers that he can neither fly like an eagle, nor get back to his homey dunghill, as, dying of hunger, he willingly renounces pride.

Of the fables oriented around the possibility and the consequences of a change of habitat, none come closer to contemporaneous social reality than those that focus upon the relationship between animals in the countryside and those in town. These constitute a grouping inherited from the classical animal tale, which can be traced as far back as Aesop, a genealogy that might seem to work against the historical specificity of Marie's interest in the motif. Yet, rather than discount the specificity of Marie's focus upon the advantages of rural versus urban habitat, the longevity of the motif merely reinforces the dynamic role of the fable at moments of intense negotiation between country and town, of which the second half of the twelfth century was certainly one.[68] In "The City Mouse and the Country Mouse" (no. 9), the urban rodent's visit to the country is capped by an invitation for "her country friend" to visit her "fancy rooms," which dazzle until the butlers enter and send both scampering. The moral of the tale is not different from that of "The Hares and the Frogs"—that fear is to be found everywhere and that one is better off in his or her natural home: "I prefer my woods, alone,/In safety and without distress/To grand rooms and unhappiness" ("Meuz amereie al bois par mei,/A seürté e sanz destresce,/Que en tes solers od tristesce" [v. 50]). A companion piece is to be found in "The Wolf and the Dog" (no. 26), in which the wolf, lured to town with the promise of food and a life of ease, balks as soon as he catches a glimpse of the dog's collar and leash. The wolf claims, in this tale without a formal moral, that he would rather live as a free wolf in the woods than luxuriously on a chain (v. 37). In what appears as a reversal of the proverb that "the air of the city makes free," the wolf asserts his own freedom of choice in rejecting the city's constraint: "Ja chaëne ne choiserai!" (v. 36).

SOCIAL MOBILITY

To the extent that the subgroup of tales involving a change of habitat presents a series of lessons in staying home and adaptation, they are part and parcel of what we have identified as Marie's existential bent. Indeed, here she seems to assert the primacy of accommodation to one's natural milieu, which might even take the form of a cross-species acclimation. In "The Lamb and the Goat" (no. 32), for example, a lamb raised by a goat that urges it to return to its natural parents claims that the goat is more his mother than the sheep: "'My reasoning, I think, is good:/My mother's she who gave me food,/For that's a better one than she/Who carried, then abandoned me'" ("'M'est avis que meuz deit estre/Ma mere, cele que me sot pestre;/Meuz que cele ke me porta/E qui de li me desevera.'" [v. 13]). "The Lamb and the Goat" is a significant but tricky fable: significant in that it counterbalances the series of tales touting the foolishness or the danger of changing habitat; tricky in that the apparent prevalence of nurture over nature contained in the moral is, in reality, a blending of the two such that the goat's adopted mother is naturalized by virtue of virtuous habit. To the degree that the goat, having adapted to his new milieu, has made the move of which the hares (no. 22), the crane (no. 81), the horse (no. 63), and the beetle (no. 75) are incapable, Marie relativizes such displacements, which are, as with almost everything in the *Fables,* situational, a function of context and not of nature. Both the lamb's birth mother and her adopted mother might, through their own behavior, be naturalized.

The motif of changing habitat, or even body type, is a thinly veiled metaphor for the changing of social station, which may from the start be built into the generic expectations of fable. In the epilogue to book 2, Phaedrus contrasts Aesop's birth and his worth, linking the latter, if not to social ascension during his lifetime, at least to the ascent of his reputation after death: "The Athenians set up a statue in honour of the gifted Aesop, and by so doing placed a slave on a pedestal of everlasting fame, that all men might know that the path of honour lies open and that glory is awarded not according to birth, but according to merit."[69] So too, the *Pancatantra,* written at the time of the rise of the civil administration as part of ancient Indian feudalism, emphasizes the rewards of individual effort as opposed to fate or birth: "The goddess of Wealth approaches (comes to abide with) the lion-like (eminent) man who is industrious. It is the weak-minded (lazy persons) who say it is fate, it is fate (that gives); setting aside fate entirely, put forth manly effort to the best of your strength, for if after an effort is made, there be no success, where is the fault in the case?"[70]

In the specific historical context of twelfth-century Anglo-Normandy, the metaphorics of natural places and newfound homes, and even changing bodily parts, are unquestionably linked to the anxieties of social promotion and the development of a professional administrative class—of *curiales* or *ministeriales*—at the Plantagenet and then the Angevin court of Henry I and that of his grandson Henry II.[71] And almost all who comment on life at court praise or protest what was perceived even at the time to be new opportunities for, and forms of, social mobility. Orderic Vitalis complained about Henry I in the 1120s that "he pulled down many great men from positions of eminence. . . . He ennobled others of base stock who had served him well, raised them, so to say, from the dust, and heaping all kinds of favour on them, stationed them above earls and famous castellans."[72] John of Salisbury in the 1170s lamented the courtiers who tried "to find some way whereby they can lift themselves aloft on one side or the other, whereby they can become more powerful than others."[73] Raoul le Noir reproached Henry II for having conferred high office upon "bastard slaves and simple soldiers."[74] Gerald of Wales asked of Henry II, "Who behaved more nobly to commoners and more ignobly to the aristocracy? Who raised the lowly higher or depressed the high so low?"[75] Those who chronicled the English court decried the new men who were coming increasingly to occupy places in the king's inner circle, places that once belonged to the baronage, members of old landed families who exemplified feudal values and rights—the most germane of which was the right to violence, to settle their disputes by recourse not to trial but to judicial combat and to private armies and war. The right, in short, to make their own law, which resembled nothing so much as Marie's law of the strongest characteristic of the animal world.

As opposed to the fixed social categories that have traditionally been associated with what for better or worse is known as the feudal world, philosophically subtended by what D. E. Luscombe terms the "Platonic examplarism" of the early Middle Ages, the Anglo-Norman court is perceived by contemporary chroniclers as a dynamic place where the potential for social advancement, fed by the principle of envy as a lubricating, motivating force, was compared by Walter Map to Augustine's concept of time itself: "'In time I exist, and of time I speak,' said Augustine: and added, 'What time is I know not.' In a like spirit of perplexity I may say that in the court I exist and of the court I speak, and what the court is, God knows, I know not. I do know however that the court is not time; but temporal it is, changeable and various, space-bound and wandering, never continuing in one state."[76]

While historians debate whether the new social mobility began with Henry I and was merely continued by Henry II, as well as the extent to which great landholding families were actually displaced by new men, that is, the extent to which the chronicler's complaints are exaggerated, of this there can be no doubt: the perception of the possibility of social mobility at the Anglo-Norman court was accompanied by altered means of achieving social success, both of which are related to the tension apparent in the *Fables* between logic and appetite.[77] The first to benefit were the chroniclers themselves. Walter Map, born to the middle class, rose from clerk to canon and eventually represented Henry II at the Third Lateran Council of 1179. John of Salisbury, possibly of common origins, rose through the ranks by having studied with the most celebrated masters of the day—Abelard, Robert of Melun, Thierry of Chartres, Peter Helias, Gilbert de la Porrée. Gerald of Wales was, in the phrase of Egbert Türk, the "erudite reject of a line of powerful lords."[78] Peter of Blois belonged to the "petite noblesse" of Brittany settled in Blois. So too, those whom the chroniclers observe rise or fall from the rank to which they were born: small and middle knights became great magnates, petty clerks, bishops, as Henry I and Henry II relied increasingly upon capable managers, regardless of origins, for the administration of the realm—Hugh de Gundeville, Robert Marmion, Richard de Canville, Gerard de Canville, Saher de Quincy, Fulk Painell, William Fitz-Hamo, Thomas Bardulf, Robert de Stuteville, Geffroy Ridel, Gilbert Fitz Reinfred, or Robert of Harcourt.[79] Geoffrey Fitz Peter rose from humble origins to the highest office in the kingdom; William de Sainte-Mère-Eglise, from clerk to bishop. The career of William Briwerre, in the phrase of Ralph Turner, "covers half a century, c. 1175–1226, and charts an extraordinary rise from obscurity to the highest councils of government."[80] The great example of the reign of Henry II remains, however, that of Thomas Becket, whose parents were privileged Londoners, who studied in London and Paris, and who worked in the office of the archbishop of Canterbury before passing into the king's chancellery and assuming the ecclesiastical honor that would cost him his life. So too, Richard of Ilchester, who began as a royal clerk, became the archdeacon of Poitiers, served as Henry II's ambassador to Rome and to the German emperor, was nominated to succeed Becket in Henry's famous dictum, "I order you to hold a free election, but forbid you to elect anyone but Richard my clerk," and ended up, along with Thomas Brown, as the King's Remembrancer and Lord Treasurer's Remembrancer of the Exchequer.[81]

If life at court carried the potential for social ascension, it also bore the risk of decline. Nigel Wireker, the author of a long unclassifiable poem—part beast epic, part social satire entitled *The Book of Daun Burnel the Ass*, recounts the story in his *Tractatus contra curiales et officiales clericos* of a cleric who tries to invest his nephew with the office he occupies and in so doing takes a fall. The prelates of the bishop, scheming with the king's clerks, inform him that in order for a prebend to be attributed to another, the position must be vacant and he must therefore resign; and as soon as he does, the royal representative rises to remind the canonical court that only the king disposes of a vacant ecclesiastical office, whereupon the overly ambitions cleric loses all and dies destitute.[82]

If the new social order of the Anglo-Norman monarchy bore with it increased social mobility, such mobility implied a set of criteria based less upon inherited function and birth than upon merit and personal worth. John of Salisbury, who includes morals and character alongside nature in the determination of rank, wonders if merit were not a prerequisite even for kingship: "For the office of prince is not due to blood, but to merit; and there is no advantage in the rule of one who is born a king without being a king by merit."[83] Among the chief means of demonstrating merit was, of course, education. Walter Map articulates the relationship between learning and social ascension and, responding to a question posed by Glanvill, complains that "the gentry of our land are too proud or too lazy to put their children to learning, whereas of right only free men are allowed to learn the arts, which for that very reason are called 'liberal.'" He goes on to acknowledge that even those of servile status, "the villeins . . . (or rustics, as we call them) vie with each other in bringing up their ignoble and degenerate offspring to those arts which are forbidden to them; not that they may shed vices, but that they may gather riches."[84]

Though Walter's complaints might apply to the class of great landed magnates and villeins, they are less appropriate to the lower and middle levels of the knightly class or to the London patriciate to which many of the career administrators of the Angevin monarchy traced their origins. Of these, growing numbers were educated in the business schools or *ars notaria* at Oxford (and elsewhere), where they learned the skills—accounting, legal procedure, some Latin—that enabled them not only to enter royal service but to serve as the stewards of large estates.[85] Under Henry II education was increasingly a key to success, and it can be no accident that so much of Nigel Wireker's *Book of Daun Burnel the Ass* is taken up with the question so dear to Marie of the relationship between learning, animal nature, and rank.[86] Like Marie's tale "The Ass Who Wanted to Play with His Master" (no. 15) or "The Ass and the Lion" (no. 35), *Daun Burnel* poses the question of the limits of species, that is, of class;[87] it features, again like Marie's *Fables,* a long narrative about changing body parts ("Concerning the Ass That Wished to Have a Longer Tail"); but most of all, a large portion of the narrative of *Daun Burnel* is consumed by concern with the effects of education upon status. After being discouraged from seeking to shorten his tail by the tale within the tale of the cows Bicornis and Brunetta, Burnel resolves to sharpen his mind and to improve his condition by study:

> I'll make my way to Paris to devote
> Ten years to liberal arts—I'll not delay.
> Then to Bologna I'll return, if God
> Directs, to gain a knowledge of the law.
> The Holy Scriptures and decretals shall
> Complete my efforts, if my life is spared.

And so I'll have the title "Master" placed
Before Brunellus, and I'll thus be called.

. . . .

I'll be a public speaker without peer.
The Senate and the people will rush forth,
The rank and file will cry, "The master's here!"[88]

Despite the fact that "he had completed almost seven years" of schooling,
Burnel—like the wolf in Marie's fable of "The Preacher and the Wolf" (no.
82) which, repeating his ABCs, can only spell "lamb"—learns little. "Yet ab-
solutely nothing had he learned/Of what his master taught except "hee-
haw!"[89] To a degree uncharacteristic of Marie, Nigel Wireker seems to be on
the side of nature and indeed to demonstrate, as in his account of the mayor
of his town who has stolen a sack of grain, the difficulty of surpassing nature's "canine ways":

To strive with nature and its canine ways,
How difficult it is, no one can say.
To wipe away the marks of servile rank
Cannot be done by doctors nor by drugs.
The product always shows and cannot hide
What nature really is and whence it came.[90]

Rather, Wireker has hit upon something more cynical and profound, that
is, the strength of the principle of birth or how easily one generation's social
ascension is transformed into the next generation's inherited status even
when that status involves administrative function.[91]

To resume, what all this suggests is that the motif of changing habitat,
changing rulers, changing bodily attributes that constitutes a virtual subgenre of Marie's *Fables* is the expression of a wider anxiety having to do with
the transformation—beginning with Henry I, but especially under Henry
II—of Anglo-Norman society from the highly personalized pre-Conquest
system of shires and hundreds, ferms, danegeld, wapentake and hidage, toll
and team, watch and ward, sac and soc, francpledge, infangthief, king's
council or witan, into something on the order of an administratively efficient state in which individuals might—to some degree and in exceptional
cases—distinguish or extinguish themselves according to unique merit
rather than birth. Such a shift, which we associate with the rise of a managerial bureaucracy and rationalization of the state, which will occur only
slightly later in France as a result of contact with the Anglo-Norman model
after the French conquest of Normandy in 1203–4, implies in both instances

a depersonalization of power based upon the distinction, unthinkable within the world of provincial earldoms in England or independent duchies in France, between authority and its wielder, between the royal household and a royal administration capable of collecting taxes and keeping accounts, rendering legal judgments and enforcing sentences throughout an expanded and more unified realm.

I am not, of course, proposing that twelfth-century Anglo-Normandy knew anything on the order of what we think of as the bureaucratic meritocracies that arose in the wake of the democratic revolutions of the eighteenth century; rather that the possibility of changing one's status, even when the numbers are relatively small, produced an uneasiness to which the fable form lends itself in a particularly powerful way.[92] Indeed, the principle of species, and of the relationship of the individual member of a species to its class, upon which the animal tale is predicated, offers a potent vehicle for the articulation of anxious concern about just how personal personal power or worth really is. Which is another way of posing the question of the interchangeability of species as well as the question of the interchangeability of individuals within a particular group. For if, as Walter Map insists, the court is a place where individuals prey upon each other, it is also the case that, where function is concerned, they are interchangeable; and it is no accident that the vocabulary that Walter uses to describe how the court survives despite the fact that some of its members are constantly replacing others is drawn from the range of Aristotelian categorical terms, passed to the Middle Ages via Porphyry and Boethius, of genus and species, or the rules by which individuals belonging to the same group can—and the question is essential with respect to Marie—supplant or substitute for one another. "When I leave [the court]," Walter writes, "I know it perfectly: when I come back to it I find nothing or but little of what I left there: I am become a stranger to it, and it to me. The court is the same, its members are changed. I shall perhaps be within the bounds of truth if I describe it in the terms which Porphyry uses to define a genus, and call it a number of objects bearing a certain relation to one principle."[93] It is the idea of anonymity that produces concern in the knightly world in which a man is only as good as his name, and, as Walter makes clear in the story of a worthy knight whose identity remains a mystery, provokes the terror of the obscure conquering the unknown.[94]

CHAPTER SIX

Marie's *Fables* and the Rise of the Monarchic State

The question of geographical displacement as well as change of species and of bodily type has special significance for a society that is itself coming out of centuries of migration, invasion, territorial competition, and a lack of geographically fixed and rationalized institutions, a society that is, in fact, settling down, settling in as well as developing, as I have maintained elsewhere, the spatially fixed political and legal institutions that bring with them the elements of regularized judicial procedure as well as some notion of internal psychology according to which the individual is increasingly obliged to adapt his own will to collective norms.[1] In this light, the change of habitat subgroup that we outlined in the previous chapter can be seen as a negotiation not only between city and forest, nurture and nature, but between the reason associated with Marie's logical, relativizing, existential side and the demands of the body associated with appetite. This is another way of describing the difference between that which she conceives to be human and that which is not human, for the animal fable is a genre whose defining subtext is the place and role of the country/beast in the city/human, the place of the wolf in the dog. The *Fables* are about nothing if not about the taming of the feudal beast, the institutionalization of the violence of the feudal world, in which, as in the animal kingdom, the law of the strongest prevailed; and this within the new civil space of city and court in which the predatory instinct, as we have also seen, takes the form of envy.

The conflict in the *Fables* between logic and the body, or between what we have identified as Marie's relativizing of perspective and the absolutism of appetite, is, at bottom, a matter of the presence and role of the animal appetites in human relations, a question of the internalization of nature—

more precisely, the inherence of a nature—in the human beast. By nature I mean that specific quality of a being that differentiates it from all others in its class, "each thing's peculiar difference," in the words of Hugh of Saint-Victor, which allows us to predict how it will behave.[2]

Among the different types of medieval animal literature, Marie's *Fables* are best understood in contrast to the bestiary, which works to identify the natures or virtues in each beast. Pierre de Beauvais, for example, whose *Bestiary* is the closest to the common source of medieval bestiaries in the second-century *Physiologus,* lays out the natures of the lion:[3]

> Physiologus says that the lion possesses three natures. The first is that it dwells willingly in the mountains. . . . The second virtue of the lion resides in the fact that when it sleeps its eyes, ever on the watch, remain open. . . . The third virtue of the lion is that when the lioness gives birth to its young, she bears it stillborn and keeps it three days.[4]

The catalogue of animal natures contained in the bestiary is relevant to human behavior to the extent to which the natures that inhere in, say, the lion, are also proper to man: "Man possesses a part of the nature of the lion, for this one will not become enraged unless he is wounded. . . . Men of high rank should bear in mind this example of mercy, and spare the poor and weak."[5] In keeping with the "Platonic examplarism" of the early Middle Ages, the bestiary, like the lapidary, functions as a glossary of natures, or of animal traits projected upon the world of humans. Richard de Fournival's *Bestiaire d'Amour,* for example, which posits the behavior of lovers upon that of animals, attributes three natures to the wolf, whose "neck is so straight that he cannot turn it without turning his whole body," "who never captures prey near its she-wolf," and "who enters sheepfolds so quietly that if its foot makes a noise breaking a branch, it venges itself upon its own foot by biting it very cruelly."[6] All three natures, Richard maintains, are to be found in a woman's love:

> For when she loves she gives herself to it entirely; this fulfills the first nature; and, according to the second, if it happens that she loves a man, she will do so to excess when he is far away, but when he is nearby, she will give no sign of it. And according to the third nature, if she goes too far in speaking such that the man notices that she loves him, just as the wolf will avenge himself by its mouth upon its foot which has been too noisy, she withdraws the word that has gone too far. For willingly would she know from another what she would not want one to know of her. And she wants resolutely to protect herself against a man whom she does not believe loves her.[7]

As the example shows, it is not simply that the she-wolf and the woman re-semble each other; but the wolf's conduct, articulated at the level even of bodily gesture, can be said to belong to the same behavioral substance as that of its human analogue. The human can be said to be a trope of the animal, which is ruled precisely by tropological "turnings" of the body, which is another way of saying that humans are moved by that which is proper to the animal world, by the instincts or the senses.

Compared with the animals of the bestiary, the animals of the *Fables* do not possess a nature to the same extent and in the same ways. Marie's beasts are limited by the physical characteristics of the body: the crane cannot escape the "instrument" of his shame (no. 81), the flight of the beetle is hampered by the size of its wings (no. 75), the peacock will never sing (no. 31), the cuckoo will never have a voice suitable to rule (no. 46), the hare will never manage the horns he desires (no. 97), a mouse will never swim (no. 3), nor will the ass ever attain the size of a suitable household pet (no. 15). So too, the capacity for change among the beasts is restricted by the general behavioral tendencies of individual animal species. The wolf inhabits the same skin for a lifetime (no. 66), the wolf is unable to resist preying upon others (nos. 29, 50, 82), and this perception is difficult to shake (no. 88). The fox is clever (nos. 10, 36, 61, 69, 70, 71), as is the snake (no. 73). The ewe is weak (nos. 4, 40), as is the lamb (no. 2) and the deer (nos. 11A, 11B, 24, 69). The animals of the *Fables* are also limited by the relationship of behavioral tendencies to the ecology of their origin. Hares are more suited to "the grove that was their home" than to the swamp to which they roam ("The Hares and the Frogs," no. 22). The dog adapts more easily to the collar and the leash of life in the city than does the wolf of the woods (no. 26). The liminal bat of no. 23 and the badger of no. 77 learn that milieu is not indifferent and that it is better, sometimes even crucial, merely to assume the species to which one was born, to stick with one's own kind, which is the message, of course, of "The Vole Who Sought a Wife" (no. 74), in which the mouse who seeks to wed above his station, which is the equivalent of changing species, learns a lesson in the limits of a nature: "'I thought that I would rise so high,/But now I must turn back, so I/Can bow to my own kind,' said he" ("'Jeo quidoue si haut munter;/Ore me covient a returner/E encliner a ma nature'" [v. 79]).

It is less accurate to say that for Marie animals do not have a nature than to say that the very concept of nature in the *Fables* is attenuated. The animals of the *Fables* fall into general types with definite limits, and the individual animals that make up a particular species are, within the limits of

the type, not necessarily identical to—and, in fact, can be quite the opposite of—one another.[8] Behavior is neither a function of a nature, nor
necessarily, as in the bestiary, predictable. And this from the start and until the very end. For Marie begins with the story of a foolish cock ("The
Cock and the Gem," no. 1), which spurns the jewel found in the manure
on which he sits, and ends with the tale of a wise hen that, though excessive in its appetite, recognizes its own faulty nature ("The Woman and Her
Hen" (no. 103). "The Hares and the Frogs" (no. 22) pits the wise frogs who
recognize the foolishness of seeking to change habitat against the majority
who are convinced otherwise. Similarly, some doves are lacking in judgment, as in "The Doves and the Hawk" (no. 19); other doves are clever, as
in "The Fox and the Dove" (no. 61), in which a bird ends up outsmarting
a fox anxious to trick her with his "crafty words and lying talk" (v. 35).
Some lions are presented as strong and brutal, as in "The Lion, the Buffalo,
and the Wolf" (no. 11A) or "The Lion, the Sheep, and the Goat" (no. 11B),
in which the bullying king of the animals and leader of the hunt challenges
all comers; other lions are portrayed as weak, as in "The Ailing Lion" (no.
14). The lion of "The Lion and the Peasant" (no. 37) behaves as a restrained
pedagogue in the lesson he teaches about the difference between deeds and
their representation, just as the lion of "The Fox and the Wolf" (no. 89)
shows himself to be a subtle judge of the relative difference between the
natures of the beasts who bring their quarrel to court. The lion of "The
Lion and the Mouse" (no. 16) is depicted as clement in this tale of a frol-
icking mouse that disturbs a lion's sleep and is forgiven; the mouse later returns the favor by gnawing through the hunter's net in which the lion is
trapped. The case is interesting, for the lion, awakened suddenly, is furious.
However, upon hearing that the mouse did not act "at all deliberately," the
lion acts reasonably to "set her free." "The Lion and the Mouse" offers an
example not only of a lenient lion but of different and even contradictory
reactions and states copresent at different moments in the same beast,
whose change of heart works against the notion of a fixed nature inherent
to the species of lion.[9] So too, in "The City Mouse and the Country
Mouse" (no. 9) it is clear that the ideal milieu for a mouse is neither country nor town. That is to say, the same animal, or the same nature, is adapt-
able to more than one ecological setting. Indeed, the possibility that the
same animal may be suited to multiple environments not only destabilizes
the notion of a nature but is tantamount to a naturalizing of the importance of milieu.

When it comes to assessing the behavior of animals, Marie is a moderate nominalist. That is to say, she believes in natures or universal types that offer an indication of the general pattern and the limits of that which is observable amongst the individual members of a species.[10] She is, in fact, quite explicit at the end of "The Hawk and the Owl" (no. 80), a tale, it will be remembered, of cross-species hatching whose last two lines make a concise case for that which is obvious throughout: "From one's kind, one can deviate,/But one can never abdicate" ("Sa nature peot hum guenchir,/Mes nul ne put del tut eissir" [v. 39]).

The animals that belong to the species of the animal kingdom do, by their very name, evoke a range of behavioral expectations. Mere mention of "the fox" summons the adjective "tricky," "wolf" summons "rapacious"; but the *Fables* are also filled with exceptions: a moderate wolf in "The Wolf and the Crane" (no. 7) who withholds devouring the bird at his mercy and who upsets the trope of the wolf that cannot resist meat of "The Wolf King" (no. 29) or of "The Wolf and the Sheep" (no. 50). The wolf of no. 7 finds a kindred spirit of exception in the wolf who is cajoled in "The Wolf and the Sow" (no. 21) into sparing his potential victim and in the wolf that holds back and engages in clever speech in "The Wolf and the Boatman" (no. 79). Finally, though most of Marie's foxes are clever, exceptions are to be found in "The Fox and the Moon" (no. 58), in which the gluttonous animal, mistaking the reflection of the moon on water for cheese, ends up drinking himself to death; in "The Cock and the Fox" (no. 60), in which the bird, held in the fox's mouth, convinces him to cry out, thus releasing him to fly away; in "The Fox and the Dove" (no. 61), in which the suspicious bird is not taken in by the fox's deceptive announcement of the royal decree of a general peace; in "The Fox and the Cat" (no. 99), in which the cat with only one strategy outwits the fox and his "bag of tricks."

The nature of animals, the natures in animals, are less stable in the *Fables* of Marie than in the bestiary. Rather, where the bestiary projects the natures that inhere in animals and radiate upon the world of humans, the fable projects the nature of women and men upon the animal kingdom. A difference that would not be so crucial were it not for the fact that reason is the property or nature specific to man, whose animal nature resides in the senses. "A great thing is man," writes Augustine, "made in the image and likeness of God, not in that he is encased in a mortal body, but in that he excels the beasts in the dignity of a rational soul." So too, Hugh of Saint-Victor:

For while the nature of brute animals, governed by no rational judgment, produces movements guided only by sense impressions and in pursuing or fleeing anything uses no discretion born of understanding but is driven by a certain blind inclination of the flesh: it remains true that the actions of the rational soul are not swept away by blind impulse but are always preceded by Wisdom as their guide.[11]

For Aquinas man is like an angel in that his soul is a spiritual substance; but unlike an angel in that it is a spiritual substance designed to be united with a body that acquires its knowledge through the senses man shares with the beasts. Animals have a nutritive plus a sensing or appetizing faculty, a capacity for knowing by use of the senses: the power to pursue that which the senses grasp as desirable or to flee that which is sensed as threatening. Unlike animals, however, man has rational faculties of understanding and choosing in light of understanding, powers of intellect and of will. It is through the will that reason exercises a controlling influence upon the sentient appetites; the will controls man's lower instincts by directing the mind's attention to objects other than that to which the appetites naturally tend.[12]

To the extent that man operates according merely to the senses, he is an animal; and to the extent to which he operates according to reason, that is, to the extent his free will exercises its connatural tendency toward the good, he is human. It is, in fact, the deliberative potential of reason that lies at the core of Marie's relativizing vision of the animal as well as the human realm. Marie is concerned in the *Fables* with the part of the animal in man and with the ways in which the part of man in the animal, associated with reason and with verbal negotiation, is able to mitigate the beast, is able to resist the tropological turnings of a nature.[13] This is another way of posing the question of the place and the efficacy of the will, or of free will, in the determination of the course of the individual born to a particular species. The change of habitat, the change of ruler, the change of species, the change of body, the change of appearance subgroups point to the limits of realigning the ecology of situation and environment. And yet the contradictions and exceptions that separate some members of a species from others make it clear that Marie opens in the *Fables* some margin for the exercise of volition in the relation of individuals to their natural world and to their kind—a space, as articulated at the end of "The Hawk and the Owl" (no. 80), in which "one can deviate" without being able to "abdicate."

RIGHT REASON AND THE MORAL

The moral attached to the end of almost all the *Fables* is, in fact, the space of volition, that is, a critical distancing, a stepping back from the tale, an analysis within, and yet apart from, the story, the beginnings of an interpretation.[14] And though it is impossible to glean a single universal precept from the myriad of Marie's morals, it is nonetheless the case that almost every lesson to be learned at this strong point just outside the narrative has to do with one kind or another of willful thinking. In this Marie again joins Abelard for whom sin resides in the intention, and for whom intention is defined in terms of consent. So too for Marie the assumption that an act of will might have changed the outcome of the events contained in the narrative is written into the moral of almost every one of the fables. We shall, therefore, limit ourselves to the most irrefutable examples, those in which her use of the conditional tense, of a volitive "should," "ought," "must," or a volitive subjunctive makes manifest a potential ethical choice through which, it is implied, things might have been otherwise.

We have seen that a number of fables such as "The Bat" (no. 23) and "The Badger and the Pigs" (no. 77) make explicit on the level of theme the necessity of choice. These examples resonate with the moral of "The Fox and the Wolf" (no. 89), in which the lion who refuses to adjudicate the case between a wolf in the wrong and a truthful fox is condemned, as we have seen, for an illusory and dangerous resistance to passing sentence. "The Dog and the Cheese" (no. 5), in which the dog confuses the reflection of cheese on water with that in his mouth, implies that an awareness of one's own appetite might prevent the kind of mishap recounted in the body of the text. The moral at the end of "The Lion and the Mouse" (no. 16), a parable of mercy repaid, gives reason to think that the lion's indulgence toward the careless mouse is a lesson in the exercise of a charitable will:

> Par ceste essample nus assume
> Que essemple prengent li rich hume
> Ki sur les povres unt grant poër.
> S'il lur mesfunt par nunsaver,
> Qu'il en eient bone merci.
> Avenir peot tut autresi. (v. 45)

> And so this model serves to show
> A lesson wealthy men should know

Who over poor folks have much power.
If these should wrong them, unaware,
The rich should show them charity,
For unto them the same might be.

The moral of "The Cricket and the Ant" (no. 39) makes evident the extent
to which material survival is a function of the will to work, a choice of the
activity of stockpiling over singing. The lesson of "The Monkey and Her
Baby" (no. 51), in which the irresistible urge to brag about one's offspring
provokes its destruction, makes as powerful a case as can be made for the
voluntary nature of silence and speech. Had the monkey mother been able,
through a willful act of self-restraint, to resist boasting, the loss of her son
might have been avoided: "And for this reason you should not / Disclose
your secret or your thought" ("Pur ceo ne devereit nul mustrer / Sa priveté
ne sun penser" [v. 25]). This too is the moral to be learned from "The Cock
and the Fox" (no. 60), in which the fox loses his game by opening his
mouth. In keeping with our analysis of the speech acts contained in the
Fables, it seems that there is no more sensible act of volition, no greater exercise of the will, of self-control, than the choice of when and when not to
speak. The moral of "The Peasant and the Snake" (no. 73), in which a man
has foolishly followed the advice of his wife, transforms the act of listening
into a voluntary exercise in discretion. Finally, "The Wolf and the Kid" (no.
90), in which the kid left at home alone recognizes the voice but not the
body of its mother, makes both lying and belief into a willful choice: "Smart
people therefore should take heed: / Do not believe in bad advice, / Nor,
feigning truth, should you tell lies" ("Pur ceo chastie le sené: / Que hum ne
deie mal cunseil creire, / Ne mençuinge dire pur veire" [v. 22]).

The ending moral of the *Fables* is the place of moral choice, which, by
its very nature, is proper to the world of humans, the lack of deliberation
being precisely that which, as Abelard and others maintain, prevents animals from exercising free will.[15] Such an assertion implies, further, that the
relationship of the narrative body of the tale to the moral is to some degree
analogous to the relationship of the senses to the faculties of reason, or,
simply, of the animal to man.[16] For while the bestiary functions according
to a mode of inherence in which the animal properties that are in man cannot but produce human behavior identical to that of beasts, the *Fables* function along the lines of analogy between the animal and human realms. This
is why, alongside the volitive "would" and "should," the transition from

narrative to moral so often involves a comparative adverb: "Autresi est de meinte gent . . ." ("Many people are like this . . ." [v. 17]), "The Cock and the Gem" (no. 1); "Autresi est de mal seignur . . ." (v. 33), "The Wolf and the Crane" (no. 7); "Autresi est del traïtur . . ." (v. 49), "The Bat" (no. 23); "Ausi vet de meinte gent. . ." (v. 13), "The Hawk and the Nightingale" (no. 67).[17] Seen in terms of an analogy, a comparison, and not in terms of an imbrication of natures, the relationship between the tale and its moral, which is that of the body or the senses to the deliberative faculties or reason, reproduces formally the tension between the animal appetites and the inclination toward relativistic thinking that coincides on the level of theme with the defining drama of the *Fables*.

The identity of the formal structure of the fable and its deeper meaning, the relation of the moral to the body of the text, which duplicates the tension between the bodies shown in the text and the representation of right reason, has wide implications for our understanding of the effects of the *Fables* upon the body as well as of their wider social significance.[18] The moral provides perspective upon the narrative. It is the deliberative space of a relativizing logic, the place where the particular of the story—the once upon a time, the rooting in an individual incident or encounter of beasts— is situated within a more general framework of identical or similar situations, is given a theoretical cast, becomes generally applicable to comparable cases.[19] The moral provokes a theoretical distancing. It guides the experience of reading or of hearing the animal tale in the direction of a measured withdrawal from the particular of the narrative toward a generalizing of the particular, toward a theoretical understanding. This withdrawal reproduces the drama depicted as occurring amongst the members of the animal kingdom or between animals and men. For just as the relationship of the reader or hearer to the narrative is one of desire in which he or she is taken in, seduced, by the tale, the moral, by its transformation of the particular case into a general rule, puts that desire into perspective. Which is the equivalent of a distancing of desire from its object, a withdrawal, expressed so repeatedly on the level of theme, of the appetite from its prey.

The moral at the end of a fable compels a movement from the body to the intellect; it mimes the movement toward right reason in the tale. Regardless of the relation of the actual message of the moral, whether it corresponds or not to the apparent meaning of the narrative lesson, it can be said not so much to contain as to enact a certain relativizing truth of the fable, which is not unrelated to the message of the change of habitat, change of ruler, change of species, change of body, change of appearance subgroups. That is, though one may change environment, the limits of one's species, one's nature, or one's body, the conditions that define the animal—viz., the human—condition are everywhere and always the same. The hares that seek to diminish their fear (no. 22) discover that fear among their neighbors, the frogs in the pond, is no less than it was in the field. The frogs that seek to trade rulers are devoured (no. 18), as are their colleagues the doves (no. 19). The crane that seeks to flee its humiliation carries along its "implement of shame" (no. 81). The horse that seeks greener grass on the other side of the hedge finds that thorns are to be found there as well (no. 63). By allying themselves with other species, the beetle (no. 75), the bat (no. 23), and the badger (no. 77) learn that it is best to stick with one's own kind.

From this perspective the *Fables* seem to proffer a socially adaptive and conservative message, and they have certainly been interpreted as supportive of existing social order.[20] Given the hierarchy within the animal species, a hierarchy from which, as Marie recognizes, one can deviate but not abdicate, and given the analogy, implicit always in the *Fables,* between the world of animals and that of men, a case for the radicalness of their social effect would be hard to make. And yet when one considers what we have seen to be Marie's existential and relativizing vision, a vision predicated upon the mediation of the animal appetites by reason, when one considers the ways in which Marie destabilizes the notion of species, when one considers the extent to which Marie insists upon ethical choice, it is also clear that the *Fables* proffer a world very different in its social consequences from that of the *Lais.* And it is in this difference that one can see the myriad ways in which the *Fables* upset a politics of quietude.

Even though the *Lais* and the *Fables* seem to speak about the same universe of lord and vassal with its heavy emphasis upon lineage and loyalty, we find a different notion of human nature in the animal tale, and from this attenuated image of the nature of the human beast can be deduced a new social model. When I say "attenuated" I mean that we cannot find in the *Fables* anything like the radical shift in the idea of what the essence of human nature is that we find at the time of the democratic revolutions in the West. On the contrary, the notion of an inherited nature, which can be seen to subtend a lineal family model and the primogenital inheritance patterns that go along with it, sets the limits of free will and thus of social mobility, despite the equalizing force of envy that we equated in the previous chapter with social mobility according to individual merit.

This said, however, the *Fables* read like a book of conduct, a guide to the new society which is no longer that of "the first feudal age" (Marc Bloch) but a world in which individuals are to some degree separated from their class, and in which the rules of social comportment and position are determined by a decidedly more urban economy based upon markets and money rather than on bonds of homage and honor. Despite their rural setting, the *Fables* are a virtual catalogue of the values and institutions of towns as well as of court, and of the state institutions that went along with the reconstitution of monarchy in the reigns of Henry I in Anglo-Normandy and of Philippe I in France, but especially of Henry II (1154–89) and of Philippe-Auguste (1179–1223), which overlapped, regardless of her precise dates, with the literary life span of Marie.[21] In this Marie's *Fables* are not unique. Indeed, as we have seen in the series of tales involving the advantages of city versus country life, city mice versus country mice, dog versus wolf. Again, such fables constitute a grouping inherited from the classical animal tale and seem to belong to the "horizon of expectation" of the fable form. Indeed, the fable tends to appear at crucial municipal moments in the development of the West: in the sixth century B.C. with Aesop and the rise of the Greek city-state; in the first century A.D. with Phaedrus, Babrius, and Rome; in the "cosmopolitan culture" of Charlemagne's court; in twelfth-century Anglo-Normandy and France.[22]

Marie's emphasis upon the danger of speech that we have seen to be a defining principle of the *Lais* and her insistence upon the socially adaptive uses of speech that we have identified with the *Fables* are part and parcel of an increased awareness of the mediatory role of words—as opposed to the immediacy of violent conflict—in the redefinition of human relations that occurs within the space of town and court. In this sense the animal tale, despite its feudal vocabulary, is progressive and works against the interests of a warrior aristocracy as seen, say, in an epic like *Roland* where actions, finally, speak louder than words, and in which the weak, whose weapon is speech, have no chance against the strong.[23] In fact, there is some evidence to suggest a link between the fable form and the principle of trickiness that enables the triumph of the small over the large; and this from the start. The *Sumerian Rhetoric Collections* contains the story of the clever goat who, via wise wordplay, manages to outwit a lion:

> When the lion caught the weak goat (the goat said,) "Free me and I will give you my companion, the ewe, on returning (to the fold)." If I release you, tell me your name," (said the lion). The goat answered the lion, "You do not know my name? My name is 'I will make you wise.'" When the lion came to the fold

he said, "I have released you!" She answered from the far side of the fence, "You became wise in exchange for the various sheep which do not live here!"[24]

Though he does not focus upon the moral per se, Phaedrus recognizes that the allegorical nature of fables is related to their inherently subversive social function:

> Now I will explain briefly why the type of thing called fable was invented. The slave, being liable to punishment for any offense, since he dared not say outright what he wished to say, projected his personal sentiments into fables and eluded censure under the guise of jesting with made-up stories. Where Aesop made a footpath, I have built a highway, and have thought up more subjects than he left behind; although some of the subjects I chose led to disaster for me. . . . For in fact it is not my intention to brand individuals, but to display life itself and the ways of men and women.[25]

In the ninth century, Sedulius Scottus's "The Ram," a retelling of the Passion of Christ, is to be understood against the background of court culture in its denunciation of liars and "untruthfulness," a widespread complaint as well among the courtiers of Henry II.[26] Henry II was known as an "oath breaker": "He was always ready to break his word," says Gerald of Wales; "in slipperiness he outdid Proteus," Becket laments.[27] John of Salisbury complains that the fall from a heroic age to "the vanity of words" extends venality even to silence: "Not merely is there no act, no word, to be had without payment, but they will not even keep silent unless paid a price; silence itself is a thing for sale."[28]

Within the ethical mix of the *Fables*, of good and bad animals that commit good and bad actions and tell wicked lies and sometimes charitable truths, Marie is consistently cynical about the abuse of seigneurial power and the exploitation of the poor. Beyond this condemnation, however, we find several significant hints of a new world order. This is not to suggest that such signs are systematic or that they are always as explicit as, say, in the more realistic literary forms of the late twelfth and thirteenth century, the fabliaux or Jean de Meun's portion of the *Roman de la rose;* rather, they are hints of a social reality associated with the legal, political, and even the cultural institutions of towns and of an increasingly statelike monarchy. As rooted as the *Lais* are in the feudal past, which may account for the defining fatalism at their core, the *Fables* are turned toward the making of the future, what many consider to be the beginnings of the early modern era, the Renaissance of the twelfth century that will undergo a second phase in the sixteenth.

TOWN AND COURT AND ROYAL PEACE

The violence of the animal realm, posited at the level of nature, offers a vision of the futility of human warfare. Rather, as in everything else in the *Fables*, war in and of itself is neither good nor bad, but justifiable or to be condemned according to surrounding circumstances. Marie defends the idea of resistance in "The Butcher and the Sheep" (no. 33), in which a rapacious marauder decimates the animal herd—"Repeatedly, he took away / A sheep and killed it, one each day" ("Chescun [jur] el champ rev[en]eit, / sis en porta e ocieit" [v. 7]—until, finally, there are no sheep left. For the most part, however, the *Fables* condemn warfare, shown, as in "The Bat" (no. 23) or in "The Wolf and the Beetle" (no. 65), to be an absurd collective version of the predatory, or what on an individual scale is presented as instinct. Yet, in keeping with a relativistic ethical vision, war per se is neither wholly good nor bad. Marie condones a justifiable war of self-defense while she condemns the wars of petty lords for the sake of something that looks awfully like envy, vanity, or pride. And at least one of the fables—"The Fox and the Dove" (no. 61)—turns around the institution of the royal peace, proffered by the monarchy allied with the papacy around the time of the First Crusade, but imposed in France, along with the first royal prohibition of trial by combat, possibly in the very decade of the *Lais*. The defense of the fox, who has tried to induce the dove to descend from her perch with the announcement that royal right has prescribed that "war forever more be banned" and who flees with the arrival of hunters, is that the dogs may not have heard the "king's proclamation"; an explanation that, taken literally, might be seen to mean that some of the nobles, who resisted the royal incursion upon the right to private war from the very first and in fact up until the end of the ancien régime, did not want to hear of this extension of monarchic power.

Both the *Lais* and the *Fables* can be situated within the context of the peace movement of the twelfth and thirteenth centuries. "Guigemar" ends with an invasion, a successful castle defense, and a marriage, in a movement toward the domestic following the violence of rapt and war. "Lanval" turns around the question of the distribution of military booty, an issue, in present-day terms, of demilitarization. "Eliduc" is the story of warring lords. In "Chaitivel" we see the destructiveness of war's ludic form, the tournament. Despite the example of "Milun," in which foreign adventure serves as the vehicle for the recognition and the reconciliation of father and son, the ravages of war depicted in the *Lais* go hand in hand with the fatalism of their dark vision.

The question of warfare in the *Fables* is much more complex. For not only is the question of the justifiable war situationally determined, but the animal tale offers alternatives to war that take us into the realm of legal procedure, which, despite the court of barons at the end of "Lanval" and the fantastical judicial resolution in the arrival of the train of beautiful maidens, remains unthinkable within the *Lais*. In the *Fables* we find just and unjust trials among the plaintiffs, the defendants, and the judges of the animal world. "The Dog and the Ewe" (no. 4) contains the story of an unjust despoliation before a duly constituted court and with the complicity of false witnesses. The same is true of "The Peasant and His Jackdaw" (no. 56), in which a man who has killed the singing bird of his neighbor, having been brought to court, hides his purse under his cloak, "so that the judge would comprehend / That it was brought as bribery / If he would help him in his plea" ("Que li juges deüst entendre / Qu'il li aporte pur luier, / Que de son pleit li deive aider" [v. 14]). Marie's conclusion concerning covetous officials is a condemnation not of the system of legal pleadings but of a corrupt individual in a particular case. The suggestion is, of course, in keeping with the ethical space of the moral, which is itself a judgment or sentence rendered upon the narrative contents of the tale, that the judges who are corrupt or ineffectual are also capable of acting otherwise. More important, Marie's repeated reliance upon the pleadings of the animal court is in and of itself significant not only within the context of the legal reforms at the court of Henry II in England, but, more generally, within the context of the peace movement in France, Anglo-Normandy, and, as we shall also see (below p. 000), Ireland of the twelfth and thirteenth centuries.[29]

What I am suggesting is that, despite the predatory ethos of the animal world and despite the corruption and inefficiency of the animal court, the *Fables* are on the side of peace and of the civil procedure that implies pleading and debate. Several tales turn around an embryonic version of the scholastic *disputatio,* yet none makes a stronger case for the movement away from the violent resolution of dispute than "The Peasant and His Horse" (no. 47), the tale of a broken promise on the part of a man who agrees to allow the first man that buyer and seller meet to set the price of their transaction. When the price seems to the seller to be too low, the buyer takes him to court. This is a tale that focuses upon the validity of a contract, which is very different from, say, the question of honor and of the sacredness of oaths in the epic, the romance, or a lai like "Lanval." Indeed, once in court, the plaintiff claims breach of a prior agreement ("Cil vot mustrer raisnablement / Que bien li deit tenir covent" [v. 33]), an argument that the defendant refutes with clever speech: "Then off the man and horse did walk;/He'd saved himself through fancy talk" ("Od sun cheval s'en est alez:/Par bel parler s'est deliverez" [v. 49]). Marie's moral has to do with the ways in which words might compensate for a lack of right:

> Pur ceo volt ici enseigner
> E mustrer bien e doctriner:
> Ki que unc se sent entrepris
> E n'eit od sei ses bons amis
> Ki sacent cunseil doner,
> Que bien deit contreguaiter,
> Si parler deit devant justise,
> Que en sa parole ait tel cointise—
> Par mi tute sa mesprisun,
> Que seit semblable a la reisun.
> Li sages hume en grant destreit
> Turne suvent sun tort en dreit. (v. 51)

> This story serves to educate,
> To show us well and demonstrate
> That if one finds he's in a snare
> And none of his good friends is there
> Who could provide some wise direction,
> He'd better act with circumspection
> When he should speak before the court,
> And make quite cunning his report—
> so what he's done, however awful,
> should thereby seem both right and lawful.

"The Peasant and His Horse," seen against the historical background of royal and monarchical prohibitions of war and the advent of trial by inquest in the place of combat, mimes the movement from battlefield to court—in contemporaneous terms, to the Parlement, the place where literally one speaks and where, as the fable suggests "in the absence of friends," clever speech compensates for both right and might. We have come a long way from the fatality of language in the *Lais* to a world in which words, spoken, do not necessarily come back to slay or even to haunt, but may be taken back, respoken, a world in which self-defense, or as the prologue to the *Fables* suggests, self-improvement, is indistinguishable from an exercise of individual agency upon the world.

The *Fables*, which have been seen rightly to be a mirror of princes, might also be addressed to those most protected by the monarchic state, the inhabitants of its communes and urban centers. The fact that they seem to serve as an admonishment to the powerful to act justly and as a sanction to those belonging to the new orders of commerce, like the peasant selling his horse, to defend themselves with clever speech is another version of the perspectival thinking we have identified with Marie's most profound intent and indeed the most significant effect of the animal tale. Again, the relativizing thrust of judicial rhetoric equalizes the social differences perceived to be natural and associated with appetite. It thus disrupts the hierarchy of a food chain according to which the strong of the animal world devour, and the strong of the human world dominate, the weak. In ethical and legal terms, "The Peasant and His Horse" is a parable of the failure of commutative justice, the justice of the sale that reaches a fair price, the justice that between equals compensates for the inequality of things through an exchange of their equivalent value in money. On the contrary, without ever making it explicit, without perhaps ever having come into direct contact with it, Marie seems to advocate in the *Fables* what looks like the Aristotelian notion of distributive justice according to which the natural inequalities between species or between individuals might be recuperated by a compensatory distribution of goods.

The Fables proffer a concept of law and of justice which is no longer, as in *La Chanson de Roland* as it was in feudal society, conceived to be divine, but which is much closer to something on the order of natural law. More precisely, the twelfth and thirteenth centuries witnessed the return not only of Aristotelian philosophy with its reliance upon distinctions, but of a sense of natural law embodied in the principle of distributive justice, which becomes both in the legal thinking of the time and in Marie's animal tales a principle of social regulation. Put in simplest terms, the *Fables* articulate a moral law based upon a certain axiom of equity—that is, "what A does to B, B will do to A," or "what A does to B, C will do to A." We have seen this principle at work in "Equitan," the most bourgeois or fabliau-like of the lais, but it functions more generally in the *Fables* as a counterbalance to the rule of the predatory prevalence of the strongest. The *Fables* offer a sense of the limits of what we have seen to be a hierarchy amongst the devourers and devoured. As can be expected in such a situationally defined universe, the lesson is not universal and absolute. Often, as, for example, in "The Wolf and the Crane" (no. 7), Marie seems resigned before the abuse of seigneurial power: "With wicked lords it is this way:/A poor man his respects will pay/And then he'll ask for his reward,/He'll never get that from his lord!" ("Autresi est del mal seignur:/Si povres hum li fet honur/E puis demand sun guerdun,/Ja n'en avera si maugré nun!" [v. 33]). So too, the end of "The Lion, the Sheep, and the Goat" (no. 11B) and its moral of "winner take all": "The rich man values glory most,/And doesn't care if love is lost./If there is gain to be divided,/The rich man keeps all, that's decided" ("Li riches volt aver l'onur,/U li povres perdra s'amur./E si nul guain deivent partir,/Li riches vout tut retenir" [v. 45]). Occasionally, however, we glimpse a hint of social rebellion. At the end of "The Fox and the Eagle" (no. 10), in which a fox manages to burn and smoke out the eagle that has kidnapped his young, Marie reminds us:

> Par ceste essample entendum nus
> Que si est del riche orguillus:
> Ja del povre n'avera merci
> Pur sa pleinte, ne pur sun cri.
> Mes si cel se pust dunc venger,
> Sil verreit l'um tost suppleer. (v. 17)

> This story has a lesson which
> Tells of a man haughty and rich:
> He shows the poor no charity
> No matter what their cry or plea.
> But if the poor can wreak vengeance,
> The rich will bow in deference.

The notion of a natural balance that works against the excesses of the animal appetite, and thus against the vices with which Marie is concerned, beginning with the prologue, is embodied in the principle of natural law manifest, for example, in "The Mouse and the Frog" (no. 3), in which a frog anxious to devour a mouse is devoured by a kite instead, with the moral: "Those who torment in this way/And think that others they'll ensnare, will/Find that they place themselves in peril" ("Que de memes le turment,/Que as autres quident purchacer,/Avient lur cors a periller" [v. 90]). In "The Lion and the Fox" (no. 69), the moral has to do with a compensating equilibrium between punishment and misdeed, the vengeance of the aristocratic world transformed into the equivalent of a natural law of retributive loss for wrongful gain: "Those who plan ill for other men/Will get the same thing back again" ("Tel purchace le mal d'autrui,/Que cel meme revient sur lui" [v. 57]). A similar lesson is to be learned from "The Kite and the Jay" (no. 87), in which a sick kite begs its mother to ask a nearby jay to pray for him. The mother asks: "'How can I go?/I don't know how to beg him so./His nest you frequently have dirtied/and defecated on his birdies'"

("'Cument irai?/ Ne sai cument li prierai./ Meintefeiz as suillé sun ni/ E sur ses oiseus esmeulti'" [v. 11]). The moral of "The Doctor, the Rich Man, and His Daughter" (no. 42), a tale of innocent ruse and discovery, captures the spirit of an inculpating balance between misdeed and discovery that creeps into the *Fables* alongside the law of the strongest: "And thus it is with all beguilers;/ The same holds true for thieves and liars:/ Those who with wickedness are fraught,/ By their own deeds they will be caught" ("Autresi vet des tricheürs,/ Des laruns, des boiseürs:/ en ki la felunie meint,/ Par eus memes sunt ateint" [v. 27]).

The principle of natural law is nowhere more apparent than in the pair of human animal tales involving prayer. Thus, in "The Peasant Who Prayed for a Horse" (no. 54), a man ties his steed in front of the church, enters in order to ask God "to provide a second horse as good" ("E que un autretel cheval li donast" [v. 6]), and emerges to discover that thieves have stolen the first one instead. Marie's moral has to do with a balance between provision and need: "Nobody ought to pray, therefore,/ To have more than his needs call for" ("Pur ceo ne deit nul hum preier/ De plus aver qu'il n'a mester" [v. 17]). So too, the prayer of "The Peasant Who Prayed for His Wife and Children" (no. 55) "but no one more" is answered by a neighbor's condemnation. Both fables of prayer, the first involving commensuration between request and use and the second a failure of reciprocity according to a natural law of votive exchange, focus on the question of measure in the distribution of natural goods and of wishes for the good.

MEASURE, TIMING, AND ALERTNESS

While the *Lais* remain enmeshed in the futureless feudal institutions that account for the fatalism at their core, the *Fables* allow a glimpse of the legal and even the state institutions of the monarchic and urban world of contracts, trials, elections, pedagogical lessons, scholastic debate, and domestic dispute. They affirm a universe of new values associated with a money economy, not the least of which is measure, the just distribution of goods, and, as we see in "The Ape and the Fox" (no. 28), even of natural endowment:

> De un singe dit que demanda
> A un gupil qu'il encuntra,
> De sa kue li prestast,
> Si lui plus—u en dunast.
> Avis li fu que trop le ot grant,
> Et tuz sunt sanz jue si enfant. (v. 1)

> An ape once asked, the story goes,
> A fox he chanced to come across,
> If fox part of his tail would lend—
> Or give him—should he condescend.
> He thought the fox had too much tail
> While his ape babes had none at all.

The debate between the ape and the fox has the earmarks, again, if not of a scholastic debate, at least of a dispute. To the ape's suggestion that "if a small piece you would concede" ("si m'en voliez un poi duner" [v. 11]), it might increase the fox's running speed, the fox reminds the ape that "my tail, which is so grand, will not / Ever better your children's lot" ("Ja de ma cue, que est granz, / Ne aleverez vos enfanz" [v. 15]); and this despite the fact that the fox's tail is by his own admission of no use whatsoever. The moral of "The Ape and the Fox" has to do with the foolishness of wasting useless excess within an economy ruled by the unequal distribution of goods.

Marie insists throughout the *Fables* upon the principle of measure, good measure, fairness, equity, equilibrium, all part, again, of a literary world that parallels that of social and legal reality, in which individuals are increasingly responsible for self-regulation according to a scale of moderate means. "The Lion, the Buffalo, and the Wolf" (no. 11A) and "The Lion, the Sheep, and the Goat" (no. 11B) provide examples of the unfair consequences of the excessive appetite of the strong. Marie makes a strong case for measure in "The Sun Who Wished to Wed" (no. 6), where Destiny, in consultation with the animal community, agrees upon the limits of political power defined by analogy with the natural world:

> Issi chastie les plusurs
> Qui sur eus unt les maus seignurs,
> Que pas nes deivent esforcïer
> N'a plus fort de eus acumpainer
> Par lur sen ne par lur aveir,
> Mes desturber a lur poeir.
> Cum plus est fort, pis lur fet:
> Tuz jurs ler est en mal aguet. (v. 25)

> Thus everyone should cautioned be
> When under evil sovereignty:
> Their lord must not grow mightier
> Nor join with one superior
> To them in intellect or riches.
> They must do all they can to thwart this.

Stronger the lord, the worse their fate:
His ambush always lies in wait.

Among the tales that stress excess of appetite or political ambition, "The Flea and the Camel" (no. 38) offers a counterexample of an equilibration between the labor of a camel and a flea according to their respective size. When an appreciative flea wedged in a camel's fur thanks him for having carried her graciously on a journey that she could never have made on her own and offers even to recompense him for his labor, the camel "answered her to say/She'd been no burden anyway./He had not known that she was there;/She had not been an irksome care" ("Li chamel le ad respundu,/Que unc de li chargiez ne fu./Ne ne sot que ele fust sur lui;/Ne que ele li fesist nul ennui" [v. 11]). "The Flea and the Camel" is a perfect example of the Aristotelian concept of distributive justice, that is, an adjustment of the natural differences between individuals by a compensatory apportionment of goods with the goal of achieving some measure of equality; in this case the superior capacity of the camel for moving across long distances compensates for the flea's limited geographical scope and small proportions. "The Flea and the Camel" is paired sequentially with "The Cricket and the Ant" (no. 39), which focuses upon the regulation of production within a system not of landed wealth, rich objects and clothes, or booty, as in the *Lais,* but of labor and the accumulation of its fruits combined with the work ethic. "For everyone should do his share," reads Marie's moral, "To bring in goods must be your care" ("Sulum ceo que chescun deit feire/Se deit pener de bien atreire" [v. 25]). This is, of course, a fable about timing—of who should be doing what at what time of year: "It would in August have been best/To seek and store the year's harvest" ("Meuz fust que tu te purchassasses/El meis d'aüst e si guainasses" [v. 17]), the industrious ant reminds his pleasure-seeking cricket colleague; and timing is an important element of the principle of measure asserted throughout the *Fables.* Measure is defined in terms of timing in "The Fox and the Cat" (no. 99), which is a companion piece to "The Wolf and the Hedgehog" (no. 72), where the animals compare defensive strategies. While the fox brags of having a bag full of tricks to the cat's single tactic, the difference between them, as the cat reminds the fox under attack, is not so much who has what, but who knows when to release what he has. The fox realizes that it is too late, he has waited too long, in what amounts to the triumph of ruse over empty words. It is as if Marie were saying that correct timing is a prerequisite to survival.

There is ample evidence for the persistence of the human/animal appetites in the *Fables*. And yet, alongside such insistence on the body and an often absurd flaunting of the impotence of reason lies an equal and opposite claim if not for the mastery of the animal appetites, which are never very far from what Marie sees as the worst in humans, then at least for something on the order of the instinct toward self-preservation according to criteria that stress the best and not the beast in man. For if reason is the specific difference separating the human from the animal realm, then reason's embodiment in a range of values associated with life in towns offers further proof of the way the animal tale mediates between city and countryside. Timing may be the trick of tricks within the *Fables*, but it is only one of the myriad of values associated with the urban experience, a competitiveness of commerce and the marketplace based not on birth or on strength, but on wit, alertness, prudence, and, again in contrast to the fatal futurelessness of the *Lais*, on an anticipatory prospective vision of what it means to negotiate one's way in a world in which not everything is what it seems. The *Fables* are set within the context of vigilance; and this from the start in the Emperor Romulus's letter to his son "to take care/That no one trick him unaware." Marie seems to offer as an antidote to the intractability of the rapacious instincts of others a series of preemptive measures, as if fables might be read as cautionary tales of self-defense. First among such measures is the simple recognition of the nature of others, a correct perception of their intentions which is the equivalent of an admonition to vigilance. "Beware of appearances," she seems to say repeatedly, "stay awake," "observe carefully those around you," as we have already seen in "The Birds and the Cuckoo" (no. 46), "The Ass and the Lion" (no. 35), or "The Fox and the Lion" (no. 36), in which a lion, tired of hunting, retires to a cave from which he simply summons the animals to be devoured until a cautious fox refuses to comply on the grounds that he has not observed the exit of any who have entered therein. The moral of the tale and its analogy with the human world have to do precisely with timing, close observation, and careful assessment of appropriate action: "At royal court the scene's akin/For those who lightly go within./Better to keep away a pace/And listen first to what takes place" ("De curt a rei est ensement:/Teus i entre legerement,/Meuz li vaudreit en sus ester/Pur nuveles escuter" [v. 25]). This too is the point of the subgroup of tales oriented around the question of illusion, as in the case of "The Peasant Who Saw Another with His Wife" (no. 44), in which the wife's claim that the peasant has not seen what he believes he has is capped by a general claim of the superiority of wit—"good sense and shrewdness," urban virtues par excellence—over the traditional feudal values of wealth and family.

Marie is obsessed by what today might be called "mass psychology," not only the animal instinct, but a herd instinct toward believing collectively even the most harmful of lies. She endorses a watchfulness that is clever, quick, and courageous, an individual antidote to the collective fallacy, the conformity, of the herd. This is the lesson of the pair of tales involving prohibitions and broken promises, "The Hermit and the Peasant" (no. 53) and "The Dragon and the Peasant" (no. 52), which ends with an invitation to vigilance, a recognition of the need to discriminate between those who are trustworthy and those who are not, and a warning against placing one's faith—"precious gold, life, or treasure fine"—in the hands of those who are untrustworthy. In contrast, an example of the positive effects of vigilance lies in "The Hawk and the Nightingale" (no. 66), in which the hawk asks the nightingale to sing, but it wisely refuses to do so until the hawk moves to another tree. Or, finally, in the penultimate fable, "The Cat and the Mice" (no. 102), in which a cat sitting on top of a stove tries to convince the mice that he is their bishop and that they should approach to get his blessing. There is almost no fable in which vigilance, acuteness of perception and quickness of reaction, flexibility and adaptability, do not figure in the lesson contained in the narrative or in the moral. And, as in "The Cricket and the Ant" (no. 39), such watchfulness is, unlike the past-oriented fatalism of the lai, forward-looking. The *Fables* are filled with lessons that affirm the values of court and marketplace—vigilance, an ability to look ahead, suspicion of the others, flexibility, endurance—increasingly characteristic of the urban space of the late twelfth century as well as of the new monarchic, as opposed to feudal, state.

To sum up, the ethics of the *Fables* has to do with staying alert as a means of staying alive; with moderation, measure in one's ambitions and appetites; with self-control in keeping with a society in which the individual is increasingly responsible for him- or herself; with self-protection, as in "The Sun Who Wished to Wed" (no. 6); and with collective self-defense, as in "The Lion and the Mouse" (no. 16). Finally, Marie makes a case for prudent action in accordance with the nature of beasts, and, more precisely, with the particular nature of each individual animal in this world of crucial distinctions in which the difference between them is conceived as being not so much quantitative (in contrast to the epic, in which one of the only ways of showing moral difference is through distinctions of size) as qualitative. All of the above are, of course, dependent upon a sense of language that is completely different from that presented in the *Lais,* one that enables such distinctions, empowers the will, and, above all, distinguishes between language and action, or between words and the subsuming presence of the body, the social and conventional as against the unreflectively instinctual in the human beast. A view of language that makes distinctions between appropriate and inappropriate actions, as in "The Eagle, the Hawk, and the Doves" (no. 62) and "The Boar and the Ass" (no. 76); between appropriate and inappropriate speech, as in "The Cock and the Fox" (no. 60). But most of all, that marks the difference between language and that to which language refers.

MARIE'S SOCIAL CONTRACT

In the thinking and writing of this book I have more than once been accused of overemphasizing the place of language in Marie's work, of presenting her in the "presentist" terms of our own obsession with language at century's end, of making of her a language poet. And yet the ethics of language of the *Fables* is a determining factor in the articulation of a relativized and rationalized universe in which the will counts for something in the definition of just and unjust action, and thus of the relations between classes of men and women as well as between the individuals belonging to any of the particular groups analogized along the lines of animal species. This amounts to no less a claim than that the *Fables* proffer a rethinking of the social contract.

A rethinking, first of all, along the lines of gender. The fable has from the start been a predominantly male genre, "a means of transmitting patriarchal wisdom and culture."[30] Indeed, the masculinity of the animal tale is evident in a piece that we identified earlier as the fable of fables from the *Isopet de Lyon*—"Dou Pere qui chestoie son anfant." Marie is certainly not unaware of the maleness of the form, as we see in the prologue in the letter of the Emperor Romulus to his son as well as in such pedagogical tales as "The Crow Instructing His Child" (no. 93) or "The Knight and the Old Man" (no. 101). However, the *Fables* can also be seen to render less acute the masculinity of a genre whose rapaciousness is traditionally, and even constitutionally, male. Harriet Spiegel, who addresses the issue directly, claims that Marie is the only known fable writer who can be seen to use the "male fable form" to "question the male hierarchy" and to "explore gender roles inherent in this order." Further, the ethics that lies at the center of the *Fables,* Spiegel suggests, is divided along the lines of a gender difference between the good females who are victims and the bad exploitative males:

The females in her fables are more compassionate than the males; their re-
sponses are personal rather than formulaic—a goddess who offers comfort
to her petitioners instead of silence, or a raped female bear who cries out in
pain and despair. The female world is likewise personal, defined perhaps by
biology—the females are engendering and nurturing creatures in a domestic setting, rather than, as in the male world, ruling and serving.[31]

And yet the question of gender and bestiality is more complicated than
Spiegel allows. For if the *Fables* contain several notable tales in which iden-
tifiably female animals are victimized by males, and at least one example of
the injustice done to one female by another ("The Pregnant Hound" [no.
8]), they are also filled with a myriad of examples of males ravaging each
other and, where domestic life is concerned, the exploitation of unsuspecting husbands by their duplicitous wives. This is certainly the lesson of two
fabliau-like tales of conjugal trickery, "The Peasant Who Saw Another with
His Wife" (no. 44) and "The Peasant Who Saw His Wife with Her Lover"
(no. 45), the latter of which concludes with a moral that is surprising, appearing as it does in a collection written by a woman rather than by a male
cleric, and that is more like the antifeminist tag lines of the fabliaux: "And
so, forewarned all men should be/That women know good strategy./
They've more art in their craft and lies/Than all the devil can devise" ("Pur
ceo dit hum en repruver/Que femmes seivent enginner;/Les vezïez e li nun-
verrable/Unt un art plus ke deable" [v. 53]). Similarly, "The Peasant and the
Snake" (no. 73), a tale of bad advice whose moral also participates in the
topos of wicked wives, can be situated alongside "The Peasant and His Contrary Wife" (no. 95) and "The Peasant and His Cantankerous Wife" (no.
96). In the first, a wife's obstinate insistence that a meadow has been clipped
by shears instead of a scythe leads to the removal of her tongue, in what appears as a satirical version of the Philomena story, yet it is a punishment
Marie seems to defend: ". . . when a fool speaks foolishness/And someone
comes who talks some sense,/The fool will doubt him and get mad/Al-
though he knows his case is bad" ("Si fols parole une folie/E autre vient, que
sens li die,/Nel creit pas, einz s'en aïre;/La u il set que l'en est pire" [v. 31]).[32]
In the second, as we have seen, the contradictory wife drowns in a river that,
her husband claims, carries her upstream. Here too, the moral condemns
the argumentative wife, the word "riote" of the final line a tip-off to a virtual subgenre in Old French of the disruptive female: "And many folks
will thus argue/With their seignior their whole life through./They do not
think about or care/What trouble this may cause howe'er,/Persisting in

their disaccord" ("Issi avient: plusurs estrivent/Vers lur seignurs tant cum il vivent./Ne saver ne veulent ne sentir,/Quels maus lur peot avenir:/Leur riote tienent avant" [v. 51]).[33]

Where the ethics of gender are concerned, and regardless of whether the protagonists belong to the human or the animal realm, Marie is neither on the side of males nor on the side of females. Rather, the question of the exploitation of one sex by the other in the *Fables* belongs to the larger issue of relations between the strong and the weak, between those who prey and those who are preyed upon, irrespective of sex.[34] Such a view, which is an integral part of what we have seen to be Marie's preference for the individual over the species, for the particular case over the general rule, is the only plausible explanation for the several tales of wicked wives and the embarrassment of the four lines of mainstream classical misogyny at the end of "The Peasant Who Saw His Wife with Her Lover." Nor is the case of the *Fables* any different in this respect from that of the *Lais,* in which the malicious wife of "Le Fresne," the murderous wife of "Equitan," the perniciously adulterous queen of "Lanval," the aggressively indiscreet wife of "Bisclavret," and the unwittingly destructive fiancée of "Chaitivel" cohabit with the unjustly imprisoned wives of "Guigemar," "Yonec," and "Milun," the charitable wife of "Eliduc," and the obedient daughter of "Les Deus Amanz."

Further proof that Marie thinks in individual rather than categorical terms is to be found in the almost complete absence, with the exception of "The Peasant who Saw His Wife with her Lover" (no. 45), of generalizations about gender, either in the narrative body or in the moral of the tale. On the contrary, if the move from story to comment involves, as we have seen, a displacement from the particular to the general, the truth of the generalizations contained in the moral comes either in the form of a warning about unethical behavior or as a condemnation of the unjust exercise of power. More men than women, to be sure, are in a position to exploit those who depend upon them. But this, again, is situational, more a part of Marie's existential view of the relative positioning of individuals within the human species than a function of virtues belonging to one sex or the other. The proof of such a claim is, by definition, negative. Yet no stronger illustration is to be found than in "The Fox and the Bear" (no. 70), the story of the rape by a clever fox of a somewhat befuddled bear whom he manages to entangle in "a mass of thorns": "The fox approached her from the rear;/Cheat that he was, he jumped on her" ("Dunc revient li gupil par derere;/Sur li sailli cume trichere" [v. 23]). If ever there were an occasion for authorial comment upon the violence done by men to women, "The Fox and the

Bear" is it. And yet the moral of the tale has more to do with a suspiciousness of words than with the consistently predictable behavior of either
species or gender:

> Ceo deit ester e remaner—
> Que li pruz hum dira pur ver:
> As vezïez est bien avis,
> Que lur parole est en tel pris
> Cum li engins de meinte gent—
> Que par cunsel venquent suvent. (v. 34)

> And it must always be this way—
> As worthy men forsooth will say:
> Wise people think it's clearly true
> That their words will be equal to
> Some other person's stratagems.
> Yet they'll be vanquished by these schemes.

"The Monkey and Her Baby" (no. 51) contains the story of another bear,
this time the male and the aggressor instead of the aggressed, who pretends
to kiss the monkey child whom he devours. Here too, Marie stresses the difference between the sexes, yet moves to a more general plane in the concluding warning not to "disclose your secret or your thought" (v. 26).

In the *Fables* the question of gender is subsumed by the larger issue of
strength and weakness, empowerment and vulnerability, of which the relationship of male and female is an important category alongside that of the
feudal relation between powerful lords and those under them. It is important to bear in mind that this relation is not necessarily one of lord and vassal, as in the lais of "Lanval" and "Eliduc," which turn around the question
of military tenure, but a broader bond that may involve legal institutions or
inequality of possession. Regardless of the cause, the issues of disparity and
the unjust exploitation of the powerless by the powerful are such recurrent
themes of the interpretive space of the morals that it appears as a key to the
whole. Indeed, the ethics of the *Fables* is dominated by the category of vicious versus benevolent rulers.

The nature of seigneurial exploitation may be legal. In "The Wolf and
the Lamb" (no. 2) Marie caps the tale of wolf-eat-lamb with an analogy to
legal human despoilment: "And this is what our great lords do,/The vis-
counts and the judges too,/With all the people whom they rule:/False
charges they make from greed so cruel" ("Issi funt li riche seignur,/Li
vescunte e li jugeür,/De ceus qu'il unt en lur justise:/Faus acheisuns par

coveitise / Treovent asez pur eus confundre" [v. 31]). So too, "The Peasant and His Jackdaw" (no. 56), a tale of bribery on the part of an egregious judge. Finally, Marie rails in "The Fox and the Wolf" (no. 89) against lords whose refusal to judge constitutes an injustice analogous to the disloyalty of the bat who wants to be on the side of both the beasts and the birds (no. 23).

Elsewhere, the exploitation of lords is economic, as in the case of "The Lion, the Sheep, and the Goat" (no. 11B) and the division of spoils by the lion's hunting party: "The rich man values glory most, / And doesn't care if love is lost. / If there is gain to be divided, / The rich man keeps all, that's de-cided" ("Li riches volt aver l'onur, / U li povres perdra s'amur. / E si nul guain deivent partir, / Li riches vout tut retenir" [v. 45]). Regardless of the under-lying cause of an unjust legal or economic equation, Marie is concerned by the limits of power, the capacity of appetite, which, unchecked in the hu-man animal, risks upsetting the equilibrium of the social system. We have seen the necessity for limiting seigneurial power in "The Sun Who Wished to Wed" (no. 6), for, Marie maintains, desire knows no bounds. "This is how many folks behave: / The more they have, the more they crave" ("Issi est il de plusurs: / Cum plus unt, plus sunt coveiturs" [v. 19])—thus the ending of "The Peacock" (no. 31) makes a simple case for the regulation of the ap-petites in accordance with a formula of adequation between need and ac-quisition. This is the point of "The Fox and the Moon" (no. 58), and even more of "The Ape and the Fox" (no. 28), for this quarrel over who should have what tail reorients the balance between appetite and possession away from the individual and toward a social system in which the needs of each are connected to those of all: "If one has more than need or want, / He won't allow (indeed, he can't) / Another to be helped thereby; / He'd rather waste it day by day" ("Si il ad plus ke le n'estut, / Ne volt suffrir [kar il ne peot] / Qu'autre en ait eisse ne honur; / Meuz le volt perdre de jur en jur" [v. 23]). To the degree that increasing the size of the tail of the ape will diminish that of the fox, they are tied together. Indeed, Marie's condemnation of the fox's refusal to share his excess tail with the ape implies an ethics of intercon-nectedness and of closure.

Marie proffers in the *Fables* an ethics of interdependence according to which lords and those under their seigneurie, the rich and the poor, are linked to each other not necessarily by legal prescription but by mutual need and responsibility. In this she is again essentially an existential thinker aware of the ways in which every part of the social organism affects every other part, in other words, how harm done to one brings injury to all. Here there is no better illustration than "A Man, His Stomach, and His Members" (no. 27), in which the decision on the part of a man's hands, feet, and head to starve his stomach ("Dunc ne volstrent mes travaillier, / Li tolirent li manger" [v. 7]) results in their growing weak themselves. The moral of this great metaphor of the body politic has to do with the interdependence of the strong and the weak, of the center and extremities of a single social system composed of functionally different parts:

> Par ceste essample peot hum veer
> E chescun franc humme le deit saver:
> Nul ne peot aver honor
> Ki hunte fet a sun seignur;
> Ne li sire tute ensement,
> Pur qu'il voille hunir sa gent.
> Si l'un a l'autre est failliz,
> Ambur en erent maubailliz. (v. 19)

> This example serves to show
> What every gentleman should know:
> No man can ever honour claim,
> Whose actions bring his master shame;
> Nor does a lord deserve esteem
> Who wishes to disgrace his men.
> When to another you're untrue,
> Trouble results for both of you.

The lesson of "A Man, His Stomach, and His Members" runs throughout the *Fables* via negative and positive examples of the imbricated obligations of animals and men both big and small.

A number of Marie's fables are tales of caution directed at the great who are encouraged to respect those under them and in their care. "The Wolf and the Beetle" (no. 65), which pits the smallest insect against the largest of four-legged beasts, the wasp whose sting causes a stag and wolf to panic, renders quite explicit the reliance of superiors upon those for whom they are themselves responsible. So too, "The Lion and the Mouse" (no. 16), the story of a mouse that rescues the king of the beasts, reinforces the dependence of the powerful upon the weak according to a natural law governing the rise and fall of an individual's fortune, but also according to a division of functions such that the poor are seen to be the guardians of practical—that is to say, ethical—knowledge:

> Par ceste essample nus assume
> Que essample prengent li riche hume

Ki sur les povres unt grant poër.
S'il lur mesfunt par nunsaver,
Qu'il en eient bone merci.
Avenir peot tut autresi:
Que cil li avera grant mester
E meuz li savera cunseiller
A sun busiun, s'il est suppris,
Que li meudres de ses amis. (v. 45)

And so this model serves to show
A lesson wealthy men should know
Who over poor folks have much power.
If these should wrong them, unaware,
The rich should show them charity,
For unto them the same might be:
The rich may need the poor man who
Can better tell him what to do
When he's by sudden need hard pressed,
Than can his friends, even the best.

To those fables that stress the dependence of superiors upon those below them correspond a number of tales that emphasize the obligation of the small toward the great. "The Frogs Who Asked for a King" (no. 18) admonishes the ungrateful subjects of a benign king. In "The Thief and the Dog" (no. 20), the remarkable story of a sheep rustler's attempt to stuff the mouth of a perspicacious watchdog with an offer of bread, Marie recognizes the importance of loyalty to one's lord. And in an example that comes as close as any in the *Fables* to a class analysis of the relation between workers and owner, "The Peasant and the Oxen" (no. 85) pits the complaint of barnyard animals that they are unfairly obligated to haul their manure out of the stable against the farmer's reminder of its source. Though elsewhere Marie sanctions rebellion of the weak against the strong, the moral of this particular tale has to do with a certain passivity effect built into what we have identified as her perspectival thinking—the realization that wrongdoing is shared by both exploiter and exploited and that in such a case neither can make a moral claim that might lead to action:

Issi va del mauveis sergant
Que tut en jur va repruchant
Sun grant servise a sun seignur;
Ne prent garde del honur.
De ceu qu'il mesfet suvent

Ne li peot suvenir nïent.
Quant sun travail veut repruver,
De sun mesfet li deit remembrer. (v. 19)

With a bad servant it's this way:
He keeps complaining every day
Of his great service to his lord;
His master's honour is ignored.
His frequent impropriety
Goes quickly from his memory.
When he complains of tasks assigned,
He'd best keep his misdeeds in mind.

"The Peasant and His Oxen" drives home the extent to which the relationship between ruler and ruled does not, strictly speaking, require a lord and inferior, but is positional; that is, even the peasant, who is surely the man of someone, might also occupy the place of lord over those below him in the pecking order, the final link in the chain of dominator and dominated being that of men over beasts.

That the relationship between superiors and inferiors along the social hierarchy is relative, combined with the fact that it is reciprocal, has wider consequences for the claim that the *Fables* work a change in the social contract—or at least in the feudal and chivalric sense of polity as seen in the *Lais*. In simplest terms, Marie's projection of a uniform and mutual sense of ethical responsibility in the absence of legal obligation is the lynchpin of a moralization of the social bond and a catalyst to the formation of lateral social ties that will be even more explicitly developed in the *Espurgatoire Seint Patriz*. Historians have long noted that one of the failures of feudalism lay in the excessive personalization of ties between men, in the difficulty of delegating power in the absence of the person or office holder, and in the verticality of a social system stressing specific obligations between lord and vassal in the place of any more general notion of commonweal uniting the inhabitants of a single domain. What I am suggesting is that the ethical thrust of the *Fables* works against the vertically oriented, particularized, feudal chain of command with its specific rights and duties rooted in a specific time and place and in favor of an internalized sense of moral obligation of individuals to one another within the wider scope of the abstract persona of something on the order of the monarchic state.[35]

The claim is a large one, to be sure. It is nonetheless unavoidable as the logical conclusion to what we have seen consistently to be Marie's ethics of language, the necessary consequence of ethical judgment in action and of the internalization of general moral rules alongside the principles of practical conduct associated with life at court and in towns. For the *Fables* may proffer a vision of a rapacious human nature that, uncontrolled, leads to a dog-eat-dog world; but the limits Marie places upon the appetite of the individual, together with the universal ethical warnings and prescriptions that foster something on the order of universal behavioral norms, show the rudimentary beginnings of a generalized model of interdependence among the animal species, among the classes of men, among animal species and men; a model of cooperation between the individual beasts that make up a species, between individual men, and between the individual inhabitants of the animal kingdom and those of the human realm. The message of the *Fables* takes us back, finally, to a theme that is dear to Marie and that serves to bind them both to the *Lais* and to the *Espurgatoire:* that of memory and of the relationship of memory to obligation—in the one case, to the obligation to write within the perspective of an ontology of language, in the other, to the obligation to act in mind of others within the framework of an ethics of words. We shall see in the chapters that follow how these two visions of the relation of words to the world are combined in the *Espurgatoire.*

CHAPTER SEVEN

A Medieval "Best Seller"

That the *Espurgatoire Seint Patriz* should be the least discussed of the three works attributed to Marie's name is ironic indeed.[1] Not only does the *Espurgatoire* share a great deal with the *Lais* and the *Fables,* resolving much that is unresolved there, but the *Espurgatoire* is the most theoretically sophisticated work of a self-consciously theoretical oeuvre. Saint Patrick's Purgatory, articulated first in H. de Saltrey's *Tractatus Sancti Patricii* and soon thereafter in Marie's translation, was among the most popular legends of the High Middle Ages and among the most enduring of the fourteenth and fifteenth centuries.[2] "One of the best sellers of the Middle Ages," in the phrase of Shane Leslie, repeated by others, the *Tractatus* left behind some 150 Latin manuscripts scattered throughout Europe.[3] The plethora of vernacular copyings are no fewer. Five Anglo-Norman verse versions, of which Marie's is considered to be the first, followed H.'s *Tractatus* along with three prose renderings, the earliest of which is from the 1230s.[4]

The legend of Saint Patrick's Purgatory is the subject of a myriad of letters, diaries, treatises, and travel and chronicle accounts, some of which are contemporaneous with H.'s *Tractatus* (c. 1188). Gerald of Wales describes the "pits" of what is obviously Purgatory in his *Topographia Hiberniae* (c. 1190), Peter of Cornwell offers a fuller account of the vision of a descent from the 1180s, Jocelin de Furness mentions it in his *Life and Acts of Saint Patrick* (c. 1183).[5] Later descriptions of the legend, of the physical location, or of an actual visit to Saint Patrick's Purgatory abound. Gossouin de Metz mentions the Purgatory in his encyclopedic *L'Image dou monde* from the 1230s. Roger of Wendover describes it in his *Flores Historiarum* (before 1231); Matthew of Paris, who has been identified with Roger, repeats his description literally in the *Chronica majora.* Stephen of Bourbon uses the legend in *De Septem donis spiritus sancti,* as does Vincent of Beauvais *(Speculum Historiale),* Jacques de Voragine *(Legenda Aurea),* Caesarius of Heisterbach *(Dialogus Miraculorum),* Jacques de Vitry *(Historiae Orientalis),* Etienne de Bourbon *(Tractatus de diversis materiis praedicabilibus),* Ranulf Higden *(Polychronicon),* and John Brompton *(Chronicon).* Accounts of travels to the site of Saint Patrick's Purgatory, Lough Derg in the modern Irish county of Donegal, include those of George Grissaphan from Hungary and Apulia (1353), Louis d'Auxerre from France (1358), Malatesta, from Rimini (1358), Nicholas Beccari (1358) and Taddeo Gualandi (c. 1360) from Italy, and Ramon de Perellós from Catalonia/Aragon (1397).[6] The first reference to a pilgrim from France, contained in a few lines of the *Chronicle of the First Four Valois Kings* under the year 1352, makes mention of the fact that a nobleman who died in battle had visited Saint Patrick's Purgatory. Froissart, in an account supposedly obtained from a "knight of England" of Richard II's court, tells the story of Guillaume de Lille who is reported to have visited Purgatory in 1394–95.[7]

Though Saint Patrick's Purgatory has maintained from the start a special relation to the fictive imagination, and the distinction between documentary and literary accounts is a vexed one, the legend is the subject of poems, plays, and parodies, from Marie, whose *Espurgatoire* is, as I shall demonstrate, the first literary rendering, to Shakespeare's mention of Hamlet's father's ghost ("Yes, by Saint Patrick . . . Touching this vision here,/ It is an honest ghost, that let me tell you" [1.5.11]). The first English version is a translation of the *Tractatus* found in the *South English Legendary,* a verse collection of saints' legends from the second half of the thirteenth century. *The Vision of William of Stranton* is, however, the only visionary account in English actually by an Englishman.[8] It is with Dante's moral cosmology that Purgatory can be said to have received its most elaborate poetic rendering, yet he is not alone: Ariosto treated it in *Orlando Furioso,* Rabelais satirized it, Erasmus described Saint Patrick's Purgatory as a distant echo of the cave of Trophonius, Calderon turned it into a play that caused Shelley to experience a strange vision.[9]

However different in theme and tone the *Espurgatoire* may seem from Marie's other works, it shares numerous and important similarities with the *Lais* and *Fables.* There is, for example, a certain thematic analogy between "Le Fresne" and the story related at the end of the *Espurgatoire* of a priest about to violate a young girl he has raised as his own daughter. Catching himself at the last minute, just as Fresne's mother recognizes the true identity of her abandoned daughter immediately before her other daughter's marriage, the priest castrates himself (v. 2270). More important, the girl is placed in a convent (v. 2295), in what is for Marie a singular and signature event, given that it appears at the end of the *Espurgatoire,* just before Marie offers her name:

> Jo, Marie, ai mis, en memoire,
> le livre de l'Espurgatoire
> en Romanz, qu'il seit entendables
> a laie gent e covenables.
> Or preium Deu que par sa grace
> de noz pechiez mundes nus face!
>   Amen. (v. 2297)

> I, Marie, have put
> The book of Purgatory into French,
> As a record, so that it might be intelligible
> And suited to lay folk.
> Now we pray to God through his grace
> To cleanse us of our sins.
>   Amen.

So close is this extraordinary tale to Marie's acknowledgement of authorship, or responsibility for translating the young girl's story into Romance "in order that it be understood," that, were it not for the fact that the episode is also found in one manuscript family of H. de Saltrey's *Tractatus,* one might wonder if it were not the biographical navel of the text, indeed of Marie's work, this story of a young girl, orphaned, abandoned, raised to be literate, harassed, if not violated, and placed in a convent.

The theme of steadfastness of purpose underlies the *Espurgatoire* just as the theme of resolute love underlies many of the *Lais.*[10] So too, traces of the theme of the Otherworld journey—writ large across the anonymous Breton lais "Tydorel," "Graelent," "Guingamor," and "Tyolet"—is also to be found in those of Marie. Even in the absence of a fully developed Otherworld, several of the *Lais* are structured spatially according to separate worlds in the here and now that function as if they were noncommunicating vases: Guigemar crosses an enchanted channel; Lanval's lady appears out of nowhere; Bisclavret passes between the distinct realms of man and beast; Muldumarec's son visits a mysterious realm to slay his father's slayer in "Yonec."[11] At the very least, several protagonists of the *Lais,* Eliduc and Milun, circulate between distinct geographic zones that, despite their physicality, might as well be two separate worlds. And though we will reserve discussion of the relation of Marie's *Fables* to the *Espurgatoire* for later, when we take up the question of the legal and economic implications of a purgatorial regime for the bureaucratization of the afterlife, it is worth noting for now that the subgenre of animal tales that emphasize changing milieu, body type, or station also turn around an implicitly bifurcated structure of distinct but contiguous ecological worlds, which may, as we shall see by way of conclusion, also correspond to actual geographical migration within the Angevin Empire between Normandy, England, Wales, and Ireland.

CHIVALRIC ADVENTURE

However much the *Espurgatoire Seint Patriz* may have grown out of ecclesiastical material and even emerging doctrine concerning the afterlife, it remains first and foremost, in Marie's rendering, an extended lai, a chivalric adventure, a romance. Marie considers the *Espurgatoire* to be a tale or "cunte," and in a passage not to be found in H.'s *Tractatus,* she refers to "the tale we wish to tell" ("al cunte que cunter voluns" [v. 91]). The assimilation of the story of Purgatory to a tale of chivalric adventure is an exceedingly old one, beginning, as S. Greenblatt shows, at the time of the Reformation with Protestant attacks upon Purgatory that compare such pilgrimages to romance and "vain fables."[12] R. Easting notes that eighteenth-century copyists and audiences recognized the romance potential in Purgatory, more precisely in the manuscript known as OMI or the Auchinleck poem, and may even—through Robert Southey's ballad of 1798, based, Easting claims, on the *Espurgatoire*—have had indirect knowledge of Marie.[13] An anonymous inscription in French found on the flyleaf of a copy of a popular book on the legend of Lough Derg, F. Bouillon's *Histoire de la vie et du Purgatoire de S. Patrice* (Paris, 1676), holds that it was "as good as a novel of chivalry for the Catholic Irish."[14]

Scholars of the last century note the resemblance between the story of Purgatory and tales of knightly adventure. In a foundational article that appeared in the *Romanische Forschungen* in 1908, L. Foulet maintains that the first part of Marie's translation is awkward and uncomfortable, contains a misreading of the parallelism of H.'s short paragraphs, clumsy transitions, a tendency to flatten H.'s original sources (Augustine, Gregory), as well as a confusion of the "theological introduction" and the *narratio* itself. It is only when Marie proceeds to Owen's story, that is, to a narrative or a romance, that she hits her stride: "elle est cette fois dans son élément." A. le Braz appropriates Foulet's perception in the early 1920s, as does C. M. Van der Zanden later in the decade. H. R. Patch emphasizes the affinity between romance and the tradition of the Otherworld, and M. Curley repeats in his introduction to the English translation of the *Espurgatoire* what by now has become a received idea, that Marie recasts Owen's "purgatorial sojourn as a chivalric *aventure*."[15]

Purgatory is easily recast not only as a chivalric but as a romantic adventure as well, and even as a parody of romance turned to torment in Peter of Cornwall's account of a knight's encounter with a beautiful maiden who, at the moment of union, turns into a tree trunk. The knight's member, transformed into a twig for the purpose of arboreal intercourse, is repeatedly hammered with nails by one of the girl's father's ministers.[16] Similarly, in the account preserved only in Italian of a Frenchman who supposedly visited Lough Derg in 1358 (though he situates it in Brittany, by which he means insular Britain, including Ireland), a certain Louis d'Auxerre substitutes seductresses for the devils who torment Owen in H.'s *Tractatus*:

> At once some ladies came towards me, dancing and singing, and their beauty was so great that a man could scarcely describe it nor another man believe him. For they were dressed like queens and on their heads they wore fine gold crowns with many precious stones; their skin was whiter than milk, of a whiteness mingling as it should with the freshness of the red rose.[17]

The ease with which adventures in Purgatory blend with romance is even more compelling where Arthurian romance is concerned. Gervase of Tilbury in the *Otia Imperialia* (1210) tells of a swineherd who, searching for one of his herd, enters a windy cave, this along with the account of a servant who, while looking for his master's lost horse, is led down a narrow path to a delightful plain where he perceives a marvelous palace. The palace is the place of repose of King Arthur, who has gone there after having been wounded by Mordret—"le purgatoire d'Arthur."[18] Gervais participates in another of the legends that circulates alongside that of Saint Patrick, that the entrance to the Otherworld is to be found at the site of Mt. Etna.[19]

Beginning with J.-B.-B. de Roquefort in the 1830s, and pursued as a "singular idea" by T. Wright in the 1840s, the question of whether or not the name of H. de Saltrey's hero Owen—"Ouen," "Oven," "Ewen," "Owein"—is the same as, or even derives from, Chrétien de Troyes's "Yvain" or "Evain," or the English "Iwain," has been with us ever since.[20] Shane Leslie sees not only similar names but a larger structural and thematic resemblance between the repentant knight's prolonged attempt to return to his lady's grace and the story of Owen's adventures in the underworld.[21] Further, when one begins to look beyond onomastics, which is the weakest of links in that Yvain and Owen share little beyond the name except that they are both knights, the points of resemblance between H.'s *Tractatus,* Marie's *Espurgatoire,* and key episodes and motifs of the chivalric and courtly corpus are so numerous as to make the membrane between religious and secular romance seem porous indeed. In the broadest possible terms, Owen's Otherworld adventure is to be placed alongside those of Chrétien's Lancelot in the Land of Gorre and of the quest of Arthurian knights in the *Queste del Seint Graal,* which represents a collective ordeal of purgation.[22] On a smaller scale, the prior's attempt to discourage Owen from entering Purgatory is similar to King Evrain's attempt to discourage Erec from undertaking the adventure of the "Joy of the Court" at the end of Chrétien's *Erec et Enide* (vv. 5560–93). The wall to which Owen comes at the end of his ordeal resembles that surrounding the garden which Erec encounters before undertaking this final battle. Both historically and in degrees of delight, Owen's wall is to be compared with the entrance to the garden in Guillaume de Lorris's portion of the *Roman de la rose.* Though one is clearly situated above ground and the other below, though one is merely a vestige and the other the real thing, both partake of the fantasy of the accessibility of the earthly paradise (v. 1689). Within the walls the procession that Owen perceives, consisting as it does of both secular and religious as well as of those of every station—archbishops, bishops, abbots, monks, priests, deacons, canons, subdeacons, acolytes—, participates in the plenitude of Guillaume's garden of Love.[23] The castle to which Owen comes, filled with light and precious stones, is as close as one could imagine in an essentially religious work to the courtly *locus amoenus:* "Quant la porte vint aprismant,/un païs vit resplendissant;/la enz aveit greignur clarté/que li soleilz n'a en esté" ("As he approached the open gate,/He saw within a land/Shining with greater brilliance/Than the sun has in summer" [v. 1519]).[24] One can argue as to whether the origins of the sweet place to which Owen arrives lie in the Celtic Otherworld or in the classical rhetorical motif; yet the question of source, as preoccupying as it has been for almost all who have treated the topic, has also served as a distraction from the overwhelming significance of the resemblance—indeed the identity where deep structure and cultural effects are concerned—between religious and secular romance, between the *Tractatus/Espurgatoire* and the courtly/chivalric corpus.

If the end point of Owen's adventures evokes the end of *Erec et Enide* as well as the beginning of Guillaume's *Roman de la rose,* the trajectory that takes him there, the ordeal to which he submits, resembles nothing so much as a series of chivalric encounters. Owen's deeds of prowess in Purgatory summon those of the forest wanderings of Erec, Yvain, Lancelot, Gawain, and particularly Perceval. He is the armed warrior, the ethos surrounding him that of the *miles christi* protected by "faith, good hope, justice, and belief to conquer the Devil in battle" (v. 647). The allegorization of arms in the *Tractatus/Espurgatoire*—indeed, allegory as an arm—is pushed quite far and represents the most elaborate example of such thinking before the extended explanations to be found in the *Lancelot del Lac* of the thirteenth-century *Vulgate Cycle*. H. and Marie may, as M. Curley suggests, have been inspired by Saint Paul's Epistle to the Ephesians (6:11–17), which speaks of the "whole armor of God," the "breastplate of righteousness," "the equipment of the gospel of peace," and the "shield of faith":[25]

> Des armes Deu s'est bien armez
> e bien guarniz e aturnez:
> halberc de justise out vestu,
> par quei le cors out defendu
> de l'engin de ses enemis;
> et l'escu de fiance out pris;
> healme out, fait de ferme creance,
> l'altre armeüre, d'esperance;
> espee a del seint Espirit,
> si cum li livre le nus dit,
> c'est la parole Ihesucrist,
> ki de sun nun numer l'aprist.
> Mult li fu cil seinz nuns aidables,
> kil rescust sovent des diables. (v. 797)

> Dressed in the armor of God,
> He was fortified and protected.
> He was dressed in the chain-mail of Justice,
> To defend his body
> From the stratagem of his enemies.
> He took up the shield of Faithfulness,
> Put on his helm, forged of strong Belief,
> And other armor made of Hope;
> He has the sword of the Holy Spirit, which,
> As the book tells us,
> Is the word of Jesus Christ,
> Who taught him to call on his name.

> This holy name was very helpful to him,
> For it often rescued him from the devils.

Owen's "halberk of justice," "shield of faithfulness," "helm of belief," "armor of hope," and "sword of the Holy Spirit" recall the maternal benediction of the Lady of the Lake of Arthurian tradition, who, when bestowing arms upon the young Lancelot, explains the allegorical meaning of each:

> "Li escuz qui au col li pent, et dont il est coverz par devant, senefie que, autresin com il se met entre lui et les cox, autresin se doit metre li chevaliers devant Sainte Eglise encontre toz maxfaitors, o soient robeor o mescreant. . . . Li hauberz dont li chevaliers est vestuz et garantiz de totes parz, senefie que autresin doit Sainte Eglise estre close et avironee de la desfense au chevalier. . . . Li hiaumes que li chevaliers a el chief qui desus totes les armes est paranz, si senefie que autresins doit paroir li chevaliers avant totes autres genz encontre cels qui voudront nuire a Sainte Eglise ne faire mal. . . . Li glaives que li chevaliers porte, qui si est lons qu'il point ançois que l'an puisse avenir a lui, senefie que, autresin com la paors del glaive dont li fuz roides et li fers tranchanz fait resortir arrieres les desarmez por la dotance de la mort. . . ."[26]

> "The shield which hangs around his neck, and by which he is protected in front, signifies that, as it stands between him and blows, in the same way the knight should stand in front of the Holy Church against all evildoers, whether robbers or pagans. . . . The hauberk which the knight wears, and which protects him all over, signifies that in the same way the Holy Church should be enclosed and surrounded by the knight's defence. . . . The helm which the knight has on his head, and which can be seen above all the other armour, signifies that in the same way the knight should be seen before all others to oppose those who wish to harm or do evil to the Holy Church. . . . The lance which the knight carries, which is so long that it stabs before he can be reached, signifies that, as fear of the lance, with its strong shaft and sharp head makes men draw back for fear of death. . . ."

Once he has made his descent, the "terrifying battles" in which Owen participates "against the devils" emphasize the identity between his adventures in the Otherworld and the chivalric ordeals of other Arthurian knights; and this right down to the presence in the *Espurgatoire* of specific testing motifs. As Owen is led to the tenth torment, for example, the devils who are his guide and who maintain that all others have lied in claiming to have shown him the true entrance to hell lead him to the bridge over a "deep and stinking river from which emanate cries and a great tumult": "Cele ewe esteit tute embrasee/de flame sulphrine od fumee,/et si ert de diables pleine/ od lur turment e od lur peine" ("This river was entirely covered/With sulfuous flame and smoke,/And it was full of demons,/Torment, and pain" [v. 1329]). The bridge over which Owen "passes without difficulty" (v. 1399) has, of course, its analogies in ancient Persian, East Indian, Babylonian, Egyptian, classical, and Moslem tradition.[27] The water barrier is known among the Greeks, for whom the commonest location of the Otherworld is a blessed island or group of islands, as we see in Homer's account of the Elysian Fields (*Odyssey* 4.561ff.) or of Hades (*Odyssey,* book 11), in Plato's Underworld (*Phaedo,* 107E–108A) or that contained in Hesiod's *Works and Days* (170ff.) or Lucian's *True History* (2.4ff.). In Statius's *Thebaid,* known in the Middle Ages beginning with the Old French *Roman de Thèbes,* the Underworld surrounded by a river barrier is referred to as Avernus, Tartarus, Elysium, or Erebus (8.1–126). Virgil's descent in the *Aeneid,* similarly known via the *Roman d'Eneas,* involves his crossing of the river Styx, the region of the Mourning Fields and land of the blessed with two gates.

In the tradition of Christian visions known in the twelfth century and mentioned by H. de Saltrey, one of the stories in Gregory the Great's *Dialogues* (4.38) is that of a soldier who, in his Otherworld journey, comes to a meadow, a river, and a bridge that, like that of Owen, is the final ordeal: "This bridge was a testing bridge. If someone bad wanted to pass, he fell in the shadowy and stinking river below. The good who had no sin to prevent them crossed easily and freely over to the sweet place." Boniface's Monk of Wenlock "saw a pitch-black fiery river, boiling and glowing, dreadful and hideous to look upon. Over the river a log was placed as a bridge. The holy and glorious souls, as they left their assembly, hastened thither, anxious to cross to the other side. Some went over steadily without faltering, but others, slipping from the log, fell into the infernal stream."[28] Gregory's or Boniface's bridges were supposedly passed down to the Irish visions in the form of the broadening bridge of the *Vision of Adamnán* or that of Tnugdal who, in the twelfth century, comes to "a very long plank stretched out across the valley from one mountain to the other like a bridge. It measured a thousand paces in length but one pace in width. No one could cross this bridge unless he were one of the chosen."[29] In the period directly following the *Tractatus/Espurgatoire,* Thurkill in the Otherworld comes to "a long bridge, bristling with stakes and nails, which every soul must cross before reaching the Mount of Joy."[30]

The narrow bridge is so common that it is found in the High and later Middle Ages in the thirteenth-century French translation of a Moslem

Otherworld journey or *hadith* known as *Mohamed's Ladder* as well as in Dante. And yet, one needn't go so far from home since the Old French chivalric and courtly tradition is filled with a plethora of bridges to test the mettle of the adventurous knight. Andreas Capellanus recounts the tale of a knight who encounters a "certain river of marvellous breadth and depth, with great waves in it, and because of the great height of its banks it was impossible for anyone to reach it. But as he rode along the edge of the bank he came to a bridge which was of gold and had one end fastened to each bank."[31] In Chrétien's *Lancelot,* the hero crosses a perilous sword bridge leading to the realm of Meleanz. Lancelot's avatar in the *Lancelot del Lac* crosses a myriad of bridges, each of which, like the causeway leading to the realm of Sorelois, puts the knight errant to the test. The Perceval of the thirteenth-century *Perlesvaus* passes the Bridge of the Needle ("le Pont del Aguille"), following in the footsteps of Chrétien's Perceval on the plank bridge.[32]

Beyond these general and somewhat vague similarities between chivalric and courtly romance and Marie's *Espurgatoire,* there is one romance whose resemblance to the *Espurgatoire* is both compelling and certain—Chrétien's *Perceval.* Both the *Conte du Graal* and the *Tractatus/Espurgatoire* were written at the urging of another—Philip of Flanders and H. of Sartis. Both the *Conte du Graal* and the *Espurgatoire* (though not H. de Saltrey's *Tractatus*) begin with a title and a book: that given to Chrétien by Philip of Flanders— "Ce est li CONTES DE GRAAL,/Dont li quens li bailla le livre" (v. 65)—and that of H.'s text, which Marie translates: "vueil en Romanz metre en escrit,/si cum li livre le nus dit,/en remembrance e en memoire,/'Des Peines de l'Espurgatoire.'"[33] The dates of composition of the two works are, moreover, certainly within the same decade, Chrétien's last work having been begun after 1181 and abandoned, possibly because of his death, before the death of Philip of Flanders in 1191. This is not to suggest a direct influence or that Marie and Chrétien were working together, rather that the two works were produced in and around the final years of the reign of Henry II, who died in 1189, and that they participate in a common, and palpably appreciable, vision of the relation between this life and the next. They are of the same world and both contribute to a global shift in the conception of the beyond that has major and long-lasting implications for the political economy of the here and now.

I realize that there has been much discussion about the date of composition of H. de Saltrey's *Tractatus.* F. W. Locke claims that the "H. abbot of Sartis" at whose urging the *Tractatus* was composed and to whom it is dedicated was Henry, seventh abbot of Old Wardon (Sartis) in Bedfordshire, and that the *Tractatus* was thus written while Henry was abbot of Sartis, or "after 1208 and before 1215." R. Easting, however, maintains that "H. abbot of Sartis" is Hugh, the second abbot of Wardon / Sartis, who assumed the abbacy in 1173 and was abbot until 1185. He shows, moreover, that the Gilbert of Louth to whom Owen relates his story became abbot of Basingwerk in 1155 but did not hold that office between 1179 and 1181. Further, in one family of *Tractatus* manuscripts Gilbert speaks in the past tense of presiding as abbot which, Easting concludes, means he was no longer abbot when he passed on Owen's story to H. de Saltrey. The date of composition of the first version of the *Tractatus* must, therefore, fall either in the years 1179–81 or 1185–86. Y. de Pontfarcy tailors somewhat Easting's demonstration, maintaining that Gilbert, no longer abbot of Basingwerk, "transmitted the story of Owen's adventure to H. de Saltrey" in 1179. "In 1184, the monk wrote, at the behest of the abbot H. de Sartris, a first version of the *Tractatus,* followed by an expanded version between 1186 and 1188, or 1190 at the latest." Such a view represents a return to L. Foulet's original placement of the date of both H.'s original and Marie's translation in the late 1180s. From evidence contained in the second and expanded version of the *Tractatus,* Foulet assimilates H.'s mention in the epilogue of Bishop Florentianus to the historical figure of Florent O'Carolan, who became bishop in 1185. Foulet concludes that the *Tractatus* was completed after 1185 and that the *Espurgatoire* was translated shortly thereafter.[34]

In keeping with the historical tendency, beginning in the late eighteenth century, to make Marie younger than she was, T. Wright originally claimed that the *Espurgatoire* was written "in the early part of the thirteenth century." The general wisdom now, however, is that it was composed in the decade after the *Tractatus* and probably around 1190, "while," according to M. Curley, "interest in Saint Patrick must still have been fairly strong among members of the Anglo-Norman aristocracy."[35] Of recent commentators, only C. Carozzi, without explanation and without regard to the chronological relation between original and translation, situates the *Espurgatoire* out of the time frame of 1186–91.[36]

What this means is that Marie's *Espurgatoire* was composed—or translated—within a period no greater than half a decade from Chrétien's *Perceval,* whose terminus ad quem, based upon the dedication to Philip of Flanders, is 1191. Beyond the evidence of external literary history, however, a reading of the two side by side permits us to hone Curley's formula according to which the *Espurgatoire* represents a "purgatorial sojourn as a chivalric *aventure*" and to see it as a "purgatorial sojourn" in the mode of a

Grail romance. The resemblance of the two is in part thematic. Owen, having crossed the perilous bridge, comes to a castle that resembles both the Chateau des Merveilles and the Grail Castle of the *Conte du Graal*. Owen's castle of the Earthly Paradise is full of light and features a procession lit by candelabras:

> Encore esteit loinz de la porte,
> quant il vit croiz que l'um aporte,
> palmes orines, ço trovuns,
> chandelabres e gomfanuns.
> ent erent de religiün
> ki firent la processiün. (v. 1531)

> While yet far from the gate,
> He saw a man carrying a cross,
> Golden palm branches, we are told,
> Candelabra, and banners.
> He also observed religious folk
> Walking in procession.

So too, Perceval in the Grail castle witnesses a candle-lit display:

> Et laiens avoit luminaire
> Si grant come on le pooit faire
> De chandoiles en un hostel.
>
> . . . .
>
> Atant dui autre vallet vindrent,
> Qui candeliers en lor mains tindrent
> De fin or, ovrez a neel.[37]

> Within the hall the light from the burning candles was as bright as could be found in any castle. . . . Then two other squires entered holding in their hands candelabra of pure gold, crafted with enamel inlays.

Beyond thematics, however, the two knights—Owen, the Irishman, and Perceval, the Welshman—resemble each other in their biographical origins, a resemblance that in the context of the Cambro-Norman occupation of Ireland beginning in the late 1160s has special significance for our understanding of Patrick's Purgatory. Springing from the periphery of the Anglo-Norman Empire, Marie's Owen, like Perceval "li galois," is a rustic who is juxtaposed—and here the comparison is unavoidable—with the Irishman who approaches Patrick as he arrives in Ireland to preach, and who, at least in H.'s and Marie's version of Saint Patrick in Ireland, represents the saint's first contact with the Irish. Like Perceval at the beginning of the *Conte du Graal,* this knight, who hardly deserves the title, doesn't know the rules of chivalric conduct: that in killing he has done wrong. A first version of Owen, then, the pre-knight who has never taken Communion nonetheless confesses and tells his life story in which he has killed five men and wounded many without knowing it was a sin: "N'i parla rien d'ocisiün;/n'ert pas pechiez, ço li ert vis,/se il aveit humes ocis" (v. 236). Owen too is initially portrayed as a naive savage from the hinterland who has committed violent excess in the wars of Stephen's reign, the Irish being known for their cruelty: "kar mult aveit sovent ovré/cuntre Deu en grant cruëlté" (v. 513).

Both Chrétien's *Conte du Graal* and Marie's *Espurgatoire* are conversion narratives, romances of personal and social transformation from an initial violence associated with psychological naiveté and a childhood spent in the chaotic zone beyond the reaches of institutional order and in ignorance of the law. Perceval is born in the Wasteland to the widow of "la gaste forêt soutaine," in other words on the margins of society, the marches, far from court, far from the class of warrior knights, far from the Round Table that is the equivalent of social order. Without being a wild man, Perceval is as close to a wild child as the twelfth century might muster, the natural world of his origin being for Chrétien as well as others an unredeemed locus of violence beyond the civil polity that we have associated for the reign of Henry II with regularized judicial procedure and state formation.[38]

In Arthurian literature the Wasteland is synonymous with poverty, with famine accompanied by a violence run amok leading to depopulation. Indeed, in *La Queste del Seint Graal* Perceval's two brothers die "killed by their excess" ("ocis par lor outrage" [p. 73]), and his father dies of sorrow because of the death of his sons. It is as if, according to Perceval's aunt, the former Queen of the Wasteland, violence is so much a general rule in Wales that the Welsh, like the unconverted Irish, do not perceive killing to be wrong:

car a cel tens estoient si desreez genz et si sanz mesure par tout le roiaume de Gales que se li filz trovast le pere gisant en son lit par achaison d'enfermeté, il le tresist hors par la teste ou par les braz et l'oceist erramment, car a viltance li fust atorné se ses peres moreust en son lit. Mes quant il avenoit que li filz ocioit le pere, ou le peres le filz, et toz li parentez moroit d'armes, lors disoient cil del païs qu'il estoient de haut lignage.[39]

for in those days the people of Wales were so insensate and fanatical that if a son found his father lying in bed by reason of some sickness, he dragged him out by the head or the arms and made a summary end of him, for he would have been held dishonoured had the father died in his bed. But when it came about that son killed father or father killed son and the whole clan died a violent death, then the neighbours proclaimed them nobly born and bred.

Perceval has been raised by his mother who, upon the death of the father, has withdrawn from the world in order to protect him from the father's calling—knighthood—and his fate.

What this suggests, of course, is that Marie's Owen is a version of Chrétien's Perceval, that not only do they share origins in the outlying margins of social order, but the ordeal to which they submit and the conversion they undergo are also entwined. Perceval is in the beginning a *naif*, an *ingénu* who is slowly socialized, or brought to know the world of the father, throughout the *Conte du Graal*. He is the one who ignores the signs of the chivalric world, gained only via the encounter with knights wandering though the forest just around the time that he is old enough to want to join Arthur's court. And so it is that Perceval literally learns the name "knight": "Are you God?" ("N'iestes vos Diex?" [v. 174]), the *ingénu* asks. "No, by my faith" ("Naie, par foi"). "Who are you, then?" ("Qui estes dont?"). "I am a knight" ("Chevaliers sui"). As well as the names of the accoutrements of knighthood: first, the lance ("Sel te dirai, ce est ma lance" [v. 189]), then the shield ("Escu a non ce que je port" [v. 224]), and, finally, the hauberk. "Or me dites, fait il, biax sire,/Que c'est que vos avez vestu?/—Vallet, fait il, dont nel ses tu?/—Je non.—Vallet, c'est mes haubers" (v. 260).

Chrétien's *Conte du Graal* is a work of pedagogical chivalry in which Perceval, having learned the names of knightly arms, is instructed by Gornemans de Gorhaut, who functions as an oblique father, in their use. More important, in a series of lessons with direct bearing both upon his ordeal in the Grail Castle and upon Owen's ordeal in Purgatory, Perceval submits to a sequence of contradictory instructions from his mother and Gornemans concerning when and when not to speak. In the mother's lesson in prudent hospitality, Perceval is advised to ask the name of any companion he might have: "N'aiex longuement compaignon/Que vos ne demandez son non; . . ./Par le sornon connoist on l'ome" ("never keep company with anyone for very long, whether at an inn or on the road, without asking his name . . . , for by the name, one knows the man" [v. 557]). Gornemans's teaching, however, is exactly the opposite of the mother's: where she had urged him to speak, Perceval's second teacher stipulates that he must learn to keep silent (v. 1648). What's more, Gornemans, fed up with hearing about Perceval's mother, urges him to censor even that: "You must

never again claim, dear brother, that your mother taught or instructed you."
("—Or ne dites jamais, biax frere,/Fait li preudom, que vostre mere/Vos ait
apris rien, se je non" [v. 1675]). For the mother's teaching, and indeed for
the name of the mother, Gornemans substitutes his own lesson and his
own name: "Then what shall I say, good sir?" ("—Coment dirai dont, biax
dols sire?" [v. 1685]), asks the pupil, to which Gornemans replies: "You can
say that the vavasour who attached your spur taught and instructed you"
("—Li vavasors, ce porrez dire,/Qui vostre esperon vos caucha,/Le vos
aprist et ensaigna" [v. 1686]).

    Indeed, Perceval, remembering his teacher, refuses to speak in the Grail
Castle before the spectacle of the bleeding lance. Nor does he forget Gornemans's admonishment to silence before the Grail which keeps passing and
before which Perceval "remains more silent than he should have" (v. 3290).
It is only slightly later, in front of the maiden who has lost her knight and
who turns out to be Perceval's cousin, that he learns that he should have spoken. For his speech would have restored the Wasteland and the king's health
(v. 3583). Chrétien's *Conte du Graal* is a chivalric Bildungsroman in which
the hero learns the names and uses of the weapons of the father, but it also
contains a powerful lesson in the good and bad uses of speech, more precisely, in the art of when and when not to speak.

    In this the education of the secular knight not only resembles that of
knight Owen but can be seen to be identical in its deepest lesson, a lesson
that merits Marie's abiding attention in both the *Lais* and the *Fables*, concerning the crucial question of when and when not to speak. As he enters
the pit of Purgatory Owen receives instructions from the prior on how to
act in order to survive (v. 725). The prior's advice to Owen, which is not ter-
ribly different from that of Gornemans to Perceval, is, above all, to remember what he has learned and from whom: "Remember what you have heard
from me" ("Retien ço que tu oz de mei" [v. 730]). It is, second, to remember to be suspicious of all other teachings, especially those of the devils he
will encounter (v. 737). But, most of all, the prior's lesson entails remembering when exactly to speak and what to say:

> "Et aiez tuz jurs en memoire
> Deu ki est sire e reis de gloire!
> Quant il vus metrunt en turment,
> Ihesucrist reclamez sovent:
> par l'apel de cel nun puissant
> serrez delivres maintenant.
> En quel liu que seiez menez

> e quel turment que vus sentez,
> le nun Ihesucrist apelez:
> quardez que vus ne l'obliëz!
> Delivres serrez par cel nun,
> par la Deu grace le savum." (v. 771)

> "Always remember God,
> Who is Lord and King of Glory!
> When they torment you,
> Cry out often to Jesus Christ,
> And by calling out his powerful name
> You will be immediately delivered.
> In whatever place where you are led,
> And whatever torment you will experience,
> Call on the name of Jesus Christ.
> Take care that you do not forget,
> For you will be delivered by his name."

The instruction that Owen receives from the prior coincides uncannily with the teachings of Perceval's mother and Gornemans. Owen, however, is the one who speaks at the right time and says the right thing.

Like Perceval, Owen seeks adventure, which involves an initial verbal instruction, a journey not to the Celtic Otherworld but to Purgatory, where, like the heroes of romance, he undergoes a series of ordeals, struggles against its hideous inhabitants, and emerges eventually to tell his tale. Most striking, however, is the fact that like Perceval, who is instructed first by his mother to speak and then by the oblique father Gornemans to remain silent before failing to ask the questions in the Grail Castle that would have cured the mysteriously wounded Fisher King and restored the prosperity of the realm, Owen submits to an ordeal of silence and speech. In fact, Owen's ordeal, in the absence of any physical contact between himself and either the devils, their instruments of torture, or purgatorial fire, stands first and foremost as a verbal test. Prior to his descent, he is instructed to speak, to say the name "Jesus" in order to escape being held in Purgatory by demons. And he is repeatedly saved by uttering the "name."

The demonstration may be a bit tedious, but it is important nonetheless, for Owen is rescued from each of the ten torments to which he risks being subjected, indeed from the risk of not returning from Purgatory but remaining forever in hell, by the utterance at the right moment of the right word, which functions as his defense. Owen is saved from the first torment, that of having been plunged into fire, by "the name of his Lord":

El feu le jetent erranment,
od cros de fer enz le buterent;
hisdusement sur lui criërent.
Li chevaliers en sa dolur
apela le nun sun seignur. (v. 890)

Then [they] threw him at once into the fire,
And pushed him down into it with an iron hook,
While hideously shrieking all around him.
In his suffering, the knight
Called on the name of his Lord.

So too, memory of "the name of God" rescues Owen from the second, that of being nailed naked to the ground on one's back: "Mes il membra al chevalier/del nun Deu, ki l'out delivré,/si a Ihesucrist reclamé" ("But the knight recalled/The name of God who had delivered him,/And he cried out to Jesus Christ" [v. 974]). And from the third, according to which people are nailed to the ground on their backs with fiery dragons perched upon them "and devouring them with their burning teeth." Threatened by the devils with the same fate, Owen blurts the name that will save him: "Il apela le nun Ihesu:/par cel apel delivres fu" (v. 1031). Similarly, Owen escapes the fourth ordeal in which the tormented "both prone and supine" are affixed with so many nails that one cannot see the body "without touching a nail": "il a nomé/le nun Ihesucrist dulcement,/si fu delivres erranment" (v. 1066). And the fifth, in which the penitent are suspended upside down by burning chains in perpetual fire: "Le nun Ihesucrist reclama:/par icel nun se delivra" (v. 1117). As well as the sixth, in which they are impaled upon a wheel and lowered into burning sulfur. Seized by a devil who has managed to trap him and ready to make the plunge, Owen utters the right word just in the nick of time: "si a nomé le nun Ihesu:/tut erranment delivres fu" (v. 1167). The seventh torment features a house in which souls are plunged into "hot and burning metal, some up to their breasts, others up to their navels, others to their thighs or knees." Owen, however, remembers the name and is saved (v. 1220). In the eighth people are squatting on their toes on a mountain, then, lifted by a whirlwind, plunged into an icy river, which Owen avoids like the rest: "Li chevaliers se remembra:/le nun Ihesucrist reclama" (v. 1259). Owen is saved from the ninth torment, the pit of hell that extinguishes body and soul, by remembering not to forget "the name of his Lord": "Tant fu de cel torment hastez,/pur poi qu'il ne s'ert obliëz/de nomer le nun sun

seignur" (v. 1297). Finally, Owen crosses the perilous bridge or the tenth torment and is rescued one last time by recall of the "name": "Al chevalier a
remembré/de quel peril Deus l'out jeté:/le nun Ihesucrist reclama" (v. 1373).

One finds analogues to Owen's successful passing of the ordeal of utterance in popular culture, in the belief, found almost universally, in the magic
power of incantatory words. In a striking medieval example, William of
Newburgh recounts the story of a simple man from Yorkshire by the name
of Ketel, whom some called the "elf-seer" and who some also said "had the
laudable custom of ejaculating the name of Christ whenever anything surprised him, which always drove away the hobgoblins for the time."[40] J. Le
Goff reminds us of literary analogies in the contemporaneous marial cult
with the intercession of that other Marie, the Virgin who saves the sinner at
the last minute in the *Miracles de Notre Dame* that we have discussed in the
context of "Lanval" and the rescuing fairy lady.[41] And yet, on the basis of all
that we have seen of Marie de France's heightened awareness of language in
the *Lais* and the *Fables*, one suspects something more profound at work.

In the repeated utterance of the single syllable that rescues Owen from
impending and everlasting disaster, we detect an infallible salutary language
effect. More precisely, what we find in the *Espurgatoire* is the very opposite
of the fatalistic language of the *Lais*, the words that rebound, wound, or kill
as soon as one opens one's mouth—that is, a salvific language that has exactly the opposite consequence, that saves, a magic language that dispels
danger in the instant of speech. The salvific effect of the single word "Jesus"
has to do, moreover, with speaking at just the right time. In a work whose
profoundest meaning has to do with the proportionality between acts committed on earth and punishment in the afterlife, Owen's utterances are all
about the demonstrable effects of proportional speech delivered at the appropriate moment. So, where we find an ontology of language in the *Lais*,
an ethics of language in the *Fables*, the *Espurgatoire* promulgates a her-
meneutics of language according to which a speech act—or, more precisely,
a failure to speak—might prove fatal, but according to which saying the
right word at the right time produces a liberating result. This is a universe,
like that of *Perceval*, in which it is essential to know when to speak and
when not to, which depends upon being able to distinguish truth from
falsehood, the true from the false speech of the devils. As the monks who
greet Owen before his ordeal explain, in listening to the devils who will
tempt him, he must learn to distinguish the truth from the falsity of their
claims:

"Grant multitudine i verras
des diables, n'en dute pas,
ki tranz turmenz te musterrunt,
de greignurs te manacerunt.
Se en lur cunseil vus metez
e se creire les en volez,
il vus prometrunt veirement
que hors vus merrunt salvement
a l'entree, dunt vus venistes
quant dedenz cest clos vus mesistes;
si vus quiderunt engignier.
De ço vus vueil bien acointier:
se vus creez lur fals sermun,
si irrez en perdiciün." (v. 733)

"You will see, have no doubt,
A huge crowd of devils
Who will show great suffering to you,
And threaten you with greater suffering;
If you show trust in their advice
And believe what they say,
They will promise solemnly
To lead you back safely
To the gate by which you entered
When you first placed yourself inside this enclosure.
Thus they will think they have fooled you.
I want to inform you of this:
If you believe their false words,
You will suffer perdition."

Once in Purgatory, Owen must learn to distinguish between falsehoods. As one set of devils confides to him, other devils have lied (v. 1313). The efficacy of the name resides, in fact, not in the word itself but in the ability to recognize the difference between true and false promises:

"S'en Deu avez ferme creance
en ses nuns e en sa puissance
e ne seiez espoëntez
des menaces que vus orrez,
e les pramesses nunverables
ne creez—qu'els sunt decevables!—
mes despisiez els e lur diz,
si serrez tensez e guariz;

> puis serrez de tuz voz pechiez
> e delivres e espurgiez." (v. 751, emphasis added)

> "If, however, you keep strong your faith in God,
> In his name and in his power,
> And are not terrified
> Of the threats directed at you,
> And if you refuse to believe their false promises
> —How deceptive they are!—
> But scorn them and their words,
> You will be defended and preserved.
> Then you will be set free
> And cleansed of all your sins."

For Owen, passing through Purgatory is, then, an act of correct speaking, but, equally important, of correct interpretation, a hermeneutic and not a physical struggle.

DOORS IN AND OUT OF THE OTHERWORLD

Now, unless we read the *Espurgatoire Seint Patriz* literally as the true story of a man who traveled to the Otherworld and back, we are obliged to understand his journey in metaphorical terms. That is to say, we are obliged to enter the text on some other level, to find some other range of meaning, by which to assimilate the manifest narrative that is told. Here, I suggest that there is no more potent means of entering the world of the meaning of Purgatory than via the question of entrance itself. Indeed, Purgatory as a place is so energetically enveloped by ways in and out that it is hard not to believe that they are not begging—in so far as a text might beg—for our attention. The abbey and cemetery that contain the entrance to Purgatory are surrounded by a wall, through which one passes via a door with a lock and key left there by Saint Patrick himself (v. 343). Owen enters the pit through another door: "Bravely, and with calm expression,/He went forward into the pit./When the prior had closed the door,/They all departed from the entrance" ("Hardiement, od bon semblant,/en la fosse se mist avant./La porte a li priürs fermee,/si se departent de l'entrée" [v. 663]). Conversely, having sustained the ten torments, Owen passes to the other side of Purgatory, to the Earthly Paradise, via a door: "He saw from afar/That the wall had a gate" ("Une porte a el mur veüe,/bien l'a de loinz aparceüe" [v. 1493]). So too, as the archbishops explain, one also passes from the Earthly Paradise to

the Celestial Paradise through a similar opening (v. 1805). Moreover, just as
Owen has entered Purgatory through a door, he is shown the way out:

> Hors a la porte l'unt mené;
> a Ihesucrist l'unt comandé.
> La porte cloënt. Il s'en va
> par mi les lius, u il passa. (v. 1869)[42]

> They led him out the gate,
> Commended him to Jesus Christ,
> And closed the door. He went away
> Through the places by which he had come.

For Owen, the topography of the cosmos—the earthly realm, Purgatory,
the Earthly Paradise, and the Celestial Paradise—is permeated by a series
of doors through which his passing is a test equivalent to the defining hermeneutic ordeal of recognizing the difference between false and true entrances, between falsehood and truth.

Owen's passage in and out of Purgatory is an example of what A. E.
Bernstein terms in relation to classical culture a "porous death."[43] Owen is a
knight obsessed by entrances—ports, doors, caves, pits. When he is outside
of Purgatory, he wants in; when he's in, he wants out. The prior promises to
show him the true way in; and, once inside, the devils constantly promise
to "show him the true entrance to Hell" ("le dreit enfer vus mosterruns"
[v. 1324]). The *Espurgatoire* is a text haunted practically from the start with
going in and out, with the soul's exit from the body and the question of
what happens to it when it departs:

> Seignurs, a l'eissue del cors,
> Quant les almes s'en issent fors
> Li bon angle i sunt en present;
> Li mal [i] vienent ensement. (v. 49)

> My Lord, when souls leave the body,
> And set out on their way,
> The good angels are present
> And the evil ones come there also.

And with the possibility of return, which is of the nature of the near-death
experience contained there: "puis repairent as cors en vies/e meustrent ço
que unt veü."[44] Again, the question for Owen is not in or out, but how to get
in when he is out, and how to get out when he is in, the question of how to

recognize the true entrances through which he might pass and the false ones which he should avoid.

The question of the door can be understood historically. Witness Gerald of Wales whose account, roughly contemporaneous with H. de Saltrey and Marie, provides for an actual physical pit on "an island one part of which is frequented by good and the other by evil spirits":

> There is a lake in Ulster which contains an island divided into two parts.
> One part contains a very beautiful church with a great reputation for holiness, and is well worth seeing. It is distinguished above all other churches by the visitation of angels and the visible and frequent presence of local saints.
> But the other part of the island is stony and ugly and is abandoned to the use of evil spirits only. It is nearly always the scene of gatherings and processions of evil spirits, plain to be seen by all. There are nine pits in that part, and if anyone by any chance should venture to spend the night in any one of them—and there is evidence that some rash persons have at times attempted to do so—he is seized immediately by malignant spirits and is crucified all night with such severe torments, and so continuously afflicted with many unspeakable punishments of fire and water and other things, that, when morning comes, there is found in his poor body scarcely even the smallest trace of life surviving. They say that if a person once undergoes these torments because of a penance imposed on him, he will not have to endure the pains of hell—unless he commit some very serious sin.[45]

Marie too figures hell as a "dark prison," its entrance as a great, scary hole: "Altresi est d'enfer li lius / Desuz terre, parfunz e cius, / Si cume chartre tenebruse" (v. 133). The darkness of Purgatory appears as a dark Wasteland— "En une guaste regiün / le meinent, hors de la maisun, / dunt la terre ert neire e oscure" (v. 915)—associated with the chaos of war and of civil discord that I have suggested elsewhere expresses a fear on the part of those living on the cusp of some glimmer of institutional order of falling back into the past, a fear of regression into violence and chaos.

One might understand the door to Purgatory anthropologically. The hole in the earth is so persistent a feature of the figuring of the underworld in a variety of cultures around the globe and throughout the ages that it seems almost universal—part of the human symbolic condition. Indeed, in Greek culture the entrance to the Cave of Hades leading to the realm of shades can be found in a fissure of the earth at Taenarus (Apollonius 2.728). The Romans situated the entrance to the realms below at the Acharusia palus, by the Sibyl's cavern, and at Avernus.[46] Access was regulated via a stone-covered pit, the *mundus* or entrance to the underworld for the city's ancestors, the *manes*. The Celts located the Otherworld in the Land-beneath-the-Waves, the land beyond the mist, or the hollow hill, to be reached via a *loch* or a well.[47] The Scandinavians placed hell toward the north deep in the ground. The volcanoes of Etna, Vesuvius, and Hecla functioned in popular legend throughout the Middle Ages as rivals to Saint Patrick's hole.

The trouble with the historical and the anthropological approach to the access to the next world is that one is too literal and specific, while the other is too general to be of any use in the understanding of a particular work of the imagination, especially one as self-conscious as the *Espurgatoire*. For Marie's understanding of the question of entrance partakes, above all, of the nature of the literary, and such an understanding is, further, of a piece with the literary self-consciousness manifest in the *Lais* and the *Fables*.

Marie links the penitent's approach to Purgatory to the realm of letters, a relation also present in H. de Saltrey's *Tractatus*. Those who have confessed and shown sufficient determination enter Purgatory via writing, as the bishop sends them to the "dark hole" with letters.[48] So too, Owen, strong in his determination to repent, is dispatched bearing the bishop's written consent to the prior "instructing him / To receive the knight / At purgatory and put him within" (v. 563).

Now, the question of letters and the entrance to Purgatory enjoys a certain literal historical connection. We possess records of actual letters of safe conduct to Saint Patrick's pit. Thomas Rymer's *Foedera,* under the date of 24 October 1358, shows that Edward III granted letters to Malatesta Ungarus of Arminium (Rimini), as well as to Nicholaus de Beccariis of Ferrara. On 7 September 1397 Richard II bestowed a letter, "De salvo conducta ad visitandum Purgatorium Sancti Patricii," upon Raymond de Perellós together with twenty men and thirty horses.[49] Eventually, the question of such letters became entangled in the venality associated with Saint Patrick's Purgatory in the late Middle Ages, as seen in the story of the pilgrimage of the monk of Eymstadt who in 1494 tried to visit as a mendicant. Sent by the prior of Purgatory to the bishop for a letter, the bishop insisted upon payment, which was waived due to the monk's lack of funds. The bishop sent the monk to the prince of the county, who also demanded a fee but who also relented. Back at the entrance to Purgatory, the monk was once more obliged to resist the demands of the prior for payment before being placed in the pit, where nothing happened. (What, one is tempted to ask, would have

happened if he had paid?) Disappointed, the pilgrim from Eymstadt transformed what was a pilgrimage into a crusade and proceeded to complain to
Pope Alexander IV who, according to the Annals of Ulster, ordered the destruction of the site in 1497.[50]

IN AND OUT OF ANOTHER TONGUE

Above and beyond the question of any potential reference to the historical practice of letters of safe conduct, and in keeping with the self-reflexive
nature of the rest of Marie's literary enterprise, the *Espurgatoire* is deeply
embedded in the project of translation. Translation, first of all, in the most
literal, etymological sense of the transfer or *translatio* of souls to the other
world that is part and parcel of the narrative of the trajectory toward eter-
nity for which the passage through Purgatory is a preparation. The *Espurgatoire* is implicated historically in the process of *translatio*—yet another
etymological meaning of the word—owing to the fact that Saint Patrick's
relics were, according to Gerald of Wales, literally translated to Downpatrick in the decade preceding H.'s *Tractatus,* despite the fact that the
Tripartite Life of Patrick maintains that the saint's true burial place remains
unknown.[51]

In the medieval version of Saint Patrick's life commissioned of Jocelin de
Furness by John de Courcy, who between 1177 and 1210 controlled the territory in which the entrance to Purgatory supposedly lay, the saint is portrayed as a translator capable of composing even in the native tongue. "In
four languages, the British, the Hibernian, the Gallic, and the Latin, was he
thoroughly skilled; and the Greek language also did he partly understand,"
Jocelin maintains. "The little Book of Proverbs, which he composed in the
Hibernian tongue, and which is full of edification, still existeth."[52] The visions of the afterlife germane to Saint Patrick's Purgatory are all to some extent concerned not only with the soul's translation to the Otherworld, but
with the literal question of translation. "For your wisdom has so wished that
our pen, although uneducated, should translate the mystery which was
shown to Tnugdal, an Irishman, from the vernacular into the Latin language," writes Brother Marcus to the Abbess G. at the beginning of *The Vision of Tnugdal.* Thurkill, the uneducated peasant, translated back to earth
after his sojourn in the Otherworld, miraculously speaks Latin for the first
time: "But now, when Thurkill was most eagerly gazing at their beauty, suddenly St. Michael said to St. Julian, 'Take this man back to his body. . . .

And lo, at once he was in the body again, he knew not how, and sitting up in bed he said, 'Benedicte!'"[53]

Translation is explicitly thematized in the *Espurgatoire* beginning with the identification of the place of entry. The original "showing" of the hole to Patrick is associated with the bestowal of a book ("un tixte d'evangiles" [v. 287]), the first descent, with translation. Unable to understand the Irish of the old man who comes to confess to him, Saint Patrick calls a translator, a "latinier," to "show and to open that which the old man says and of which he confesses" (v. 229). Owen, upon return from the pilgrimage undertaken after his descent, becomes a translator, as Gilbert, one of H. de Saltrey's sources, is sent to Ireland by the Cistercian Gervais to found an abbey and finds himself in need of linguistic help, provided in this instance by the king:

> Li reis li dist: 'N'en dutez mie!
> Jo vus metrai en compaignie
> un produne, bon latinier.'
> Dunc apela le chevalier
> Owein, si li preia e dist
> qu'od lui alast, si l'apresist. (v. 1955)

> The king said: "Do not worry.
> I will place you in the company
> Of a fine man and a good interpreter."
> Then he called the knight
> Owen, and asked him
> To go with Gilbert and to instruct him.

Together they found the abbey of which Gilbert is the manager and Owen the official latiner.[54]

We have seen elsewhere that the points of textual entry into the *Lais* and the *Fables* are the sites of strong theoretical understanding of the work that they frame. Marie's beginnings, her prologues, the places of entry into language, as at the beginning of "Guigemar," offer a key to our understanding of the whole, and the *Espurgatoire* is no exception. The ports of entry into and escape from Purgatory—the doors, gates, pit, and cave—are the nodal points of the narrative of the *Espurgatoire,* which is structured in some fundamental sense quite literally, and this from the beginning, by the search for the entrance to Purgatory:

> vueil en romanz mettre en escrit,
> si cum li livre le nus dit,

> en remembrance et en memoire,
> 'Des peines de l'Espurgatoire'
> qu'a seint Patriz volt Deus mustrer
> Le liu u l'um i deit entrer. (v. 3)

> I wish to put into writing in French,
> The Pains of Purgatory,
> Just as the book tells us about them,
> As a collection and record,
> For God wished to show Saint Patrick
> The place where one might enter purgatory.

Here we find ourselves before an extraordinary analogy between the place where "a man should enter" ("Le liu u l'um i deit entrer") and Marie's project of translation ("voeil en romanz mettre en escrit,/si cum li livre le nus dit"), and in front of a certain truth of the *Espurgatoire:* that is, the topographic quest for an entrance to Purgatory is the thematic analogue of Marie's search for an entrance into a previous text, in this case, into the English Cistercian H. of Saltrey's *Tractatus de Purgatorio Sancti Patricii.*

Given all that we know about Marie's consciousness of the concreteness of language, and indeed her play with words and letters, it is tempting to see in the *o* of Purgatory, as my late much-beloved colleague and friend Joel Fineman has seen in the *O* of Othello, a concretization of a graphic representation of the hole around which everything in the *Espurgatoire* is made to turn.[55] Indeed, I am not the first to make such an association, also contained in Barbam's "Lay of the Old Woman Clothed in Grey" of the *Ingoldsby Legends.*[56] Nor, as soon as one begins to think along such lines, can one avoid the *O* of Owen, inherited of course from H., or Marie's conscious use of the Anglo-Norman *Jo* for the Old French *Je* in signing her own name:

> *Jo,* Marie, ai mis, en memoire
> le livre de l'Espurgatoire
> en Romanz, qu'il seit entendables
> a laie gent e covenables. (v. 2297)

> I, Marie, have put
> The Book of Purgatory into French,
> As a record, so that it might be intelligible
> And suited to lay folk.

Whether or not the *o* of *Jo* is a conscious choice, the fact remains that the linguistic drama contained in the *Espurgatoire,* and expressed on the level of theme as Owen's getting in and out of Purgatory, has to do with the question of passing in and out of another language, translation being equated explicitly in Marie's text with places of entry, of opening. Indeed, alongside Owen's search for the entrance to Purgatory lies Marie's quest for an opening in the text she is translating, an "opening up," an uncovering:

> Poi en ai oï e veü;
> Por ço que j'en ai entendu
> Ai jo vers Deu greignur amur
> De lui servir, mun Creatur;
> Pur quei jo voldrai *aovrir*
> Ceste escripture e *descuvrir.* (v. 25)

> I have heard and seen little of this subject,
> Yet, through what I have learned of it,
> I have greater love for God,
> And desire to serve him, my Creator.
> For these reasons, I want to open up this writing
> For you, and reveal its contents.

The very word Marie uses for translation is *aovrir,* as we have seen in the exchange between St. Patrick and his "latinier" or translator:

> Pur ço qu'il ne saveit comprendre
> sun language ne rien entendre,
> il fist un latinier venir,
> Pur li *mustrer* et *aovrir*
> ço que li vieilz huem li diseit
> e dunt il se regehisseit. (v. 229)

> Yet, since Patrick did not know
> His language, nor understand what he said,
> He commanded a translator to come
> To *reveal* and *disclose* to him
> What the old man had said to him,
> And to tell him what he had confessed.

In the equation of *descuvrir, aovrir, mustrer* lies an extraordinary clue to just how Marie understood translation, one that goes to the heart of the *Espurgatoire.* For no word circulates more frequently or more meaningfully, in fact, than *mustrer,* which is used no less than thirty times and which is the equivalent, from the start, of the discovery of the location of the entrance to Purgatory:[57]

vueil en romanz mettre en escrit,
si cum li livre le nus dit,
en remembrance et en memoire,
'Des peines de l'Espurgatoire';
qu'a seint Patriz volt Deus *mustrer*
le liu u l'um i deit entrer. (v. 3)

According to her own logic (or the logic of the text), if Marie seeks to translate, "to put into writing in French/the pains of Purgatory," it is because "God wished to show Saint Patrick/The place where one might enter purgatory." At the very beginning where Marie enters into her material, that is, when she enters H. de Saltrey's text, she affirms that to translate is "to show," more precisely, to show the places where "one might enter" upon the pains of Purgatory, writing being for Marie a form of purgation.

Unlike writing as a primary activity—if, in fact, one could imagine a kind of primary writing without prior writing— translation is an opening up of another text, a "showing" that is the equivalent of disclosure. Marie expresses the desire "to uncover" or "to discover" the text she translates; and she emphasizes, just as in the prologue (v. 42) to the *Lais,* where she claims to have labored late into the night, the fact that she has put into the effort "pain"—purgatorial pain?—and "care": "Vueil *desclore* ceste escripture/E mettre i, pur Deu, peine e cure" (v. 45). In places in the *Espurgatoire* the verb *mustrer* is the equivalent simply of articulation or speech. Those who wish to enter Purgatory must seek the bishop and "show him" or "tell him" their confession ("cil, ki enz voleient entrer/e l'Espurgatoire espruver,/a l'eveske durent aler/e lur cunfessiün mustrer" [v. 435]). So too, Saint Patrick, who has been "shown" the hole, shows it to others by speaking, that which is "shown" ("mustré") being the equivalent of the spoken word (v. 265). Elsewhere, *mustrer* is the equivalent of writing or accurate writing, as Marie seeks to demonstrate in her "correct" rendering of Owen's story:

El tens le rei Estefine dit,
si cum nus trouvum en escrit,
qu'en Yrlande esteit uns prozdum
—chevaliers fu, Oweins out nun—,
de qui nus voluns ci parler
e la dreite estoire *mustrer.* (v. 503)

In the time of King Stephen,
As we find it written down,

> There was a nobleman in Ireland,
> A knight, by the name of Owen,
> About whom we now wish to speak,
> And to set forth his true story.

Still elsewhere, *mustrer,* which appears repeatedly in the *Espurgatoire,* though not in H. de Saltrey's *Tractatus,* refers, as in the case of the genealogy of the tale (more later), to translation. Thus, in revealing his sources, H. de Saltrey maintains that Gilbert told Owen's story to him, and he relates it to Marie, who "shows" or "translates" through writing:

> Gileberz conta icel fait
> a l'autor, ki nus a retrait,
> si cum Oweins li out conté
> e li moignes dunt j'ai parlé,
> ço que jo vus ai ici dit
> *e tut mustré par mun escrit.* (v. 2057)

> Gilbert told this matter
> To our author, who reported to us
> (Just as Owen told him [Gilbert]
> And the monks of whom I have spoken)
> What I have told you here
> *And shown thoroughly in my writing.*

Again, just as what God "shows" to Saint Patrick, and the premise upon which Purgatory rests, is a "big, deep, dark hole" (v. 301), what Marie "shows"—uncovers, opens, discloses—in H. de Saltrey's text are its holes. All of which returns us to the most basic concept of what the writing of the ancients—or any writing for that matter—is for Marie as announced in the prologue to the *Lais:* gaps or obscurities, holes into which those who come after are obliged to insert their own "surplus of sense."

MAKING THE DEAD SPEAK

This little study of the semantic field of the verb *mustrer* underscores what one might think of as the "echolalia effect" of a near-death vision like the *Espurgatoire,* that is, the sense it proffers of voices—Owen's, Gilbert's, H. de Saltrey's, Marie's—speaking or translating through each other. In this respect translation is a means of communicating with the dead, of making the dead speak, but also of speaking for the dead via a literal blending or appropriation of their voice. Nor is such a genealogy of oral transmission

direct, but becomes in H.'s epilogue—present in version B, but not in A—
a virtual chorus. There H. claims to have spoken with two abbots who also
contribute to his story:

> Ego autem, postquam hec omnia audieram, duos de Hibernia abbates, ut
> adhuc certior fierem, super his conueni. Quorum unus, quod numquam in
> patria sua audierat talia, respondit. Alius uero, quod multotiens hec audierit
> et quod essent omnia uera, affirmauit. Sed et hoc testatus est quod idem pur-
> gatorium raro quis intrantium redit.[58]

And which Marie translates:

> Puis parlai jo a dous abez
> (d'Irelande) erent, bons ordenez,
> si lur demandai de cel estre
> se ço poeit veritez estre.
> Li uns afirma que veirs fu
> de l'Espurgatoire e seü
> que plusurs humes i entrerent,
> ki unkes puis n'en retornerent. (v. 2063)

> Thereafter, I myself spoke to two abbots,
> Good, ordained men, from Ireland,
> And asked them if these events
> Could be true.
> One of them pronounced true
> All that has been said about purgatory,
> And commented that he knew several men
> Who went there but who never returned.

A reading of the Latin and the vernacular alongside each other makes it clear
that more is involved in passing from H. to Marie than a simple transfer
from one language to another. Their juxtaposition poses a thorny problem
of voice. Elsewhere Marie speaks of H. as the "auctor" whom she trans-
lates/transmits. Her own voice ("je"), therefore, cannot be the same as his.
Here, however, she simply adopts H.'s "je"; and were we not to have H.'s text
before us, we would have no way of telling that Marie's "jo" was not that of
H. himself. Nor, in the absence of the source text, would there be any way
of telling if it were H. or Marie who has spoken to the two Irish abbots.

If H.'s voice speaks through Marie, other voices speak through him.
Take, for example, H.'s conversation with Bishop Florentien, the nephew of
the "third Saint Patrick" ("Nevos fu al tierz seint Patriz" [v. 2073]). "Nuper
etiam affatus sum episcopum quendam, nepotem sancti Patricii tertii,"

reads manuscript B of the Latin,[59] whereas Marie's use of the pronominal *jo* blends her voice with that of H.: "En cel an meïsmes trovai / un eveske, a qui jo parlai" ("This year I also spoke / To a bishop whom I met" [v. 2071]). Again, there is no way of knowing, absent the Latin original, that it is not Marie who spoke with the bishop.[60] Or, again, asked if the stories about Purgatory are true, Florentien responds to H. in the first person: "De quo cum curiosius inquirerem, respondit episcopus: 'Certe, frater, uerum est. Locus autem ille in episcopatu meo est'" ("Indeed, brother, this is true. This Purgatory lies in my diocese and many have died there").[61] And in her translation Marie appropriates that person as her own: "Ententivement, li enquis / se ço fust veirs, que l'en ert vis. / E il me dist, certainement / que c'esteit veirs, e dist coment" ("I asked him eagerly if what I heard / Was true, and what his opinion of it was. / He said that it was all indeed true, / And told me how he came to learn of the place" [v. 2081]). The commingling of a "je" or a "jo" and an "ego," which is sometimes H. and at other times Marie, creates a ghostlike atmosphere in the *Espurgatoire:* ghosts, having been translated to the realm of death, seem, through translation from one language to another, to speak, indeed to have returned from the dead.

Some will object that I have used a metaphor to describe a phenomenon that might better be described in more neutral terms. Yet, how can one speak of the silent emptiness of death—the beyond, the hole, absence, the real—without recourse to metaphor, the medieval term for which was precisely translation, *translatio?* Nor, finally, does Marie's understanding of translation, as seen in the *Espurgatoire* and not in H.'s *Tractatus,* allow us to move very far away from the question of literature itself. In a world in which the reworking of sources rather than the originality of testimony is the mark of authenticity, literature in general, and the Otherworld journey in particular, is a way of allowing the dead to speak, of communicating with the dead, and, thus, of maintaining a relation to the dead. Through the fiction of such communication, which is assimilable, finally, to the nature of fiction itself, the dead are somehow not entirely dead, they are less dead.

The ventriloquism implicit in vision literature, by which the dead who speak and speak in a dead language are thus translated back to the land and the language of the living, is also a matter of cultural translation. C. Carozzi notes that most near-death visions involve social elevation in that they happen to simple and illiterate souls whose experiences are not only recorded but inevitably interlaced with such literate interpolations as to make it clear that it is an erudite author, and not the visionary, who speaks.[62] This is true of Bede's story of the vision of Dryhthelm in the seventh century, and is just as true of the vision of Tnugdal, which supposedly took place around the same time (1148 or 1149) as that of Owen (1153). Though Tnugdal may be a knight and "brought up in the manner of the court," he relates his story to Brother Marcus, who excuses himself for his lack of linguistic mastery: "I am incompetent and almost ignorant of Latin eloquence, but I am not unhappy to offer this story, for God loves a happy giver, supposing that my small and meagre talent were able to recount it."[63] Nor does Marcus's voice become any less mingled with that of Tnugdal than that of Marie with H.

The question of translation is for Marie generally assimilable to that of literature, or, simply, of how to put oneself into the voice of another. And it entails, in keeping with Marie's theory of literature as an introduction of a "surplus of meaning" into the obscurities of another's writing, an excess. For her search for an entrance to H.'s text cannot be disassociated from a search for a voice, for a place of entry, for the feminine voice within a masculine world; and in cultural terms, it cannot be detached from the search of a feminine voice on the side of the vernacular for a place by which to enter the masculine Latin tradition. Owen's hunt for a place to enter Purgatory expresses on the level of theme Marie's own attempt literally to find the places at which to insert a voice, a self, a *je,* within her Latin model. Indeed, such an assertion can be taken on the most literal level as an attempt to introduce pronouns, that is, the first person pronoun singular—*je*—into the inflected forms of Latin, the attempt to find the places, the holes, the ports of entry for a self, a "je," into an inflected tongue. This is a simple point, one so obvious that to give examples is almost to retranscribe both Henry's and Marie's texts in their entirety. When, for example, Henry writes, "Licet enim utilitatem multorum per me provenire desiderem" ("Although it is my wish that many may find improvement through me"),[64] Marie renders the pronoun implicit in the person contained in the present subjunctive "desiderem" by "Jeo desir": "Ja seit iço que jeo desir/De faire a grant profit venir/Plusurs genz e els amender" ("However much I might want to cause many people/To come to great profit" [v. 17]). She literally introduces a self, an "I," into Henry's Latin model. And this process of interjecting a vernacular voice into the Latin tradition that on the most basic level of syntax involves introducing the *je* into Latin's inflected morphological forms is equivalent to the entrance and exit of Owen to and from Purgatory, which are, as we have seen, figured consistently in terms of writing.

The story of Owen's entrance to, adventures in, and return from Purgatory is the story of a purgation. A purgation, first of all, of the Latin language and the cultural model it implies. For Latin hangs over the *Espurgatoire* like the insistent devils seeking to drag Owen down. Indeed, subservience to the Latin text is one of the obsessive tics of the *Espurgatoire,* and Marie constantly draws our attention to the determining presence of "li escriz," the already written: "Ici trovum *en nostre escrit*" (v. 141); "Seignur, si cum dit *li escriz*" (v. 421). Whereas H. of Saltrey seems merely to recount in some more immediate sense the events contained in the narrative of the *Tractatus*— "Contigit autem his temporibus nostris, diebus scilicet Regis Stephani, militem unum nomine Owein, de quo presens est narratio . . ." ("In this our time, that is in the days of King Stephen, it happened that a knight called Owein, who is the subject of this narrative . . .")[65]—the *Espurgatoire* is mediated through H. to whom Marie remains in some fundamental sense beholden: "In the time of King Stephen,/As we find it written down,/There was a nobleman in Ireland . . ." ("El tens le rei Estefne dit,/si cum nus trovum *en escrit,*/qu'en Yrlande esteit uns prozdum" [v. 503]). For Marie, hell is figured as a "dark prison":

> Altresi est d'enfer li lius
> desuz terre, parfunz e cius,
> si cume chartre tenebruse,
> a cels qui mesfunt perilluse. (v. 133)

> Likewise, the location of hell is
> Beneath the earth, deep and dark,
> Like a gloomy prison,
> Perilous to those who do evil.

The "gloomy prison"—"chartre tenebruse"—is also represented as a "shadowy charter," the prison a charterhouse, assimilated in the *Espurgatoire* to the constraining effects of Latin, as well as of its predominantly male tradition, upon Marie both as a vernacular writer and as a woman. After all, the limiting "escrit" does not stop with H. de Saltrey, but extends beyond the "autor" to his own sources, which are mentioned by name and rooted as far back as the Church Fathers, beginning with Augustine: "We find in our book/That they remain there in delight./Elsewhere, Saint Augustine tells us . . ." ("ici trovum *en nostre escrit*/qu'iluek demuerent a delit./Aillurs nus dit Seinz Aüstins . . ." [v. 141]). And moving forward in time to the seventh century with Gregory the Great, whose *Dialogues,* book 4, are one of the great sources of vision literature in the West: "Saint Gregoires dit altresi,/en ses livres, qu'avuns oï" (v. 151).

Alongside its defining debt to the patristic past, the *Espurgatoire* also carries the possibility of a liberation, a raising of the vernacular to the status of

Latin, an endowing of the Anglo-Norman tongue with grammar, with rules, with a memory that we have seen elsewhere to be an integral part of Marie's project of cultural reclamation. Indeed, we have a good example in the phrase just examined of what escapes the constraining model, since an understanding of the "shadowy charter" as both a prison and a charter works in Old French, but does not work in Latin, which distinguishes *carcer* from *charta:* "Et quod infernus subtus terram, uel infra terre concauitatem, quasi carcer et ergastulum tenebrarum a quibusdam esse creditur, narracione ista nichilominus asseritur" ("Furthermore, this account confirms what is believed by some, that hell is under the earth, or rather at the bottom of a cavity in the earth, like a dungeon or a prison of darkness").[66] That which escapes the Latin model, the added meaning of *chartre/charter* as paper, is an addendum, an emendation that Marie associates in the beginning of the *Espurgatoire* with the "amendation" of character via purgation; it is, in other words, one of the supplemental semantic resonances in Old French that is thoroughly assimilable to the process of glossing that figures so centrally in the prologue to the *Lais,* one of the "surpluses of sense" that Marie equates not only with translation but with the understanding of literary works through time and with writing. Translation is for Marie de France a "breaking out" of the prison house of language.

Then too, as I have suggested, among the independent semantic resonances of Old French that escape "li escriz," the Latin model, none is more significant than the incantatory invocation—"le nun Ihesucrist"—which is for Owen "the name of Jesus" and for Marie "the *no* of Jesus": "En quel liu que seiez menez/e quel turment que vus sentez,/le nun Ihesucrist apelez" ("In whatever place where you are led,/And whatever torments you will experience,/Call on the name of Jesus Christ" [v. 777]). Here, again, the homonym obvious in the vernacular does not work in the Latin which reads simply, "Semper igitur in memoria habeas Deum, et cum te cruciauerint, inuoca Dominum Ihesum Christum" ("Always remember God and when they torture you call upon the name of the Lord Jesus Christ, for through the invocation of his name you will immediately be delivered from the torture").[67]

For France's first woman poet, translation involves a hermeneutic struggle analogous to Owen's recognition of the difference between truthful and deceiving devils, true and false entrances. It is indissociable from the writer's ordeal of correct reading and, ultimately, of correct writing. The devil's promise "to show" to Owen "the real hell" ("le dreit enfer vus mosterruns" [v. 1324]) is assimilable to Marie's promise "to show" the real story

found in "writing," that is, in H. de Saltrey's text (v. 503). Avoidance of the
pains of Purgatory implies a recognition of true interpretations and a purg-
ing of false ones. Indeed, Marie understands translation as an act of correct
interpretation or reading of a prior text, a reception of certain elements and
a rejection of others. For Owen's "nun," which is also a "no," can be seen as
a resistance to, an elimination of that which is left behind and will not pass
from one language to another as well as a process of inserting meanings—
"surpluses of sense"—in the original. In this, translation entails the creation
of a parallel universe, what Virginia Woolf, in her famous essay by the same
title, refers to as a "room of one's own." Marie titles her book "Les peines
de l'espurgatoire," the "pains of purgatory," in which the alert English
reader—among whom I include Marie—is tempted to see not only the
"pains," but the "pens of purgatory," the word *pen* first attested in English
in the twelfth century from the Old French *penne;* nor can it be an accident
that she uses the word *espurgatoire* instead, simply, of *purgatoire.* It is difficult not to imagine that she imagined writing her way "out of purgatory"—
es + purgatoire—via the vernacular tongue.

CHAPTER EIGHT

Between Fable and Romance

Given the richness of the medieval tradition of Otherworld visions, what is Marie's contribution? Why did she choose the *Tractatus* for translation? How does such a choice fit with what we have seen of the *Lais* and the *Fables?* In moving from the documentary character of the *Tractatus* to the literary ethos of the *Espurgatoire,* what elements of doctrine pass into the generic mold, or at least fulfill the generic expectations, of fable and of romance?

The *Espurgatoire* serves, first of all, as a dissemination of the legend in the vernacular. The translation from Latin to Anglo-Norman French works a cultural translation in so far as it asks the question, also posed in the *Lais,* of what might pass back and forth across the channel between English and French, of what might pass from the increasingly firm doctrine of Purgatory, as articulated among the monks and theologians of the twelfth century, into popular culture, and into a popular culture increasingly given to the expression of its own aspirations in various narrative forms. What the *Espurgatoire* does in converting a supposedly documentary treatise on the origins and workings of Purgatory into a tale of knightly deeds is significant, for it is a translation not just between languages but between different cultural discourses, or, again, between a work that aspires to the status of verifiable truth and one that resonates with romance. For H. de Saltrey's *Tractatus* is just that, a treatise, the written record of a series of oral depositions. Marie's *Espurgatoire,* on the other hand, is more sharply focused upon the literary; and where H. maintains a certain documentary relation to the testimony of witnesses it records, the primary relation of the *Espurgatoire*—and herein lies its literary specificity—is to another written text. Marie's alternate blending with the voice of H. and distancing from the written

record, "li escriz," offer certain proof that we are in the realm of textual relations, in the orbit of what Harold Bloom terms an "agony of influence"
between strong literary presences. Given how careful Marie is, as we have
seen in the *Lais,* concerning the choice of what she chooses to translate,
given how anxious she is about her effect upon others, the conscious choice
of the *Tractatus*—and by this time I hope the reader will have been convinced that everything Marie does is conscious—tells us something fundamental about the integral body of her work as well as about the persona that
we are in the process of reconstructing from it.

It is my claim, argued in what follows, that the *Espurgatoire,* so clearly
posited between two cultures, clerical and lay, stands, finally, as a negotiation between the *Lais* and the *Fables.* My first instinct in writing this sentence was to use the word *synthesis* to describe the way that the *Espurgatoire*
mediates between them. Yet "synthesis" is a bit too neat, a trifle too wrapped
up, and perhaps also a tad too laden with intention to describe what appears
as an attempt on Marie's part to resolve that which remains incomplete,
troubling, and untenable in her other two works.

I realize that I am taking for granted the chronology of Marie's literary
production—that the *Lais* were written before the *Fables,* and the *Fables* before the *Espurgatoire.* Even were such a series not well established on philological and historical grounds, I think that the claim could be made on the
basis of the logical consistency of moving from the mental universe of the
Lais to that of the *Fables* and to the *Espurgatoire* in terms of an internal logic
of their relation, a continuum of the will expressed as a particular relation
to language, and according to which each work responds to and grows out
of that which precedes.

Simply put, we find in the *Lais* a certain theological absolutism according to which life in the flesh is conceived to be unthinkable and, concur-
rently, a fatalism of language such that one is wounded or dead in the
instant one speaks. Though I am more than a little wary of such broad
generalizations, it is the case that such a literary vision could be associated
with a Platonic-Augustinian worldview characteristic of the early Middle
Ages, one that operates under the assumption of a radical separation between this world and the next that cannot be bridged by degrees of being
and therefore cannot be mediated by mind or reason. The *Fables,* in contrast, show the glimmerings of an efficacy of the will in a social world in
which a myriad of potential good and bad speech acts carry the burden of
ethical action. And yet even here a certain lingering fatalism lurks in the un-
predictability of the body—animal and social—ready to make itself felt

whenever appetite usurps right reason. If in the *Lais* one is condemned merely for being alive, in the *Fables* one is subject to the limits of one's own species in relation to other species within the context of a fickle fight for survival. What is satisfactory about the *Lais* is precisely their incorporation of the theological; what is excluded is the possibility of life on this planet. What is appealing in the *Fables* is the possibility of escaping—via an exertion of the will—the fatalism of the *Lais,* yet what remains missing, in the struggle between the big and the little, the strong and the weak, is precisely some general and absolute standard by which particular bodies might be restrained.

The present chapter speaks to the identity between the language theater of the *Espurgatoire* and that of the *Lais,* while that which follows takes up the social effects of Purgatory encountered in the *Fables.*

MAKING THE DEAD SEE

The drama of language that we identified in the *Lais* as a conflict between the desire for fullness and integration and the knowledge of the partial and contingent nature of linguistic expression is no less present in the *Espurgatoire,* where it is expressed in terms of an anxious awareness of the inadequacy of articulation   of the difficulty of making the invisible visible and of giving the visible articulate form. On the one hand, Marie is conscious of the fragility of the enterprise, wrapped in the making of literature itself, of making the dead speak, and, on the other, she is no less tempted to buttress the unsubstantiality of the literary by recourse to the seemingly certain techniques of testimony, transcription, and, of course, her old identifying shibboleth of memory and reassembly or "remembrement."

The genre of the medieval Otherworld voyage or near-death experience is enveloped in the issue of making death—some might say the void, others the real—palpable and involves a complicated cycle in the *Espurgatoire* between the invisible and the visual, the oral and the written. The story of Owen's and others' descent and return turns around making the Otherworld visible in order that it might take material shape in the imagination, might become real, might be credible. This is why the little word *mustrer* is so important and why, meaning both "to show" and "to tell" or "to describe," it functions at the interstices of that which is heard and that which is seen. However, as Marie is well aware, the world of the imagination and that of words are only partially, and sometimes even dangerously, connected. The "Say it and you lose it" of "Lanval" and the "choose one and lose them all" of "Chaitivel" hover as emblems over the *Lais*. They capture in some very compressed sense the hazardous consequences of an incommensurability between words and things characteristic of the linguistic fatalism of the *Lais* and evident in the sense of liability and of loss in speech, the perilous gap between that which can be thought, sensed, or seen and that which can be said. Marie is constantly aware of the reductive, contingent, material nature of words alongside the expansive, universal wholeness of the imagination or of an idea.

The deadly drama of language writ so large across the *Lais* also spills over to the *Espurgatoire* in the inadequation between what the mind might conceive or the body might sense, and even might suffer as the pains of Purgatory, and the words, regardless of number, expressive of that conception or sensation. No fullness of language, and here Marie is categorical, might capture the reality of lived, bodily experience:

> Tels sunt les peines enfernals
> e les mesaises e les mals
> que nuls nes porreit anumbrer
> plus que gravele de la mer. (v. 1411)

> The pains, suffering,
> And torment of hell
> Are more numerous
> Than the sands of the sea.

The *Espurgatoire* is inscribed in a contradiction between the necessity of making the invisible visible and the translation of visibility into human language that, recognized to be deeply flawed, remains inadequate.

In this Marie draws upon a topos practically synonymous with medieval vision literature, and especially visions of the Otherworld. Tnugdal's tongue remains unequal to that which he hears and sees: "After a long time, alone in such dangers, he heard the shouts and howls of a huge crowd, and a thunder so horrific that neither our humble person could comprehend it nor, as Tnugdal admitted, was his tongue able to relate it." The Monk of Evesham, whose vision related in Roger of Wendover's *Flowers of History* supposedly took place in 1196 or within a decade of the *Tractatus/Espurgatoire,* admits to being incapable of articulating, or even remembering, that which he has experienced: "And what we saw as we went on, the tongue cannot reveal or human weakness worthily describe. . . . But how glittering was the inconceivable brightness, or how strong was the light which filled all those places, let no one ask of me, for this I am not able to express in words, nor even to recollect in my mind."[1] More important, the "inexpressibility topos" found in the visions of Tnugdal, of the Monk of Evesham, and in the *Espurgatoire* participates, as we have seen, in a deeper medieval drama of language manifest not only in the *Lais* but in the verbal epistemology of the period between Augustine and the scholastics of the thirteenth century and the terminists or modists of the fourteenth. Put in simplest terms, this drama is founded upon a recognition of the incommensurability between the universality of an idea, and even an idea accessible to the mind, and its expression in verbal—oral or written—form, a recognition of a disparity between what writers and thinkers *know* about human language as an essentially flawed, irrecuperable, conventional (socially determined) medium and what they *feel* as a deep nostalgia for the wholeness of beginnings when the word corresponded to the thing.[2]

Throughout the Middle Ages, in visions like the *Espurgatoire,* the medieval drama of language is expressed in terms of a mind/body, or rather a soul/body, split attached to the question of Purgatory and having to do with the difficulty of knowing with certainty whether it is the soul or the body that voyages to, that beholds, the Otherworld. Given the fallible nature of the senses, if it is the body that travels to the beyond, then the question naturally arises as to the trustworthiness of the perceptions that it brings back. And, on the other hand, if it is the soul that voyages, then the question remains as to how a soul, absent the bodily faculties of perception, might actually see anything in the Otherworld or might know what it has seen.[3]

In the case of the Monk of Wenlock it is the soul that travels and the body that remains. In terms that would not have surprised Plato, Wenlock "said that the extreme pain from a violent illness had suddenly freed his spirit from the burden of his body" and speaks of the lifting of "the veil of the flesh."[4] Dryhthelm too leaves his body behind and eventually returns to it with some regret. "When he [his guide] had finished speaking," Dryhthelm reports, "I returned to the body with much distaste, for I was greatly delighted with the sweetness and grace of the place I had seen and with the company of those whom I saw in it."[5] "As soon as he had shed the body and knew for sure that it was dead, the soul became frightened," Tnugdal confesses; yet, once having glimpsed the Earthly Paradise, his soul begs to remain: "But the angel said: 'You must go back to your body and retain in your memory everything you saw, for the benefit of your neighbour.'"[6] In the rubric that reads, "How the same monk was separated from the body, and entered the first place of punishment," it is clear that the Monk of Evesham undergoes an out-of-body experience.[7] So too, when Thurkill departs,

Saint Julian urges him to leave his body behind and, given the greater realism of the age, allows for infusing it with a simulation of life: "And when Thurkill began to rise, the saint said 'Let thy body rest here awhile, only thy Soul will depart with me. But that thy friends may not think thee dead, I will send a breath of life into thee.' And so saying he breathed into Thurkill's mouth: and they both, as it seemed to the man, left the house, and set forth straight towards the east."[8]

H. de Saltrey is conscious of the paradox of the insentient soul traveling to the beyond, and he focuses upon the materiality of that which is seen there according to Gregory the Great, who "says that souls taken away and returned to the body tell of visions and revelations made to them either of the torments of the sinners or the joys of the just. However, everything mentioned in their tales is concrete or similar to material elements."[9] In his own voice H. reminds us that "these torments cannot be defined by men because they have no means whatsoever of knowing them."[10] Marie too focuses upon the dilemma of seeing the truth of Purgatory with fallible eyes in the first mention of the possibility of souls visiting the Otherworld contained in the *Espurgatoire*. Those who have been to the beyond and "then return to the living body and show what they have seen" ("puis repairent as cors en vies/e meustrent ço que unt veü" [v. 73]) do so only because "they see spiritually that which appears corporeally" ("Els veient espiritelment/ ço que semble corporelment" [v. 77]).

And they do so only because that which is seen spiritually is given corporeal substance through words. The torments of Purgatory may be hidden to the senses "since they are spiritual and men are mortal"; but, through verbalization, that which is spiritual and inaccessible to the eye can be seen. It becomes, and here the phrase is key, "like a corporal substance":

> Icist turment sun esconsé,
> a la gent ne sunt pas mustré
> pur ço qu'il sunt espiritel
> e que li hume sunt mortel.
> E si par revelaciünsveient e par avisiüns
> plusurs des almes meinz granz signes
> (solunc iço qu'eles sunt dignes),
> quant eles sunt des cors ravies.
> Par Deu revienent a lur vies
> e diënt bien, pur la mustrance
> de cele espiritel sustance,
> *que semblable est* a corporel

ço qu'il veient espiritel.
E si nus dit qu'ume mortel
unt ço veü e corporel
si cume en forme e *en semblance*
de vive corporel sustance. (v. 163)

These torments are hidden,
And not manifest to people
Since they are spiritual,
And men are mortal.
And thus by revelations
And by visions
Many souls see numerous great signs,
According to their worth
When they are rapt from their bodies.
With god's help, they return to their lives,
And tell clearly, as an illustration
Of spiritual substance,
That what they perceive as spiritual
Is similar to the corporeal.
They even say that a mortal,
Material man saw spiritual things
In the form and *appearance*
Of live material substance.

The trajectory of passage to the world inaccessible to the senses ("Icist turment sun esconsé,/a la gent ne sunt pas mustré") and return accompanied by a making of that which cannot be seen accessible to the eye ("la mustrance/de cele espiritel sustance") is a sleight of hand or eye, the equivalent of a magic trick, and, indeed, what we might think of as an instance of the literary, a giving of visual form to that which is invisible and of verbal form to that which can henceforth be seen. For here it is clear that we are dealing with the nature of metaphor, the literary magic residing not in the identity of the bodily and the spiritual, the seen and the unseen, but in the "being like"—the "que semblable est," the "si cume," the "semblance" which H.'s Latin renders: "Unde et in hac narratione a corporali e mortali homine spiritualia dicuntur uideri quasi in specie et forma corporali."[11] The difference between "quasi in specie et forma corporali " ("under the aspect and form of material things") and Marie's "semblance" and "as if," the former indicating a relation between two distinct modes of physical things and the second a relation of material reality to illusion, contains all the difference between

H.'s *Tractatus,* which is a record of Owen's adventure, and Marie's *Espurgatoire,* which is a literary reworking of that record. Saint Patrick's Purgatory is not simply another story of an Otherworld vision but a paradigm of the literary. Whether entering into the gaps in the language of the ancients as in the prologue to the *Lais,* or entering a fissure in the earth as in the *Espurgatoire,* the descent, the expiatory pains, the emergence, dictation, transcription, and translation of the "semblances" of the Otherworld are, unless we are willing to take them literally as believable and real, on the order of a dramatization and an allegory, a dramatization of death and an allegory of the describability of death as a great "epistemological barrier"—an empty hole—about which anything that can be said is of the nature of fiction itself.[12]

Again, I am not the first to sense the deep identity between the story of Purgatory and the making of fiction, to take the describability of the beyond as an allegory for the birth of art. In what remains a foundational article on medieval vision poems, H. R. Jauss equates allegory with making the invisible visible. With specific reference to Otherworld journeys, C. Zaleski compares the relation they establish between seeing and telling about that which is inaccessible to the senses with "a work of the narrative imagination." With still more specific reference to Saint Patrick, S. Leslie observes that the story of Purgatory fulfills the human longing for ghost stories while sharing in the mysterious draw of the detective genre.[13] So too, S. Greenblatt, in a book on the relationship between Protestant attacks upon Purgatory and the ghosts that reappear upon the Renaissance stage, shows with consummate rigor and elegance that there is something specific in the nature of Saint Patrick's story that, above and beyond the material causality that we may associate with it, partakes of, is attached to, crystallizes around, the nature of fable "in the way that fables seize hold of the mind, create vast unreal spaces, and people those spaces with imaginary beings and detailed events."[14]

The literary sleight of hand that I have associated with the origin of Purgatory, the making of something out of nothing and the usurpation of that something by others that haunts Marie, the fictitious dialogue with the dead that is of the nature of fiction itself, explains, I think, the concern expressed about the formation of the legend of Saint Patrick on the part of those responsible for its compilation. The author, or authors, of the *Tripartite Life,* recognizing the fragility of the "thread of narration," seek to establish a continuous line of transmission via a series of names whose repetition is intended to ground the legend's authority.[15] Jocelin de Furness, like a nineteenth-century philologist, is concerned with the "establishment" and provenance of the text:

> And of all those things which so wonderously he did in the world, sixty and six Books are said to have been written, whereof the greater part perished by fire in the reigns of *Gurmundus* and of *Turgesius*. But four books of his virtues and his miracles yet remain, written partly in the Hibernian, partly in the Latin language; and which at different times four of his Disciples composed;—namely, his successor the blessed *Benignus;* the Bishop Saint *Mel;* the Bishop Saint *Lumanus,* who was his nephew; and his grand-nephew Saint *Patricius,* who after the decease of his uncle returned unto Britain, and died in the Church of Glascon. Likewise did Saint *Evinus* collect into one volume the acts of Saint Patrick, the which is written partly in the Hibernian, and partly in the Latin tongue. From all which, whatsoever we could meet most worthy of belief, have we deemed right to transmit in this our work unto after-times.[16]

Owen's fictional voyage to Purgatory shows a similar anxiety concerning origins and an anxiousness to establish, if not the truth, then a credible account of its own transcription and transmission.

TESTIMONY AND TRANSCRIPTION

If, as we have seen, those who enter Purgatory do so via writing, sent by the bishop to the "dark hole" with letters, the return of those who do return is also marked by the written word that serves as the guarantor of experience. And this from the start in the practice, initiated by Saint Patrick, of testimonial transcription:

> Enz entrerent seürement.
> Mult sufrirent peine e turment
> e mult virent horrible mal
> de la dure peine enfernal;
> aprés icele grant tristesce
> virent grant joie e grant leesce.
> Ço qu'il voldrent cunter e dire
> fist seinz Patriz iluek escrire. (v. 355)

> And [they] entered securely.
> They suffered great pain and torment,
> And witnessed much of the horrible agony
> Of bitter infernal pain;
> After this great sorrow,

They witnessed great joy and happiness.
Whatever they wished to recount and tell,
Saint Patrick had written down on the spot.

The question of the immediacy of transcription is one that vexes the Otherworld experience to be captured as freshly as possible. In transmitting the
vision of Dryhthelm, for example, Bede assures us that the man who took
direct testimony, Brother Haemgisl, is still alive and that "He would often
visit this man and learn from him, by repeated questionings, what sort of
things he saw when he was out of the body; it is from his account that these
particulars which we have briefly described came to our knowledge." In addition, Dryhthelm, like Owen, frequents a royal patron: "He also told his
visions to King Aldfrith, a most learned man in all respects. . . . at the king's
request he was admitted to the monastery already mentioned. . . . Whenever the king visited that region, he often went to listen to his story."[17] Boniface, writing to "the blessed virgin and best-loved lady, Eadburga," assures
her of the freshness of his account of the Monk of Wenlock's vision by
telling her that it is not a matter of hearsay but that "I myself spoke recently
with the aforesaid resurrected brother when he returned to this country
from beyond the seas. He then related to me in his own words the astounding visions which he saw in the spirit while he was out of the body."[18]
Thurkill's vision is witnessed openly by the entire community: "on the day
of All Saints and on the day of All Souls, he proclaimed all that he had seen,
consistently and clearly, in the English tongue; in the presence of Osbert de
Longchamp, the lord of the village, and his wife, and the rest of the parishioners; all being utterly astonished at the eloquence of the man, who had always before been bashful and nearly tongue-tied." His words are faithfully
recorded as soon as they are uttered: "I have striven to write down the Vision of this simple man in simple speech, just as I heard it from his own
mouth," the scribe, whom some believe to be Ralph of Coggeshall, proclaims.[19]

The question of ocular witnessing is at the origin of the cult of Saint
Patrick and the legend of Purgatory attached to it. According to popular belief, Patrick, having failed to convert the Irish by preaching, was called upon
to make visible his words concerning heaven and hell. Whereupon the Lord
appeared to him and showed him a pit, saying: "Whatever man, being truly
penitent, and armed with a lively faith, shall enter that pit, and there remain
for a day and a night, shall be purged from all his sins, and going through it
shall behold the states of bliss and woe."[20] The importance of visual per-

ception persists throughout the period in question. In the prologue to his account of his pilgrimage to Lough Derg in 1397, for example, Ramon de Perellós insists upon the conviction of the eye over the ear:

> It is a fact that everyone desires to learn about things which are strange and wonderful and that, naturally, those things are more pleasing when one can see them for oneself rather than learn of them by hearsay alone. For this reason, I, brought up in my youth by King Charles of France, in whose care my father, who was his admiral and chamberlain left me, in his Court—with all the knights and squires of his kingdom and of other Christian kingdoms— was eager to know and learn about the wonderful, diverse and strange things which exist in the world: and my heart was set on seeing those things rather than merely hearing about them from many and divers knights.[21]

Both H. de Saltrey and Marie emphasize that the "fickle bestiality" of the Irish is synonymous with a disbelief cured by God's showing Patrick "the pit which he could show to the people": "Mult fu haitiez de sun seignur/que il aveit veü le jur,/e de la fosse veirement,/qu'il poeit mustrer a la gent" (v. 331). As we have seen in the context of the little word *mustrer,* Purgatory, or rather the belief in Purgatory, is deeply rooted in the visual, in God's showing the hole ("Deus . . . li mustra . . . une fosse tute roünde" [v. 301]) and in the pilgrim's actually seeing it rather than merely hearing about it.

The writing begun at the time of Patrick's discovery of the entrance to Purgatory is quickly converted into an established scribal institution:

> Seignur, si cum dit li escriz,
> plusurs genz el tens seint Patriz
> e en altres tens altresi,
> issi cum nus avuns oï,
> dedenz l'espurgatoire entrerent
> e puis après s'en returnerent.
>
> . . . .
>
> Cil ki revindrent tut cunterent
> e li chanoigne l'embreverent,
> pur edifiër altre gent
> e qu'il n'en dutassent nïent. (vv. 421, 429)
>
> My Lord, the book says that
> Several people in the time of Saint Patrick
> And in other times as well,
> Just as we have heard,
> Entered into purgatory,

And afterwards returned.

. . . .

Those who returned recounted all they had seen,
And the canons took it all down
To edify other people,
And leave no doubts about purgatory.

The written record of those who return from Purgatory is for the "edification of others" ("pur edifiër altre gent"), and is, in a fabulously explicit example of how writing shapes cultural memory, the basis of the instructions
passed on to Owen at the time of his descent. As the prior sets out what the
penitent knight will see and will encounter in Purgatory, he is careful to note
that "we only know what we know because those who have gone before have
recounted their adventures which have been put into writing" (v. 635). As
soon as Owen is on the other side of experience, Marie reminds us of H. de
Saltrey's source, the book that will come from the transcription of the
knight's words (v. 1401). And though the moment of actual writing will occur only once Owen has also passed through the Earthly Paradise, has fasted
and prayed, his return conforms to Saint Patrick's rule of obligatory testimony and transcription:

> A la porte vint de cler jur.
> Encuntre lui vint li priür,
> ki volentiers l'a receü;
> mult fu liez, quant il l'out veü.
> En l'iglise le fist entrer
> e quinze jurs la demorer
> en jeünes, en oreisuns,
> en veilles, en aflicciüns.
> puis reconta ço que il vit,
> e il le mistrent en escrit. (v. 1903)

> At the gate he saw the light of day.
> The prior came forward,
> And being very happy to see him,
> Eagerly received him.
> He had him enter the church,
> And remain there for fifteen days,
> Fasting, praying, keeping vigils,
> And performing acts of mortification.
> Then he [the knight] recounted what he had seen,
> And they set it down in writing.

In fact, the recorded testimony dictated to ecclesiastical scribes is only the first of a series of retellings, as Owen, having descended into Purgatory and returned, and then having undertaken a pilgrimage to the Near East, recites his tale at the royal court (v. 1917). In this, Owen, the rude knight guilty of cruelty before being reformed, before the purgation of his violent impulses, resembles the hero of Arthurian romance, the one who, like Chrétien's Erec, undergoes a series of adventures at the end of which he becomes capable of telling his own tale. And he participates in a process of transcription, seen throughout the prose romances of the thirteenth century, in which the Arthurian knight who leaves the court is obliged, according to the formula dictated by Merlin to Arthur at the time of the bestowal of the Round Table, to take an oath to "tell the truth, upon return, about all the things that have happened to him and that he will have found in his quest, whether they be to his honor or shame."[22] In keeping with Merlin's bureaucratic prescription for good information gathering and thus good government, the *Lancelot Prose Cycle* is filled with testimonials on the part of knights who, like Owen, dictate not to the ecclesiastical but to the royal scribes of Arthur's court.[23]

Just as the knights' adventures are transcribed by the Arthurian *greffiers* or stenographers, the underworld adventure of Owen, the oral account of the lived experience of Purgatory, the testimony of a witness, is, shortly after his return, transformed into a written record. The place of entrance to and return from Purgatory is, again, the place of writing, a place of testimony, a place where testimony is transcribed and accumulated, the beginnings of cultural memory in the form of the archive: "Ipsius autem beati patris tempore multi penitencia ducti fossam ingressi sunt, qui regredientes et tormenta se maxima perpessos et gaudia se vidisse testati sunt. Quorum relationes iussit beatus Patricius in eadem ecclesia notari" ("And in the days of this blessed father, many people, driven by repentance, entered the pit and, on their return, testified that they had both seen the joys and endured the greatest torments. And blessed Patrick ordered that their accounts be recorded in the same church").[24] More important, the geographic hole in the earth through which the penitent enters, and which I have equated with the philological holes through which Marie's Old French might penetrate H.'s Latin, the place of origin of the tale, its umbilicus, is, in the context of Marie's project of endowing the vernacular with the status of literature, also quite literally the place at which the inchoate status of orality is fixed:

> E pur ço que Deus demustra
> a seint Patriz e enseigna

primes cel liu, est issi diz
"l'Espurgatoire Saint Patriz."
Rigles a nun, la u fu mise,
li lius, e fundee l'iglise. (v. 372)

And since God showed
This place first to Saint Patrick,
And taught him about it, it is called here
Saint Patrick's Purgatory.
The place where the church was founded
And established is called *Rigles*.

The place of entry to Purgatory and to writing is the place of grammar, of regularity, of rules, of the permanence engendered by writing as a means of preserving cultural memory. Memory is, in fact, one of the obsessive issues not only of the prologue to the *Lais,* but of the *Espurgatoire,* where Owen is constantly reminded to remember the name of Jesus as well as to remember what has happened to him in his journey that will end at the place of testimony and transcription, a memory place, memory being a place in the sense of a *locus,* a "lieu" of the written trace, in contrast to the unordered—dark and scary—hole of unarticulated lived experience, as the *Espurgatoire* reproduces the drama we encountered in the *Lais* defined, where the language effect is concerned, by a contrast between a longing for unity and "remembrement" and a fear of dispersion and loss of meaning. This is why it can be no accident that the abbey itself is called "Rules," "Rigles": "*Rigles* a nun, la u fu mise,/li lius, e fundee l'iglise" as a rendering of H.'s Latin: "Locus autem ecclesie Reglis dicitur" ("But the place of the church was called Reglis").[25]

I am not the first to have focused upon the name of the abbey built at the place of entry to and return from Purgatory. The etymology and the meaning of "Rigles" have, in fact, not only kindled some debate, but offer a fabulous example of the coincidence of philology and topography in the medieval tradition of rooting names, more usually the patronym of a family, in land.[26] The question of the origin of "Reglis," its translation from Latin, and possible links to Old Irish determines the question of its reference and has fed the discussion of where exactly the entrance to Purgatory is located in the medieval past as well as where one should look for it in the present. Some maintain that the word "Reglis" used by H. derives from the Irish *reiclés,* from the Latin *reclusum,* and originally referred to an oratory or small church, a monastic cell or anchorite's hut. Y. de Pontfarcy, for example, points to the origin of "Reglis" in the "monastic cell" of a cenobitic settlement as proof of the existence of an anchoritic community on Station Island, one of the two islands of Lough Derg.[27] Others, however, trace the roots of "Reglis" to the Latin *ecclesia*, which would indicate a larger church, or to the Latin *regula*, which reflects a church of the canons regular, an abbey church, the regular canon's house, or a monastery, and thus a more likely location of the entrance to Purgatory not on Station Island but on Saints' Island.[28] The uncertainty surrounding the origins and meaning of the little word "Reglis" makes any topographical conclusion based on etymological evidence more than suspect. But it does point in the direction of something that has been hovering in the margins of my argument all along, and that has to do with the resonance of H.'s "Reglis" and Marie's "Rigles" with the notion of "rules" itself, the *regula* of Latin, regardless of its actual geographical reference or meaning in Old Irish, being the equivalent of grammar. In fact, I don't see how one can avoid such an association, given that the Abbey of Rigles, the site of writing and of archival information, the place of testimony and of transcription, is the locus of a double transformation—of the visual into an oral account, and of the oral account into written form.

Within the inscribed genealogy of both H.'s and Marie's text the transcription has a double function and works at two levels: to make the past visible and to preserve for future generations a record of that which has been seen.

GENESIS OF THE TALE

If the transcription of the pilgrim's words at Rigles reveals a desire to capture lived experience in fixed form, which recalls Marie's anxious concern for the capriciousness of meaning encountered especially in the *Lais*, the *Espurgatoire* is no less freighted by the question of reception, what happens to words in the ear, mind, and mouth of another. The Archbishop's invitation to Owen to "tell the meaning" of what he has seen is merely the beginning of a process of interpretation and transmission that is central to our understanding of the *Espurgatoire*, which contains a genealogy of its own origin, moving as it does from Owen's and others' testimony to Marie's translation of H'.s text, and moving at the same time away from the fixity of beginnings.

The premise of Purgatory is that of a story out of a hole, which, despite the religious trappings, captures something of the essence of the creation of a literary fiction. This is not to suggest that the *Espurgatoire* comes out of nowhere, rather that Marie's choice of the *Tractatus* to translate is not arbitrary but a conscious opting, like that in the prologue to the *Lais* to translate from the Breton rather than from Latin, in favor of the tale of tales where it comes to literary creation. Further, if the archetypal tale of Purgatory is complicated at the outset, the story of its transmission from the lived experience of God's showing Saint Patrick the hole and the knight Owen's purgation, to H.'s text, and then to Marie's rendering of H., is no less complex. Indeed, once one begins to ask the philological questions of what happened in between the fictive origin of Purgatory and the single manuscript of the *Espurgatoire* (BN fr. 24407, folios 102r–122v), one becomes even more convinced of the self-consciously literary parameters of Marie's undertaking.

H. de Saltrey's *Tractatus* is not the work of a single consciousness but a collective project, an amalgam of oral and written sources, tellings and retellings, writings and rewritings, on the part of the *relatores* and *scriptores* who have contributed to the making of the legend of Purgatory and to the final narrative account of one knight's trip to the beyond.[29] The oral record of Owen's adventures in Purgatory, which supposedly took place in 1148 or 1149 ("In the time of King Stephen"), was, according to the internal account contained in the *Espurgatoire*, transcribed by the scribes of Rigles shortly after the event: "Then he [the knight] recounted what he had seen,/And they set it down in writing" ("Puis reconta ço que il vit,/e il le mistrent en escrit" [v. 1911]). Things do not end there, however, for this initial rendering is supplemented by subsequent oral accounts. Indeed, Owen, having completed a pilgrimage to the Middle East shortly after the event, brings his story to court and retells it to the king: "He recounted to the king,/In proper order, the true course of his life" ("Tut en ordre li a cunté/de sa vie la verité" [v. 1921]).[30] Like the Arthurian narrator-knight, Owen not only recounts the story of his life but shapes his account according to what medieval rhetoricians would have considered to be a natural narrative, one whose order follows the chronological sequence of events. I realize that the reading may be a little subtle, but it is clear that something on the order of the literary, that is to say a rhetorical ordering or composition, has occurred between Owen's initial testimony as a witness and the subsequent royal retelling. This is all the more significant, given the fact that Marie has done something similar. For the episode of Owen's retelling of events, Owen's debut as a teller of tales at court, is not present in H.'s *Tractatus,* which moves directly from the knight's question to the king about whether or not he should take the robes of religion to the arrival of Gilbert, sent by Gervais to found a sister house.[31] It is, in other words, Marie who has introduced the tale of Owen's telling his tale at court; it is Marie who has transformed the knight into something of a performer, a poet.

Among the oral sources of the internal genealogy of the *Tractatus,* Gilbert stands as the primary authority for H.'s tale. In fact, H. speaks preemptively of a presumably oral source of his story whose name he will reveal in the end: "Quis uero eam mihi retulerit et quomodo eam agnouerit, in fine narrationis indicabo. Quam quidem narrationem, si bene memini, ita exorsus est."[32] H. refers, of course, to his oral source Gilbert, who founded the abbey together with his translator Owen and must have heard Owen's story from him, since, after the monks leave Reglis to found another house at "Louth in England" (v. 1991), Gilbert continues to tell the tale: "Cist Gilberz conta sovent/cez choses devant meinte gent" (v. 1997). It is Gilbert, in fact, who not only tells Owen's story to H. but combines it with others.[33] Gilbert too is a performer of the tale of Purgatory, which he buttresses, like a jongleur whose credibility is challenged, with the story of the monk who has struggled with devils and is himself somewhat of a mime. "As he narrated his story," Gilbert claims in narrating his own, "I myself saw the wounds of this monk and touched them with my own hands" ("Huius monachi uulnera uidi et manibus meis attrectataui").[34]

Gilbert's oral account of Owen's adventures is supplemented by that of the two Irish abbots whom H. has also consulted, one of whom testifies to having heard stories of Purgatory and the other of whom claims to have often heard such tales, as well as by the testimony of Bishop Florentien, "a nephew of the third Saint Patrick and the companion of Saint Malachy," whom H. has encountered in the same year as the two Irish abbots.[35] Florentien, in turn, tells the story of a hermit living near him who has spoken often with demons, "and often heard their stories" ("e ot lur cuntes mult sovent" [v. 208]), which stories are incorporated within the tale related orally by Florentien along with the story of his chaplain who continues the tale of the hermit.[36] In fact, behind the chaplain's account of the hermit's account of the story of the devil's seduction of another hermit lies the tale of the priest, pushed by devils into seducing a young girl, and saved, as we have seen (above p. 208), only at the last minute by castrating himself.

Here we have it: in the seemingly infinite regress of H. de Saltrey's oral sources in Owen, Gilbert, the two Irish abbots, Bishop Florentien, Florentien's chaplain, and the two hermits, the ultimate literary source turns out to be devils. In the compilation of his account it is not as if H. de Saltrey is not suspicious of his sources. Indeed, in the gathering of testimony, he quizzes Bishop Florentien about the truth of Purgatory (v. 2076). Yet, the more H. seeks to document his account of Purgatory, to fortify his treatise with the oral testimony of witnesses, the further he gets from what he might have considered to be documentary proof; and, moving as he does from first-, to second-, and even third-hand testimony, which verges in the end upon the hermit's tale of self-castration, the closer he seems to get to the fictive, to the literary, to demons.

Alongside the multiple oral accounts that constitute the core of H.'s text, the *Tractatus* draws upon a number of written sources. It will be remembered that at the time of the "showing" of the entrance to Purgatory, a written copy of the Gospels is transmitted by Jesus to Saint Patrick along with a stick, which are, H. insists, "up to this day still fittingly venerated in Ireland as great and precious relics" ("que hucusque pro magnis et preciosis reliquiis in Hybernia, ut dignum est, uenerantur").[37] So too, in the A group of manuscripts of the *Tractatus* we learn about the genealogy of this part of H.'s story, which he supposedly read in another written source with which we are already familiar, *The Life of Saint Malachy,* Malachy being the "companion of the third Saint Patrick," uncle to Bishop Florentien, a historic figure whose life was written in 1149 or shortly after his death in 1148 by Bernard of Clairvaux. Further, H. refers to St. Patrick's stick as the "stick of Jesus" ("baculus est Ihesu uocatus"), which repeats verbatim Bernard's phrase.[38] Thus, either H. de Saltrey read Bernard's *Life of Malachy* and integrated it into his text, or the attribution to Malachy was added by a subsequent scribe who knew the source of the story in Bernard's account. The "stick of Jesus" is also mentioned in the *Tripartite Life,* where it seems to be waiting for Patrick's arrival like Galahad's weapons in Arthurian tradition,[39] as well as in Jocelin de Furness's *Life and Acts of Saint Patrick* where the saint acquires it in Tuscany on one of his trips to Rome.[40] What is most relevant to our purpose, however, is that Marie knew and translated from the manuscript family with the reference to Saint Malachy: "The Life of Malachy tells us/About this, have no doubt" ("ço nus mustre Malachias/en sa Vie, n'en dutez pas" [v. 299]).

Among the written sources acknowledged by H. figure two references to Gregory the Great, whose *Dialogues* (book 4) contain a number of tales from the beyond.[41] H. also seems to be aware of Augustine's writings about the afterlife, and indeed seems to contrast Gregory's view that "good angels or bad angels accompany the souls according to their merits and drag them to torments or lead them to a restful abode" ("In multis enim exemplis que proponit ad exitum animarum angelorum bonorum siue malorum presentiam adesse dicit, qui animas pro meritis uel ad tormenta pertrahant uel ad requiem perducant")[42] with Augustine's view of the great *refrigerium* in which the soul will reside between the time of death and resurrection. Could it be that H. knew Augustine's statement in the homily on Psalm 36 having to do with the instant of death: "as you will be in leaving this world, so will you be in the next life"?[43]

H.'s version is an amalgam of oral and written sources, some of which, as in the case of Gilbert, the two Irish abbots, Florentien, or Florentien's chaplain, are second- or thirdhand. The written accounts contained in the *Tractatus* are of uncertain provenance. There is no indication—that is, no direct citation—that H. has primary knowledge of the writings of Augustine or Gregory the Great. H.'s *Tractatus* turns, moreover, around a lost written document. We never learn the fate of the transcription made at the time of Owen's return from Purgatory, which is supplanted by Gilbert's subsequent oral version, or the fate of the putative record that might have been made by the king at the time of Owen's return from the Middle East and oral rendering at royal court, to which are added the various testimonials of the Irish abbots, Florentien, his chaplain, and the chaplain's hermits. In fact, the story of Owen's purgatorial adventure circulates in both written and oral form, gaining in length via interpolation, between the time of his descent and the composition of H.'s *Tractatus,* or, if we follow the chronology contained in the text, almost forty years. This is not unusual within the context of medieval literary visions. As Claude Carozzi points out, the recording of the Otherworld journey rarely takes place in close temporal proximity to the event. Of the twenty "literary visions" that he considers in *Le voyage de l'âme dans l'au-delà d'après la littérature latine (Ve–XIIe siècle),* just over half are edited in the years directly afterward; the other transcriptions take place at a temporal remove of between ten and forty years.[44] Or, if we are to assume that H. knows Owen's story only from Gilbert's account, what, it may be asked, has happened between the time Owen has confided it to him, which may be reasonably assumed to have been four or five years after the event, and the relating of the knight's tale to H. some thirty years later?[45] At which time H., at the request of another H., H. de Sartris, the "pater uenerande" of the prologue, the H. to whom the *Tractatus* is dedicated, composed a first version, which within a period of two to four years was expanded, that is, amplified to include the homilies and anecdotes printed on pp. 154–58 of the Warnke edition.[46]

H. surrounds himself with "a network of names" (Greenblatt)—Augustine, Gregory, Patrick, Gilbert, Florentien, his chaplain, the abbots, hermits, kings, and even the devils, all of whom to a lesser or greater degree contributed to the shaping of the *Tractatus,* composition being the equivalent of an assembling of accounts, which will ultimately be reassembled in a longer version that will serve as the basis of another reworking by Marie in the vernacular. Finally, what is most striking, and here the attentive reader must have seen this coming, is the extent to which the process of literary creation displayed in the internal genealogy of the *Tractatus Sancti Patricii* resembles Marie's notion of "remembrement," a dialogue with the dead and a remembering that is also a purposive collation, a rewriting of the disparate elements of H.'s text in the process of translation. The question of what passes through translation and what doesn't, what is to be taken from H.'s varied sources and what is to be left behind, the question of what remains in the first person and what is converted to the indirect third person voice are, at bottom, editorial decisions on the translator's part, a reminder that the enormous project of cultural memory contained in the *Espurgatoire* is a work of gathering against the fear of fragmentation with which we began this journey into the world of Marie de France, a "remembering" that is literally a "remembrement."

REMEMBERING WHAT THE DEAD HAVE SAID AND SEEN

Within the framework of Marie's translation, or "remembering," of Owen's adventures in Purgatory, she too has her sources. Some point to an oral origin and seem to make the dead of Purgatory speak, and, by the odd ventriloquism of translation, a taking on of the voice of another, to make that other speak another language. For often, in the regress of voices from the grave, in their successive translation, it is difficult to determine who speaks the words we read. Marie's written sources are, of course, easier to identify, since the textual genealogy of H.'s "remembrement"—from Owen, to Gilbert, to H., and then to her—is made explicit in the end:[47]

> Gileberz conta icel fait
> a l'autor, ki nus a retrait,
> si cum Oweins li out conté

> e li moignes dunt j'ai parlé,
> ço que jo vus ai ici dit
> e tut mustré par mun escrit. (v. 2057)

> Gilbert told this matter
> To our author, who reported to us
> (Just as Owen told him [Gilbert],
> And the monks of whom I have spoken)
> What I have told you here,
> And shown thoroughly in my writing.

Moreover, H.'s own written sources, mixed with the oral, are encased in the *Espurgatoire* like a series of sedimentary layers stretching back over a period of some forty years; in the case of Saints Augustine, Patrick, and Gregory, they extend even further. And if the ghosts of the patristic and the chivalric past speak through H., they pass via Marie's translation into the vernacular. The dead speak, and when they do, they speak Anglo-Norman French.

The passage from H. to Marie entails a confusing mixture of the written and the oral, of texts and voices. Where H. promises in the beginning, for example, to reveal his source in Gilbert,[48] Marie offers a vague affirmation of the truth of the tale that follows (v. 181), along with a reference to her source, which confuses the oral with the written:

> Si j'ai bien eü en memoire
> Ço que j'ai oï en l'estoire,
> Je vus dirai veraiement
> En ordre le cumencement. (v. 185)

> If I have well retained in memory
> What I have heard in the story,
> I shall truly recount to you
> The beginning, in an orderly fashion.

In treating the question of source, Marie conflates hearing and reading, what she has "heard in the story" with what she has "read in the story"; and this confusion cannot, within the context of her broad understanding of the question of "remembrement," be dissociated from that of remembering and forgetting. Indeed, the project of translating H.'s *Tractatus,* itself a "remembrement" or an assemblage of various elements from written and oral sources, entails revision, changes in the form of interpolation, the equivalent of false memory, and changes in the form of deletion, the equivalent of forgetfulness.

In Marie's understanding, composition is a question not of invention but of acts and lapses of recall, memory, inseparable from the question of faithfulness to H.'s text, being more than a simple psychological activity. On the contrary, it strikes to the core of the literary endeavor—creation by accretion; creation by taking and leaving elements of a previous text, as one passes from one language to another, which I have equated with the core theme of the *Espurgatoire,* the passing into and out of Purgatory; the making of fiction as a process of assembling and reassembling the various elements of oral and written tradition.

The *Espurgatoire* is framed by the question of memory, which marks its very beginning. "I wish to put into writing in French,/The Pains of Purgatory,/Just as the book tells us about them,/As a recollection and record," Marie promises ("vueil en Romanz metre en escrit,/si cum li livre le nus dit,/en *remembrance* e en *memoire,*/'Des Peines de l'Espurgatoire'" [v. 3]). So too does memory mark its very end: "Jo, Marie, ai mis, en *memoire,*/le livre de l'Espurgatoire/en Romanz, qu'il seit entendables/a laie gent e covenables" ("I, Marie, have put into memory and into French/The Book of Purgatory,/So that it might be intelligible/And suited to lay folk" [v. 2297]). Memory frames the *Espurgatoire* and lies at the core of Owen's repeated recall of the salvific name in which memory can be said to be on trial. The Abbey of Rigles is a memory palace in which the ordeal of recall will itself be remembered because of the written record that is made there and that stands as a reminder that writing in the *Tractatus,* as well as translation in the *Espurgatoire,* is an ordeal of "remembrement" analogous to that of Owen. The *Tractatus* is a remembering or reassembling of names, just as the *Espurgatoire* is a remembering of the *Tractatus,* more precisely, a realignment of the words of one language with those of another which is the essence of translation.

This is why the question of voice is so important; for not only does H.'s *Tractatus* speak through Marie's *Espurgatoire,* but the voices of all who speak there—Saint Patrick, the old man whose confession he hears, Owen, Gilbert, and the other witnesses—speak through her as well, producing a layered effect that Carol Zaleski, discussing the thirteenth-century vision of Thurkill, associates generally with the nature of medieval Otherworld adventure.[49] The origin of the journey beyond is always obscure. One never captures directly the experience, or even the first testimony of the visionary. As we have seen, those whose names are associated with death and return are more often than not illiterate, and none actually write their own account, which, like that of Owen, is transcribed and then passes through multiple revisions—translations in the literal sense of passage from one language to another, but also translations in the much looser sense of recensions. The Otherworld voyage is a multilayered production, the product of several voices and even multi-authorship, so much so that it is often difficult to say who is speaking through whom. This is true of the vision of Dryhthelm, where Bede learns the story from a witness, Haemgisl, who lives in a neighboring cell and whom he meets in the course of a trip to Lindisfarne. It characterizes the Vision of Wettin put into verse in 827 by Walahfrid Strabon on the basis of a written version of Haito, bishop of Basel and abbot of Reichenau, who himself heard it from Wettin in 824. Tnugdal's vision, told by the Irish Brother Marcus, gives no indication how he came into contact with the story; Peter of Cornwall's account (1200) of knightly adventures in Purgatory, which occurred during the reign of Henry II (c. 1170), was related to Bishop Laurence, whose companion Walter then told them to Bricius, who then related them to Peter, who seems also to have known H. de Saltrey's *Tractatus*.[50] Given the obscurity of its origins and the multiplicity of authors, translations, and recensions through which it passes, the Otherworld vision is, again, an instance of the literary. "Saint Patrick's Purgatory is a tangle of fictions."[51]

In fact, what can be said of the collated quality of the individual vision, the product of multiple narrative layers in the making, can be said to characterize the history of our understanding of the genre as a whole. This is why so many of the books and essays on the Otherworld journey seem so insistent upon tracing the sources of each work in terms of those that have gone before, no matter how distant, as if every vision ever written spoke through each and every other.[52] In some cases, those who trace the sources of the legend of Saint Patrick's Purgatory go as far back as the Persian legend of Ishtar's descent, the nocturnal journey of the Egyptian sun god Ra, the Jewish *Apocalypse of Baruch*, or the mysteries of the Orphic cult.[53] They hark back to the mythic heroes Orpheus, Hercules, Theseus, to Plato's underworld in the *Phaedo* (107E–108A) and to the myth of Er in the *Republic*, as well as Macrobius's *Dream of Scipio*, to Homer's account of the Elysian Fields (*Odyssey*, book 4) and of Hades (*Odyssey*, book 11), to Aeneas's underworld journey in the *Aeneid*, Statius's Avernus in the *Thebaid* (8.1–126), and Plutarch's story of Thespesios in the *Moralia*. They point to Christ's own descent, to the *Vision of St. Paul*, and to that of Peter. Augustine's vision of Curma along with his mention of the *Apocalypse of St. Paul* in the *Tractatus 98 on the Evangile of John* or the *Vision of Perpetua* (Tertullian) set the background for a "second wave" of monastic visions beginning in the seventh

century with those contained in Gregory's *Dialogues,* Boniface's vision of
the Monk of Wenlock, and Bede's vision of the lay person Dryhthelm, as
well as the Vision of Furseus, alluded to by Bede and translated into Anglo-
Saxon by Archbishop Alfric in the tenth century, along with that of Baron-
tus from the seventh. Among Carolingian visions cited as possible sources
of H.'s *Tractatus* are found the *Vision of the Poor Woman* attached to the
Reichenau of Haito's time (818 or 822), the *Vision of Wettin* (827), and the
vision of Charles the Fat found in William of Malmesbury's *History.*[54]
Those closer to H. include the *Vision of Tnugdal* (1149) and the vision of the
Boy William (1144). Then too, some see in the Irish visions or "Imrama" a
special vein of influence upon H. de Saltrey, citing the "Voyage of Bran Son
of Febal" (eighth century, manuscript c. 1100), "Voyage of Maeldúin," "Voyage of Snedgus," "Adventures of Connla the Fair," "Sick-bed of Cuchu-
lainn," "Adventures of Art Son of Conn," "Voyage of St. Columba's Clerics,"
and "Voyage of Brendan," found in a manuscript of the tenth century.[55]

Though all the above have been mentioned as potential antecedents of
H.'s *Tractatus,* and thus of Marie's *Espurgatoire,* we know relatively little
about what H. may or may not have read in the way of other Otherworld
visions, what he may have heard recited orally, or what he may have known
in the way of legend. Even the references to Gregory the Great, to Augustine, or to Malachy offer no certain proof that H. actually came into direct
contact with their writings or writings about them, and it is entirely possible
that he might have known of the visits to the Otherworld contained in
Gregory's *Dialogues* merely by hearsay. Thus, the potential influences upon
H. stretch like a litany of ghostly voices that speak potentially through one
another, eventually through him, and, finally, through Marie. H. is surrounded by a "network of names" that, again, make the *Tractatus* the end
product of an irretrievable process of textual accretion, that make it, in fact,
a paradigm of medieval literary creation as a program of reception and
reworking. Marie too is surrounded by the same network of ghostly influences, plus one—that of H. And, according to her own definition of
what it is to write, seen in the prologue to the *Lais* as an insertion of one's
own meanings into the received—and sometimes lost—meanings of others and as a process of remembering, rememberment, or reassembling,
Marie, who is also concerned that she not be forgotten, places her name—
"Jo, Marie"—into cultural memory.

My thesis is very simple: that the *Espurgatoire* stands midway between
the *Lais* and the *Fables,* its salvific language suspended between the linguistic fatalism of the *Lais* and the relativized language of the *Fables,* its assumed

universe combining metaphysics with ethics in such a way as not only to respond to the inadequacies of each, but, within the givens of Marie's constant themes—memory, translation, the relation of the oral to the written and of words to all other aspects of human endeavor—to offer a synthesis of its own. I am not suggesting that Marie set out intentionally to write a work that would answer to the inadequacies of the *Lais* and the *Fables,* that would meld their merits; rather, that she elected to translate H.'s *Tractatus* because the concept of Purgatory coincided with an overarching desire present in her previous works, though insufficiently expressed, to integrate the theological and the social. My contention is that Marie seized upon the notion of Purgatory because she sensed—consciously or not—that it contains a third way, which also happens to correspond to a third social space, neither the castle nor the court, but the town. For the idea of Purgatory as it developed in the second half of the twelfth century, as it crystallized in H.'s *Tractatus* and was disseminated in the vernacular, among which Marie's *Espurgatoire* was the first beacon, went hand in hand with the development of urbanized intellectual, social, economic, legal, and political institutions at the time of the emergence of the monarchic state.

Stated most plainly, the *Espurgatoire Seint Patriz* can be seen to continue Marie's interest, visible in the *Fables,* in the rationalization of the social bond, but it combines this interest with that which seems to be lacking in the *Fables* but present in the *Lais*—a sense of the divine, more precisely, a sense of divine justice. Put the other way around, the *Espurgatoire Seint Patriz* can be seen to continue Marie's interest, visible in the *Lais,* in the world beyond or the divine, but to combine this interest with that which seems to be untenable in the *Lais* while present in the *Fables*—a sense of the possibility of living within the bounds of a rationalized human community.

Of course, Marie de France did not invent Purgatory. Yet she did choose to translate H.'s *Tractatus* among what must have been a plethora of possibilities. What all that we have seen thus far suggests is that this choice was motivated, first, by the fact that the concept of Purgatory responded so perfectly to the unresolved issues of the *Lais* and the *Fables,* serving to complete that which is lacking, and to combine that which is present, in each. In converting an essentially ecclesiastical document into a secular work of imagination Marie must have sensed the possibility of continuing the project of literary and cultural transformation. Her focus upon the *Tractatus* was stimulated by the extent to which H.'s text represented something new, Purgatory being a novel concept, certainly no older than the 1170s.[56] The concept of Purgatory, fully crystallized for the first time in the *Tractatus,* corresponds to what we identified from the start as the active, future-oriented quality of her work, her modernism. Finally, as we shall see in the next chapter, the "birth of Purgatory" (J. Le Goff) was inscribed in a specific historical moment, captured in H.'s documentary rendering and projected in Marie's literary rendering upon a fantasized future in a stunning example of the way in which cultural superstructure might work in the shaping of a perceptual world, perceptions might be translated into institutions, and institutions into actions. Stated bluntly, the legend of Saint Patrick represents a significant ideological weapon in the conquest and colonizing of Ireland in the last two decades of the reign of Henry II. In the specific historical context of the colonial expansion of the Angevin monarchy, the legend of Saint Patrick's Purgatory is linked to the attempt—aided by Irish ecclesiastical reform— to bring Ireland into the Anglo-Norman orbit.

CHAPTER NINE

The Anglo-Norman Conquest of Ireland
and the Colonization of the Afterlife

Against the always difficult, necessarily speculative, and willingly unfulfilled ambition of establishing the historical context for a work of art—much less a thematic or generic type such as the Patrick Purgatory narratives—we begin from a significant premise: Where Patrick is associated with the afterlife before the *Tractatus/Espurgatoire* there is no mention of Purgatory; and where the afterlife is associated with Purgatory there is no mention of Patrick.

It is true, of course, that the legend of Patrick, like that of many saints, involves raising the dead. As the anonymous author of "The Lebar Brecc Homily on S. Patrick," one of the assorted documents constitutive of the legend, reiterates, "He used to ordain, anoint, consecrate, and bless. He used to cure lepers, the blind, the lame, the deaf, the dumb, and folk of every disease besides. He used to cast out devils; he used to raise the dead to life."[1] One of the first miracles of the *Tripartite Life* is the resuscitation of his sister who, like the Monk of Wenlock, Dryhthelm, Thugdal, Gunthelm, the Monk of Evesham, or Thurkill, undergoes a near-death experience. Having fallen and "struck her head against a stone, so that death was nigh unto her," she is raised by Patrick's making of "the sign of the cross over the wound, and healed . . . without any illness."[2] In Jocelin de Furness's *Life of Saint Patrick,* the youthful Patrick not only wipes away his sister's wound with a bit of spittle from "the thumb of his right hand," but, in a series of similar miracles, brings his foster father, the husband of his nurse, back from death.[3] Indeed, Patrick's arrival in Dublin, a Norwegian city, as Jocelin is careful to point out, is associated with the raising of the dead as an essential element of his conversion of the Irish. The King of Dublinia, having lost both son and daughter that very day, promises "that if God at the prayers of the Saint would restore the children of his age, he and all his people would worship him."[4]

Though Patrick may travel throughout Ireland raising the dead, the dead whom he raises do not visit Purgatory; nor is Purgatory synonymous, as it will be beginning with H. de Saltrey, with an underground cavern. The Patrick of legend is associated with fountains: the converted of Dublin, "rejecting their Idols and all the abominations of the Devils, were converted unto Christ, and were baptized at *The Fountain of Saint Patrick,* at the Southern side of the City, which the Saint, striking the earth with *The Staff of Jesus,* had caused to arise."[5] In his capacity as a resuscitator of the dead he is aligned with the grave or with a pit. One finds in Jocelin's *Life* the topos of struggle between Patrick and the demons over the souls of sinners. One finds, even, the idea of preemptive prayer as a means of avoiding hell. Yet in the geography of the afterlife as it is represented in the legend of Patrick, Purgatory cannot be said to exist as a site: neither does the principle of purgational purification by fire, nor the system of remission by the suffrages of one's friends and relations play the slightest role in the life of the saint. On the contrary, in Jocelin's figuring of the afterlife, Saint Patrick's Purgatory is mentioned only once, where it is represented as a mountainous height, "on the summit of which, many are wont to watch and to fast, conceiving that they will never after enter the gates of Hell; the which benefit they account to be obtained to them of God through the merits and the prayers of Patrick. And some who have thereon passed the night relate them to have suffered grievous torments, whereby they think themselves purified of all their sins; and for such cause many call this place *The Purgatory of Saint Patrick.*"[6]

Conversely, the visions of the afterlife in which purgatory takes the shape given to it in H.'s *Tractatus* and Marie's *Espurgatoire*—as a distinct underworld zone of cleansing torment—have nothing to do with Patrick. Tnugdal is led through Purgatory by an angel. In the vision of the Monk of Evesham, it is Saint Nicholas's Purgatory, which the itinerant soul learns only incidentally: "Amongst [the souls] I recognized a certain goldsmith who had been well known to me in life. . . . As he frequently cried out, 'Holy Nicholas, have pity on me,' I was pleased to recognize the name of my dear protector, St. Nicholas, from whom I hoped to obtain salvation both of body and soul."[7] Gunthelm, whose vision is dated 1161, is conducted through the Otherworld by Saint Benedict and the Archangel Raphael.[8] Thurkill is issued into the next life by Saint Julian the Harbourer, who is assisted by a host of other saints: James, Michael, Paul, who "led the white Souls along a narrow grassy path, between the flames across the pool, and over the bridge, up to the Mount of Joy," and, finally, Saint Peter, who struggles with Satan in the theatricalized judicial court.[9] Gerald of Wales, who could have known the *Tractatus/Espurgatoire*—or might even have come into contact with Marie at the court of Henry II—does not, in his description of the lake in Ulster that produces a "purgatory-effect" (above p. 000) in those who spend a night of torment in one of its pits, link the site to Saint Patrick, though the specific siting of Purgatory in Northern Ireland is not without significance. Gerald, whose mention of Purgatory in the *Topographia Hiberniae* locates the entrance to the Otherworld on one of the islands of Lough Derg, not only recorded in his *Expugnatio Hibernica* the story of the Anglo-Norman conquest of Ireland, but was either related by blood or knew personally most of the participants in the campaign beginning in the late 1160s by which Ireland became an English colony—and from which, in some profound sense, history has yet to recover. His quite remarkable description of Ireland and account of the complex political and military interaction of native Irish, English, Welsh, and Norman chiefs point, I think, to a fuller understanding of the colonizing potential of the legend of Saint Patrick within the givens of a new economy of salvation.

Patrick is the child of migration and conquest, the son of "a French Damsel named Coneussa, niece of the blessed Martin, Archbishop of Tours," and an English father. His ancestry captures the migratory move across the English Channel and reflects the Anglo-French connection. Born in the shadow not only of Ireland ("near the town of Emphor, . . . nigh unto the Irish sea") but of the Roman colonization of Britain, the son of Politus, "a Presbyter, by nation a Briton, living in the village of Taburnia (that is, the field of the Tents, for that the Roman army had there pitched their tents)," Patrick is himself English. And not only English, but a colonizer, liberating as he does Ireland from the pestilence of snakes, driving as he does the demons from the land,[10] but, most of all, moving as he does from tribal territory to tribal territory converting the Irish to Christianity. "What shall we do?" one of the exiled demons complains to another; "this man, the destroyer of our Gods, the persecutor, nay the extirpator of our Sect, worketh many miracles; if we let him go thus, all the people of Hibernia through him will believe in his God, and the Christians will come and they will remove our laws."[11]

The demon's question and fear of the displacement of one set of laws by another are to be understood in the context of Anglo-Norman ambitions in

Ireland and of their ideological consequence in what is figured as the civilizing mission of the English. Saint Patrick, having crossed once to Ireland and returned to his father's house, has a vision in which he is called "by the voice of the Irish," in the phrase of Jocelin, to liberate the island:

> he beheld in a vision of the night, a man of comely garb and countenance, bearing many letters as if from Ireland, and holding out to him one of them to read; which taking, he read and found therein thus written: "This is the Voice of the Irish." But when he would have continued to read, he seemed in the spirit to hear the Irish Infants which were yet unborn crying unto him with a loud voice—"*Oh holy youth* Patrick, *We beseech thee come unto us, and abide with us, and release us!*" And Patrick being pierced therewith in his heart, could not finish the letter, but awaking gave infinite thanks to God; for he was assured by the vision, that the Lord had set him apart, even from his Mother's womb, had by his grace called him to convert and to save the Irish Nation, which seemed to desire his presence among them.[12]

As liberator, the anonymous author of "The Lebar Brecc Homily on S. Patrick" compares Patrick to Christ and Moses.[13]

From what, it may be asked, is Patrick called to liberate the Irish?

First and foremost, it turns out, from themselves, or from the primitiveness of national character. The Irish are obdurate, the first attempt at conversion, that of Palladius sent "with many books, the two Testaments, with the relics of the Apostles Peter and Paul, and of numberless Martyrs," having failed: "the Irish not listening to, but rather obstinately opposing, Palladius in his mission, he quitted their country, and going towards Rome, died in Britain near the borders of the Picts."[14] The Irish are morally lax. Their marriage practices do not conform to Christian practice: "they did not contract legitimate marriage nor make confession," complains Saint Bernard in the *Life of Malachy.*[15] Most of all, however, the Irish are barbarous, they are cruel. We have seen that the knight who first approaches Patrick in the *Espurgatoire* has never taken Communion and does not know that killing is wrong; so too, Owen has often acted "against God and with great cruelty" ("kar mult aveit sovent ovré/ cuntre Deu en grant cruëlté" [v. 513]).

The cruelty Owen exhibits, presumably in the wars of King Stephen's reign in which he has participated, is hardly original. On the contrary, the savagery of the Irish is a widespread cliché of the Anglo-Norman world that runs like a rich vein throughout Otherworld visions, hagiographic literature, chronicles, and literary works. Brother Marcus, having described the physical properties of Ireland after the fashion of Bede, focuses in the

Vision of Tnugdal upon its "cruel battles." Saint Bernard, whom Marcus claims to have encountered at Clairvaux while in the process of writing the *Life of Malachy,* insists upon the saint's "rude origin" ("Our Malachy was born in Ireland of a barbarous tribe"), which, cured by a French education, makes his return to Ireland to preach all the more dramatic: "Once he had begun to exercise his office the man of God realized that he had been sent not to men but to beasts."[16] Gerald of Wales repeatedly decries the savagery of the Irish in battle, of which Dermot Mac Murrough's slaughter of the men of Osraige in 1168 offers a particularly vivid example:

> Groups of Irish foot soldiers immediately beheaded with their large axes those who had been thrown to the ground by the horsemen. In this way the victory was won, and about two hundred heads of his enemies were laid at Diarmait's feet. When he had turned each one over and recognized it, out of an excess of joy he jumped three times in the air with arms clasped over his head, and joyfully gave thanks to the Supreme Creator as he loudly revelled in his triumph. He lifted up to his mouth the head of one he particularly loathed, and taking it by the ears and hair, gnawed at the nose and cheeks— a cruel and most inhuman act.[17]

Diarmait hates the citizens of Dublin, Gerald specifies, "for in the middle of a large building, where it was their custom to sit as if before the *rostra* in the *forum,* they had buried his father, whom they had killed, along with a dog, thus adding insult to injury."[18] William of Newburgh claims that Ireland sports a "population that is uncivilized and barbarous, almost entirely ignorant of law and discipline and lazy in agriculture."[19] Gervase of Tilbury is in agreement concerning "that land, that from ancient times had sustained itself from the milk of animals, neglected the Lenten fast, consumed raw meat, given itself up to foulness and despised religion."[20] Finally, the literary account of the Cambro- and Anglo-Norman invasion of Ireland, the *Conquête d'Irlande* or the *Song of Dermot and the Earl,* portrays a state of unrelenting cruel warfare among various tribal chiefs as well as between the Irish and the Welsh and English.

If Patrick is the liberator, ridding Ireland of demons and snakes, it is the Irish who are demonized and driven out. The portrait of the cruel Irish is used, in a mixture of religious messianism and political aspiration, to justify the invasion and occupation that engaged Henry II practically from the beginning of his kingship in 1154 until his death in 1189, three and a half decades that correspond uncannily to the chronological poles of Marie de France's literary career. Gerald of Wales is unabashedly candid concerning the relationship between collective moral character and conquest: "the Irish people have deserved to suffer the confusion attendant on invasion and conquest by foreigners, since their misdemeanours and vile practices demanded this punishment."[21]

What this suggests is that the birth of Purgatory and its apportionment to Saint Patrick can be situated in the context of the Anglo-Norman invasion of Ireland and, further, that the relationship between military and political history, on the one hand, and cultural representation, on the other, reaches beyond the realm of negative stereotype such as that of the cruel Irish deep into that zone where institutional and literary forms are conjoined.[22] Put in simplest terms, the legend of Saint Patrick, according to which Ireland is liberated from itself, serves to rationalize conquest. When joined, as we shall see, to the purgatorial bureaucratization of the afterlife, legend works to shape the vision of that which is conquered along the lines of a rationalized administrative system that coincides spectacularly with the institutions developed by the Angevin monarchy in its pursuit of a mechanism by which the tools of war might be transformed into those of state.

For Henry II Ireland was a persistent problem, one with a long history, reaching back at least to the Conquest, and one that he dealt with in several stages. The origins of Ireland's wildness in English and Norman eyes lie, according to Marie Therese Flanagan, in the phenomenon of British exiles seeking asylum in Ireland, in the "particular attraction" of the Hiberno-Norse towns of Dublin, Waterford, and Wexford "for political exiles intent on attempting a restoration of their former position in Britain," and in the ease with which mercenaries operated between southern Ireland and adjoining areas of the mainland, the area, in fact, where Patrick was born— "near the town of Emphor, . . . nigh unto the Irish sea."[23] Godwin, earl of Wessex, banished by Edward the Confessor, sought refuge there in 1051; two of his sons, Harold and Leofwine, fled to Ireland via Bristol; after the battle of Hastings in 1066, the sons of the slain King Harold, son of Godwin, likewise sought aid from Diarmait mac Máel mBó, the great-grandfather of the very Dermot who, as we shall see, sought aid from Henry II when in the course of territorial wars he was exiled from Ireland in 1166.[24]

The exile of Dermot, which is the subject of the extraordinary Old French *Conquête d'Ireland,* is not only usually identified as the terminus a quo of Henry II's direct intervention in Ireland, but itself begins like a courtly romance. Vanquished by his rival Tiernan O'Rourke, whose wife Dermot had seduced and carried off some seventeen years earlier,[25] Dermot turned to Henry II who, preoccupied with consolidating his own territory on the continent, sanctioned Dermot's recruitment of Welsh mercenaries for the task. In August 1167 Dermot returned to Ireland with a knight of Pembrokeshire, Richard Fitz Godebert, and a small band of troops, recovered his hereditary kingdom, and came to terms with those (Rory O'Conor, Tiernan O'Rourke, Dermot O'Melaghlin, and the Ostmen of Dublin) who had originally ousted him.[26] In 1168 Dermot, anxious to expand his original holdings, sought the help of Robert Fitz Stephen, who arrived in May 1169 with a force of thirty knights and sixty other horsemen in coats of mail as well as three hundred archers on foot. Finally, determined to rule as high king of Ireland, Dermot issued an invitation to Richard Fitz Gilbert de Clare, lord of Strigoil and earl of Pembroke, also known as Strongbow, who, in the phrase of A. J. Otway-Ruthven, "enjoyed an almost independent power in the marches of South Wales," to assist him in return for his daughter's hand in marriage and succession to the kingship of Leinster after his death.[27] When, however, Dublin fell on 21 September 1170, Henry II, despite his original support of Dermot's cause, became alarmed at the prospect of an independent Cambro-Norman kingdom in Ireland; and when Dermot died in 1171 he decided to invade. In the simple phrase of the author of the *Conquête*, "Le rei henri est dunc passez / En yrlande od ses nefs" ("King Henry passed over then to Ireland with his ships" [v. 2585]).

In fact, Henry II had contemplated a trip to Ireland as early as 1155 at the Council of Winchester. John of Salisbury speaks in the *Metalogicon* of the bull known as the "Laudabiliter" of Pope Adrian IV, authorizing the "illustrious king of the English, Henry II, . . . to proclaim the truths of the Christian religion to a rude and ignorant people, and to root out the growths of vice from the field of the lord," and insuring "the hereditary possession of Ireland."[28] The papal demonizing of the Irish was repeated at the time of Henry's invasion of 1171 in the form of three letters issued by Alexander III, who speaks of the "enormities and crimes *[enormitates et vicia]* of the Irish," and who, despite the contemporaneous controversy with Henry over the murder of Becket, in the wider spirit of the ecclesiastical reform of Ireland, again legitimates Anglo-Norman claims.[29]

Consisting as it did of five hundred knights, three or four hundred archers, numerous horses, provisions, and ready-made siege towers, the size of Henry's invading force, in an age and place in which as few as ten armed knights and thirty archers were sometimes able to rout local territorial chiefs, testifies to the seriousness with which the monarch viewed the situation. The campaign was an immediate success. Upon Henry's entering Waterford, Strongbow surrendered the city and did homage for all of Leinster.[30]

Most of the Irish kings followed suit. According to Gerald of Wales, "all the princes of southern Ireland individually submitted to Henry," as did those of the north, he adds, except for the princes of Ulster.[31] With the exception of the tribes of the Cinel Owen and the Cinel Connell, the chiefs of Ireland, having accepted Henry II as their overlord, were his guests at a Christmas court in 1171 at which, Gerald claims, they were impressed by "the sumptuous and plentiful fare of the English table and the most elegant service by the royal domestics." Gerald then adds a detail that is significant in that it signals the transformation of the spectacle of hospitality into a civilizing rite. "Throughout the great hall, in obedience to the king's wishes," the chronicler notes, "they began to eat the flesh of the crane, which they had hitherto loathed."[32] Elsewhere, in the *Topographia,* Gerald speaks of the crane as a symbol of virtue. It is, then, as if by forcing the Irish chiefs to eat that which they loathed, Henry II were symbolically forcing virtue down their throat.

Henry II's initial conquest of Ireland was effectively completed in 1175 via the Treaty of Windsor at which Rory O'Connor, the provincial king of Connacht, came to an agreement by which he would pay a tribute of one hide for every ten animals but by which Henry also renounced the right to intervene personally in Irish internal affairs. The Treaty of Windsor, as Marie Therese Flanagan maintains, was essentially a peace agreement, as is clear from the terms in which it is recorded in the Annals of Tigernach: Cadla Ua Dubthaig, archbishop of Tuam and one of Rory's representatives at the negotiations, "came out of England from the son of the Empress, having with him the peace of Ireland, and the kingship thereof, both Foreigner and Gael, to Ruaidrí Ua Conchobair, and to every provincial king his province from the king of Ireland and their tributes to Ruaidrí."[33] Though there is some question not so much as to whether but as to how long the Treaty of Windsor held, it is clear that Henry II sought to reaffirm the Angevin lordship in Ireland when in 1177 he invested his youngest son John, then only nine years old, king of Ireland. At the same time, Henry made "speculative grants" to Anglo-Norman vassals in the kingdoms of Cork or Desmond and Limerick or Thomond, that is to say, fiefs that still required capture, thus setting off another round in the cycle of conquest, rebellion, and reconquest characteristic of English-Irish relations in the second half of the twelfth century. Indeed, as soon as John was old enough to be knighted, he undertook a campaign that landed him at Waterford in 1185 and that by all accounts was a horrendous failure, serving to reunite the chief kings of the south and west of Ireland, Donnell O'Brien, Dermot Mc Carthy, Rory

O'Connor, and leading to renewed rebellion of others.[34] At the end of eight months John was forced to leave Ireland to which he did not return until the more successful campaign of 1210.

The Anglo-Norman conquest of Ireland was, of course, above all a military undertaking. The Welsh invaders had succeeded originally because of superior military equipment, organization, and experience. That is, they possessed arrows, long lances, and defensive armor, were aligned along the lines of a chivalric fighting corps, and had amassed almost a century of experience in fighting the Norman invaders of England. As the author of the *Conquête d'Irlande,* whom Ian Short characterizes as "an outstandingly mediocre poet," proclaims, in assessing the disadvantage of the 1,700 Irish against the 300 well-armed Welsh who accompanied Dermot's men when they arrived at Bannow Bay in 1169, "the traitors are quite naked."[35] Colonization, however, was a different matter, requiring deep and lasting changes in political organization. It was the attempt to rule the Irish "along standard lines of Norman feudalism," in the phrase of A. J. Otway-Ruthven, that characterized the Angevin presence after 1171–72. Henry II's occupation of Ireland for better or worse—better in the coastal lowlands than in the interior, worse under renegade and free-booting vassals than under loyal governors—tested the administrative limits of his reign.

Occupation involved, first of all, a change in the principles of land ownership, from the loose possession of the tribal warrior band to the infeudation and subinfeudation of large tenancies. When Earl Richard or Strongbow surrendered Waterford in 1171, he did homage to Henry for Leinster, and "the rich king granted to him / Leinster in fee" ("Leynistere lui ad grante / Li riche reis en herite" [*Conquête,* v. 2621]). The earl, in turn, distributed fiefs to others, as did the other great landholders such as Hugh de Lacy, who, as chief governor of Ireland from 1172 to 1173, "enfeoffed his barons, / Knights, serjeants, and retainers" ("il feffa ses baruns, / Cheualers, serianz e garsunz" [(*Conquête,* v. 3126]).[36] The Anglo-Norman occupation involved a change in the modes of political submission, from the exchange of hostages and cattle to the feudal relation of lord and vassal; it entailed new forms of social organization and spaces around castles, manors, and towns; it involved ecclesiastical reform and reorganization of the Irish Church along the centralized lines of Canterbury as opposed to a more autonomous system of monasteries; it brought a transformation in the modes of marriage and inheritance; it meant augmentation and regularization of economic exchange between Ireland and England; it carried a change in the fundamental rule of law from the old Brehon custom of reciprocal vengeance and "necessary homicide" to something resembling the rationalized legal patterns of the Anglo-Norman state. In sum, alongside military conquest and political reorganization, colonization involved a pacification and administration of the conquered territory in keeping with the trend toward state formation that we have identified with Marie's *Fables,* and which, as we shall see by way of conclusion, is even more fully developed in the *Espurgatoire.*

PATRICK THE ADMINISTRATOR

Patrick was not only the moral conqueror of Ireland, but, having converted the Irish, as Jocelin de Furness makes clear, he became a surveyor, a builder, a collector of taxes or tithes, an administrator: "he caused the whole Island to be divided with a measuring line, and all the inhabitants, both male and female, to be tythed; and every tenth head, as well of human kind as of cattle, commanded he to be set apart for the portion of the Lord.—And making all the men Monks, and the women Nuns, he builded many Monasteries, and assigned unto them for their support the tythe of the land and of the cattle."[37]

Further, Jocelin's description of Patrick the surveyor and administrator, associated with Henry II's invasion and pacification of Ireland, resonates uncannily with Richard Fitz Nigel's description of William's tactics after the Conquest of 1066:

> When the famous William, "the Conqueror" of England, the Bishop's near kinsman, had brought under his sway the farthest limits of the island, and had tamed the minds of the rebels by awful examples, to prevent error from having free course in the future, he decided to bring the conquered people under the rule of written law. . . . Lastly, . . . after taking counsel he sent his most skilful councillors in circuit throughout the realm. By these a careful survey of the whole country was made, of its woods, its pastures and meadows, as well as of arable land, and was set down in common language and drawn up into a book; . . . This book is metaphorically called by the native English, Domesday, i.e. the Day of Judgment, . . . not because it contains decisions on various difficult points, but because its decisions, like those of the Last Judgment, are unalterable.[38]

In the suppression of a native population by terror ("awful examples"), in the advent of "the rule of written law," in the survey and the making of a record, in the absolute judgment of Judgment Day which, like the *Tractatus/Espurgatoire,* grounds the legalism of this world in the fear of the next, the legend of Saint Patrick's Purgatory can be said to do for the Anglo-Norman conquest of Ireland what the Domesday Book did for the Norman Conquest.

Part of what Henry II's army carried across the Irish Channel was linguistic as well as military. Occupation represented a significant territorial extension, despite the use of French for administrative documents, of the English tongue.[39] The conquest was partially cultural. Henry encouraged poems both in Latin and in the vernacular concerning the principal events of his reign—Benoît's *Chronique des Ducs de Normandie* and Jordan Fantosme's poem about the defeat of the king of Scotland by Henry's barons in 1174 were joined by the anonymous *Conquête d'Irlande,* Gerald of Wales's *Expugnatio Hiberniae,* and Jocelin de Furness's *Life and Acts of Saint Patrick.* What I am suggesting, however, is slightly different—that the conquest was also ideological and that within the perspective of a changed figuring of the relationship between this world and the next, the concept of Purgatory in its founding articulation in H. de Saltrey's *Tractatus* and disseminating expression in Marie de France's translation was a powerful speculative tool in the Anglo-Norman pacification and colonization of the conquered foe. To the degree that the entrance to Purgatory is a physical, geographic site, and not just a site but "perhaps the only entrance on earth accessible to mortals to the underworld,"[40] the claim to it is the equivalent of a powerful territorial claim, one comparable symbolically to the present-day conquest and prospecting of space, the planting of a flag on the moon, or the patenting of specific genes within the exploration of the biological territory of the genome.

Alongside the military conquest and pacification of Ireland, the *Espurgatoire* can be understood as an ideological catalyst to the suppression of violence and a moralization of the social bond. As a conversion narrative, like that of Dryhthelm, Tnugdal, and Thurkill, the story of Saint Patrick's Purgatory in general, and of Owen's descent and return in particular, represents a spectacular symbolic burial of violence in a hole. So too, the Otherworld stories contained in Marie's text are those of transformed lives, first that of the old warrior who comes to confess to Patrick, and then that of Owen, who has been excessively violent in the past and who, because of his entrance and exit journey, is reformed. The fact too that both are at the time of their arrival at Saint Patrick's hole unaware that killing is wrong indicates a coming into consciousness of the law. But the conversion of the Irish knight and of Owen is symptomatic of more than the socialization of a single knight, or even of two knights. It points, however embryonically,

toward the transformation of a culture of killing into something on the order of a judicially defined state.

In keeping with a more general trend toward social conversion that I
have maintained elsewhere is the essence of the romance, we see, from the
chivalric works of Chrétien to the prose romances of the thirteenth century,
a regular cycle involving the knight's departure from court, conquest of rob-
bers, rapists, and renegades in the forest, and dispatching of his captives
back to court.[41] In Marie's *Espurgatoire* it is as if the king who sends the
unsocialized knight to Saint Patrick's hole were dispatching him to a locus
of transformation that cannot be disassociated from the conversion of a violent past into a more peaceful future. This is something that Matthew of
Paris understood in the preface to his story of Owen written some four
decades later:

> A certain knight Hoenus by name who served many years under King
> Stephen, obtained the King's leave to set out to his native land in Ireland to
> visit his parents. When he had tarried some time in that land he began to
> think over his disgraceful life: how from his cradle he had wasted his time in
> arsons and rapine, and, what he grieved over the more, how he had been a
> violator of churches and invader of ecclesiastical property besides many sin-
> ful enormities lying in his breast.[42]

As does Ranulf Higden, who wrote over a century after Matthew of Paris
and who, in the *Polychronicon,* treats directly the question of pacification:

> Touching Patrick his Purgatory, take heed that the second St Patrick, that
> was Abbot and not Bishop, while he preached in Ireland, studied well fast
> busily for to turn those wicked men, that lived as beasts, out of their evil life
> for dread of the pains of Hell and for to confirm them in good life by hope
> of the great bliss of Heaven; and they said that they would not turn but some
> of them might know somewhat of the great pains and the bliss that he spake
> of, while they were here in life.[43]

Seen in the context of the legal transformation of the twelfth century, the
conversion of Knight Owen and all who follow his example is deeply embedded in the civilizing thrust of romance. It is indicative of a shift from a
vendetta society functioning according to the principle of collective guilt
and reliant upon immanent modes of proof by ordeal to the state institutions in which the monarchy or the large feudatory princes, including those
who, like Henry II, tried to subdue Ireland, retain the right to make war and
to judge according to a more rationalized evidentiary system of proof by in-

quest as well as according to individual and not collective criteria of legal responsibility.

THE NORMAN AND IRISH PEACE MOVEMENT

Where pacification was concerned, the dukes of Normandy and kings of England were far in advance of the French monarchy, which appropriated Anglo-Norman judicial institutions after the reconquest of Normandy in 1203–4.[44] According to an inquest conducted in 1091 by Robert Curthose and William Rufus, William I had enacted, as early as 1075, a "Duke's Peace" limiting blood feuds and placing numerous restrictions upon the conduct of any but his own expeditions.[45] The *Consuetudines et Iusticie* of the Conqueror prohibited seeking one's enemy with hauberk, standard, and sounding horn; it forbade the taking of captives and the expropriation of arms, horses, or property in the course of a feud. Burning, plunder, and wasting of fields were forbidden in disputes involving the right of seisin. Assault and ambush were outlawed in the duke's forest; and, except for the capture of an offender in flagrante delicto, no one was to be condemned to loss of life or limb without due process in a ducal court. William's law had a double effect: to control wars of vendetta and to reserve jurisdiction over certain cases of serious infraction for the duke's own court, thus bypassing the local seigneurial judge who would ordinarily have enjoyed cognizance over crimes committed within his fief.

The effects of William's effort to control private war and to extend ducal prerogative through a special peace and reserved jurisdiction are evident in the earliest custumal: the *Très Ancien Coutumier de Normandie* prohibits military response to offenses normally requiring vendetta and instead enjoins the offender to trial:

> Nus hom n'ost fere guerre envers autre; mes qui leur fera tort, si se plaignent al duc e a sa justice, e se ce est cause citeaine, il fera amander le mesfet par chatel; se elle est criminnal, il le fera amander par les membres.[46]

> No man dares make war against another; if someone does him wrong, let him complain to the duke and his justiciar, and if the matter is civil, he [the justiciar] will cause the wronged party to be recompensed in chattel; and if it is criminal, he will cause recompense to be made in limbs.

The *Grand Coutumier* marked a number of crimes—homicide, theft, rape, arson, assault at home or on the duke's highway, counterfeiting—for the duke's justice. In addition, the duke alone was responsible for maintaining the Norman Truce of God; any infractions of his peace reverted automatically to his court.

In Normandy something resembling a regular inquisitional procedure had been in place since the beginning of the twelfth century and really since the Conquest. There the archaic Frankish *inquisitio* had developed into the sworn inquest, which functioned along the same lines as the English Domesday and fiscal surveys of the eleventh century. Thus, in disputes involving ownership or custom, a defendant had the right to reject a wager of battle, insisting instead upon a jury trial. The elders of the district were then convoked with a mandate to produce a collective ruling. The first known sworn inquest occurred in 1133 when Henry I assembled the Norman court in order to determine the possessions of the bishop of Bayeux. Geoffrey Plantagenet regularized the procedure, extending its cognizance to all disputes involving ecclesiastical fiefs. In an effort to recover lands lost to the Norman bishops, "good men" of the vicinage were required to confirm under oath the possessions of a particular see. Henry II, upon accession, further extended the sworn inquest to recover lands and rights lost by Stephen during the years of chaos of his reign, which correspond historically to the years just before Owen's conversion in the *Espurgatoire*. By the end of the first decade of Henry II's reign, the very decade during which Marie de France most likely began to write, the pertinence of the inquest had grown to cover almost every aspect of civil and criminal procedure. An 1159 charter stipulates that no decision is to be pronounced in ducal courts without the "evidence of neighbors."[47] More important for our purpose, however, is the fact that one of the privileges granted the towns of Ireland after the conquest of 1171–72—and indeed, as A. J. Otway-Ruthven points out, one of the inducements to migration from England to the occupied territories—had to do precisely with the freedom of the town based primarily, he maintains, on the custom of Breteuil, a Norman town whose laws served as a model for the legal organization of southwest England, Wales, and Ireland.[48] A charter of the town of Dublin in 1192 specified that those who lived within the walls of the city were not obliged to submit to external justice except in matters involving extramural tenancies and "that they might clear themselves on any appeal by compurgation, instead of by wager of battle."[49] Those living within the free territories or liberties had in the first quarter of the thirteenth century gained the right to a trial by jury instead of battle in cases having to do with land held by free tenure.[50]

What this suggests is that the thrust toward pacification seen in the

Fables and continued in the *Espurgatoire* goes hand in hand with the historic peace movement of the High Middle Ages which enjoyed a parallel history in Ireland. Indeed, around the middle of the eleventh century Donnchad, son of Brian Bóruma, king of Munster, declared a prohibition against theft, armed combat, and manual labor on Sundays. According to Marie Therese Flanagan, the church may not have been directly responsible for Donnchad's ordinance, but "its provisions are reminiscent, on the one hand of the *Cáin Domnaig*, a ninth-century ecclesiastical ordinance on Sunday observance, and on the other hand, of the contemporary peace and truce of God movements fostered by ecclesiastics in France."[51] Before his exile, in fact sometime between 1162 and 1165, Dermot issued a charter to the monastery of Killenny in which he threatened to punish those who transgressed against monastic property or persons. So too Gerald of Wales's prescription for ruling the Irish after conquest involves neither laxness nor vengeance, but justice and a keeping of the peace: "Thus the rewards offered by such a policy may encourage them to obey, and to aim at the benefits which go hand and hand with peace, while the inevitability of punishment may constantly deter them from embarking on rash ventures." Peace, of course, involves disarmament, for "as soon as this race has fully submitted to the yoke of obedience, then like the people of Sicily it should be completely forbidden the use of every sort of arms by public edict, and a severe penalty should be laid down for any contravention of this law."[52]

ECCLESIASTICAL REFORM AND THE CISTERCIAN PRESENCE

The pacification and legal transformation of occupied Ireland was unthinkable without the ecclesiastical reform that occurred in Ireland even before the conquest. Some movement toward reform had begun much earlier, in the consecration of Irish bishops at Canterbury in the eleventh century, at the first synod of Cashel 1101, the synod of Rathbreasail (1111), and the synod of Kells (1152), at which Ireland was divided administratively into four bishoprics. Some historians think, in fact, that it was the church that pushed Henry II toward colonization as early as the Council of Winchester in 1155.[53] The history of this reform has been well documented, and there is no reason to rehearse such a vast topic here, except, that is, in so far as the *Tractatus/Espurgatoire* might be situated within a nexus involving the Cistercian orbit in Ireland alongside the Anglo-Norman conquest.[54]

That the Cistercians, who under Bernard of Clairvaux had favored the Angevin cause in the struggle against Stephen, fed Henry II's ambitions in

Ireland is beyond question.[55] Even before his assuming rule, Bernard in his
Life of Malachy (1148) portrays the saint among the Irish "beasts" as a re-
former continuing in the twelfth century the civilizing work of Patrick in
the fifth:

> You might say he was a fire burning the briars of crime. You might say he was
> an axe or a mattock hacking down bad sprouts in uprooting barbarous rites,
> supplanting them with the Church's. He abolished all outmoded supersti-
> tions (the place abounded with them) and wherever he found them, he drove
> out tribulations sent by evil angels. . . . He laid down laws filled with justice,
> moderation and honesty. He established again the apostolic sanctions and
> rulings of the holy fathers and in particular the customs of the Holy Roman
> Church. From that time to this they observe chanting and psalm-singing at
> the canonical hours according to universal custom. There was very little of
> this done before that, even in the city. . . . Then too, Malachy re-instituted
> that most wholesome use of confession, the sacrament of confirmation and
> the marriage contract—something again about which they knew nothing
> and cared less.[56]

Dermot, supposedly on the side of reform, founded the Cistercian Abbey
de Valle Salutis at Baltinglass and received from Bernard a letter praising his
good works.[57]

Alongside the oaths of loyalty extracted from the Irish chiefs shortly after the conquest, Henry organized a synod held at Cashel in the winter of
1171–72 at which the bishops made a similar promise. This council was
presided over by Christian O'Conarchy, legate of the pope and bishop of
Lismore, who had also been a monk at Clairvaux under Saint Bernard, and
who had served as the first abbot of the Irish Cistercian house of Melli-
font.[58] The rulings that came out of Cashel covered a wide range of issues
dealing with the church's attempt to discourage cohabitation and the depre-
dation of church property and to encourage marriage within the permitted
canonical degrees, baptism and catechism, tithing, confession, the making
of wills, and, in consonance with the econo-purgatorial regime, the payment of "due obsequies with masses and vigils." Above all, the Constitu-
tions of Cashel, in keeping with the global project of assimilating Irish
social forms, laws, administrative practice, and ecclesiastical organization to
those of England, provided that "all divine matters shall henceforth be conducted according to the observances of the Anglican Church."[59] Gerald
summarizes succinctly the way in which Henry, "fired with an ever greater
desire to increase the glory of God's church and the worship of Christ in

those parts," sought, under the guidance of the Cistercians and what he hoped would be the abiding pressure of the Irish clergy, to bring Ireland into the English pale.[60]

The Cistercians served as a guiding ecclesiastical presence in the Anglo-Norman occupation of Ireland, and their influence hovers like a beacon over the legend of Saint Patrick as well as the *Tractatus/Espurgatoire*. John de Courcy, who, acting somewhat on his own, in 1177 captured Down (now Downpatrick), the capital of the kingdom of Ulaid, to which he had Patrick's relics translated in 1186, founded a Cistercian monastery at Inch, to which he imported monks from Furness in Lancashire, one of whom was Jocelin, author of *The Life and Acts of Saint Patrick*.[61] So too the Cistercian influence was especially strong at Lough Derg, which, long before the invention of Purgatory, had been a center of Celtic monasticism. Purgatory remains firmly within the Cistercian orbit. Jacques Le Goff maintains that the concept of Purgatory appeared in two places—among Parisian intellectuals at the cathedral school of Notre Dame and at the Abbey of Saint-Victor, on the one hand, and at the Abbey of Cîteaux, on the other.[62] Following in the tradition of the Visions of Gunthelm and preceding the "Vision of Thurkill," both Cistercian tales, the *Tractatus* was produced at the request of the Cistercian H. de Sartris from the Cistercian monastery in Bedfordshire by the Cistercian H. de Saltrey, whose source, Gilbert, is from the Cistercian abbey of Louth. Further, as we have seen, Malachy, the Cistercian dispatched to Armagh and the man most responsible for Irish ecclesiastical reform, is mentioned (*Espurgatoire*, v. 2074) specifically by H. de Saltrey as the companion of the third Saint Patrick and the uncle of Bishop Florentien, one of H.'s sources.[63] With the arrival of Malachy more regular orders appeared in Ireland, with the result, in the phrase of Shane Leslie, that "the Irish took to the Cistercian Order like ducks to water."[64] Owen, like Gunthelm and Tnugdal, seeks refuge among the Cistercians. Caesarius of Haesterbach urges conversion to the white monks in his version of Purgatory, as does Helinand de Froidmont much later in his transposition of Dryhthelm from a seventh-century Northumbrian into a Benedictine who becomes a Cistercian monk.[65] Though in Latin, H. de Saltrey's *Tractatus* can be seen as a means of promoting Cistercian, that is, French culture.[66] Cornelis van der Zanden considers it a "Cistercian manifesto" that demonstrates that the white monks are the worthy successors of Saint Patrick in what Carol Zaleski delicately terms the "task of taming Ireland."

THE CIVIL GOVERNANCE OF CAPTURED LAND

While the Cistercian colonization and ecclesiastical reform of Ireland represented the spiritual arm of invasion, civil occupation was dependent upon judicial reform. More than judicial reform, the legal transformation that occurred in Anglo-Norman England, and that the Angevins attempted to impose upon a conquered Ireland, carried a fundamental change in the nature of judicial encounter and legal responsibility that not only had long-range implications for the building of the managerial monarchy but also coalesced to an extraordinary degree with the concept of Purgatory and its rapid dissemination in both Latin and vernacular texts.

Following the example of the Anglo-Norman experience in Wales of capture (1165) followed by negotiation, Henry II applied a strategy in Ireland of conquest, which was really more of a show of force, diplomacy, and, above all, the imposition of a system of legal and economic administration based upon the English model. This was not an easy matter, however, for Ireland existed in a much more fragmentary state of political organization than just about any other part of Europe, a local situation of tribal warfare being the primary cause of Henry's intervention in the first place. Ireland had never come up against Roman institutions, and even Scandinavian settlement had been more superficial than on the Continent, restricted as it was to the southern coast from Dublin to Arklow and the areas around Wexford, Waterford, Cork, and Limerick.[67] The "tribalism" of Ireland at the time of the Norman conquest was a double-edged sword: neither was there a centrally organized command by which the Irish might effectively resist, nor was there an institutionally developed sovereignty to which the invaders might merely be assimilated in order to rule. Henry II's difficulties in Ireland began almost with his departure following rapid victory. Called away in April 1172 by the prospect of reconciliation with the pope over the lingering matter of the death of Becket and by the threat of rebellion in Normandy, Henry left behind a series of fiefs held either directly or indirectly by the Crown and an administration headed by Hugh de Lacy, the first in a long series of governors with the power to make war, proclaim royal service, summon tenants-in-chief to serve in person, or, that failing, to pay scutage.[68] Most of all, the governor was the chief justiciar, that is, the chief administrative officer, assisted by a baronial council like that of the king, responsible for keeping the peace and enforcing justice throughout the land.

Though the historians of medieval Ireland argue over whether Henry II intended to run Ireland as a regional administration headed by a true justiciar or as a stewardship or household office along the lines of Normandy and Brittany, the fact remains that the governors of Ireland—and the list is an impressively long one even in the time between conquest and Henry's death in 1189[69]—were at the head of a system of central judicial institutions that was situated in Dublin and whose county courts, shire courts, and hundred courts ran, again, on the English model; and whose law, at least for the "free Irish" living in the conquered territories, was that of England: "the laws of our land of Ireland and of England are and should be identical," reads a proclamation of the English royal government from 1223.[70]

Information about the English governance of Ireland is much more scanty for the period under consideration than for the period following the administrative reforms of 1234.[71] Nonetheless, one discerns in the period following the conquest the outlines of both local government and its offices of sheriff, coroner, and keepers of the peace and some version of an Irish chancery with its clerks and treasurers responsible for collecting revenue, keeping accounts and records, pipe rolls and memoranda rolls, and issuing writs and seals. By the early thirteenth century we find mention of barons of the exchequer, which include, alongside the justices, the offices of treasurer, chamberlain, marshal, and escheator, the last of particular interest to the Crown because of his role in the collection of feudal revenues. The question of the Irish exchequer is a vexed one, the difference between judicial and fiscal offices, the roles of justiciar and head of the exchequer, being difficult to discern in the early years. The Dublin exchequer was the sole body of central administration, reproducing on a smaller scale the equivalent administrations of England and Normandy, auditing the king's accounts, but also eventually hearing and deciding disputes under its jurisdiction. Before the thirteenth century the exchequer was, according to H. G. Richardson and G. O. Sayles's masterful *Administration of Ireland, 1172–1377*, primarily a department of finance that may also have supplied clerks to serve the justiciar in the drafting of charters and writs.[72] Pleas of the Crown, that is, those having to do with infraction of the king's peace or his rights, were presumably first tried locally, though they might find their way to the exchequer, and, eventually, by right of appeal, to the king's bench in England.[73]

THE INVENTION OF PURGATORY AND
THE BUREAUCRATIZATION OF THE AFTERLIFE

The thematics of pacification that we have seen in the *Espurgatoire*—that is, the burying of violence in a hole, the conversion of the once unruly

knight into a translator, which is Marie's way of representing the transfer of
violent impulse into words—can be situated in the context of Henry II's
campaign to establish in Ireland, as he had done elsewhere, regularized judicial and economic institutions. The "porous death" of Owen the knight,
his dialogue with the dead that is of the essence of the literary, Owen's translation to Purgatory and back linked to Marie's conscious project of translation are part and parcel of a larger change in the constellation of relations
between the living and the dead that Jacques Le Goff, in the reigning book
on Purgatory, has powerfully linked to the bureaucratization of the afterlife beginning in the second half of the twelfth century. We have seen in
Chapter 5 the affinity between the animal tale and the rise of a managerial
class, more precisely, the ways in which Marie's *Fables* seem to nourish a vision of rational state formation. Where the ideological sustenance of the administrative institutions of the Angevin monarchy is concerned, the *Espurgatoire* can be seen to continue in the direction of the *Fables* by grounding
metaphysically several key concepts by which the everyday interactions of
individuals with one another as well as with the state seem to gain legitimacy
in a great exchequer of the beyond.

Purgatory and the Rationalization of Time.   In a curious passage that
appears while Owen is in the interim space of the Earthly Paradise, after he
has successfully completed his ordeal yet before his return, he comes upon
a group of the truly dead who do not seem dead at all. On the contrary, they
appear just as they were on earth. While the souls in the process of being
purged are naked, these are dressed; and Owen is able to recognize their
earthly status according to what they are wearing:

> Si diverse ert lur vesteüre
> cum les esteiles par figure
> diverses sunt en lur luur,
> l'une mendre, l'altre greignur.
> Li un l'orent tute d'or fin,
> li altre vert u de porpin,
> li un de jacincte colur
> u bloie u blanche cume flur.
> Cist Oweins sout de celes genz
> par la forme des vestemenz,
> de quel mestier orent esté
> e en quel ordre orent finé. (v. 1613)

The folk differed in their garb
As the stars differ
In the appearance of their light:
Some were faint, others were bright;
Some were of pure gold,
Others green or purple,
Some like hyacinth in color,
Others blue or white like a flower.
Owen knew by the appearance
Of the clothing of this folk,
What had been their profession,
And in which order they ended up.

Within the tripartite Otherworld, consisting as it does of hell, Purgatory, and the Earthly and Celestial Paradise, this passage indicates that one will return to one's earthly state before passing to eternal beatitude. The fact that the inhabitants of the Earthly Paradise are dressed as they were in life makes the ordeal of Purgatory seem like a stage production, a torture chamber, a house of horrors, after which one will bathe, dress, and resume one's earthly identity, or the identity one enjoyed at the time of death.[74] All of which makes Owen's voyage in and out of Purgatory seem extraordinary in one sense, but less so in another. For if the normal trajectory of the truly dead ends in the resumption of their earthly status, it seems that nothing has changed at all. Rather, the variable is not status—the form of their clothes, their profession, or the order in which they finished—but the length of the ordeal through which they have passed, the duration of the purgatorial fire to which they have submitted before resuming their previous shape. Time is a key element of the doctrine of Purgatory.[75]

With H.'s *Tractatus* Purgatory is no longer a state. It becomes a place and is spatialized in terms of an actual hole in the ground located at a specific geographical site. So too the afterlife is temporalized. Purgatory is not the eternal forever of heaven and hell but a transitory stage through which those who are eligible for salvation pass on their way to the Earthly, and eventually the Celestial, Paradise. Degrees of innocence and guilt are expressed through a temporalizing of the seriousness of infraction over time in an equilibration that resembles nothing so much as the calculation of time within the space of towns: bourgeois time, the time of financial transactions, of the counting of payments and interest, the time of accounts. Neither the seven ages of man, nor eschatological time, nor liturgical time, nor the agricultural time of the seasons, nor the popular time of carnival and Lent, nor feudal time marked by springtime levies and the dates for payment in kind, nor the great assemblies of Pentecost and Toussaint seen in Arthurian romances, the time of Purgatory is a linear, successive, regular measure by which time, work, and money can be calibrated and equilibrated with one another.[76]

Purgatory can be said to lubricate the mental machinery of towns in so far as it engages thinking according to which time can be converted into commodities and labor as well as into the various actions and moral states that require penance in the hereafter. As the archbishop explains to Owen in a phrase that we will later see in relation to the legal concept of equity, one gets out in terms of punishment what one puts in in terms of sinful behavior:

> Mes pur iço que nus pechames
> e de pechié nus encombrames,
> le nus estut espeneïr,
> einz que ci peüssuns venir
> e estre en l'espurgaciün
> selunc ço que fait aviün.
> La penitence que preïmes,
> que devant la mort ne feïmes,
> en cez lius la nus estut faire
> par unt vus eüstes repaire.
> Vus i veïstes les tormenz
> as chaitis ki furent dedenz;
> tels en a greignurs, tels menurs,
> solunc les uevres des plusurs:
> cil ki plus pechierent el munt
> greignurs tormenz iluec avrunt. (v. 1720)

> Because we sinned,
> And encumbered ourselves with sin,
> We were required to expiate our sins,
> And suffer purgation
> According to our deeds
> Before we were able to come to this place.
> That penance which was imposed on us,
> But which we did not perform before death,
> We had to perform in the places
> Through which you have come.
> You witnessed the torments

Of the wretches dwelling there;
Some suffered greatly, some less so,
According to their works.
Those who sinned most in the world
Will have greater torments in purgatory.

What any individual will suffer in Purgatory—as well as the length of suffering—is based upon a delicate calibration of sin and punishment as well
as upon the extent of penance achieved before death as opposed to after.
Purgatory is the repository for venial sins and for "regretted sins," sins that
linger, that have been confessed but for which penance is not yet complete.

Time in Purgatory becomes an object of negotiation between this world
and the next: one serves more time in Purgatory for sins committed while
alive, less time for good deeds; less time for penance carried out while alive,
more time for penance left undone.[77] Thus seen, Purgatory implies a compensatory relationship between justice in the here and now and that of the
beyond, an equilibration between time spent on earth in a state of sin and
time to be spent in Purgatory in a state of pain. Not only does the next
world serve in final terms as a corrective upon this one, but the fear of a preemptive correction in the here and now makes this world a better place. Purgatory offers a world of accounts, a system of debt and payment, of moral
balances conceived along temporal lines—a more-or-less in which time
is fungible. Indeed, the idea of commensurability between a portionable
quantity of sin and an equivalent amount of measurable, adjustable, and
just time in Purgatory is a question of translation not unrelated to that of
linguistic conversion, or of finding equivalent words or expressions between
one language and another. The time of Purgatory is the time of translation.

Purgatory and the Corporation.   If the accounts of Purgatory imply a
translation of one's own moral status before death into one's physical state
after death, they also entail—indeed, are the foundation of—one's relations
to the dead as well as to the community of others while still alive. Historically, the idea of praying for the dead as a means of alleviating their pain in
the afterlife is to some extent part of Christian culture from the start and is
to be found in the writings of the Fathers—Tertullian, Cyprian, Origen,
Gregory of Nyssa, Ambrose. Perpetua prays for her younger brother who
has died at age seven and who she hopes will by her prayers be delivered
from torment. Augustine comments on the efficacy of prayer for "those
who, having been regenerated in Christ, did not spend their life so wickedly

that they can be judged unworthy of such compassion, nor so well that they can be considered to have no need of it."[78]

The continued negotiation of one's status after death and the time one will spend in the middle afterlife are not important elements of eschatological thought before the twelfth century. As we have seen (above p. 259), Augustine's statement in the homily on Psalm 36 having to do with the definitiveness of the instant of death makes the negotiation of time seem less than worthwhile. Beginning with Gregory, however, time seems to become more plastic. In scorning the world, in taking the Eucharist daily, in pardoning others their sins, and in practicing forgiveness, one might, Gregory maintains, lessen one's torture in the hereafter. Gregory recounts the story of a monk in his monastery named Justus, who, dying, confides to another brother, Copiosus, that he "secretly had in his possession three pieces of gold." Gregory orders that he be placed in quarantine and that he be buried not in the monastic cemetery but on a dung heap along with his concealed treasure. Thus, Gregory pretends to "kill two birds with one stone," to punish and to make a lesson. However, thirty days after Justus's death he feels compunction and orders out of charity that Justus be helped out with prayers for another thirty days. One night after that Justus appears to Copiosus who asks, "'Well! Brother, how go things with you?'" to which Justus replies, "'Up until now I was badly off, but now I am fine, because today I received Communion.'" Gregory concludes that it is clear that the dead brother escaped his torment thanks to the beneficial offering, which he transforms into a general rule: "If after death sins are not unpardonable, the offering of the beneficent host aids souls even after death, to such a degree that sometimes the souls of the departed themselves show that they require it."[79] According to the seventh-century Julian of Toledo, true sinners go to hell in perpetuity; yet those who are not wholly good or wholly bad submit to "medicinal" pain before joining the elect in the celestial realm.[80]

The negotiation of time-off in the afterlife as a result of the good deeds of others becomes especially important in the twelfth century. With an increasing sense of continuity in the relations between the living and the dead increasingly subject to a mentality of calculation attached to the development of monetary institutions in the urban centers of northern Italy and Anglo-Norman France, the concept of Purgatory can be seen to support the idea of the corporation whose very essence is that of a social bond transcending the earthly existence of any individual member. We saw in Chapter 6 the ways in which Marie's *Fables* work as a catalyst to the formation of lateral social ties, and thus against the excessive personalization of vertical bonds between men that is part of a feudal world more visible in the *Lais*, in, for example, the complicated relations of Lanval to Arthur and of Eliduc to his lord. Again, the *Espurgatoire* can be seen to continue in the same direction. In the doctrine of Purgatory the ways in which the living and the dead might affect each another are dynamized in terms of a calculation of the duration of purgatorial pain in the afterlife according to the good works of others, thus yielding a glimmer of something on the order of a commonweal. Not only do one's own good deeds shorten one's own time there, but the good actions, alms, and prayers of family or of others might lessen time spent in purgatorial fire.

Marie is categorical on this account, insisting no less than three times that it is the duty of the living to remember the dead, more particularly, to remember them by deeds—masses and prayer, alms and charitable donation, in short, the suffrages that might shorten their pain:[81]

> Cil ki par lius sunt en torment
> ierent delivré veirement
> par messes e par oreisuns
> e par almosnes e par duns
> qu'um dune a povre gent pur els. (v. 1441)

> They who are in torment
> Will surely be set free
> By masses and prayers,
> By offerings and gifts,
> Which we bestow upon the poor in their favor.

In particular, Purgatory prolongs relations with family members after death. As Marie makes clear, aid provided "dead relatives" is an extension of the obligations of earthly family life:

> Pur ceo vus vueil amonester
> que des turmenz deiez penser
> e si aidiez a voz amis
> ki laienz sunt en peine mis.
>
> . . . .
>
> En tels tormenz sunt nostre pere,
> meres, sorurs, parent e frere;
> atendant sunt a noz bienfaiz,
> tant que d'iluec les ait Deus traiz. (vv. 1433, 1449)

> Therefore, I want to advise you
> To consider these torments,

And to help your friends
Who are subjected to them.

. . . .

Among the tormented ones are our fathers,
Mothers, sisters, brothers, and relatives.
They await our acts of mercy,
By which God will set them free.

The souls who continue to circulate in the beyond, preserving in some instances, as Owen bears witness in the Earthly Paradise, the clothes that be-
speak their earthly social status, remain connected to this world.

In this Marie is not, of course, alone. An eleventh-century homily cited
by Thomas Wright contains a particularly clear statement of the terms of
purgatorial negotiation:

> Some are there long, some a little while, according to what their friends do
> for them here in life, and according to what they earned before in life. Each
> knows another, and those who come to rest know truly both those whom
> they knew before and those whom they knew not, because they were in good
> deeds before alike.[82]

Saint Bernard tells the story in his *Life of Saint Malachy* of how the Irish
saint, angry with his sister, at first stops praying for her after her death, but
feels remorse when one night a voice informs him in a dream that she has
not tasted a thing for thirty whole days. Malachy realizes that this is the
"very length of time since he had stopped offering the living bread from
heaven on her behalf." He begins to pray for her again, and "she first comes
to the threshold of the church not yet able to come in and wearing a dark
garment." He sees her a second time in an off-white garment, admitted to
the church but not near the alter. Finally "the third time she was seen in the
midst of the white-clothed choir, arrayed in bright clothing." "Would it not
seem to you," Bernard asks, "that the prayer of Malachy took the place of a
burglar at the very gates of heaven, in that a woman deep in sin procured
through her brother's prowess what was denied her on her own merits?"[83]
So too the Monk of Evesham, contemplating a flock of souls in the course
of his purgatorial journey, learns that "each of them was treated according
as they were benefited or impeded by their former actions, or by the good
works of their friends."[84] In the "Vision of Thurkill" Saint Julian, verging
on the venal, describes "all the places of torment and the mansions of the
Just, he told all the parishioners of the state of their fathers and mothers,
and their brothers and sisters; and for how many suffrages and how many

masses they could be redeemed from Purgatory."[85] Peter Lombard states around 1160 that the church's masses celebrated for the dead mitigate the pain of the moderately bad and "for the moderately good they are worth full absolution."[86]

Working generally to foster "the communal commitment to caring and assistance that conjoins the living and the dead" (Greenblatt), working more particularly to foster bonds between living and dead members of the same family, Purgatory serves more particularly still to foster a sense of the corporate identity of the individual self. Not only do those who do good deeds and penance before death serve a lesser sentence in Purgatory, but those who, like Owen, visit Purgatory before death and survive the ordeal are exempt from any further purgatorial pain after death, thus implying a relation between the living and the dead self. Nor should there be any doubt about the extent to which the purgatorial visions of the twelfth century proffer a relationship of the living self to the dead self that is deeply economic. Though individuals die, they continue to live economically, to enjoy an economic identity and a persona that not only survives death but unites them with the family and community whose corporate identity also transcends the physical disappearance of any individual member. Tnugdal's vision originates in an economic exchange. Raised at court and trained in the martial arts, Tnugdal cared nothing for God's Church, "did not even want to see Christ's poor," and squandered "whatever he had on jesters, players, and jugglers." His vision occurs in the course of a trip undertaken for the purpose of recovering an unpaid debt.[87] When the debtor, who also happens to be a friend, cannot acquit himself, Tnugdal falls into a rage, yet agrees nonetheless to stay for dinner, in the course of which "God's mercy forestalled his appetite" and called him to a vision of the next world. Tnugdal's return to his body is marked, like that of Dryhthelm, who distributes all he has to his wife, his family, and the poor, by economic disbursement: "by written deed he gave away and distributed to the poor everything he had." The vocabulary of Tnugdal's vision is laden with economic terms, the relationship between the self while alive and the self after death being one of a "settling of accounts."[88]

In the vision of the Monk of Evesham the economics of purgatorial accounts is mixed with that of memory: recollection and collection—repayment of a debt at some future date, and even in the afterlife—are blended. As the Monk gazes upon the place reserved for sodomites, in a passage that prefigures Dante's placement of usurers and sodomites together in the *Inferno*, canto 15, he recognizes a lawyer whom he knew in life and whose tortures are a "recollection" of his fault: "Therefore none of the thousand kinds of torments which I daily endure, tortures me so much as the recollection of my fault, because I am actually compelled to be a slave to the baseness of my former weakness." There is a logic in the punishment of the lawyer: that which he has done on earth is done to him—"Those therefore were continually attacked by huge monsters of a fiery appearance and horrible beyond description, which, notwithstanding their opposition, committed on them the damnable crimes of which they had been guilty on earth"—in what amounts to a postponement of moral debt, a settling of accounts with the self, under a purgatorial regime that posits the afterlife in terms of an economic relation to the self.[89]

It is in the "Vision of Thurkill" that the economics of Purgatory as an extension of the financial self is most fully developed. Of all the sins that the simple rustic might have committed, those reported in his purgatorial confession, a speaking from the interior, focus upon his debt to the church: "He confessed also before all the people how he had tithed his harvest unfairly." Reminded repeatedly of this debt ("'Methinks,' quoth St. Julian, 'thy crops are not fully tithed'"), Thurkill pleads poverty and is consoled only by the saintly dictum to the effect that "full tithings bring full harvests." More important, as Thurkill's second guide, Saint Michael, leads him out of the "Theatre of Devil's Plays and Suffering of Souls" and past the south side of the basilica of a church where they encounter "multitudes of Souls, with their faces turned fixedly towards the church, and all wearied, as it were, with long waiting for the suffrages of their living friends," they come "towards the gate of the church" to those who died in a state of debt. Startlingly, Thurkill, who, as we have seen, will give testimony concerning his vision in the presence of his current lord Osbert de Longchamp and his wife, recognizes, "his former lord, Roger Picoth, who was barred from approaching the entrance, because of a sum of forty *denarii* that was still owing to his labourers; and also because he had retained a certain annual rent, due to the canons of St. Osith." Purgatory is the place for Roger to settle his accounts, and in the presence of Thurkill he "sent word to his son William, charging him to clear off the debts, and thus bring him nearer to his place of rest." This is an extraordinary moment. For not only is Thurkill admonished to liquidate his obligations before his true death, but, since he was one of Roger Picoth's men, it may be assumed that Roger's son, under instructions from the father, will pay Thurkill his portion of the forty "denarii" that are due his former laborers. Purgatory is the place where debts are paid, but also, in the case of Thurkill, where they are collected. The exchange with

Roger Picoth is only reinforced by Thurkill's meeting with his own father who, "beholding him, made full confession to his son, how he had cheated men in certain bargains," and by the negotiation that ensues. When Saint Michael informs Thurkill that thirty masses are required to free his father, the rustic again pleads poverty, with the result that "two thirds of them were remitted. . . . Thurkill joyfully consented; and bound himself to pay." In all of this Michael functions almost comically as an intermediary, a middleman who knows the price of each sin, the means of each sinner, and who does not hesitate to haggle: "And whenever Thurkill recognised any of the Souls waiting here, St. Michael told him how many masses would help them to reach the gate."[90]

The negotiation of time in and around the concept of Purgatory goes hand in hand, of course, with urban organization within the more general context of the political, economic, judicial, and even intellectual institutions of the postfeudal era. As Le Goff observes, the fine distinctions to be made between those sins that can be purged and those that cannot, the relative worth of venial versus mortal sins, the time value of particular sins, and their convertibility into particular degrees of pain in the afterlife show a refinement and a sophistication nourished by the scholasticism that we have also seen at work in the *Fables*.[91] With the sophistics of Purgatory, time becomes a commodity to be bought and sold; it is, in effect, denatured. Despite the theological growth of the doctrine of Purgatory, which received papal sanction in 1254, the ransoming of the duration of the soul's pain, the purchase of time which becomes a fungible instrument, brings it dangerously close to the practice of usury, the selling of time via interest condemned by theologians precisely because time as a natural commodity belongs to God alone.[92] Most of all, however, alongside the dialogue with the dead implicit in the purgatorial sojourn, the concept of Purgatory implies an extension of the life of the individual beyond physical death that cannot be detached from the corporate mentality characteristic of the collective institutions—communes, guilds, universities, chartered municipalities, in addition to monastic communities—of the Anglo-Norman world. Through the extension of the economic existence of the individual beyond the grave, Purgatory offered nothing less than a renegotiation of the social contract along the lines of an abstraction of individuals, their coalescence into a community both preceding the birth of each of its members and surviving his or her death. On a more global level, Purgatory works to legitimate the abstraction of the state, to legitimate the idea of the state as a corporate entity capable, unlike that of the feudal world, of acting like a person—in the levying of taxes and armies, and maintenance of justice and peace—on its own behalf.

The prolongation of the economic life of the individual beyond death, communication between the living and the dead, travel between this world and the next are the manifestations of an abstraction of the person of the individual, who in some sense never really dies. And although the pains of Purgatory may seem concrete, the concept of Purgatory is abstract and serves, within the overall social transformation of the High Middle Ages, to subtend the kind of theoretical thinking, to add to the symbolic substance, of the abstract entities whose reason for being is dependent upon the economic dependence of individuals upon one another and whose existence is increasingly part of a larger movement toward political abstraction in the coming into being of the fictive persona of the monarchic state. In the system of assets and debts that it entails between the members of groups of the living—families, members of the same parish, monastic communities, guilds, corporations—the concept of Purgatory signals a broad shift in mental structures, what Le Goff, under the spell Dumézil's ternary patterns but nonetheless cognizant of something fundamental in the shifting nature of twelfth-century political culture, has characterized in terms of the displacement of the binary structures and "mental habits" of "feudal Christianity" (inferior/superior, clerical/lay, and an absolute opposition between heaven and hell) by the "ternary logical structures" that Georges Duby also articulates in terms of the "three orders" of the High Middle Ages. Purgatory goes hand in hand with "abstracted," primarily urban, intellectual, social, and economic institutions. Finally, the triadic model of the afterlife, according to which heaven and hell are separated by a space in which time is negotiable according to a sophisticated schema of proportionality, sustains the notion of just measure and a changing idea of justice itself.

PURGATORY AND THE LAW

The Tailoring of Fire.   Part of the appeal to Marie of H.'s *Tractatus* and of Purgatory was, I think it can be argued, the equilibrium that they establish between this world and the next, the rationalization of a system of transgression and punishment that responds to a lack in both the *Lais* and the *Fables*. In the *Lais,* with the possible exception of "Equitan" and the ending of "Le Fresne," there is no sense of earthly justice, so absolute is the sense of condemnation for living—and speaking—in the flesh. In the *Fables* too, alongside a number of tales involving the corruption of judges and obvious social injustice based upon a natural difference in bodily size or force, we find a series that seems to assert a sense of equity based upon the principle of common sense. And yet the *Fables* display no overarching awareness of any ultimate legal recourse. Within the material world of competition between individuals of differing species, there is no redeeming principle or agent of reward and punishment, only, as we have seen, something on the order of fairness—the good will of the big and the strong not to exploit the small and the weak. This is where the concept of Purgatory can be said to respond to the limits of the principle of "voluntary justice" in the *Fables,* for the well-equilibrated paradigm of reciprocity between sin and penalty that it affirms makes it possible to imagine a place for both the exercise of the ethical will and the punishment of failures of the will.

What I am suggesting, again, is that one of the reasons that Purgatory became so quickly part of the belief system of the High Middle Ages, producing as it did an astounding number of manuscripts both in Latin and in the vernacular, had to do with the way it coincided with a shift in the notions of time and of community, but also with the legal transformation in the twelfth and thirteenth centuries that I have outlined elsewhere.[93] The gradual displacement of a feudal system of immanent procedure featuring trial by combat, the *judicium Dei,* and ordeal by a more rational system of judgment by inquest, testimony, evidence, and debate can be seen in the differing representations of legal proceedings in the *Lais* and the *Fables*—from the supernatural judgment made manifest by the fairy lady of "Lanval" to the more regularized, though often corrupt, tribunals of "The Dog and the Ewe" (no. 4), "The Peasant and His Horse" (no. 47), "The Sick Lion, the Deer, and the Fox" (no. 71), and "The Fox and the Wolf" (no. 89). Where the concept of judicial fairness in Purgatory is concerned, the *Espurgatoire* continues the move in the direction of a rationalized notion of equity coupled with the immanent principle of divine retribution. It is, in fact, in Purgatory that corrupt judges are themselves penalized, as in the theatrical acting out witnessed by Thurkill of one of the Chief Justiciars of England, who is "forced by fiends to cram coins down his greedy throat" for taking bribes "from both sides."[94] And it is in Purgatory that, as the Angel explains to Tnugdal, even excessive mercy is tempered by justice: "Although God is merciful, He is nevertheless just. Justice repays everyone according to his merits; mercy allows forgiveness of many offences which deserve punishment. . . . if God pardoned everything why would man be just? And if he were not terrified of the torments, why would the sinner restrain himself?"[95]

The radicalness of Purgatory has to do, as C. Zaleski has noted, with the ways in which the afterlife is tailored to each individual, whose "progress through the regions of the otherworld is governed by a separate time-table."[96] Indeed, Purgatory works against the undifferentiated absolutism of the notion of original sin, the inherited sin of the first parents with which the individual, guilty by nature, is born and against which he can do nothing. The deemphasizing of the will, the condemnation to be in the flesh, which we have identified with the linguistic fatalism of the *Lais,* is also collectivist in that everyone submits to the same condition and, where the afterlife is concerned, presumably ends up occupying a communal space.

There is some distinction in classical culture between the "morally neutral" death of those who are assigned to the collective spaces of the afterlife such as the resting place of Homer's shades and a more "functionalist" idea of penalty and reward.[97] Plato argues, for example, in a sentence that would not have been unfamiliar to the author of the above citation from *Tnugdal,* that the thought of punishment after death acts as a deterrent to evil and that a lack of punishment of the wicked would constitute a failure of justice.[98] So too Virgil's Aeneas confronts the neutral, the curable, the blessed, and the incurably evil in the course of his descent to the underworld. Within Christian culture the great *refrigerium interim* of the early Middle Ages, where souls wait together for the Last Judgment, partakes of an essentially collectivist approach to redemption at the end of human time.

With the advent of the concept of Purgatory, the soul enters not only an economic negotiation with a future self after death as well as with others, but a legal negotiation as well, one that is less communal and more personal. The purgatorial model of the afterlife entails a double judgment, first at the moment of death and again at the end of human time.[99] Death marks the beginning of a fight between angels and demons for the soul which is submitted to a judicial procedure and a rendering of accounts:[100]

> Seignur, a l'eissue del cors,
> quant les almes s'en issent fors,
> li bon angle i sunt en present,
> li mal i vienent ensement.
> Li bon angle, c'en est la sume,
> receivent l'alme del produme,
> en joie e en repos la metent;
> e li diable s'entremetent
> des males almes turmenter
> e en peril od els mener:

solunc ço qu'eles unt ovré
lui iert iluec gueredoné. (v. 49)

My Lord, when souls leave the body,
And set out on their way,
The good angels are present,
And the evil ones come there also.
The good angels, to sum it up,
Receive the soul of the good man
And place it in joy and in rest.
The devils undertake
To torment the wicked souls,
And to lead them into danger.
The souls' rewards will accord
With their toil.

Purgatory is conceived as collective only in the sense that more or less every-one will pass through it. The duration and degree of punishment of any par-ticular passage are tailored to the individual. Purgatory is a place of distinc-tions and degree: it is not for the wholly good, who go to heaven, or for the wholly bad, who go to hell, but for the not wholly bad and not wholly good—those, in other words, who still possess a lingering debt of venial sins to be redeemed in the intermediate zone between heaven and hell.

To the degree that the pains of Purgatory are shaped to fit the moral worth—the ethical assets and liabilities—of the individual soul, Purgatory appears in some fundamental sense to be democratic. Democratic, first of all, because, as Marie repeats like a mantra at the beginning of almost every torment, those who submit to it are of all ages: number 3, "De chascun eage de gent/out en cel champ diversement" ("There were people of every age/Mingled together in this field" [v. 983]); number 4, "De tute maniere d'eé/i aveit gent trop grant plenté" ("There he found a multitude/Of people of all ages" [v. 1037]); number 7, "Grant multitudine de gent/i a veü, di-versement/de tute maniere d'eé" ("He saw gathered there/A great crowd of people,/Of all different ages" [v. 1199]) (see also vv. 1225, 1267). It is not simply that Purgatory includes those who are younger and older, but the phrase "de tute maniere d'eé" carries with it a sense of "of all kinds" of men, of all status or degree. Purgatory serves, moreover, to link the prosecutory power of divine justice to justice within the human realm through an in-creased emphasis upon the sinfulness of individual acts. This is what is lack-ing in the *Lais,* where individuals are condemned for reasons beyond their control and beyond their understanding. In fact, one finds there the very opposite of a just system of punishment and reward: the best—Lanval and Eliduc, for example—are punished because they are good, since their goodness, as Marie insists, only elicits the envy of others. In the *Fables* the question of punishment and reward is individualized but left somewhat arbitrarily to chance, depending on one's situation, surroundings, and the goodness of those in one's immediate vicinity. There is, finally, no penalty for those who unjustly despoil or eat others, as is evident from the start in "The Wolf and the Lamb" (no. 2). In the *Espurgatoire,* however, acts are linked not only to consequences but to a system of measured punishments and rewards, and this too from the beginning, in Saint Patrick's original preaching on Purgatory, of joy and pain "in keeping with one's works," a lesson that is repeated by both the prior and the archbishop (vv. 761, 1721):

> De ço furent la genz creanz
> que seinz Patriz esteit disanz
> par cels ki esteient venu
> de cel liu, u orent veü
> e les joies e les dolurs
> sulunc les uevres des plusurs. (v. 363)

> Thus the people came to believe
> What Saint Patrick preached to them
> Through those who returned
> From the place where they had witnessed
> The joys and sufferings of many folk,
> In keeping with their works.

The relation between punishment and penalty, good deeds and reward, was not, of course, invented by Marie; and yet it explains, I think, the enormous appeal of the concept of Purgatory, which both, as in the *Fables,* allows for the exercise of the will, and, as in the *Lais,* anticipates supernatural consequences for a failure to do so. The result is a combination of voluntarism with fair, measured, and ultimate consequences for the individual who willingly respects or disregards the consequences of ethical choice. For here there can be no doubt: Purgatory functions according to a system of belief and of fear that serves to keep the potential sinner in check:

> Ki serreit si fols ne desvez,
> hors de sun sen e afolez
> qu'il alast la u ne seüst
> quels mals avenir li deüst?
> De l'alme est il tut altresi;

nus n'en savuns nië ici,
puis que ele est hors del cors traite:
c'est solunc l'uevre qu'ele a faite.
Mais male morz, n'en dutum mie,
ne vient pas aprés bone vie.
Nepuroek nus sumes certeins
que solunc l'uevre a plus u meins
des peines de l'Espurgatoire. (v. 101)[101]

Who would be so foolish or crazy,
Out of his senses and mad,
As to go where he did not know
What evils might befall him?
The same is true for the soul.
After it is drawn out of the body,
We know nothing of it here:
Everything rests on the work it has performed.
But a bad death, let us leave no doubt,
Does not follow a good life.
Nevertheless we are certain
That we will suffer more or less of the pains
Of purgatory according to our works.

Theoretically, the pains of Purgatory function according to degree. Unlike the fatal absolutism that reigns in the *Lais* and the equally fatal relativism of the *Fables,* punishment in the *Espurgatoire* is modulated, as can be seen in the archbishop's discourse, according to a gradated scale:

Si cum li chaitif en torment
sunt travaillié plus longement
pur les granz pechiez que il firent
tant cum il el siecle vesquirent,
si sunt li altre meins pené
ki meins firent d'iniquité.
Si est de nus ki sumes ci:
solunc ço qu'avum deservi
devuns ici plus demorer,
einz qu'a greignur joie munter. (v. 1771)

Just as the wretches in torment
Are punished longer,
The greater the sins they committed
While they lived in the world,

So those are punished less
Who committed fewer iniquities.
And so it is with us.
We must remain here,
According to the period we have deserved,
Before rising up to greater glory.

In fact, the torments to which Owen is witness are distinguished more by quantity, or the length of time they are endured, than by kind. There are no categories of sinners, as in Dante, united by a particular torment corresponding to the specific nature of their sin, no punishment that represents in a contrapunctual way the appearance of the dead itself. Nonetheless, the seventh torment proffers the possibility of a gradation in the degree of punishment according to the extent to which the body is immersed in burning liquid and metal. Though all are plunged into the same flaming pit, some are in it more than others:

Tuit furent plungié il alquant
en cel metal chalt e ardant.
E tels i out de ci qu'as piz,
e tels i a desqu'as numbriz,
tels as quisses, tels as genuz:
grevuse peine i out a tuz.
Tel a gambes e tel as piez
el metal esteient fichiez;
tel i teneient l'une main,
tel ambes dous, de dolur plain. (v. 1203)

They were all plunged
Into this hot and burning metal,
Some up to their breasts,
Others up to the navels,
Others to their thighs or knees.
They all experienced grievous pain.
Some were immersed in the metal
Up to their feet, or to their legs,
Some held one hand in it,
Others both hands, with pure pain.

The distinct degrees of immersion in the seventh torment point to a calibration, a fine-tuning of the relationship between punishment and infraction that, again, can be situated between the absolutism of the *Lais* and the relativism of the *Fables:* punishment is sure, but it is measured. In this the

Espurgatoire can be said to offer a synthesis of the unresolved issues of Marie's previous works and to point to the great social and legal transformation of the High Middle Ages. The measured quality of the seventh purgatorial pain suggests that the *Espurgatoire Seint Patriz* can best be understood in terms of "a new mental landscape" (Le Goff) that not only accompanied but enabled the gradual abandonment of the immanent institutions of a warrior's world—the feudal rights of resistance and private war, judicial combat, and the ordeal of God—in favor of the more rationalized romanized procedures and abstract ideological underpinnings of the monarchic state.

The Personalization of Legal Responsibility.   The imposition in Ireland of the substance of English laws and the form of English institutions would not be so pressing upon the connection between the invention of Purgatory in H. de Saltrey's *Tractatus* and the dissemination of a purgatorial regime in Marie's *Espurgatoire* were it not that those laws and institutions represented a fundamental change in the nature of legal responsibility as well as in the subject's legal identity and relation to the state. In keeping with the individualization of the afterlife of the purgatorial regime, the tailoring of punishment to fit each individual instance of sin or infraction, the gradual advent of an inquisitory mode of procedure and proof served to transform the nature of the judicial encounter from a symbolic struggle between two groups—clans, counties, duchies, monarchies, and even monasteries—to a struggle of an individual against the increasingly comprehensive body of the state. For the potential violence of clannish vendetta—the violence of some against some—royalty attempted to impose a violence of all against one. The feudal trial had depended upon the accusation of an injured party or of a member of his immediate family or of the *comitatus* to which he belonged in order for the court to assume cognizance; that cognizance, as can be seen in epics like *Roland, Raoul de Cambrai, Les Quatre Filz Aymon, La Chevalerie Ogier* or in a romance like *La Mort Artu,* was nothing more than a regularized means of substituting single combat for the clash of entire armies. Trial by inquest, on the other hand, may depend upon the presence of an accuser, upon denunciation, or upon the judge's own initiative. As this last alternative, the ex officio indictment, became more and more common in the thirteenth and fourteenth centuries, it led to the creation of an independent judicial function, the *promotor* or public prosecutor.

By the time of the appearance of the Old French epics, which are the most abundant source of information we possess about the feuds of the period between the collapse of Carolingian polity and the revival of the state in Italy and Anglo-Normandy, the ethos of vendetta which they portray may already have disappeared. Nonetheless, there is sufficient evidence of resistance to ducal and royal prohibition of clannish wars of revenge to indicate not only their survival, but their arresting effect upon the formation and legal governance of larger social bodies. For the feud and the feudal right of war and resistance function according to a principle of collective legal responsibility in which each member of a clan is responsible to it, and it is responsible for him; each knight is liable to the warrior group, the other members of which are obliged to avenge the death of a "friend by blood."[102] Similarly, pecuniary reparation or composition money was paid by the whole group when one of their number was at fault; and it was divided equally when they had been wronged. In what is the prime literary example, Ganelon's thirty relatives rise to his defense at the end of *La Chanson de Roland* and are condemned collectively after his conviction. And literary representation is not very far from the historical record: more than a century after the poem's composition, the seneschal of Normandy felt compelled to prohibit his agents from executing a criminal's kin along with the felon: "nus n'em doit estre mis em painne fors li malfeteurs." Even after the duke's court had decided to pardon a murderer, it first had to obtain the permission of the victim's family: "Li dus ne puet fere pes d'omecide envers celui qui l'a fet, se il n'est avant reconciliez as amis a celi qu'il ocist."[103] Pressure brought to bear by relatives and friends was, in many instances, the only way of forcing a guilty party to court and of guaranteeing the court's decision. Conversely, an accord between warring individuals often specifically promised compliance of the entire family group.

Nor was the individualization of legal responsibility restricted to Anglo-Normandy and England. The old Brehon or chief's law in force at the time of Henry II's arrival in Ireland did not distinguish between wrong done to individuals and a crime against the state. Pragmatic to an extreme, it existed merely to try to stop a quarrel between tribes, and, where possible, to assess the damage to be paid according to a scale that provided for a "body fine," fixed for all free men at seven *cumals* or twenty-one cows, and an "honor price," set according to the dignity of the victim from one *cumal* for a *boaire* or cow chief, the highest of the nonnoble classes, to twenty-eight *cumals* for the chief king.[104] Moreover the Brehon law distinguishes between murder and homicide via the difference between "necessary" or obligatory killing, one that is carried out to avenge the death of a member of the tribe or family, and "unnecessary" killing, which lacks the legitimating motive of revenge.[105] Only in the latter case was responsibility individual. Liability for an obligatory homicide was shared by those who might share in the "man price" attached to the victim whose death obligates his relatives to the "sacred duty" of vengeance. "In the case of unnecessary or non-obligatory crimes," as G. H. Orpen shows, "the liability fell primarily on the criminal and on his movable property, and the family might either deliver up the criminal and keep his land or give the land for his crime."[106] If only in theory, this last category provides an opening toward the designation of the individual in distinction to the clan as a locus of legal obligation.

The individualization of legal responsibility, which is assimilable to the purgatorial particularization of the individual's fate in the afterlife, coincided with the return of a money economy and the ideological interests of the bourgeoisie; but it also suited the long-range political interests of monarchy.[107] Monarchic policy was directed toward weakening the unity of the feudal clan through the restriction of its legal autonomy. And this through the attempt to impose direct ties of dependence between each inhabitant of the royal domain and royalty itself, thus circumventing the intermediate jurisdiction of aristocracy. Beginning in the twelfth century, the individual assumed a distinct legal personality by which he became less responsible to the clan, which was less liable to and for him. Where the warrior group was once responsible for fighting for the rights of each of its members, avenging their deaths, making sure they were not involved in faulty causes, and paying reparation when they were, the individual grew increasingly accountable to the state only for himself. The fragmentation of legal responsibility, its focus upon the individual, was thus designed to undercut the power of nobility by encouraging loyalty to a higher and more central authority.

Inquisitory legal procedure and outlawing of trial by battle, advent of the office of public prosecutor, "reserved cases," by which some causes were reserved in the first instance for royal jurisdiction, and, above all, a system of appeal, by which any case might eventually end up in royal court, contributed to a recentering of the judicial encounter from a conflict between opposing families to a contest between the individual and the body politic, subsumed under the increasingly abstract notion of public peace, public order, or commonweal. Concomitantly, the democratic inclusiveness of the concept of Purgatory, the emphatic linking of transgression and consequence, the calibration of infraction and punishment according to a quantifiable scale of degrees, the negotiations of time and pain, the calculation of familial and communal support, in short, the legalism of purgatorial space, also served, as we saw with the animal tale, the general trend toward civil polity. Along with the ecclesiastical peace movements of the tenth through the twelfth century, Purgatory stands as an ideological element of the move, favored by monarchy and by an increasingly legalistic bourgeoisie, toward pacification and the construction of a juridical state.

Interiorization of the Law.   In the general move toward the suppression of violence that I have assimilated to the conquest and pacification of Ireland and the installation of a purgatorial regime, one can find no better example of the internalization of the law than that contained in that most unlikely of places, Richard Fitz Nigel's *Dialogue of the Exchequer.*

> The noble King of the English, Henry is styled the second of that name, but is considered to have been "second to none" in dealing with a crisis. For from the very beginning of his rule he gave his whole mind to crushing by all possible means those who rebelled against peace and were "froward," and sealing up in men's hearts the treasure of peace and good faith.[108]

The *Dialogue of the Exchequer* is a document that comes right out of the Anglo-Norman "Curia" and can thus be connected directly to the will of Henry II. More important, one could not dream of a better image for the transformation of violent rebellion and "frowardness" or stubbornness into docility than that of a "sealing up in men's hearts the treasure of peace and good faith," what today in Freudian terms we would call repression.

The question of the heart or of inner intention in the assessment of legal responsibility is to be understood alongside a parallel evolution within the realm of ecclesiastical attitudes toward sin and penance. The twelfth and thirteenth centuries witnessed a move away from the solemn penance invoked once in a lifetime under special circumstances—after serious wrongdoing or before death—toward the regular remission of sins at periodic intervals.[109] The Fourth Lateran Council (1215) declared it the duty of every Christian to confess once a year and to the same confessor, with the result that emphasis upon the material act of transgression itself tended to yield to stress upon the intention behind the act, and thus upon the individual's responsibility for wrongdoing. We have seen the ways in which Abelard privileges the notion of consent; the temptation to do evil becomes sinful only when it submits to inner sanction. Intention becomes the foundation of ethical theory in the penitentials that appear in the twelfth and thirteenth centuries—those of Bartholomew of Exeter, Roger de Saint-Pair, Alain de Lille, Robert of Flamborough—and that focus upon the particular nature of each individual sin. Alexander of Stavensby, bishop of Coventry from 1224 to 1237, outlines a methodical series of questions—*quis, quid, ubi, quibus, auxiliis, cur, quomodo, quando*—to be used in the assessment of every infraction, as the penalties affixed to sin were, in contrast to the fixed tariffs of earlier punishment or the *wergeld*, "personalized" in a way thoroughly in keeping with the personalization of the afterlife in Purgatory.

Deep in that zone where psychology can be said to intersect with the social relations it also subtends, Purgatory, or the legalization of the afterlife, participates in the moralization of the social bond. And this via increased emphasis upon the efficacy of the will and the internalized—personal—nature of responsibility, the very notion of responsibility itself constitutive of a sort of "social glue" between individuals.[110] Purgatory is linked to the relativism and voluntarism of twelfth-century ethics, as, for example, in Anselm's distinction between voluntary sins and sins of ignorance; but it is also related to ethical practice, as in the contemporaneous doctrine of contritionism, the necessity of offering external proof of inner repentance. For Abelard, Saint Bernard, and the Victorines, the remission of sin occurs once the sinner has agreed voluntarily to receive divine grace, which causes actual physical tears of contrition. Self-examination is one of the important themes of the age.[111] Abelard equates Christian morality with self-knowledge in the *Ethics*. William of Saint-Thierry adopts the Delphic dictum "Man, know thyself" in the prologue of his treatise on the nature of body and soul. Aelred of Rievaulx asks rhetorically, "How much does a man know if he does not know himself?" And John of Salisbury offers an answer in the *Policraticus:* "no one is more contemptible than he who scorns a knowledge of himself."[112]

This is, finally, why memory is so important in the *Espurgatoire*. The ability to remember one's sins for the purpose of the confession necessary for penitence and absolution, the setting and settling of accounts with oneself, is the lynchpin of an interiorization of the penitential system; and it is key to the development of the psychology—that is, the constitution of the individual as an inner locus of the will—that dominates not only the *Espurgatoire*, but the *Lais* and the *Fables* as well.[113] We have seen in Abelard's *Ethics* a relativized and "psychologized" notion of responsibility tailored to the particular situation of the individual and to the context of each particular sin. So too in the *Dialogue of a Philosopher with a Jew and a Christian,* Abelard asks how it is possible that souls without bodies can move around locally and how physical elements like fire can attack souls in their incorporeality. "Such a possibility cannot be easily expressed in words or understood," Abelard affirms, yet he seems to resolve the issue of the reality of the visionary's visions via a third term—conscience, "a certain inter gnawing of their souls by which they are already tormented in their consciences by the hopelessness of forgiveness and the increase of future punishment."[114] Purgatory may exist as a "third place" between heaven and hell, but it also points to the opening of a "third space" between body and soul, the psychological, that is to say, the space of interiority, a place of reflection and of self-reflection by which instinct might be detached from action, a place where appetite might be mediated. It is in this sense that the *Espurgatoire* might be seen to respond to the *Fables,* where, it will be remembered, the struggle between the body and reason ends, as often as not, in a foreclosing act of destruction, the devouring of small animals by larger ones.

Beginning with the *Roman d'Eneas* and Chrétien's *Erec et Enide,* the structure of romance as a reversible narrative proffers—in contrast, say, to the unidimensionality of character and history in *Roland*—a reversible model of the personality in which each and every individual life is imagined as a series of self-corrections along a continuous path of the will. This would not be so important, or so relevant to the topic at hand, if it were not for the fact that the idea of Purgatory stands as the conceptual or ideological premise on which the biographically defined life as a reversible narrative is built. Purgatory is a place for the undoing of previous acts on the part of the individual—the pilgrim but also everyman—for whom life itself is seen as a perpetual purgatorial struggle for what M. Foucault, in the context of the ancient world, calls the diligent "care of the self."

It is my contention that the power of this structure, in which destiny and psychology coalesce, goes a long way toward explaining the appeal of H.'s *Tractatus* to the Marie of the *Lais* and the *Fables*. The romancing of the afterlife implicit in H.'s text provided for Marie the possibility of a romancing of the here and now, the transformation of the narrative of a life into life as a narrative in which time is both linear and reversible. With the concept of Purgatory Marie introduces "a plot into the individual history of salvation";[115] she introduces a sense of the self's closure upon itself that we have identified with psychology, reversible steps along a voluntary continuum. Indeed, the concept of Purgatory provides for an ongoing account of the self with the self, in which punishment is imposed not as in the epic from without, by a vengeful God or a more powerful lord, but from within— sanction at a later date according to prior behavior. The purgatorial life is to be reckoned as a series of moral assets and debts to be settled in the fullness of time but before the great collective day of final accounts.

This is why the question of self-correction, self-improvement, or amendation is so important to Marie and, once again, remains so deeply enmeshed in the conditions of literary production. The *Espurgatoire* is a didactic work whose aim of converting orality into writing cannot be detached from the aim of moral conversion. The reversibility of fate implicit in the purgatorial voyage as well as the internal mixing of "horrible pain" and "great joy" is explicitly linked to writing—that is, the transcription that occurs, as we have seen (v. 355, above p. 249), upon return and with which cultural knowledge of Purgatory begins. So too in Marie's intense thinking of the world in terms of the relation of orality to transcription, writing upon return from Purgatory for the edification of others is also for the self and the start of a process of self-correction: "Já seit iço que jeo desir/de faire a grant profit venir/plusurs genz e els amender" (v. 17). One cannot separate the desire to change or to "amend others" from self-improvement or amendation. The Prior, prior to Owen's descent, encourages him to amend his life without actually risking the perils of Purgatory: "You can amend your life right here" ("bien pucz ci ta vie amender" [v. 597]). Such a recommendation, moreover, could be based only upon the experience of others as previously recorded, the written testimony of witnesses of which the records from the time of Saint Patrick would be one example and the *Tractatus* of H. as well as the *Espurgatoire* another. Indeed, the connection is there in the text of the *Espurgatoire* to be made between the idea of conversion or self-correction, the record of an amended self, and the warning that such a record makes manifest—between, in other words, *amender* and *amonester*. Witness the homily just after Owen emerges from the tenth torment:

> Pur ceo vus vueil amonester
> que des turmenz deiez penser
> e si aidiez a voz amis
> ki laienz sunt en peine mis. (v. 1433)

> Therefore, I want to advise you
> To consider these torments,
> And to help your friends
> Who are subjected to them.

The warning about self-correction contained in the verb *amonester* is, moreover, related to the process of demonstration captured in the verb *mustrer* which, as we have also seen, lies at the heart of the showing of Purgatory and of writing as a showing, a making visual of that which must be seen to be believed. For Marie the literary experience is synonymous with improvement, translation being a profound and sustained process of correction, amendation being the equivalent of emendation. As stated from the outset, the goal of her translation is to improve the behavior of others by correcting another's writing:

> Pur ço plus ententivement,
> pur amender la simple gent,
> vueil desclore ceste escripture
> e mettre i pur Deu peine e cure. (v. 45)

> Thus, I want to disclose
> This writing very carefully,
> And to put effort and care into it for the sake of God,
> In order to improve the simple folk.

I don't know how much closer one could get to an assimilation of the idea of self-correction to that of translation than in the project of "amending simple folk" ("pur amender la simple gent") by discovering, revealing, or opening another text ("vueil desclore ceste escripture"), which opening is the word Marie uses most insistently for translation. Indeed, we have assimilated Owen's descent into the hole of Purgatory with Marie's interjection of the vernacular into H. de Saltrey's Latin, which here can also be seen to be a version of textual emendation, an opening ("desclore") and an insertion ("mettre i"), both of which serve, on the level of Marie's consciousness of the concreteness of language in general and of writing in particular, to bolster a definition of a narrativized life as a process of successive self-openings, in keeping with the reader's interjection of his or her own "surpluses of sense" present from the outset in the prologue to the *Lais,* and of self-corrections.

Conclusion

Part of what makes Marie de France so fascinating is not only that her three works—unlike, say, those of Chrétien de Troyes, Robert de Boron, or the Tristan poets—are so different, but that their difference rides the cusp of one of the great moments of transformation the West has ever known. Even if we cannot say with absolute certainty that Marie is conscious of the global shift at work around her, one that is manifest in every area of institutional and cultural life, the horizon of her perception becomes conscious in and through the *Lais,* the *Fables,* and the *Espurgatoire* which, at over eight centuries remove, can be seen both to portray and to participate in the workings of historical change. This is partially a function of the public nature of the literary enterprise before the advent of literacy and the individual reader. Because of the dynamic participatory relationship between creator or performer and public, poetry necessarily expresses shared social dilemmas and aims at the articulation of viable solutions. It is also a function, as I have maintained throughout, of a uniquely percipient writer whose works, read chronologically, can be seen to capture the movement of the changing world they depict. In this Marie de France is no different from, say, Balzac of the Restauration, or Proust, whose portrait of the Belle Epoque charts the end of what we think of as "La Vieille France" and defines our image of it.

If Marie's works contribute to our view of the High Middle Ages, they also shape our vision of her, or the person to whom we refer when we use the name "Marie," and who, despite the lack of external biographical givens, is not so anonymous after all. I think it can safely be said at the end of this little tour in and around the *Lais,* the *Fables,* and the *Espurgatoire* that we know their author from within. She has spoken and continues to speak to us as part of what we might think of as a literary biography not too unlike the slightly fuller accounts attached to the life of Christine de Pisan, Charles d'Orléans, or François Villon. Indeed, where the vexed question of the influence of a life upon an oeuvre is concerned, one might well ask if we know that much more about the specific qualities of Christine's *Livre de la mutacion de Fortune*, the *Avision Christine*, or *Cité des Dames* by knowing where she was born, who her father was, and that she was married and widowed young. Do we understand more fully the poetic qualities of Charles d'Orléans's ballads and *chansons* by knowing the date of his capture at Azincourt or the perambulations of his English exile? Do we know more about Villon's uniquely personal voice in the *Lais* and *Testament* from the documents that surface from his brushes with the law? Again, such a line of reasoning is not uniquely medieval and a function of the documentary darkness of the end of the Dark Ages. To wit, our awareness of the conditions of Kafka's employment hardly explains his bureaucratic paranoia. That Flaubert had been taken by his father to a surgical theater sheds little light upon his attachment to realistic detail and the *mot juste*. We would be hard pressed to explain Joyce's fragmenting vision in *Finnegans Wake* on the basis of his eye trouble. Nor, finally, do we understand in some clinching evidentiary sense Virginia Woolf's reluctant modernism from knowing that she had free rein to explore her father's library and was—like Marie?—denied a university education.

One suspects that in equating the external givens of a life with a life's work, which is the only reason for interest in biography in the first place, one always moves backward—from the work to the life, and, beyond the life, to the culture at large. Indeed, what I have offered here is a psychological portrait of Marie from the point of departure of salient aspects of her works, a reconstructed internal portrait and a cultural biography based upon a great artist's language as a "sensitive index" (F. O. Matthiessen) to the world around her. So too, in contrast to almost all that has been written or said about Marie to date, and which we reviewed by way of Introduction, we have encountered an extraordinarily coherent, sophisticated poet whose words still resonate—or, more precisely, have begun to resonate again—with what we think of as the sensibility of our own times. I have assumed all along that Marie is a modern and that, without neglecting scholarly method, we might read her as a contemporary. We have taken her as being as serious, authentic, and as subjectively agonized and unified as any writer writing in the so-called age of authorship.

From within, we detect in Marie a body of work whose cohesiveness runs deeper than the philological questions of ascription of manuscripts, identification of specific historical figures in their dedications, or localization of place-names and dates. I have insisted upon the thematic unity of the *Lais,* the *Fables,* and the *Espurgatoire* along with a coherence of personality, as if the rule of reliably consistent memory transformed into a legal principle in the *Espurgatoire* were a cautionary hint at the persistent traits, the little tics of character and the dominant themes, associated with Marie's name: that is, an obsession with the plasticity and the concreteness of language, with the difference between ordinary discourse and poetic verse, with orality versus writing, with the question of when and when not to speak, with the intention of speakers or writers and the reception of meaning in the mind of another, with the ways words might escape intention and take on an unpredictable life of their own, and with the ways in which transmission, memory, and especially "remembrement" or reassembly might counter the disseminating effects of misunderstanding, misappropriation, translation, or even plagiarism at an extreme. Marie is conscious of the capriciousness of words in the *Lais,* of their trickiness in the *Fables,* and of the parameters of the literary enterprise along with the salutary potential of words—and even of a word—in the *Espurgatoire.* And if she has been traditionally tagged by her critics as being more modest and more attentive to detail than other vernacular poets of the High Middle Ages, it is because throughout Marie tracks more insistently than any of her contemporaries the observable psychological and social effects of both writing and speech. Marie participates in what might be thought of as a literary sensibility in which poetic practice and theory coincide.

If on the basis of a consistent network of reflexes and concerns we have been able to characterize Marie internally, we have at the same time managed to circumscribe an external field of potential literary, intellectual, cultural, and even political appropriations and affinities. In terms of literary association, Marie is more than her potential sources, however direct they may seem. She participates in a wider web of cultural life than has heretofore been suspected. Her *Lais* situate her among the romancers of antiquity, the authors of the *Eneas, Roman de Thèbes,* and *Roman de Troie,* as well as the first generation of chivalric and courtly novelists—Chrétien, Thomas, and Béroul. Her *Fables* place her in the rich tradition of classical and medieval wisdom literature in the vein of the allegorized animal lore, the *Physiologus,* and the bestiaries of Pierre de Beauvais, Philippe de Thaon, and Richard de Fournival as well as the more realistic animal tales, the classical Romulus line, and the so-called *Isopets* of Paris, Chartres, Lyon, and the Avionnet. In another cultural register altogether, Marie locates herself within the more orthodox circuit of H. de Saltrey, more precisely in the tradition of medieval vision literature, the voices that speak through her from Gregory's *Dialogues,* Bede's *Dryhthelm,* and Boniface's *Monk of Wenlock,* as well as the more contemporary *Tnugdal, Evesham,* Thurkill, Irish Imrama, and Bernard's *Life of Malachy.*

We have seen that the intellectual force field in which Marie moves extends beyond the generic bounds of the lai, the fable, or the Otherworld vision. Though it is imprudent to posit anything like direct contact or reading, she moves in a wide circle of ideas that are part of the ambient intellectual milieu of the twelfth century, much as at present the thought of Rousseau, Nietzsche, or Freud infuses the assumptions and perceptions of those who have read their works as well as of those who have not. Thus, the universe of the *Lais,* its defining core of dangerous language so indissociable from a condemnation of the material world, is steeped in the theological thinking of the Church Fathers as well as in the more secular world of early grammarians for whom the primacy of origins implies a sense of loss and a nostalgia for a fantasized moment when the word was imagined to be joined to meaning, and meaning to the thing. The *Fables* place Marie within the contemporaneous circle of the intellectual life of her time, between the first glimmers of ethical and philosophical relativism in the early twelfth century and the flowering of scholasticism in the thirteenth. Though she writes in the vernacular, Marie participates in the intellectual renaissance of the High Middle Ages and is of a piece with its defining ingredient, the return of Aristotle to the West, after, but also alongside, Abelard, whose *Ethics* provides a fuller understanding of the "existentialism" of the animal tale. The *Espurgatoire* establishes Marie within the orbit of the Cistercians as they migrated in the twelfth century to England from France and of their renunciation, in the phrase of Etienne Gilson, "of everything except the art of writing well."

Aware of the grain of conjecture involved in such a leap, comparable to the conviction of an accused on the basis of circumstantial evidence that is nonetheless admissible, we have positioned Marie socially and politically within—or, if not directly within, certainly within the sphere of influence of—the court of Henry II. The concern with social ascension and the rapacious envy of courtiers, which resonates so strongly with a model of social comportment in the *Lais* and is naturalized in the *Fables,* aligns her with the chroniclers and satirists of the Angevin circle, men who, like the peripatetic

Henry, studied, wrote, and traveled on both sides of the Channel. For where culture is concerned, Marie was, above and beyond the demonstrated quadri-lingualism of her mastery of Breton, English, Latin, and French, a translator in the broadest sense of the term, that is, the forger of a linguistic and cultural synthesis coterminous with the Anglo-Norman world, the first in a series of avatars of the universe recognizably our own.

What emerges from all this is a much fuller vision of Marie de France as a writer more deeply embedded in surrounding culture, both learned and popular, than heretofore acknowledged and as a complex figure that is just the opposite of the simple, natural, spontaneous, and moderate image that has flourished since the eighteenth century. More complicated than Chrétien de Troyes who is all romance, or the Tristan poets Thomas and Béroul, who play on only one string of the violin of agony, she is not a simple girl. On the contrary, the range of her languages and works along with consciousness of the literary enterprise makes for a very complex case, which is why, I think, she appeals so insistently to our own sensibility and why in the end she elicits, as we have seen throughout, such a plethora of contemporary approaches. Marie's sophistication can be seen in the variety of critical languages we have used to understand her, to speak about her, an observation with broader implications for medieval studies and for literary studies in general. For it has been my assumption all along, give or take a few philological pockets of knowledge and tricks open to anyone with an Old French and a Latin dictionary, that Marie remains an author accessible to today's reader and, what's more, can be read as a contemporary according to the languages of literary analysis applicable to any thickly woven text, classical, medieval, or modern.

Thus, we have at various moments invoked the methods of standard philology in the teasing out of the variant spellings, etymologies, and semantic range of key words like *lai, aventure, traire, sens, plait, lectuaire, aouvrir, mustrer,* as well as phrases that offer a structural clue to the literary enterprise as Marie understood it: "gloser la lettre," "surplus de sens," "remembrer/remembrement." We have explored the associations connected to proper names and name pairings ("Laüstic," "Lanval," "Yonec," "Bisclavret," "Eliduc," "Tristram," "Guildeluëc" and "Guilliadun," "Codre" and "Fresne") and to the place names ("Düelas," "Avalon," "St. Malo," "Pisteis," "Excestre," "Rigles") that sometimes literally seem to ground wider meaning in the soil. The care Marie exerts in the preparation of prologues and epilogues as well as the attention she devotes to titles—"Bisclavret" or "Garwaf," "Gotelef" or "Chevrefoil," "Laüstic," "Russignol," or "Nihtegale,"

"Chaitivel" or "Les Quatre Duels"—points to an eager editorial husbanding of her work that is not entirely unlike the first stages of a modern critical edition.

In our milking of meaning from the words and names rich enough to
sustain such analysis, we have invoked, if not the methods, at least the
mindset of what has come to be known, for better or worse, as deconstruction. In fact, the literalness of philology is but a cousin of the plays of the
letter of deconstruction, and a careful reading of Marie's works makes clear
just how close the medieval sense of the concreteness and plasticity of words
is to deconstruction's sense of the aporia of the signifier, of the undecid-
ability of meaning, of language's difference from itself. The assumptions of
deconstruction concerning the autonomy of language, itself allegorized and
given a life and a will of its own, are not so far from Marie's acknowledgment of the failures of communication, of a sense of loss in language, of
a betrayal of presence and being characteristic of the linguistic fatalism of
the *Lais*. Admittedly, deconstruction works better for the *Lais* than for the
Fables or the *Espurgatoire;* and, this being the case, throws the issue back to
us in the form of a question: What is the relationship of what we think of
as deconstruction, growing out of philosophy and particularly out of a philosophy of language, to medieval theology and to the dominant perception
from the early Church Fathers to the Renaissance that, in the phrase of Augustine, "words merely teach us other words, less than that, a sound and a
simple voiced noise"?

Marie has elicited the methods of structural analysis, as in our discussion
of the architectonic framing of the *Lais* in terms of a formal analogy with
the thematics of containment and dispersion. Marie's performatives of ambiguity, such as the impossibility of determining with certainty what Tristan writes on the stick of "Chevrefoil," do to the reader what they represent
as occurring in the consciousness of the protagonists of the tale. So too, we
have posited a formal analogy between the dual structure of many of the
fables, the body of the tale doubled by its interpretive moral, and the
fable's deeper meaning in the theme of bodily appetite versus right reason,
the senses versus logic, the animal in the man versus the man in the animal.
The *Espurgatoire* too offers a stunning formal analogy between Marie's insertion of the pronouns and prepositions of the vernacular into the inflected
categories of Latin and, on the level of theme, Owen's entrance to and exit
from the Otherworld.

To the extent to which our approach to Marie has been guided by her
own awareness—there from the very beginning of the prologue to the

Lais—of the projection of the reader's subjective meanings and desires upon temporally distant works, we have invoked the categories and concepts of psychoanalysis. Even by way of introduction we used the chronological record of how others have viewed Marie's works as a historical mirror of the scholar's desire, which reveals, in the characteristics projected upon her, a deep wish to associate her anonymity with the feminine; this on the part of members of a scholarly community composed until after World War II primarily of men, with perhaps the exception of a few bluestockings in the British Museum who have always struck me as Marie's long-lost granddaughters. Where my own analysis of the *Lais* is concerned, I suggested that Marie displays an astonishing engagement, whether conscious or not, with the question of desire, the desire of lovers, but also, again in keeping with the patristic casting of concupiscence as an inordinate love of letters, the desire for language, and for wholeness, and for wholeness in language. (In this respect she is more of a Lacanian than a Freudian.) Marie is aware, as we saw in "Yonec," of the somatization of inner states upon the body, and, more generally, of the imbricated interpersonal dynamic at work in the attempt to understand the underlying subtle sources of human motivation: the wife in "Bisclavret" may unconsciously seek her husband's secret because she has one of her own; the wife's gossipy barb in "Le Fresne" is perhaps the unconscious sign of her husband's infidelity; Arthur's suspicion of Lanval reveals not so much the knight's desire for Guinevere as his unconscious perception of the queen's desire for the knight, a desire grounded, moreover, in her unarticulated perception that Lanval has a secret love of his own that makes him appear fuller, more desirable, than he really is. This is complicated stuff read between the lines of the *Lais*, but it points in the direction of a more explicit analysis of the mechanism of pervasive social envy evident in the *Fables*. At its outer limit, envy might be understood as a version of oedipal rivalry among brothers at court under the rule of the father king as well as a jealous rivalry among poets. Marie denounces those who would steal her work as well as her detractors, one of whom, Denis Piramus, left, as we saw, a trace of his resentment of her. Finally, to understand the psychological component of the legal revolution of the *Espurgatoire*, we had recourse to the psychoanalytic concept of repression figured symbolically as a burial of aggression in a hole in the ground.

Where social psychology yields to anthropology, we found that the *Lais* are a valuable source of information about marriage practice and the inheritance patterns of the aristocracy of the High Middle Ages. The *Espurgatoire* exposes the Christianized rituals of entering the Otherworld and of return, the initiate or pilgrim transformed by his ordeal. Where anthropology itself yields to sociological and even political analysis, the *Fables* deliver a privileged glimpse into the role of literature in the service of a value system stressing measure and moderation, timing, alertness, endurance, flexibility, hypothetical and prospective thinking, all qualities associated with the revival of markets, towns, and an urban economy as well as of state formation. Marie is fascinated throughout by the social dynamics between individuals as well as by the comportment of classes. Rendered in the animal tale as a destabilized notion of species as well as an urge to change bodily attribute or habitat, the individual who rises or falls from the class to which he was born or the group that seeks to move from "its home grove" bespeaks a potential for increased social aspiration and mobility that was historically an integral part of the consolidation of the Angevin monarchy and the alliance of the communes of Anglo-Normandy with the Crown. The *Lais, Fables,* and *Espurgatoire* are deeply embedded in the legal transformation of the twelfth and thirteenth centuries. No less than a literary rewriting of the social contract and a moralization of the social bond, they contribute to remedying one of the great failures of military feudalism through increased emphasis on lateral social ties.

Underneath our analysis lie, of course, the questions and tools of feminist analysis, a consciousness of Marie's subject position, of the difference of a feminine voice against the background of a social, political, and cultural world that was overwhelmingly male. Her works induce a constant awareness of the dynamic of power relations between the sexes, especially of the ways in which a secular, aristocratic model of marriage worked to the detriment of women and contributed to the suffering of the "mal mariées" of the *Lais*. Moreover, if Marie displays a degree of self-consciousness more developed than that of her peers, and even hints in "Les Deus Amanz" at women's secret knowledge, it is a function of the self-distancing that is, finally, the most convincing proof—above and beyond the thematic obsession with unhappy marriage that is, after all, not unknown to the Tristan poets or to Chrétien—that Marie was indeed a woman. A difference of gender stands as the handmaiden of an energizing, heightened perspective, as a source of awareness of the opacity of much that remains transparent—that is, invisible—to the horde of male poets and courtiers of the Anglo-Norman world.

Having thrived for over twenty years in the intellectual petri dish of the University of California at Berkeley, nourished by the peppery phage of *Representations,* my approach to Marie, as indeed to much of what I understand about the relation of literature to the surrounding world, is conditioned by the New Historicism, that is, by a sense that not everything is language or can be reduced to words, that every work has a specificity all its own, is an artifact rooted in a particular time and place. Even though we know so little about her, Marie de France is not paradigmatic; and though we know about her life only through her work, its details, its defining revelatory moments, verbal tics, and thematic obsessions produce a distinctness that is at once very personal and culturally specific. So too, in keeping with the procedures of New Historicism, we have placed Marie's diverse poems in contact with all kinds of other texts and discourses—other literary works in both Latin and the vernacular as well as the customals, theological and ethical treatises, satire, and chronicles belonging to a wider world of social and cultural relations. In what is always something of a tautology, but one that is nonetheless inherent to the study of the Middle Ages, we have seen the multiple ways that the *Lais,* the *Fables,* and the *Espurgatoire* aid in understanding their surrounding milieu as well as the degree to which that milieu is defined by the very works it illuminates.

To the extent that the system for dating and recording events, alongside an inattention to the minutiae of everyday life, makes the New Historicism inappropriate to the study of the Middle Ages, I have stretched a bit the orthodoxy of a method that, in fact, never existed *strictu sensu* as such. Nonetheless, I have persisted in the attempt to locate what I consider to be the representative anecdotes of Marie's life as they reveal themselves in the details that are part of her work and that, either via repetition or via poignant relief, reveal how we might understand the rest: that is, the back and forth across the Channel in "Eliduc"; the confessions of constraint in the prison bedrooms of "Guigemar" and "Yonec"; the claustrophobic "mal mariée" who resorts to writing as an escape in "Milun" and turns, like Lanval, to the liberating fairy of fiction; the acknowledgment of authorship, a signature event, appearing as it does just after the story of a young girl, orphaned, abandoned, raised to be literate, harassed, and then consigned to a convent in the *Espurgatoire.* It is only a small step to complete the syllogism suggested by the writing prisoners of "Milun" and Purgatory and to infer that they—again like Marie?—have found a way out, a translation, via writing in a room of their own.

Finally, Marie's last work seems unmistakably linked to a specific historical event, the English conquest of Ireland, which is where the New Historicism and its attentiveness to power relations yield to a stunning example of the relevance of postcolonial to medieval studies. The *Espurgatoire* shows, as we have seen in our last chapter, how a cultural artifact, whether literary or not, might serve to justify morally the project of conquest, to legitimate the territorial claims of the conqueror, to ideologically and institutionally buttress the long-range project of occupation.

Some years ago the journal of the Medieval Academy of America *Speculum* printed a special issue on the New Philology. The overwhelming majority of the articles pleaded in one way or another for the application of current literary theory and methods in the social sciences to medieval works, part of a wider movement, begun a decade earlier, to recognize the modernism of the Middle Ages. What I have proposed in the volume at hand is a step beyond this original rejuvenating perception: that is, that we might read a medieval work simultaneously on its own and on our own terms and that we might use all that we can muster in the way of other fields of inquiry to understand these mysteriously rich objects of continued fascination. The range of disciplinary approaches pertinent to the reading of Marie— philology and textual studies, structuralism and deconstruction, psychoanalysis, anthropology, sociology, feminism, New Historicism, and postcolonialism—bear witness to the complexity of her creation. That the *Lais,* the *Fables,* and the *Espurgatoire* might sustain the questions belonging to such disparate domains of inquiry points in the direction of a new eclecticism, one whose ultimate payoff is not contradiction and inconsistency; rather, a fuller picture of a thickly plotted oeuvre whose origin, meaning, and effects cannot be contained by any one perspective, whose "surplus of sense" is, finally, inexhaustible. After all, it is only humanists who, in the absence of data observable by all and oblivious to the criterion of the reproduction of results, willingly limit their vision to a single approach. Scientists are in this respect much more open to and cognizant of the fact that disciplinary cross-fertilization is the means by which a field may prosper, witness in our time the spectacular growth of molecular biology out of the modes of research once belonging to chemistry, physics, and classical genetics. Literary studies, and perhaps the humanities more generally, have painted themselves into the corner of specialization and of doctrinal rigidity in which the fundamental delight of reading and of discovery, the opening of a text not to another text, but to the body, to others, and to the world have been lost. If Marie has taught us anything, it is that the time has come for both the pleasures of the text and its deeper plurivalent significance to be reclaimed.

Notes

INTRODUCTION

1. Claude Fauchet, *Recueil de l'Origine de la Langue et Poesie Françoise, Ryme, et Romans* (Paris: Mamert Patisson, 1581), p. 163.

2. Cited Richard Baum, *Recherches sur les oeuvres attribuées à Marie de France* (Heidelberg: Carl Winter, 1968), p. 62.

3. Thomas Tyrwhitt, *The Canterbury Tales of Chaucer* (London: T. Payne, 1775–78), 4.164–68.

4. De la Rue's *Dissertation* appeared in *Archaeologia: or Miscellaneous Tracts Relating to Antiquity* (London: Society of Antiquaries of London, 1797), vol. 13.

5. *Journal des Savants* 132 (1820): 400.

6. Gaston Paris, "Lais Inédits—De Tyolet, De Guingamor, De Doon, Du Lecheor et De Tydorel," *Romania* 8 (1879): 37.

7. Emil Winkler, *Französische Dichter des Mittelalters*, vol. 2: *Marie de France* (Vienna: Hölder, 1918); p. Chabaille, "Marie de France," in *Nouvelle biographie générale* (Paris, 1857–66), vol. 33, col. 732; Eduard Mall, *De aetate rebusque Mariae Francicae nova quaestio instituitur* (Halle: Halis Saxonum, 1867); *La vie Seint Audree: poème anglo-normand du XIIIe siècle*, ed. Östen Södergard (Uppsala: A.-B. Lundequistska Bokhandeln, 1955); Constance Bullock-Davis, "Marie, Abbess of Shaftesbury, and Her Brothers," *English Historical Review* 80 (1965): 314–22; Jessie Crosland, *Medieval French Literature* (Oxford: Basil Blackwell, 1956), p. 97; John Charles Fox, "Mary, Abbess of Shaftesbury," *English Historical Review* (1911): 317–26; Antoinette Knapton, "A la recherche de Marie de France," *Romance Notes* 19 (1978): 248–53; Ezio Levi, "Maria di Francia e le abbazie d'Inghilterra," *Archivum Romanicum* 5 (1921): 472–93; Urban T. Holmes, "New Thoughts on Marie de France," *Studies in Philology* 29 (1932): 1–10; Urban T. Holmes, "Further on Marie de France," *Symposium* 3 (1949): 335–39; p. N. Flum, "Additional Thoughts on Marie de France," *Romance Notes* 3 (1961–62): 53–56.

8. La Rue, *Dissertation*, p. 44.

9. J.-B.-B. de Roquefort, *Poésies de Marie de France, Poète Anglo-Normand du XIIIe Siècle ou Recueil de Lais, Fables et Autres Productions de cette Femme Célèbre* (Paris: Marescq, 1832), 1:6. This quotation is repeated integrally by Sainte-Beuve in his *Ancienne littérature (partie médiévale), cours professé à l'Université de Liège, 1848–1849),* ed. Françoise Dehousse (Paris: Les Belles Lettres, 1971), p. 543.

10. Gaston Paris, *Histoire littéraire de la France* (Paris: Imprimerie Nationale, 1888), 30:8.

11. *La Grande Encyclopédie: Inventaire raisonné des sciences, des lettres et des arts par une société de savants et de gens de lettres* (Paris: Société Anonyme de la Grande Encyclopédie, 1885–1901), 23:112; Ernest Hoepffner, *Les Lais de Marie de France* (Paris: Boivin, 1935), p. 177.

12. Jean-Charles Payen, *Le lai narratif* (Turnholt: Brepols, 1975), p. 63; Milena Mikhaïlova, *Le présent de Marie* (Paris: Diderot, 1996), p. 60.

13. The Abbé La Rue writes: " 'Marie ai non, si suis de France, &c.' If we consider well the latter verse, there will be no difficulty in perceiving that Mary wrote in England. Indeed, it was formerly a very common thing for authors to say that they were of such a city, and even to assume the name of it. This we can easily conceive; or even that, when writing in Latin, they should state themselves either natives of England or of France. But when an author writes in France, and in the language of the country, he does not say that *he is of France.* Now this precaution on the part of Mary implies that she wrote in a foreign country, the greater part of whose inhabitants spoke her native language; and where shall we find the French tongue more used at the time than in England?" (*Dissertation*, p. 50).

14. See Ian Short, "Patrons and Polyglots: French Literature in Twelfth-Century England," *Anglo-Norman Studies* 14 (1991): 240; Lucien Foulet, "English Words in the *Lais* of Marie de France," *Modern Language Notes* 20 (1905): 109–11.

15. "In the case of *Milun* the swan helps to establish the actual district from which the story stemmed. . . . As the average weight of a young male swan is fifteen pounds or more, the squire, if he had to 'carry' it, which is more than likely, for it was obviously not pinioned, could not have had very far to go; so that what Milun said about his loved-one living near seems to be confirmed." As to her sources, Bullock-Davis is "indebted to Mr K. G. Clark, Assistant Secretary to the British Trust for Ornithology for details concerning the weight and life-span of swans." Constance Bullock-Davies, "The Love-Messenger in 'Milun,'" *Nottingham Medieval Studies* 16 (1972): 22, 25.

16. Glyn Burgess, *The Lais of Marie de France: Text and Context* (Athens: University of Georgia Press, 1987), p. 22.

17. Gustave Cohen, *La vie littéraire en France au moyen âge* (Paris: Tallandier, 1949), pp. 114–15. This passage reproduces an earlier article of 1936.

18. Emil Levi, "Il Re giovane e Maria di Francia," *Archivum Romanicum* 5 (1921): 448–71; "Ainsi, conformément aux conventions de l'éloge, la rhétorique de la dédicace ne retient absolument rien de la personne historique du roi. Seule la figure importe" (Roger Dragonetti, "Le lai narratif de Marie de France" in *La musique et les lettres* [Geneva: Droz, 1986], pp. 36–37).

19. *Die Fabeln der Marie de France,* ed. Karl Warnke (Halle: Niemeyer, 1898); Axel Ahlström, *Marie de France et les lais narratifs* (Göteborg: Flanders, 1925), p. 15; Madeleine Soudée, "Le dédicataire des *Ysopets* de Marie de France," *Les Lettres Romanes* 35 (1981): 183–98; Sidney Painter, "To Whom Were Dedicated the *Fables* of Marie de France?" *Modern Language Notes* 48 (1933): 367–69. See Glyn Burgess, introduction to *Lais, ed.* Alfred Ewert (Bristol: Bristol Classical Press, 1995), p. ix; Emmanuel Mickel, *Marie de France* (New York: Twayne, 1974), pp. 19–21.

20. For the question of Marie's dates, see Burgess, *introduction,* pp. vii–viii; and for the question of the internal chronology of the *Lais,* see his *Lais of Marie de France: Text and Context,* pp. 1–34.

21. Lucien Foulet, for example, was convinced that Marie was at the origin of both; see "Marie de France et les lais bretons," *Zeitschrift für Romanische Philologie* 29 (1905): 19–56, 293–322.

22. Ezio Levi, "Marie de France e il romanzo di *Eneas,*" *Atti del Reale Istituto Veneto di Scienze, Lettere ed Arti* 81 (1921–22): 645–86.

23. Payen, *Lai narratif,* p. 56.

24. *Dictionnaire des lettres françaises—Le Moyen Age* (Paris: Fayard, 1992), pp. 795, 68.

25. "Ces chroniques constituent deux documents précieux pour l'histoire de France et pour l'histoire d'un genre littéraire naissant, l'historiographie en prose française" (ibid., p. 68).

26. See Bernard Cerquiglini, *Eloge de la variante: Histoire critique de la philologie* (Paris: Seuil, 1989).

27. No question is more vexed than that of the authorship of the earliest works or "monuments" of French literature. Works belonging to the prehistory of Old French are the object of a speculation that makes the mist surrounding Marie seem like clarity itself. Despite the name—Nithard—attached to the earliest example of a Romance language, the *Serments de Strasbourg,* we know very little about the conditions surrounding the production of this first text. The same is also true of the vernacular works from the ninth, tenth, and eleventh centuries—the "Séquence de Sainte Eulalie," the "Serment sur Jonas," the "Vie de Saint Alexis," all of which remain anonymous. On the difficulty of establishing authorship, see my article "The First Document and the Birth of Medieval French Studies," in *A New History of French Literature,* ed. Denis Hollier (Cambridge: Harvard University Press, 1989), pp. 6–13; Renée Balibar, *L'institution du français: Essai sur le colinguisme des Carolingiens à la République* (Paris: Presses Universitaires de France, 1985); Bernard Cerquiglini, *La Naissance du français* (Paris: Presses Universitaires de France, 1991).

28. Alistair Minnis, *Medieval Theory of Authorship: Scholastic Literary Attitudes in the Later Middle Ages* (Philadelphia: University of Pennsylvania Press, 1988), p. 22.

29. Ibid., pp. 29, 42.

30. *Vie de seint Edmund le rei,* ed. Hilding Kjellman (Göteborg: Elanders, 1935), v. 35.

31. Glyn Burgess, *Marie de France: An Analytic Bibliography* (London: Grant and Cutler, 1977, supplements in 1986 and 1997).

32. Hoepffner, *Lais,* p. 176; Leo Spitzer, "The Prologue to the *Lais* of Marie de

France and Medieval Poetics," *Modern Philology* 61 (1943): 102; Edgard Sienaert, *Les Lais de Marie de France: Du conte merveilleux à la nouvelle psychologique* (Paris: Champion, 1978), p. 209.

33. Philippe Ménard, *Les Lais de Marie de France* (Paris: Presses Universitaires de France, 1979), pp. 10, 149.

34. Paula Clifford, *Marie de France: Lais* (London: Grant and Cutler, 1982), p. 18.

35. Ménard, *Lais*, p. 11.

36. Burgess, *Lais of Marie de France: Text and Context*, p. 68.

37. De Roquefort, *Poésies*, 1:15.

38. Ménard, *Lais*, pp. 11, 101, 149.

39. De Roquefort, *Poésies*, 1:21.

40. Lucien Foulet, "Marie de France et la Légende du Purgatoire de Saint Patrice," *Romanische Forschungen* 22 (1908): 626; Hoepffner, *Lais*, p. 71.

41. Ménard, *Lais*, p. 110.

42. Hoeppfner, *Lais*, p. 79; Ménard, *Lais*, p. 111.

43. Hoepffner, *Lais*, p. 91; Ménard, *Lais*, p. 127.

44. Edmond Faral, "Marie de France: Les lais," in *Histoire de la littérature française illustrée*, ed. Joseph Bédier and Paul Hazard (Paris: Larousse, 1923), 1:23; Hoepffner, *Lais*, p. 166; Ménard, *Lais*, pp. 237, 11, 129.

45. De Roquefort, *Poésies*, 1:22. Sainte-Beuve repeats this sentence literally in his *Ancienne littérature*, p. 550.

46. *Histoire littéraire de la France: Ouvrage commencé par des religieux bénédictins de la Congrégation de Saint-Maur, et continué par les Membres de l'Institut (Académie royale des Inscriptions et Belles-Lettres)* (Paris: H. Welter, 1895), 19:792.

47. Gaston Paris, *La poésie du moyen âge* (Paris: Hachette, 1895), p. 42; Joseph Bédier, "Les Lais de Marie de France," *Revue des Deux Mondes* 107 (1891): 858.

48. Hoepffner, *Lais*, p. 79; Ménard, *Lais*, p. 205.

49. S. Foster Damon, "Marie de France: Psychologist of Courtly Love," *PMLA* 44 (1929): 976.

50. Süheylâ Bayrav, *Symbolisme médiévale: Béroul, Marie, Chrétien* (Paris: Presses Universitaires de France, 1957), pp. 63, 72.

51. Ménard, *Lais*, p. 211.

52. William S. Woods, "Femininity in the *Lais* of Marie de France," *Studies in Philology* 47 (1950): 6; Mickel, *Marie de France*, p. 133.

53. Ménard, *Lais*, p. 211.

54. Ibid., 232.

55. Rupert Pickens, "Thematic Structure in Marie de France's *Guigemar*," *Romania* 95 (1974): 332.

56. Roger Dragonetti, introduction to Mikhaïlova, *Le présent de Marie*, p. 28. See also Jean-Charles Huchet, "Nom de femme et écriture féminine au Moyen Age: Les *Lais* de Marie de France," *Poétique* 48 (1981): 407–30.

57. Walter Benjamin, "Unpacking My Library: A Talk about Book Collecting," in *Illuminations* (New York: Schocken Books, 1969), pp. 61–62.

58. Gaston Paris, *Esquisse historique de la littérature française au moyen âge* (Paris: Armand Colin, 1926), p. 131.

59. See Marjorie M. Malvern, "Marie de France's Ingenious Uses of the Authorial Voice and Her Singular Contribution to Western Literature," *Tulsa Studies in Women's Literature* 2 (1983): 37.

60. Virginia Woolf, " 'Anon' and 'The Reader': Virginia Woolf's Last Essays," ed. Brenda Silver, *Twentieth Century Literature* 25 (1979): 397.

61. See Brian Stock, *The Implications of Literacy: Written Language and Models of Interpretation in the Eleventh and Twelfth Centuries* (Princeton: Princeton University Press, 1983).

62. Guillaume de Lorris and Jean de Meun, *Le Roman de la rose,* ed. Daniel Poirion (Paris: Garnier-Flammarion, 1974), v. 11187. The English translation is that of Frances Horgan, *The Romance of the Rose* (London: Penguin, 1994), p. 172.

63. R. Howard Bloch, "The Dead Nightingale: Orality in the Tomb of Old French Literature," *Culture and History* 3 (1988): 63–78; "The Medieval Text—'Guigemar'—as a Provocation to the Discipline of Medieval Studies," *Romanic Review* 79 (1988): 63–73; "New Philology and Old French," *Speculum* 65 (1990): 38–58; "The Lay and the Law: Sexual / Textual Transgression in the *Lais* of Marie de France," special issue of *Stanford French Review* on transgression, ed. Kevin Brownlee and Marina Brownlee (1990): 181–210; "Das Altfranzösische Lai als Ort von Trauer und Gedächtnis," in *Gedächtnis als Raum,* ed. Renate Lachmann and Anselm Haverkamp (Frankfurt: Suhrkamp, 1991), pp. 189–206.

64. See the chapter on the trial of Ganelon in Eugene Vance, *Reading the Song of Roland* (Englewood Cliffs, N.J.: Prentice-Hall, 1971).

65. Bédier, "Lais," p. 857.

66. Denis Piramus, *Vie de seint Edmund le rei,* v. 43.

CHAPTER ONE

1. Stephen G. Nichols, "Marie de France's Commonplaces," *Yale French Studies,* Special Issue (1991): 135; see also Sarah Spence, "Writing in the Vernacular: The *Lais* of Marie de France," in *Texts and the Self in the Twelfth Century,* ed. Sarah Spence (Cambridge: Cambridge University Press, 1996), p. 120.

2. "Puis que des lais ai comencé, / Ja n'iert par mon travail laissé: / Les aventures que j'en sai / Tut par rime les cunterai" ("Yonec," v. 1); "Cil qui ceste aventure oïrent / Lunc tens aprés un lai en firent" (v. 549).

3. As Jean Frappier points out, the term "aventure" is used to designate the principle of unity of the lai; see "Remarques sur la structure du lai: Essai de définition et de classement," in *La littérature narrative d'imagination, des genres littéraires aux techniques d'expression* (Paris: Presses Universitaires de France, 1961), p. 31.

4. See Erich Koehler, *Ideal und Wirklichkeit in der Höfischen Epik* (Tübingen: Max Niemeyer, 1956), pp. 66–99.

5. Cited in Jean Maillard, *Evolution et esthétique du lai lyrique des origines à la fin*

du XIVe siècle (Paris: Publications de l'Institut de Musicologie de l'Université de Paris, 1963), p. 24. Maillard's translation is as follows: "Une hai d'arbres m'entoure; pour moi, en vérité, le merle agile chante son *loîd.* Sur mon livre réglé chante pour moi le *trîrech* des oiseaux."

6. "Le français *lai* vient vraisemblablement de l'irlandais *loîd,* plus tard *laîd:* c'est l'Irlande qui nous offre les exemples les plus anciens de ce genre de poésie et du mot par lequel on le désigne." Achille d'Arbois de Jubainville, "Mélanges: Lai," *Romania* 8 (1878), p. 422.

7. See Richard Baum, "Les troubadours et les lais," *Zeitschrift für Romanische Philologie* 85 (1969): 1.

8. Maillard, *Evolution,* p. 27. On the Celtic origins of the word, see Ernest Hoepffner, *Les Lais de Marie de France* (Paris: Boivin, 1935), p. 42.

9. Still another etymological strain claims that one must seek the origin of *leich* in tropes of the liturgical Kyrie designated by the vocable "leis," second syllable of *eleison* (Maillard, *Evolution,* p. 28).

10. Ibid.

11. Two forms also used in Old High German are *liet* which means "words with melody" and *leih* which means "melody with words" (ibid., p. 28).

12. Baum, "Les troubadours," p. 40.

13. So too the word is used in Miracles of Gautier de Coinci to designate the poetic form of the miracle itself: "Entendez tuit ensemble et le clers et li lai / Le salu de Nostre Dame, nus ne sait plus douz lai. / Plus douz lais ne puet estre qu'est *Ave Maria:* / Cest lai chanta li angres quant Diex se maria." Jacques Chailley, *Les Chansons à la Vierge de Gautier de Coinci* (Paris: Heugel, 1959), p. 184.

14. "Ung gros exemple em porroit metre / As gens *laiz* qui n'entendent lettre (*Roman de la rose,* ed. Daniel Poirion [Paris: Garnier-Flammarion, 1974], v. 17,393); "Les laies gens n'on autre escrit" (Gautier de Coinci, *Miracles de Notre Dame,* ed. V. Frederic Koenig [Geneva: Droz, 1961], 2:22.

15. "Mout ont gemi, mout ont ploré / Ançois que raconté lor ait / Comment de son savoreus lait / La mere Dieu l'avoit gari." Gautier de Coinci, *Miracles de Notre Dame,* 3:141.

16. "Trois torz torna an molt po d'ore, / une vague li vint desore, / qui la fiert an l'un des lez, / les borz a fraiz e decassez." *Roman d'Eneas,* ed. Salverda de Grave (Paris: Champion, 1964), v. 245.

17. See my *Etymologies and Genealogies: A Literary Anthropology of Medieval French Literature* (Chicago: University of Chicago Press, 1983), pp. 37–44.

18. Philo, *On the Cherubim,* ed. F. H. Colson (London: Heinemann, 1929), 2:43.

19. Dante, *De vulgari eloquentia,* ed. Pio Rajna (Florence: Le Monnier, 1896), p. 16.

20. For the medieval debate about the ancients and moderns, see M.-D. Chenu, *Nature, Man, and Society in the Twelfth Century,* trans. Jerome Taylor and Lester Little (Chicago: University of Chicago Press, 1968), chap. 9. For a discussion of Priscian and Marie, see Mortimer J. Donovan, "Priscian and the Obscurity of the Ancients," *Speculum* 36 (1961): 78; Tony Hunt, "Glossing Marie de France," *Romanische Forschungen* 86 (1974): 396–418; D. W. Robertson, "Marie de France, *Lais,* Prologue, 13–16," *Modern*

Language Notes 64 (1949): 338; Leo Spitzer, "The Prologue to the *Lais* of Marie de France and Medieval Poetics," *Modern Philology* 41 (1943): 96.

21. Augustine, *De doctrina Christiana,* ed. G. Combès and J. Farges (Paris: Desclée de Brouwer, 1949), p. 258.

22. Augustine, *De genesi ad litteram,* ed. p. Agnësse and A. Solignac (Paris: Desclée de Brouwer, 1972), 2:122.

23. Augustine, *De doctrina,* p. 300.

24. I am not the first to have noticed Marie's obsession with the opacity of words: see Brewster Fitz, "Desire and Interpretation: Marie de France's 'Chievrefoil,'" *Yale French Studies* 58 (1979): 186; Robert Sturges, "Texts and Readers in Marie de France's *Lais,*" *Romanic Review* 71 (1980): 244.

25. See Anne Paupert, "Les femmes et la parole dans les *Lais* de Marie de France," in *Amour et merveille: Les 'Lais' de Marie de France,* ed. Jean Dufournet (Paris: Champion, 1995), pp. 169–70.

26. Hugh of Saint-Victor, *Didascalicon,* trans. Jerome Taylor (New York: Columbia University Press, 1968), p. 43; see Brewster Fitz, "The Prologue to the *Lais* of Marie de France and the *Parable of the Talents:* Gloss and Monetary Metaphor," *Modern Language Notes* 90 (1975): 558–64.

27. "Qui sages est nel deit celer,/mais pur ceo deit son sen monstrer/que, quant serra del siecle alez,/en seit puis toz jours remembrez" (*Le Roman de Thèbes,* ed. Francine Mora-Lebrun [Paris: Lettres Gothiques, 1995], v. 1); "Salemons nos enseigne et dit,/Et sil lit hon en son escrit,/Que nus ne deit son sens celer" (Benoît de Sainte-Maure, *Le Roman de Troie,* ed. Emmanuèle Baumgartner and Françoise Vielliard [Paris: Lettres Gothiques, 1998], v. 1).

28. *L'Isopet de Lyon,* ed. Julia Bastin, *Recueil général des Isopets* (Paris: Champion, 1929), 2:85. See also the beginning of the *Isopet I—Avionnet* (ibid., p. 203).

29. *Le Bestiaire d'Amour suivi de la Réponse de la Dame,* ed. C. Hippeau (Geneva: Slatkin Reprints, 1969), p. 51; *Le Lai d'Ignaure,* ed. Rita Lejeune (Liège: H. Vaillant-Carmanne, 1938), v. 1. See also Guillaume de Normandie, *Le Bestiaire divin,* ed. M. C. Hippeau (Caen: A. Hardel, 1852), p. 303; *Athis et Prophilias,* ed. Alfons Hilka (Dresden: Gesellschaft für romanische Literatur, 1912–16), 1:1; *Aymeri de Narbonne,* ed. Louis Demaison (Paris: Firmon Didot, 1887), v. 2; *Guillaume de Palerne,* ed. Alexandre Micha (Geneva: Droz, 1990), v. 1; Wace, *La Vie de Saint Nicholas,* ed. Einar Ronsjö (Lund: Etudes Romanes de Lund, 1942), v. 27; *The Life of St. Catherine, by Clemence of Barking,* ed. William Macbain (Oxford: Blackwell, 1964), v. 1.

30. Chrétien de Troyes, *Erec et Enide,* ed. Marie Roques (Paris: Champion, 1963), v. 1. The translation is that of Carleton W. Carroll, *Chrétien de Troyes: Arthurian Romances* (London: Penguin, 1991), p. 37.

31. "Quant de lais faire m'entremet,/Ne voïl ublïer Bisclavret" ("In my effort to compose lais I do not wish to omit 'Bisclavret'" ["Bisclavret," v. 1); "De *Bisclavret* fut fet li lais/Pur remembrance a tut dis mais" ("The lai was composed about Bisclavret to be remembered for ever more" [v. 316]); "Talent me prist de remembrer/Un lai dunt jo oï parler" ("I am minded to recall a lai of which I have heard tell" ["Chaitivel," v. 1]); "Del aventure de ces treis/Li auncïen Bretun curteis/Firent un lai pur remembrer,/

Qu'hum nel deüst pas oblïer" ("From the story of these three the ancient courtly Bretons composed a lai to be remembered" ["Eliduc," v. 1181]).

32. See Milena Mikhaïlova, *Le présent de Marie* (Paris: Diderot, 1996), p. 60.

33. See Mary J. Carruthers, *The Book of Memory: A Study of Memory in Medieval Culture* (Cambridge: Cambridge University Press, 1990), p. 218.

34. Varro, *De lingua latina*, ed. R. G. Kent (Cambridge: Harvard University Press, 1951), p. 14.

35. The anonymous author of the so-called "Bestiaire de Gervaise," for example, claims to "walk only with the aid of a cane" and to "extract a book into romance": "GERVASES, qui ne puet aler/Que ne li covieigne porter/.I. baston por soi apuier,/Vuet .j. livre en roman traitie[r]" ("Le Bestiaire de Gervaise," ed. Paul Meyer, *Romania* 1 [1872]: 426, v. 29). Here the word *traire* is the equivalent of "to extract" meaning from one language to another: "Li livres a non Bestiaire./A Barbarie est [en] l'armaire/Li latins qui mult est plaisanz;/De illuec fu estraiz li romanz" (v. 33, p. 426).

36. See Roger Dragonetti, "Le lai narratif de Marie de France," in *La musique et les lettres* (Geneva: Droz, 1986), p. 33.

CHAPTER TWO

1. See S. Foster Damon, "Marie de France: Psychologist of Courtly Love," *PMLA* 44 (1929): 968–96; John A. Frey, "Linguistic and Psychological Couplings in the Lays of Marie de France," *Studies in Philology* 61 (1964): 3–18.

2. Of all her commentators, Milena Mikhaïlova is the only one of whom I am aware who links Marie's morbidity not only to the wound but to the sense of dispersion and loss defined as a linguistic drama as well. See *Le présent de Marie* (Paris: Diderot, 1996), p. 60.

3. Though her identification of a precise geographical site for the action of "Lanval" may seem overly literal, Elizabeth A. Francis nonetheless affirms the topographic association of the name and "down the valley" or "downhill." See "Marie de France et son temps," *Romania* 72 (1951): 87–88.

4. On the question of narrative structure and endings in the *Lais,* see Evelyn Birge Vitz, "The *Lais* of Marie de France: 'Narrative Grammar' and the Literary Text," *Romanic Review* 74 (1983): 396.

5. See R. Howard Bloch, *Etymologies and Genealogies: A Literary Anthropology of the French Middle Ages* (Chicago: University of Chicago Press, 1983), pp. 70–83.

6. See Georges Duby, *La société aux XIe et XIIe siècles dans la région mâconnaise* (Paris: Armand Colin, 1953), p. 280; "Structures de parenté et noblesse dans la France du Nord au XIe et XIIe siècles," in *Hommes et structures au moyen âge* (Paris: Mouton, 1973), p. 270; "Situation de la noblesse au début du XIIIe siècle," in *Hommes et structures,* p. 344.

7. See Georges Duby, *Medieval Marriage* (Baltimore: Johns Hopkins University Press, 1978), chap. 1; and *La société aux XI et XIIe siècles dans la région mâconnaise,* p. 436; Charles Donahue, "The Policy of Alexander the Third's Consent Theory of Marriage," *Proceedings from the Fourth International Congress of Medieval Canon Law* (Vatican: Biblioteca Apostolica Vaticana, 1976), pp. 256, 257; Michael M. Sheehan, "Choice of Mar-

riage Partner in the Middle Ages: Development and Application of a Theory of Marriage," *Studies in Medieval and Renaissance History* 1 (1978): 1–33; Juliette Turlan, "Recherches sur le mariage dans la pratique coutumière (XIIe–XIVe siècles)," *Revue historique du droit français et etranger* 35 (1957): 477–528.

8. R. Howard Bloch, "Tristan, the Myth of the State, and the Language of the Self," *Yale French Studies* 51 (1975): 61–81.

9. The following lines are not in the Harley 978 manuscript in the British Museum, but are to be found in BN fr. 2168. I have followed the transcription of the Warnke/ Ewert/Burgess edition, p. 178.

10. Andreas Capellanus, *The Art of Courtly Love,* trans. J. J. Parry (New York: Columbia University Press, 1969), pp. 106–7.

11. For a discussion of the legal ramifications of the question of secrecy and exposure, see John M. Bowers, "Ordeals, Privacy, and the *Lais* of Marie de France," *Journal of Medieval and Renaissance Studies* 24 (1994): 1–31.

12. See Erich Koehler, *Ideal und Wirklichkeit in der Höfischen Epik* (Tübingen: Max Niemeyer, 1956), p. 25, and my *Medieval French Literature and Law* (Berkeley: University of California Press, 1977), pp. 220–38. Koehler's insight, from which I drew my own, is to be set against a whole tradition that considered Lanval to be merely homesick and such homesickness to offer proof that Marie was herself living at a foreign court. See Ernest Hoepffner, *Les Lais de Marie de France* (Paris: Boivin, 1935), p. 50; Paula Clifford, *Marie de France: Lais* (London: Grant and Cutler, 1982), p. 57.

13. See Georges Duby, "Les 'jeunes' dans la société aristocratique dans la France du Nord-Ouest du XIIe siècle," in *Hommes et structures,* pp. 213–26.

14. C. S. Lewis, *The Allegory of Love* (New York: Oxford University Press, 1958), p. 13.

15. The deepest discussion of the question of the broken promise is to be found in Shoshana Felman's *The Literary Speech Act: Don Juan with J. L. Austin, or Seduction in Two Languages,* trans. C. Porter (Ithaca: Cornell University Press, 1983).

16. For a comparison of the two *récits,* see Jean Rychner, "La présence et le point de vue du narrateur dans deux récits courts: Le *Lai de Lanval* et la *Châtelaine de Vergi*," *Vox Romanica* 39 (1980): 86–103.

17. For a historically defined discussion of the judicial procedure of Lanval's trial, see Jacqueline Eccles, "Marie de France and the Law," in *Les Lieux Interdits: Transgression and French Literature,* ed. Larry Duffy and Adrian Tudor (Hull: University of Hull Press, 1998), p. 17; Elizabeth A. Francis, "The Trial in *Lanval,*" in *Studies in French Language and Mediaeval Literature Presented to M. K. Pope* (Manchester: Manchester University Press, 1939), pp. 115–24.

18. See R. Howard Bloch, *Etymologies and Genealogies,* pp. 133–36; Alexandre Leupin, "Ecriture naturelle et écriture hermaphrodite," *Diagraphe* 9 (1976): 119–41; Eugene Vance, "Désir, rhétorique et texte," *Poétique* 42 (1980): 137–55; Jan Ziolkowski, *Alan de Lille's Grammar of Sex* (Boston: Medieval Academy of America, 1985), pp. 40–43.

19. Glyn Burgess suggests that *laustic* derives from the Breton form *éostic,* via *aostic, austic. The Lais of Marie de France: Text and Context* (Athens: University of Georgia Press, 1987), p. 10.

20. In the abutment of the lovers' houses we find the fantasy of presence: "Kar pres esteient lur repere,/Preceines furent lur maisuns/E lur sales e lur dunguns;/N'i aveit bare ne devise/Fors un haut mur de piere bise" ("Their houses, halls, and keeps were close by each other and there was no barrier or division, apart from a high wall of dark-hued stone" [v. 35]). Because of such proximity oral communication is envisaged as possible: "Des chambres u la dame jut,/Quant a la fenestre s'estut,/Poeit parler a sun ami/ De l'autre part, e il a li" ("When she stood at her bedroom window, the lady could talk to her beloved in the other house and he to her" [v. 39]).

21. "Cele aventure fu cuntee" ("Laüstic," v. 157); "Nul hum n'en oï plus parler,/Ne jeo n'en sai avant cunter" ("Lanval," v. 645).

22. Laurence de Looze has discussed the two names in terms of two family branches that correspond to separate manuscript families; see "Marie de France et la textualisa-tion: Arbre, enfant, oeuvre dans le Lai de 'Fresne,'" Romanic Review 82 (1990): 396–408.

23. See Roger Dragonetti, "Le lai narratif de Marie de France," in La musique et les lettres (Geneva: Droz, 1986), p. 39; Jean-Charles Huchet, "Nom de femme et écriture féminine au Moyen Age: Les Lais de Marie de France," Poétique 48 (1981): 407–30.

24. First, Bisclavret, "De si qu'il a le rei choisi;/Vers lui curut querre merci" ("As soon as he saw the king he ran up to him and begged for mercy" [v. 145]); and then the King, "A grant merveille l'ot tenu/Et mut le tient a grant chierté./A tuz les suens ad co-maundé/Que sur s'amur le gardent bien/E li ne meffacent de rien,/Ne par nul d'eus ne seit feruz;/Bien seit abevreiz e peüz" ("He considered the wolf to be a great wonder and loved it dearly, commanding all his people to guard it well for love of him and not to do it any harm. None of them was to strike it and plenty of food and water must be pro-vided for it" [v. 168]).

25. Joseph Loth, "Le Lai du Bisclavret: Le sens de ce nom et son importance," Revue Celtique 44 (1927): 300–307; Heinrich Zimmer, "Histoire littéraire de la France, tome XXX," Göttingische Gelehrte Anzeigen 20 (1890): 800ff.; Th. M. Chotzen, "Bisclavret," Etudes Celtiques 2 (1937): 33–44; H. W. Bailey, "Bisclavret in Marie de France," Cam-bridge Medieval Celtic Studies 1 (1981): 95–97; William Sayers, "Bisclavret in Marie de France: A Reply," Cambridge Medieval Celtic Studies 4 (1982): 77–82. See also Burgess, Lais of Marie de France, p. 9.

CHAPTER THREE

1. See Brewster Fitz, "The Storm Episode and the Weasel Episode: Sacrificial Casu-istry in Marie de France's 'Eliduc,'" Modern Language Notes 89 (1974): 542–49.

2. On the doubleness of the title and the thematics of "Eliduc," see Leo Spitzer, "Marie de France—Dichterin von Problem-Märchen," Zeitschrift für romanische Philologie 50 (1930): 38; on the question of names in the Lais, see Matilda Tomaryn Bruckner, "Strategies of Naming in Marie de France's Lais: At the Crossroads of Gen-der and Genre," Neophilologus 75 (1991): 31–40.

3. I am grateful to Margaret Pappano for this suggestion.

4. See R. Howard Bloch, Etymologies and Genealogies: A Literary Anthropology of the French Middle Ages (Chicago: University of Chicago Press, 1983), pp. 137–49.

5. Jean de Meun, *Le Roman de la rose,* ed. Daniel Poirion (Paris: Garnier-Flammarion, 1974), v. 5535.

6. "Icil kil porterent avant,/Quatre Dols l'apelent alquant, . . . Le Chaitivel ad nun en us" (vv. 233, 237).

7. Roger Dragonetti, "Le lai narratif de Marie de France," in *La musique et les lettres* (Geneva: Droz, 1986), p. 49.

8. This is why, I am convinced, silence is such an obsession in Old French literature: every written work silences a voice.

9. See Spitzer, "Marie de France—Dichterin von Problem-Märchen," p. 52.

10. Stephen Nichols links this passage to the beginnings of feminine writing in the *chanson de toile* "Bele Doette," which begins with the singer's reading of a book before learning of her lover's death and ends with her building an abbey for unhappy lovers; see Stephen G. Nichols, "Medieval Women Writers: *Aisthesis* and the Powers of Marginality," *Yale French Studies* 75 (1988): 82.

11. See Jacqueline Eccles, "Marie de France and the Law," in *Les Lieux Interdits: Transgression and French Literature,* ed. Larry Duffy and Adrian Tudor (Hull: University of Hull Press, 1998), p. 15.

12. Cited in Jean Maillard, *Evolution et esthétique du lai lyrique des origines à la fin du XIVe siècle* (Paris: Publications de l'Institut de Musicologie de l'Université de Paris, 1963), p. 30. Maillard in turn cites two sources, one of which, Paulin Paris's 1833 edition of the poem, does not contain the passage, and the other of which I have not been able to consult.

13. See Maillard, *Evolution,* pp. 30–34.

14. In a psychoanalytically shaped reading of "Chevrefoil," Doris Desclais Berkvam discusses this scene of writing in which "the subject is played out" in terms of Tristan's desire for writing itself; see "La 'Vérité' déplacée dans le 'Chevrefoil,'" *Neophilologus* 73 (1989): 14–22; Thomas L. Reed offers a reading in terms of the difficulty of assessing motivation in "Chevrefoil" and the question of literary interpretation; see "Glossing the Hazel: Authority, Intention, and Interpretation in Marie de France's Tristan, 'Chievrefoil,'" *Exemplaria* 7 (1994): 99–143.

15. For an excellent summary of various scholarly positions, see Glyn Burgess, *The Lais of Marie de France: Text and Context* (Athens: University of Georgia Press, 1987), pp. 67–69. See also Maurice Delbouille, "Ceo fu la summe de l'escrit," in *Mélanges de langue et de littérature du moyen âge et de la Renaissance offerts à Jean Frappier* (Geneva: Droz, 1970), pp. 207–16; Jean Frappier, "Contribution au débat sur le lai de 'Chèvrefeuille,'" in *Mélanges de linguistique et de littérature romanes à la mémoire d'István Frank* (Saarbrücken: Universität des Saarlandes, 1957), pp. 215–24; Anna G. Hatcher, "Lai du 'Chievrefueil,' 61–78; 107–13," *Romania* 71 (1950): 330–44; Leo Spitzer, "La 'Lettre sur la baguette de coudrier' dans le lai du 'Chievrefueil,'" *Romania* 69 (1946–47): 80–90.

16. Ana-Mariá Valero, "El 'lai' del 'Chievrefueil' de María de Francia," *Boletín de la Real Academia de Buenas Letras de Barcelona* 24 (1951–52): 173–83.

17. See Maurice Cagnon, "'Chievrefueil' and the Ogamic Tradition," *Romania* 91 (1970): 238–55; Grace Frank, "Marie de France and the Tristram Legend," *PMLA* 63 (1948): 405–11.

18. See Frappier, "Contribution au débat," p. 223.

19. See Michelle Freeman, "Marie de France's Poetics of Silence: The Implications for a Feminine *Translatio*," *PMLA* 99 (1984): 860–83.

20. Dragonetti, "Le lai narratif," p. 45.

CHAPTER FOUR

1. A. de Courde de Montaiglon, *Recueil général et complet des fabliaux* (Paris: Librairie des Bibliophiles, 1972–90), 5:171.

2. For an excellent discussion of the relationship of the word *fable* and its etymology to the question of talking, lying, and fiction, see Jan M. Ziolkowski, *Talking Animals: Medieval Latin Beast Poetry, 750–1150* (Philadelphia: University of Pennsylvania Press, 1993), pp. 16–17.

3. *Aiol,* ed. Jacques Normand and Gaston Raynaud (Paris: Firmin Didot, 1877), v. 7. A similar barb is to be found in the so-called "Bestiary of Gervaise," ed. Paul Meyer, *Romania* 1 (1872): v. 1.

4. The project of translation is for Marie linked to that of teaching or enlightenment with which we began, a point nowhere more explicit than in another prologue to a collection of fables, the *Isopet de Chartres* from the end of the thirteenth century, in which the move from Latin to French seems to be equated with the dispersal of darkness. See Julia Bastin, *Recueil général des Isopets* (Paris: Champion, 1929), 1:116.

5. For the theme of labor, nocturnal labor in particular, see Stephen G. Nichols, "Marie de France's Commonplaces," *Yale French Studies* (1991): 40–41.

6. *Babrius and Phaedrus,* ed. Ben Edwin Perry (Cambridge: Harvard University Press, 1965), p. 139. The King Alexander mentioned in this passage is, according to Perry, "a petty king of that name appointed by Vespasian in Cilicia, according to a statement made by Josephus in his *Antiquities of the Jews*" (p. xlviii).

7. "My feelings have carried me beyond the limit that I intended; but it is hard for a man to contain himself when he is aware of his own untainted integrity and is weighed down at the same time by the insults of those who seek to injure him. 'Who are they?' you ask. They will be seen in time. As for me, as long as my wits remain unshaken, I shall keep well in mind a maxim that I once read as a boy: 'It is sacrilege for a man of low birth to murmur in public'" (ibid., p. 239).

8. The classic article on the relationship between the true animal fables and those involving human characters is that of Jürgen Beyer, "Die Schwank-Fabeln im Esope der Marie de France," in *Schwank und Moral: Untersuchungen zum altfranzösischen Fabliau und verwandten Formen* (Heidelberg: Winter, 1968), pp. 34–50; see also Jessie Crosland, *Medieval French Literature* (Oxford: Basil Blackwell, 1956), p. 92.

9. John of Salisbury, *The Statesman's Book,* trans. John Dickinson (New York: Knopf, 1927), pp. 64–65.

10. See Jean-Claude Schmitt, *The Holy Greyhound: Guinefort, Healer of Children since the Thirteenth Century* (London: Cambridge University Press, 1983).

11. Aesop, *The Complete Fables,* trans. Olivia Temple and Robert Temple (New York: Penguin, 1998), p. 65.

12. See Léopold Hervieux, *Les fabulistes latins* (Paris: Firmin-Didot, 1893), 1:475–95; Bastin, *Recueil,* 2:ii; Ziolkowski, *Talking Animals,* p. 20.

13. "Cil qui une foiz m'a malmis / Saiche ne suis pais ses amis" (Bastin, *Recueil,* 2:132, 133).

14. *Isopet I,* ibid., 2:252; *Isopet III,* ibid., 2:404.

15. Ibid., 2:30.

16. Ibid.

17. Ibid., 1:110.

18. Ibid. A similar lack of attention to the question of voice and of the trickiness of language is to be found in the *Isopet de Chartres* (ibid., 1:179–80), as in its source, the *Novus Aesopus* of Alexander Neckam, the moral of which reads: "Consiliis nos ista monent parere parentum, / Qui nostrae causas utilitatis habent" (ibid., 1:30).

19. A curious paradox emanates from the comparison of the status of language in the *Lais* and in the *Fables:* that is, while language is fatal in the former, it is not an object of suspicion, as if the very unconsciousness of the danger surrounding it were the guarantee of a certain blind risk. And while language in the *Fables,* in contrast, is rarely fatal, it is the object of constant apprehension: even sounds are the object of deep mistrust, as we saw in "The Birds and the Cuckoo" (no. 46) and in "The Ass and the Lion" (no. 35), two tales that reveal a certain antirhetorical bias on the part of Marie.

20. "The Dog and the Cheese" appears in the *Aesopic Fables* of Babrius, the *Romulus ordinaire,* the *Isopet de Paris, Isopet de Chartres, Isopet I—Avionnet, Isopet de Lyon,* the *Romulus* of Walter l'Anglais, and the *Fables* of Odo of Cheriton.

21. Aesop, *Fables,* p. 47.

22. There are numerous versions of the wolf in school motif, the story of a wolf who tries to learn the alphabet or the psalms and who thinks only of lambs. There is even a Jewish rendering of the tale in which the wolf adds his study of the letters "aleph, beth, gimel" to spell "sheep" (*Fables of a Jewish Aesop Translated from the Fox Fables of Berechiah ha-Nakdam,* trans. Moses Hadas [New York: Columbia University Press, 1967], p. 213). See Ziolkowski, *Talking Animals,* p. 207; Arnold Clayton Henderson, "'Of Heigh or Lough Estat': Medieval Fabulists as Social Critics," *Viator* 9 (1978): 276–77.

23. Aesop, *Fables,* p. 29; *Babrius and Phaedrus,* p. 67.

24. Bastin, *Recueil,* 1:74.

25. Ibid., 1:139–40.

26. I am grateful to Margaret Pappano for suggesting this phrase to me in connection with Marie's *Fables.*

CHAPTER FIVE

1. The only critic to recognize the existential nature of the fables is Sahar Amer in a remarkable book that I encountered only after having written the first draft of this chapter. See *Ésope au féminin: Marie de France et la politique de l'interculturalité* (Atlanta: Rodopi, 1999), p. 110.

2. Julia Bastin, *Recueil général des Isopets* (Paris: Champion, 1929), 2:210.

3. Ibid., 2:211.

4. Ibid., 2:268.

5. Robert S. Falkowitz, "Discrimination and Condensation of Sacred Categories: The Fable in Early Mesopotamian Literature," in *La fable: Huit exposés suivis de discussion* (Geneva: Fondation Hardt, 1983), p. 2.

6. See Thomas Newbigging, *Fables and Fabulists: Ancient and Modern* (London: Elliot Stock, 1895; rpt. Ann Arbor: Gryphon Books, 1971), p. 68.

7. See the introduction to *Babrius and Phaedrus,* ed. Ben Edwin Perry (Cambridge: Harvard University Press, 1965).

8. John Vaio, "Babrius and the Byzantine Fable," in *La fable: Huit exposés,* p. 199.

9. *Babrius and Phaedrus,* p. 233.

10. Quintilian, *Institutio oratoria,* ed. H. E. Butler (Cambridge: Harvard University Press, 1969), 1:156.

11. Macrobius, *Commentary on the Dream of Scipio,* ed. William Harris Stahl (New York: Columbia University Press, 1952), pp. 84–85.

12. Priscian, *Opera,* ed. Augustus Krehl (Leipzig: Libraria Weidmannia, 1820), 2:423.

13. See Jan M. Ziolkowski, *Talking Animals: Medieval Latin Beast Poetry, 750–1150* (Philadelphia: University of Pennsylvania Press, 1993), p. 22.

14. Harriet Spiegel, "The Male Animal in the Fables of Marie de France," in *Medieval Masculinities,* ed. Clare A. Lees, Thelma Fenster, and JoAnn McNamara (Minneapolis: University of Minnesota Press, 1994), p. 112.

15. Amer, *Esope au féminin,* pp. 33, 37.

16. Karen K. Jambeck, "The *Fables* of Marie de France: A Mirror of Princes," in *In Quest of Marie de France: A Twelfth-Century Poet,* ed. Chantal Maréchal (Lewiston, N.Y.: Edwin Mellen Press, 1992), pp. 59–106. For a discussion of the *Pancatantra,* see G. U. Thite, "Indian Fable," in *La fable: Huit exposés,* pp. 33–53.

17. See Ziolkowski, *Talking Animals,* p. 20.

18. The parental context of the fables is also rendered in the *Isopet I—Avionnet* "De la Chievre et du Loup" (no. 29); see Bastin, *Recueil,* 2:251.

19. Ibid., 2:168, 169.

20. Ibid., 2:170, 173.

21. See Ziolkowski, *Talking Animals,* pp. 46, 145.

22. Bastin, *Recueil,* 2:330.

23. Ibid., 1:180.

24. Ibid., 1:181.

25. "Issi deit fere li bon sire:/Il ne deit pas juger ne dire,/Si si hume, que de lui tient,/Ireement en sa curt vienent" ("No good seignior should be this way:/No judgment pass, no verdict say,/If men under his sovereignty/Should come to court most angrily" [v. 19]).

26. On the question of the transmission of Aristotelian ethics to the Middle Ages, see Vernon J. Bourke, *History of Ethics* (Garden City: Doubleday, 1968), pp. 30–32; Fernand van Steenberghen, *Aristotle in the West* (Louvain: E. Nauwelaerts, 1955), pp. 36–41.

27. See Robert Blomme, *La doctrine du péché dans les écoles théologiques de la première moitié du XIIe siècle* (Louvain: Publications Universitaires de Louvain, 1958),

p. 337; D. E. Luscombe's introduction to *Peter Abelard's Ethics* (Oxford: Clarendon Press, 1971), p. xviii.

28. For a discussion of what he calls "Christian Socratism," see Bourke, *History of Ethics,* p. 62. The question of whether or not the *Fables* participate in what might be termed a Christian ethics is disputed. Karen Jambeck claims that "Marie's *Fables* also inculcate fundamental medieval Christian values. Perhaps the most subtle indicator of this tendency is the adaptation of ancient fables for a Christian, though not necessarily a clerical, audience" ("The *Fables,*" p. 76). Jürgen Beyer, however, disagrees: "Die Fabelmoral bietet der christlichen Ethik keinen Spielraum" ("Die Schwank-Fabeln im Esope der Marie de France," in *Schwank und Moral: Untersuchungen zum altfranzösischen Fabliau und verwandten Formen* [Heidelberg: Winter, 1968], p. 46).

29. This is the view of one of Abelard's most powerful modern commentators: D. E. Luscombe, *The School of Peter Abelard: The Influence of Abelard's Thought in the Early Scholastic Period* (Cambridge: Cambridge University Press, 1970), p. 308.

30. *Peter Abelard's Ethics,* pp. 39–41.

31. Jean Cottiaux claims that the *terminus ante quem* of the *Ethics* is 1138, the year that William of Saint-Thierry brought it to the attention of Saint Bernard, thus initiating the procedure of condemnation against Abelard; see Jean Cottiaux, "La conception de la théologie chez Abélard," *Revue d'histoire ecclésiastique* 28 (1932): 259.

32. Sahar Amer has also hit upon the resemblance between Marie and Abelard when it comes to the relativizing of ethics; see *Ésope au féminin,* p. 125.

33. "In fact the same thing is often done by different people, justly by one and wickedly by another, as for example if two men hang a convict, that one out of zeal for justice, this one out of a hatred arising from an old enmity, and although they certainly do what it is told to do and what justice requires, yet, through the diversity of their intention, the same thing is done by diverse men, by one badly, by the other well" (*Peter Abelard's Ethics,* p. 29).

34. Ibid., p. 45.

35. Ibid., p. 53; see Blomme, *La doctrine du péché,* pp. 138, 291.

36. *Peter Abelard's Ethics,* p. 9.

37. See, for example, Anselm of Canterbury, *Truth, Freedom, and Evil: Three Philosophical Dialogues,* ed. and trans. Jasper Hopkins and Herbert Richardson (New York: Harper Torchbooks, 1967), p. 162.

38. Ibid., p. 179.

39. "In the voluntary action there are two acts, namely the interior act of the will and the exterior act, and both of these acts have their objects. The end is properly the object of the interior voluntary act, and that with which the exterior act is concerned is its object. Therefore, just as the exterior act takes its species from the object with which it is concerned, so the interior act of will takes its species from the end as its proper object. However, that which is taken from the side of the will relates formally to that taken from the exterior act, because will uses the members in action as instruments, nor do exterior actions have the note of morality except insofar as they are voluntary. Therefore, the species of the human act is formally considered taken from the end and materially

considered taken from the object of the exterior action" (Thomas Aquinas, *Summa theologica,* Ia: IIae, q. 19, a. 6, c).

40. *Peter Abelard's Ethics,* p. 7.

41. Jean Batany, "Animalité et typologie sociale: Quelques parallèles médiévaux," in *Epopée animale, fable, fabliau: Actes du IVe colloque de la Société internationale renardienne, Evreux, 7–11 septembre 1981,* ed. Gabriel Bianciotto and Michel Salvat (Paris: Presses Universitaires de France, 1984), p. 48.

42. *Chronicle of Battle Abbey,* ed. Eleanor Searle (Oxford: Clarendon Press, 1980), p. 212; see also W. L. Warren, *The Governance of Norman and Angevin England, 1086–1272* (London: Edward Arnold, 1987), p. 95.

43. John of Salisbury, *Entheticus Maior and Minor,* ed. Jan van Laarhoven (Leiden: Brill, 1987), 3:190, par. 86, vv. 1301ff.

44. *Materials for the History of Thomas Becket,* ed. J. Craigie Robertson and J. Brigstoke Sheppart (Rolls Series 67) (London, 1875–85), 1:5–6.

45. See Egbert Türk, *Nugae Curialium: Le règne d'Henri II Plantagenêt (1154–1189) et l'éthique politique* (Geneva: Droz, 1977), pp. 176–78.

46. Boethius, *Consolatio Philosophiae,* ed. L. Bieler, Corpus Christianorum, serie Latina 94 (Turnhout, 1957), 1:4, para. 13. For a comparison of the two courts, see Türk, *Nugae,* p. 189.

47. Alain de Lille, *Plaint of Nature,* ed. James J. Sheridan (Toronto: Pontifical Institute of Toronto, 1980), p. 190.

48. As exceptions, Eduard Mall, who thought Marie to have lived in the thirteenth century at the court of the English Henry III, picks up on the theme of envy which he ascribes to her foreign status: "Mariam invidiam hominum timuisse, quod esset in terra aliena" (Eduard Mall, *De Aetate Rebusque Mariae Francicae nova quaestio instituitur* [Halle: Halis Saxonum, 1867], p. 7). Recently, Sarah Spence maintains apropos of the *Lais* that "all of the tales, it can be argued, are about envy and the problems that stem from it" ("Writing in the Vernacular: The *Lais* of Marie de France," in *Texts and the Self in the Twelfth Century,* ed. Sarah Spence [Cambridge: Cambridge University Press, 1996], p. 127). Richard Baum speaks of a topos in Old French of "médisance par envie" ("Les troubadours et les lais," *Zeitschrift für Romanische Philologie* 85 [1969], pp. 133–35).

49. Walter Map, *De Nugis Curialium,* ed. and trans. Montague Rhodes James (Oxford: Clarendon Press, 1983), p. 247.

50. See Türk, *Nugae,* p. 19. Alain de Lille too picks up the "worm of envy, . . . by whose gnawing the sound mind grows diseased and wastes away in corruption" (*Plaint,* pp. 188–89).

51. Map, *De Nugis,* p. 13. Nor are monks immune from the prey mentality of the court, which Walter also sets forth in ornithological terms (p. 85).

52. John of Salisbury, *Entheticus,* p. 216, para. 113, v. 1719.

53. Abelard, *Historia Calamitatum,* in *The Letters of Abelard and Heloise,* trans. Betty Radice (New York: Penguin, 1974), pp. 60–63.

54. John of Salisbury, *Policraticus,* trans. John Dickinson (New York: Knopf, 1927), p. 116.

55. "Besides, since envy is tearing apart and depreciating our *Topography,* a work by no means to be scorned, I have considered it not improper to insert here some words in its defence. There is unparalleled, unvarying and general praise for its stylistic elegance, redolent of the schools. Envy, quite against its own nature, breaks into words of praise, and is both ashamed and afraid of carping at the first and third book." Giraldus Cambrensis, *Expugnatio Hibernica: The Conquest of Ireland,* ed. A. B. Scott and F. X. Martin (Dublin: Royal Irish Academy, 1978), p. 5.

56. Ibid., p. 11.

57. Hue de Roteland, *Prothesilaus,* ed. Franz Kluckow (Dresden and Halle: Gesellschaft für romanische Literatur, 1924), v. 7179.

58. Glyn Burgess is somewhat more courageous in suggesting a precise timetable for Marie's arrival in England, though Henry II was also often in France: "Everything suggests that, between writing her first group of lays and beginning the second, Marie had come to Britain, either as a result of marriage or because she wished to further her career and possibly attract the patronage of Henry and Eleanor." *The Lais of Marie de France: Text and Context* (Athens: University of Georgia Press, 1987), p. 18.

59. According to the historian W. L. Warren, "in the thirty-four years of his reign Henry II spent Christmas at twenty-four different places. He crossed the English Channel at least twenty-eight times and the Irish Sea once." *Henry II* (Berkeley: University of California Press, 1973), p. 302.

60. Richard de Fournival, whose *Bestiaire d'amour* superimposes the natural and the courtly world, depicts human society in terms of beast eating beast, or of seduction, and specifically of seduction with words in which clerics are compared to birds of prey, "and one does well to be on the lookout if one can." *Le Bestiaire d'Amour suivi de la Réponse de la Dame,* ed. M. C. Hippeau (Geneva: Slatkin Reprints, 1969), p. 93.

61. The fable "The Ailing Lion" finds an unlikely parallel in Richard Fitz Nigel's *Dialogus de Scaccario: The Course of the Exchequer,* where the man who restored Henry II's books and the son of the man who put the English accounting system into place for Henry's grandfather urges us "to serve [kings] by upholding not only those excellencies in which the glory of kingship displays itself but also the worldly wealth which accrues to kings by virtue of their position. . . . Their power indeed rises and falls as their portable wealth flows or ebbs. Those who lack it are prey to their enemies, those who have it prey upon them." *Dialogus de Scaccario: The Course of the Exchequer,* trans. Charles Johnson (Oxford: Clarendon Press, 1983), p. 1.

62. "To sell justice is therefore iniquity; to sell injustice is not only iniquity but insanity." John of Salisbury, *The Statesman's Book,* trans. John Dickinson (New York: Knopf, 1929), p. 125; see also pp. 171-79.

63. Ibid., p. 153.

64. John of Salisbury, *Entheticus,* p. 190, vv. 1315ff.

65. Map, *De Nugis,* p. 247.

66. Warren, *Henry II,* p. 336. The following paragraph essentially follows Warren's presentation of the law of the "assize of novel disseisin."

67. Ibid., p. 338.

68. It is no accident that the genre as we know it was born in the West with Aesop, who is reported to have lived in the middle of the sixth century B.C. or around the time of the rise of the Greek city-state. John Jacobs senses the liminal quality of the animal tale between country and city in the biography of Odo of Cheriton that he imagines; see *The Fables of Odo of Cheriton,* ed. and trans. John C. Jacobs (Syracuse: Syracuse University Press, 1985), p. 10.

69. *Babrius and Phaedrus,* pp. 247–49.

70. *Pancatantra,* 2.130, cited in Thite, "Indian Fable," p. 43.

71. See Hans Robert Jauss, *Untersuchungen zur mittelalterlichen Tierdichtung* (Tübingen: Max Niemeyer, 1959), pp. 33–40, for a treatment of the topic of nature versus social station, which Jauss considers in terms of a condemnation in a Christian context of the sin of pride.

72. Orderic Vitalis, *Historia Ecclesiastica,* ed. and trans. Marjorie Chibnall (Oxford: Clarendon Press, 1968–80), 6:16. Thus the title of Ralph Turner's masterful *Men Raised from the Dust: Administrative Service and Upward Mobility in Angevin England* (Philadelphia: University of Pennsylvania Press, 1988). See also Turner's *The English Judiciary in the Age of Glanvill and Bracton, c. 1179–1239* (New York: Cambridge University Press, 1985), pp. 4–5; Warren, *Governance,* p. 85.

73. John of Salisbury, *Policraticus,* p. 283.

74. Raoul le Noir, *Chronicon,* ed. Robert Anstruther (New York: B. Franklin, 1967), p. 167.

75. *Giraldi Cambrensis Opera,* ed. J. S. Brewer, J. F. Dimock, and G. F. Warner, 8 vols., Rolls Series (London, 1861–91), 5:199.

76. Map, *De Nugis,* p. 3.

77. See Judith A. Green, *The Government of England under Henry I* (New York: Cambridge University Press, 1986), chap. 7; Richard Southern, "The Place of Henry I in English History," in *Medieval Humanism and Other Studies* (Oxford: Blackwell, 1970), pp. 208–28.

78. Türk, *Nugae,* p. 103.

79. See Warren, *Henry II,* pp. 309–10.

80. Turner, *Men Raised from the Dust,* p. 71.

81. Warren, *Henry II,* p. 311.

82. Nigel Wireker, *Tractatus contra curiales et officiales clericos,* ed. André Boutemy (Paris: Presses Universitaires de France, 1959), pp. 164–65.

83. John of Salisbury, *Policraticus* p. 55; see also p. 77.

84. Map, *De Nugis,* p. 13.

85. See Ralph Turner, "The *Miles literatus* in Twelfth- and Thirteenth-Century England: How Rare a Phenomenon?" *American Historical Review* 83 (1978): 941–45.

86. The question of whether or not Marie and Nigel Wireker might have known each other, or at least known either each other's work or a common source, occurs from the start of *The Book of Daun Burnel the Ass* where Nigel begins with the motif of the hidden gem—the essence of Marie's fable no. 1, "The Cock and the Gem"—in order to illustrate the moral that great hidden worth may lie in humble form. *The Book of Daun*

Burnel the Ass: Nigellus Wireker's "Speculum stultorum," trans. Graydon W. Regenos (Austin: University of Texas Press, 1959), p. 29.

87. "An ass may reign and hold the lion's sway,/And judgment give; he'll always be an ass." Wireker, *Daun Burnel,* p. 31.

88. Ibid., p. 78.

89. Ibid., p. 85.

90. Ibid., p. 97.

91. "'Brunellus is my name,' replied the ass,/'Quite widely know by name and deed alike./My country's princes and the kings themselves/I serve, yet do not lead a servile life./My father and grandfather always served/The kings and will for all the time to come./I'm in the king's employ by family right,/And all the court requires my services.'" Ibid., p. 59.

92. For a discussion of the historical relation, especially at the time of the Renaissance, between politics and the fable form, see Annabel Patterson, *Fables of Power: Aesopian Writing and Political Power* (Durham: Duke University Press, 1991).

93. Map, *De Nugis,* p. 3.

94. "At Louvain in the march of Lorraine and Flanders, at the place called Lata Quercus, there were assembled (as is still the custom) many thousands of knights to play together in arms after their manner, a sport which they call a tournament, but the better name would be torment." A knight, leaning on his spear, keeps sighing and when asked why replies, "'Good God! What work I shall have to beat all those who have gathered here to-day!' Which he does." Yet, as he departs the field, "he was pierced to the heart by an obscure knight of no account who opposed him, and died in a moment. Both sides were called apart, and when he was disarmed and shown to each and all of either party, no one could recognize him, and to this day it has not been ascertained who he was." Ibid., p. 165.

CHAPTER SIX

1. R. Howard Bloch, *Medieval French Literature and Law* (Berkeley: University of California Press, 1977), pp. 162–249.

2. Hugh of Saint-Victor, *Didascalicon,* trans. Jerome Taylor (New York: Columbia University Press, 1968), p. 57.

3. See Florence McCulloch, *Medieval Latin and French Bestiaries,* Studies in the Romance Languages and Literatures, no. 33 (Chapel Hill: University of North Carolina Press, 1962).

4. *Bestiaires du moyen âge, mis en français et présentés par Gabriel Bianciotto* (Paris: Stock, 1992), pp. 20–21.

5. Ibid., p. 21. The bestiary is an essentially allegorical genre, of course; and each nature is subject to the appropriate sacred interpretation. See the introduction to Guillaume de Normandie, *Le Bestiaire divin,* ed. M. C. Hippeau (Caen: A. Hardel, 1852), p. 50; Philip E. Bennett, "Some Doctrinal Implications of the *Comput* and the *Bestiaire* of Philippe de Thaun," in *Epopée animale, fable, fabliau: actes du IVe colloque de la*

Société Internationale Renardienne, Evreux, 7–11 septembre 1981, ed. Gabriel Bianciotto and Michel Salvat (Paris: Presses Universitaires de France, 1984), p. 98.

6. Richard de Fournival, *Le Bestiaire d'Amour suivi de la Réponse de la Dame,* ed. M. C. Hippeau (Geneva: Slatkin Reprints, 1969), p. 8.

7. Ibid.

8. Sahar Amer is to my knowledge the first to recognize not only the existentialism of Marie's thought, but the individuality of the animals of the *Fables.* Indeed, she contrasts the fable and the bestiary in terms of individual and general types; see Sahar Amer, *Ésope au féminin: Marie de France et la politique de l'interculturalité* (Atlanta: Rodopi, 1999), pp. 139ff.

9. See Arnold Clayton Henderson, "'Of Heigh or Lough Estat': Medieval Fabulists as Social Critics," *Viator* 9 (1978): 271.

10. Jean Batany suggests that the fable participates in an archetypal representation of the individual members of a species, a concept that is intriguing but not wholly accurate where Marie's *Fables* are concerned; see "Détermination et typologie: l'article et les animaux de la fable (de Marie de France à La Fontaine)," in *Au bonheur des mots: Mélanges en l'honneur de Gérald Antoine* (Nancy: Presses Universitaires de Nancy, 1984), p. 42.

11. Augustine, *On Christian Doctrine,* trans. D. W. Robertson (New York: Bobbs-Merrill, 1958), p. 18; Hugh of Saint-Victor, *Didascalicon,* p. 51.

12. Thomas Aquinas, *Summa theologica,* 75.7, 96.2.

13. This is, of course, nothing new in the West. On the contrary, beginning with Plato we find that the ideal of social behavior developed in terms of the mastery of animals by humans; see *Phaedrus,* 246 and 253, in the *Collected Dialogues of Plato,* ed. Edith Hamilton and Huntington Cairns (New York: Pantheon Books, 1961), pp. 493, 499–500, as well as the *Republic,* book 4, 431–439, in ibid., pp. 672–82.

14. See Arnold Clayton Henderson, "Medieval Beasts and Modern Cages: The Making of Meaning in Fables and Bestiaries," *PMLA* 97 (1982): 40.

15. See Odon Lottin, *La théorie du libre arbitre depuis s. Anselme jusqu'à s. Thomas D'Aquin* (Louvain: Abbaye du Mont-César, 1929), p. 12.

16. To some degree in the Christian West the animal appetites have always been associated with vice, the senses with the part of the animal in man. And this from the start, not only in the founding theological formulation of the Church Fathers but in their understanding of the ethical beginnings of mankind. Augustine suggests an analogy between the senses and the serpent at the time of the fall; see Augustine, *The Trinity,* ed. Stephen McKenna (Washington: Catholic University of America Press, 1963), pp. 359–60. Hugh of Saint-Victor, who was a contemporary of Abelard, predicates the relationship between bodily desire, the pleasure that desire engenders, and consent to desire upon the relationship of the snake, the woman, and the man; and it is this model of original sin that is reenacted whenever the rational faculties cede to appetite; see Robert Blomme, *La doctrine du péché dans les écoles théologiques du la première moitié du XIIe siècle* (Louvain: Publications Universitaires de Louvain, 1958), pp. 306–7.

17. For a slightly different view of this linguistic shift as it is played out in the

bestiary, see Gabriel Bianciotto, "Sur le *Bestiaire d'amour* de Richart de Fournival," in Bianciotto and Salvat, *Epopée animale,* pp. 107–17.

18. Among contemporary critics, Morton Nojgaard has articulated the relationship of the body of text and the moral in terms of the instincts or body and moralization; see "La moralisation de la fable: D'Ésope à Romulus" in *La fable: Huit exposés suivis de discussion* (Geneva: Fondation Hardt, 1983), pp. 224–25. See also Karen K. Jambeck, "The *Fables* of Marie de France: A Mirror of Princes," in *In Quest of Marie de France: A Twelfth-Century Poet,* ed. Chantal Maréchal (Lewiston, N.Y.: Edwin Mellen Press, 1992), p. 59.

19. This is in keeping with one of the famous definitions of the fable, that of Lessing: "Und nunmehr glaube ich meine Meinung von dem Wesen der Fabel genugsam verbreitet zu haben. Ich fasse daher alles zusammen und sage: *Wenn wir einen allgemeinen moralischen Satz auf einen besondern Fall zurück führen, diesem besondern Falle die Wirklichkeit ertheilen, und eine Geschichte daraus dichten, in welcher man den allgemeinen Satz anschauend erkennt: so heisst diese Erdichtung eine Fabel.*" "Von dem Wesen der Fabel," in Erwin Leibfried and Josef Werle, *Texte zur Theorie der Fabel* (Stuttgart: J. B. Metzlersche, 1978), p. 56.

20. Harriet Spiegel, for example, states that Marie seems to endorse "the established social hierarchy"; see "The Male Animal in the Fables of Marie de France" in *Medieval Masculinities,* ed. Clare A. Lees, Thelma Fenster, and Jo Ann McNamara (Minneapolis: University of Minnesota Press, 1994), p. 114; see also pp. 116, 118. Karen Jambeck, following the lead of Arnold Henderson, speaks of "an upper-class bias on the part of Marie and her audience" ("The *Fables,*" p. 91). Hans Robert Jauss considers Marie to be essentially pro-monarchist and conservative; see *Untersuchungen zur mittelalterlichen Tierdichtung* (Tübingen: Max Niemeyer, 1959), p. 52; see also Charles Brucker, "Société et morale dans la fable ésopique du XIIe et du XIVe siècle," in *Et C'est la Fin pour quoy sommes ensemble: Hommage à Jean Dufournet* (Paris: Champion, 1993), 1:281–92.

21. This is said with full consciousness of the fact that the *Fables* have traditionally been considered to be a mirror of the feudal world, beginning with Aristide Joly's "Marie de France ne peint pas l'humanité, mais la féodalité" (Aristide Joly, *Marie de France et les fables au moyen-âge* [Caen: Legoste-Clérisse, 1863], p. 34), and including Hans Robert Jauss's claim that they express the "Ideal der höfisch-ritterlichen Welt" (*Untersuchungen zur mittelalterlichen Tierdichtung,* p. 28).

22. See François Laserre, "La fable en Grèce dans la poésie archaïque," in *La fable: Huit exposés,* pp. 61–96; Chester G. Starr, *The Economic and Social Growth of Early Greece, 800–500 B.C.* (New York: Oxford University Press, 1977), pp. 97–146; Anthony M. Snodgrass, *Archaic Greece: The Age of Experiment* (London: J. M. Dent, 1980); Jan M. Ziolkowski, *Talking Animals: Medieval Latin Beast Poetry, 750–1150* (Philadelphia: University of Pennsylvania Press, 1993), p. 51.

23. Even Hans Robert Jauss, who sees Marie's *Fables* as essentially conservative and pro-monarchist, recognizes an increased emphasis upon what is the essentially urban value of cunning; see *Untersuchungen zur mittelalterlichen Tierdichtung,* p. 54.

24. Cited in *La fable: Huit exposés,* p. 6.

25. *Babrius and Phaedrus,* ed. Ben Edwin Perry (Cambridge: Harvard University Press, 1965), pp. 255–57.

26. See Ziolkowski, *Talking Animals,* pp. 69, 76.

27. W. L. Warren, *Henry II* (Berkeley: University of California Press, 1973), p. 217.

28. John of Salisbury, *The Statesman's Book,* trans. John Dickinson (New York: Knopf, 1927, p. 116; see also John's *Entheticus Maior and Minor,* ed. Jan van Laarhoven (Leiden: Brill, 1987), p. 202.

29. See my *Medieval French Literature and Law,* pp. 108–20; Marc Bloch, *Feudal Society* (Chicago: University of Chicago Press, 1966), 1:413; Yvonne Bongert, *Recherches sur les cours laïques du Xe au XIIIe siècle* (Paris: A. and J. Picard, 1944), pp. 234–35; Georges Duby, *La société au XIe et XIIe siècles dans la région mâconnaise* (Paris: Armand Colin, 1953), p. 199; Adalbert Esmein, *Cours élémentaire de droit français* (Paris: Sirey, 1930), p. 251; Charles Petit-Dutaillis, *Les communes françaises* (Paris: Albin Michel, 1970), pp. 44–58.

30. Spiegel, "The Male Animal," p. 111. See also "The Woman's Voice in the *Fables* of Marie de France," in Maréchal, *In Quest of Marie de France,* pp. 45–46.

31. Spiegel, "The Male Animal," pp. 111, 113.

32. For a discussion of the medieval Philomena, see Jane Burns, *Bodytalk: When Women Speak in Old French Literature* (Philadelphia: University of Pennsylvania Press, 1993), pp. 115–50.

33. See my *Medieval Misogyny and the Invention of Western Romantic Love* (Chicago: University of Chicago Press, 1989), pp. 13–22. In a case of nondomestic exploitation, the witch of "The Thief and the Witch" (no. 48) manages to maliciously and seemingly gratuitously trick the male, though virtue resides on neither side. In "The Wolf and the Sow" (no. 21), the female outwits her male aggressor.

34. See Hans Ulrich Gumbrecht, *Marie de France Aesop: Eingeleitet, kommentiert und übersetzt* (Munich: Wilhelm Fink, 1973), pp. 36–43.

35. See Henderson, "'Of Heigh or Lough Estat,'" p. 269.

CHAPTER SEVEN

1. The *Espurgatoire* has been the object of only a handful of articles and, to my knowledge, no monograph or book-length study.

2. Since the name Henry for H. of Saltrey was a later addition of chroniclers, I will use "H." instead.

3. Shane Leslie, *Saint Patrick's Purgatory: A Record from History and Literature* (London: Burns Oats and Washbourne, 1932), p. xvii.

4. See Hugh Shields, "The French Accounts," in Michael Haren and Yolande de Pontfarcy, *The Medieval Pilgrimage to St. Patrick's Purgatory: Lough Derg and the European Tradition* (Enniskillen: Clogher Historical Society, 1988), pp. 83–98; Kurt Ringger, "Die altfranzösischen Verspurgatorien," *Zeitschrift für romanische Philologie* 88 (1972): 389–402.

5. See Leslie, *Saint Patrick's Purgatory,* pp. 6–17; George Philip Krapp, *The Legend*

of Saint Patrick's Purgatory: Its Later Literary History (Baltimore: John Murphy, 1900), pp. 2–7; Robert Easting, "Peter of Cornwall's Account of St Patrick's Purgatory," *Analecta Bollandiana* 97 (1979): 397; D. D. K. Owen, *The Vision of Hell: Infernal Journeys in Medieval French Literature* (Edinburgh: Scottish Academic Press, 1970), p. 38.

6. See Haren and Pontfarcy, *Medieval Pilgrimage*, pp. 5–6; Krapp, *Legend*, p. 2; Jacques Le Goff, *La naissance du Purgatoire* (Paris: Gallimard, 1981), pp. 267–77; D. M. Carpenter, "The Pilgrim from Catalonia/Aragon: Ramon de Perellós, 1397," in Haren and Pontfarcy, *Medieval Pilgrimage*, pp. 99–119.

7. Sire de Beaujeu *Chronique des quatre premiers Valois (1327–1393)*, ed. Simeon Luce (Paris: V. J. Renouard, 1862), p. 22; *Chroniques de Froissart*, ed. Kervyn de Lettenhove (Brussels: V. Devaux, 1871), 15:145–46.

8. See Robert Easting, "The English Tradition," in Haren and Pontfarcy, *Medieval Pilgrimage*, pp. 62, 67.

9. Carol Zaleski, "St. Patrick's Purgatory: Pilgrimage Motifs in a Medieval Other-wold Journey," *Journal of the History of Ideas* 46 (1985): 472.

10. See Michael J. Curley, Introduction, *Saint Patrick's Purgatory* (Binghamton: Medieval and Renaissance Texts and Studies, 1993), pp. 33–34.

11. For relation of the *Lais* to the Celtic Otherworld, see Howard Rollin Patch, *The Other World according to Descriptions in Medieval Literature* (Cambridge: Harvard University Press, 1950), pp. 243–56.

12. Stephen Greenblatt, *Hamlet in Purgatory* (Princeton: Princeton University Press, 2001), p. 37.

13. "By a variety of additions and omissions, the authors of this version make the most of the narrative's romance potential: the adventures of a knight encountering the ultimate perils and delights of the otherworld." Easting, "English Tradition," p. 64.

14. Cited in Shields, "French Accounts," n. 1, p. 83.

15. Lucien Foulet, "Marie de France et la Légende du Purgatoire de Saint Patrice," *Romanische Forschungen* 22 (1908): 625; Anatole le Braz, *La légende de la mort chez les Bretons armoricains* (Paris, 1922), 1:xxxix; Cornelis Mattheus Van der Zanden, *Etude sur le Purgatoire de Saint Patrice* (Amsterdam: H. J. Paris, 1927), p. 64; Curley, Introduction, p. 23; see also Patch, *Other World*, p. 230.

16. Easting, "Peter of Cornwall's Account," p. 404.

17. Cited Shields, "French Accounts," p. 91. The story is to be placed alongside the account of the devils who enter the hermit's cell in the passage at the end of the *Espurgatoire* in the form of naked women: "en semblance de femmes nues/se mustrent, ki la sunt venues/pur lui deceivre e engignier/e faire sun propos laissier" ("To fool and deceive him,/And to force him to abandon his calling,/They appeared to him/In the guise of naked women" [v. 2112]); see also L. L. Hammerich, "Le pèlerinage de Louis d'Auxerre au Purgatoire de S. Patrice," *Romania* 55 (1929): 118–24.

18. Cited Le Goff, *Naissance*, p. 277.

19. Le Goff, *Naissance*, p. 279; Patch, *Other World*, p. 234.

20. J.-B.-B. de Roquefort, *Poésies de Marie de France, Poète Anglo-Normand du XIIIe Siècle ou Recueil de Lais, Fables et Autres Productions de cette Femme Célèbre*

(Paris: Marescq, 1832), 2:405; Thomas Wright, *St. Patrick's Purgatory: An Essay on the Legends of Purgatory, Hell, and Paradise Current during the Middle Ages* (New York: New World Press, 1844), p. 21.

21. Leslie, *Saint Patrick's Purgatory*, p. xix.

22. "Nus en si haut servise ne doit entrer devant qu'il soit netoiez et espurgiez de totes vilanies et de toz pechiés mortex," specifies the old man who addresses Arthur's knights who have taken the oath of the quest (*La Queste del Saint Graal*, ed. Alfred Pauphilet [Paris: Champion, 1975], p. 19). "For no man may enter so high a service until he is cleansed of grievous sin and purged of every wickedness" (*The Quest of the Holy Grail*, trans. Pauline Matarasso [London: Penguin, 1969], p. 47).

23. The motif is, of course, more general than that, and one might also extend the comparison to the gardens of Love in Jean de Condé's *La Messe des Oisiaus;* the *Panthère d'Amours;* Watriquet de Couvin's *Li Mireoirs as Dames;* Machaut's *La Fonteinne Amoureuse, Dit dou Vergier, Jugement dou Roy de Behaingne,* and *Dit dou Lyon;* Jean Froissart's *Paradys d'Amours;* Eustache Deschamps's *Lay du Desert d'Amours.*

24. The same is true of the vision of Tnugdal, who finds himself at the end of his purgatorial voyage before a tree that could be right out of the Garden of the God of Love of the *Roman de la rose;* see *The Vision of Tnugdal,* trans. Jean-Michel Picard (Dublin: Four Courts Press, 1989), p. 151.

25. Curley, Introduction, p. 87, n. 10.

26. *Lancelot do Lac: The Non-Cyclic Old French Prose Romance,* ed. Elspeth Kennedy (Oxford: Clarendon Press, 1980), 1:143. The translation is that of Corin Corley, *Lancelot of the Lake* (Oxford: Oxford University Press, 1989), p. 53.

27. Patch, *Other World,* p. 8.

28. Gregory the Great, *Dialogues* (Paris: Editions du Cerf, 1980), 3:130; *The Letters of Saint Boniface,* trans. Ephraim Emerton (New York: Columbia University Press, 2000), p. 6.

29. *Vision of Tnugdal,* p. 119; see also p. 123. See Carol Zaleski, *Otherworld Journeys: Accounts of Near-Death Experience in Medieval and Modern Times* (New York: Oxford University Press, 1987), p. 69; Owen, *Vision,* p. 28.

30. "The Vision of Thurkill, Probably by Ralph of Coggeshall," ed. H. L. D. Ward, *Journal of the British Archaeological Society* 31 (1875): 432.

31. Andreas Capellanus, *The Art of Courtly Love,* ed. J. J. Parry (New York: Columbia University Press, 1941), pp. 178–79.

32. Chrétien de Troyes, *Le Chevalier de la charrete,* ed. Mario Roques (Paris: Champion, 1965), v. 3010; *Lancelot,* ed. Kennedy, p. 357; Chrétien de Troyes, *Perceval ou le Conte du Graal,* ed. William Roach (Geneva: Droz, 1959), v. 8091.

33. "I wish to put into writing in French, / The Pains of Purgatory, / Just as the book tells us about them, / As a recollection and a record" (v. 3). I am grateful to Karen Jambeck for drawing my attention to this particular point of resemblance.

34. F. W. Locke, "A New Date for the Composition of the *Tractatus de Purgatorio Sancti Patricii,*" *Speculum* 40 (1965): 646; see also Curley, Introduction, p. 9; Robert Easting, "The Date and Dedication of the *Tractatus de Purgatorio Sancti Patricii,*" *Specu-*

lum 53 (1978): 780; Yolande de Pontfarcy, "Le 'Tractatus de Purgatorio Sancti Patricii' de H. de Saltrey: Sa date et ses sources," *Peritia* 3 (1984): 465; Foulet, "Marie de France," p. 616.

35. Wright, *St. Patrick's Purgatory,* p. 20; Curley, Introduction, p. 11.

36. "A l'époque où la littérature didactique en langue vulgaire évoluait ainsi, Marie de France, vers 1170, traduisait le *Purgatoire de Saint-Patrick.*" Claude Carozzi, *Le voyage de l'âme dans l'au-delà d'après la littérature latine (Ve–XIIe siècle)* (Rome: Ecole Française de Rome, 1994), p. 643.

37. Chrétien de Troyes, *Perceval,* vv. 4365, 4391; Chrétien de Troyes, *Arthurian Romances,* trans. William Kibler (London: Penguin, 1991), p. 420.

38. See my article "Wasteland and Round Table: The Historical Significance of Myths of Dearth and Plenty in Old French Romance," *New Literary History* 11 (1979–80): 255–76; Bernard Guenée, "Des limites féodales aux frontières politiques," in Pierre Nora, *Les lieux de mémoire* (Paris: Gallimard, 1986), 2:11–34.

39. *La Queste del Saint Graal,* p. 95; Matarasso, pp. 115–16.

40. Wright, *St. Patrick's Purgatory,* p. 13.

41. Le Goff, *Naissance,* p. 240.

42. See also vv. 1899 and 1903.

43. Alan E. Bernstein, *The Formation of Hell: Death and Retribution in the Ancient and Early Christian Worlds* (Ithaca: Cornell University Press, 1993), p. 84.

44. "They then return to their living bodies,/And relate what they have seen" (v. 72). Carol Zaleski notes that Saint Patrick's Purgatory's "most striking feature is the way it links terrestrial to extraterrestrial topography: the protagonist steps through a physical doorway into the other world; he insists that his was not the visionary experience of an ecstatic. This peculiar detail seems to set the Purgatory legend apart from other Christian tales of rapture and return-from-death visions." *Otherworld Journeys,* p. 35.

45. Gerald of Wales, *The History and Topography of Ireland (Topographia Hiberniae),* trans. John J. O'Meara (Atlantic Highlands, N.J.: Humanities Press, 1982), p. 61.

46. Bernstein, *Formation of Hell,* p. 105; Wright, *St. Patrick's Purgatory,* p. 33.

47. Patch, *Other World,* pp. 27, 47.

48. "Mais quant verreit certeinement/cels tenir lur purposement,/par letres les enveiereit/al priur, si li mandereit/qu'il preïst d'els e guarde e cure/e meïst en la fosse oscure" ("But when the bishop saw for certain/That they held to their purpose,/He sent them with letters/To the prior, asking him/To guard and care for them,/And place them in the dark pit" [v. 445]).

49. Thomas Rymer, *Foedera* (London, 1816–69), 3:174.

50. Krapp, *Legend,* p. 41; John Seymour, *Irish Visions of the Other World* (London: Society for Promoting Christian Knowledge, 1930), p. 174.

51. Gerald of Wales, *Expugnatio Hibernica,* ed. A. B. Scott and F. X. Martin (Dublin: Royal Irish Academy, 1978), p. 235; *The Tripartite Life of Patrick,* ed. Whitley Stokes (Liechtenstein: Kraus Reprint, 1965), pp. 255–57.

52. Jocelin de Furness, *The Life and Acts of Saint Patrick, the Archbishop, Primate and Apostle of Ireland,* ed. J. C. O'Haloran (Philadelphia: Atkinson and Alexander, 1823),

p. 227. See Yolande de Pontfarcy, "The Historical Background to the Pilgrimage to Lough Derg," in Haren and Pontfarcy, *Medieval Pilgrimage*, p. 33; Pontfarcy, "Le *Tractatus*," p. 479; Zaleski, *Otherworld Journeys*, p. 34; Zaleski, "St. Patrick's Purgatory," p. 471.

53. *Vision of Tnugdal*, p. 109; "Vision of Thurkill," p. 437.

54. "Cil dui funderent l'abeïe/e mistrent genz de bone vie./Gileberz en fu celeriers/e Oweins fu sis latiniers" (v. 1977). The figure of the knight turned translator is also to be found in the curious epic account of the history of contemporaneous Ireland *La Conquête d'Ireland*, also known as *The Song of Dermot and the Earl*, in that the author claims to have received his material from Morice Regan, the hero Dermot's latiner. See *La Conquête d'Irlande: Song of Dermot and the Earl*, ed. Goddard Henry Orpen (Oxford: Clarendon Press, 1892), v. 1. Interestingly too, in the delicate negotiations between enemy chiefs translators are used as messengers and negotiators. Ibid., vv. 1656, 2994.

55. Joel Fineman, "The Sound of O in Othello: The Real of the Tragedy of Desire," *October* 45 (1988): 76–96.

56. "Now it seems that there's a place they call Purgat'ry, so/I must write it, my verse not admitting the O./But as for the venue I vow I'm perplext/To say if it's in this world or if in the next." Cited Leslie, *Saint Patrick's Purgatory*, p. xxxii.

57. With respect to the word *mostrar*, I am indebted to David Pike for pointing me in the direction of one of the essential differences between H.'s Latin version and Marie's translation as a difference between H.'s concern with recounting events and Marie's concern with the truth-value of H.'s account, a perception that coincides with a view of the *Espurgatoire* as a hermeneutic struggle: "For along with the courtly vocabulary, what Marie primarily adds to the Latin text is a string of adjectives and adverbs, along with the verb 'mostrar,' all of which serve to call attention to the truth-claims the poem requires as artifact, an attention that the Latin text, which in its language is all about actions, seems to feel very little need to pay" (p. 4 of an unpublished paper presented at the "Journée de Travail—Marie de France," Columbia University, 20 April 1996). For a discussion of the relationship between the concept of opening and writing in Old French, see Roger Dragonetti's introduction to Milena Mikhaïlova, *Le présent de Marie* (Paris: Diderot, 1996), pp. 17, 24–25.

58. H. de Saltrey, *Tractatus Sancti Patricii*, in *Das Buch vom Espurgatoire S. Patrice der Marie de France und seine Quelle*, ed. Karl Warnke (Halle: Max Niemeyer, 1938), p. 150.

59. Ibid., p. 150.

60. This is something that is noted by Foulet, "Marie de France," p. 619.

61. *Tractatus*, ed. Warnke, p. 152. The translation is that of Jean-Michel Picard, *Saint Patrick's Purgatory* (Dublin: Four Courts Press, 1985), p. 74.

62. Carozzi, *Voyage*, p. 233.

63. *Vision of Tnugdal*, p. 109.

64. *Tractatus*, ed. Warnke, p. 3; trans. Picard, p. 43.

65. Ibid., ed. Warnke, p. 36; trans. Picard, p. 50.

66. Ibid., ed. Warnke, p. 10; trans. Picard, p. 45.

67. Ibid., ed. Warnke, p. 54; trans. Picard, p. 54.

CHAPTER EIGHT

1. *The Vision of Tnugdal,* trans. Jean-Michel Picard (Dublin: Four Courts Press, 1989), p. 135; Roger of Wendover, *Flowers of History, Comprising the History of England from the Descent of the Saxons to A.D. 1235, formerly Ascribed to Matthew Paris,* ed. and trans. J. A. Giles (London: Henry G. Bohn, 1869), 2:161–62.

2. See my *Etymologies and Genealogies: A Literary Anthropology of the French Middle Ages* (Chicago: University of Chicago Press, 1983), pp. 44–63.

3. For a fuller discussion of this question, see Claude Carozzi, *Le voyage de l'âme dans l'au-delà d'après la littérature latine (Ve–XIIe siècle)* (Rome: Ecole Française de Rome, 1994), pp. 540–57.

4. *The Letters of Saint Boniface,* trans. Ephraim Emerton (New York: Columbia University Press, 2000), p. 3.

5. Bede, *Ecclesiastical History of the English People,* ed. Bertram Colgrave and R. A. B. Mynors (Oxford: Clarendon Press, 1969), p. 497.

6. *Vision of Tnugdal,* pp. 114, 155.

7. Roger of Wendover, *Flowers of History, p. 153.*

8. "The Vision of Thurkill, Probably by Ralph of Coggeshall," ed. H. L. D. Ward, *Journal of the British Archaeological Society* 31 (1875): 427.

9. H. de Saltrey, *Saint Patrick's Purgatory,* trans. Jean-Michel Picard (Dublin: Four Courts Press, 1985), p. 44. "Raptas etiam et iterum ad corpora reductas uisiones quasdam et reuelationes sibi factas narrare dicit siue de tormentis impiorum siue de gaudiis iustorum et in hiis tamen nichil nisi corporale uel corporalibus simile recitasse" (*Tractatus Sancti Patricii,* in *Das Buch vom Espurgatoire S. Patrice der Marie de France und seine Quelle,* ed. Karl Warnke [Halle: Max Niemeyer, 1938], p. 6).

10. *Tractatus,* trans. Picard, p. 45; "que quidem ab hominibus non possunt diffinire, quia ab eis minime possunt sciri" (ed. Warnke, p. 12).

11. Ibid., ed. Warnke, p. 14. "That is why, in this account, a mortal and material man tells how he saw spiritual things under the aspect and form of material things" (trans. Picard, p. 45).

12. See Yolande de Pontfarcy, *Le "Tractatus de Purgatorio Sancti Patricii" de H. de Saltrey: Sa date et ses sources, Peritia* 3 (1984): 476; Carozzi, *Voyage,* pp. 642–43; Howard Rollin Patch, *The Other World according to Descriptions in Medieval Literature* (Cambridge: Harvard University Press, 1950), p. 17.

13. Hans Robert Jauss, "La transformation de la forme allégorique entre 1180 et 1240: D'Alain de Lille à Guillaume de Lorris," in Anthime Fourrier, *L'humanisme médiéval dans les littératures romanes du XII au XIV siècle* (Paris: Klincksieck, 1964), pp. 107–46; Carol Zaleski, *Otherworld Journeys: Accounts of Near-Death Experience in Medieval and Modern Times* (New York: Oxford University Press, 1987), p. 7; Shane Leslie, *Saint Patrick's Purgatory: A Record from History and Literature* (London: Burns Oats and

Washbourne, 1932), p. xxxiv; see also Alan E. Bernstein, *The Formation of Hell: Death and Retribution in the Ancient and Early Christian Worlds* (Ithaca: Cornell University Press, 1993), p. 96.

14. Stephen Greenblatt, *Hamlet in Purgatory* (Princeton: Princeton University Press, 2001), p. 33; see also pp. 85–86.

15. *The Tripartite Life of Patrick,* ed. Whitley Stokes (Liechtenstein: Kraus Reprint, 1965), p. 257.

16. Jocelin de Furness, *The Life and Acts of Saint Patrick, the Archbishop, Primate and Apostle of Ireland,* ed. J. C. O'Haloran (Philadelphia: Atkinson and Alexander, 1823), pp. 229–30.

17. Bede, *Ecclesiastical History,* p. 497.

18. Boniface, *Letters,* p. 3.

19. "Vision of Thurkill," pp. 426–27.

20. Cited St. John Seymour, *Irish Visions of the Other World* (London: Society for Promoting Christian Knowledge, 1930), p. 176.

21. Dorothy M. Carpenter, "The Pilgrim from Catalonia/Aragon: Ramon de Perellós, 1397," in Michael Haren and Yolande de Pontfarcy, *The Medieval Pilgrimage to St. Patrick's Purgatory: Lough Derg and the European Tradition* (Enniskillen: Clogher Historical Society, 1988), p. 104.

22. *Huth Merlin,* ed. Gaston Paris and Jacob Ulrich (Paris: Firmin Didot, 1886), 2:298. For a discussion of the relation of legal deposition and literary transcription, see my *Medieval French Literature and Law* (Berkeley: University of California Press, 1977), pp. 189–214.

23. See, for example, Oskar Sommer, *The Vulgate Version of the Arthurian Romances* (Washington: Carnegie Institute, 1909), 4:296, 5:190.

24. *Tractatus,* ed. Warnke, p. 26; trans. Picard, p. 48.

25. Ibid., ed. Warnke, p. 26; trans. Picard, p. 48.

26. See my *Etymologies and Genealogies,* pp. 75–83.

27. Pontfarcy, "Le *Tractatus,*" pp. 13–14.

28. For a fuller account of the debate about the origin of "Reglis," see Michael J. Curley, Introduction, *Saint Patrick's Purgatory* (Binghamton: Medieval and Renaissance Texts and Studies, 1993), p. 65; p. J. Dunning, "The Arroasian Order in Medieval Ireland," *Irish Historical Studies* 4 (1945): 305–6; Robert Easting, "Peter of Cornwall's Account of St. Patrick's Purgatory," *Analecta Bollandiana* 97 (1979): 402; M. Joynt, *Contributions to a Dictionary of the Irish Language* (Dublin, 1944), fasc. R, col. 32; Cornelis Mattheus Van der Zanden, *Etude sur le Purgatoire de Saint Patrice* (Amsterdam: H. J. Paris, 1927), p. 48.

29. See Curley, Introduction, p. 22.

30. In this Owen resembles Dryhthelm, who "also told his visions to King Aldfrith, a most learned man in all respects. . . . at the king's request he was admitted to the monastery already mentioned. . . . Whenever the king visited that region, he often went to listen to his story." Bede, *Ecclesiastical History,* p. 497.

31. *Tractatus,* ed. Warnke, pp. 138, 140.

32. Ibid., p. 14. "I will reveal the identity of the man who related this story to me,

and how he had knowledge of it, at the end of this narrative which, if my memory does not fail me, begins thus" (trans. Picard, p. 45).

33. *Tractatus,* ed. Warnke, version A, p. 150.

34. *Tractatus,* ed. Warnke, p. 148; trans. Picard, p. 74.

35. "Nuper etiam affatus sum episcopum quendam, nepotem sancti Patricii tertii, socii uidelicet sancti Malachie, Florentianum nomine, in cuius episcopatu, sicut ipse dixit, est idem purgatorium" (*Tractatus,* ed. Warnke, pp. 150, 152). "Also, recently I was talking to a bishop called Florentianus, a nephew of the third saint Patrick, who was the companion of saint Malachy. And he told me that this Purgatory lay in his diocese" (trans. Picard, p. 74).

36. "Hec cum dixisset episcopus, ait capellanus ei: 'Ego eundem uirum sanctum uidi et narrabo uobis, si placet, quod ab eo didici" (*Tractatus,* ed. Warnke, p. 154). "After the bishop had finished saying this, the chaplain said to him: 'I have seen the same holy man and, if you please, I will tell you what I learnt from him" (trans. Picard, p. 75).

37. *Tractatus,* ed. Warnke, p. 22.

38. Bernard of Clairvaux, *The Life and Death of Saint Malachy the Irishman,* trans. Robert T. Meyer (Kalamazoo: Cistercian Publications, 1978), p. 42.

39. As Patrick arrives in Ireland at age sixty, he meets an old woman who claims to have been there since the time of Christ, who foretold his coming, "And God left with us that thou wouldst come to preach to the Gael, and he left a token with us, to wit, his staff, to be given to thee" (*Tripartite Life,* p. 29).

40. Patrick meets a man who lives on an island in the Tuscan sea and who gives him a staff "which he declared himself to have received from the hands of the Lord Jesus. . . . And the Staff is held in much veneration in Ireland, and even unto this day it is called the Staff of Jesus" (Jocelin de Furness, *Life and Acts,* pp. 33, 36).

41. *Tractatus,* ed. Warnke, p. 4.

42. *Tractatus,* ed. Warnke, p. 6.

43. *Hom. I In Psalmum XXXVI,* 10, CCL 38, p. 344. "Dicit uero beatus Augustinus animas defunctorum post mortem usque ad ultimam resurrectionem abditis receptaculis contineri, sicut unaqueque digna est, uel in requiem uel in erumpnam" (*Tractatus,* ed. Warnke, p. 12). "On the other hand blessed Augustine says that the souls of the dead are contained in secret receptacles between the time of death and the final resurrection, either resting or suffering each according to its merits" (trans. Picard, p. 45).

44. Carozzi, *Voyage,* p. 519.

45. See Pontfarcy, "Le *Tractatus,"* p. 479.

46. Pontfarcy, "Le *Tractatus,"* p. 465; see also Lucien Foulet, "Marie de France et la Légende du Purgatoire de Saint Patrice," *Romanische Forschungen* 22 (1908): 602–4; Seymour, *Irish Visions,* p. 179.

47. Carol Zaleski, "St. Patrick's Purgatory: Pilgrimage Motifs in a Medieval Otherwold Journey," *Journal of the History of Ideas* 46 (1985): 477.

48. *Tractatus,* ed. Warnke, p. 14.

49. Zaleski, *Otherworld Journeys,* p. 86.

50. Bede, *Ecclesiastical History,* p. 497; Carozzi, *Voyage,* p. 325; Easting, "Peter of Cornwall's Account," p. 404; Pontfarcy, "Le *Tractatus,"* p. 474.

51. Greenblatt, *Hamlet,* p. 99.

52. E.g., "The Legend of St Patrick's Purgatory shows a dim Celtic doctrine grafted to the Classical lore and taken into possession by the Church to adorn the story of St Patrick's apostolate" (Leslie, *Saint Patrick's Purgatory,* p. xxv); "Almost all the possible motifs were present in the literature of oriental and classical mythology. . . . All of this material from the East was transmitted in the vision literature of the Middle Ages" (Patch, *Other World,* p. 320).

53. D. D. R. Owen, *The Vision of Hell: Infernal Journeys in Medieval French Literature* (Edinburgh: Scottish Academic Press, 1970), p. xi; Patch, *Other World,* pp. 82–91.

54. Carozzi, *Voyage,* pp. 319–20.

55. Seymour, *Irish Visions,* p. 64.

56. "Il n'y a pas de Purgatoire avant 1170 au plus tôt." Jacques Le Goff, *La naissance du Purgatoire* (Paris: Gallimard, 1981), p. 184.

CHAPTER NINE

1. "The Lebar Brecc Homily on S. Patrick," in *The Tripartite Life of Patrick,* ed. Whitley Stokes (Liechtenstein: Kraus Reprint, 1965), 2:285.

2. *Tripartite Life,* p. 13; for other examples of Patrick raising the dead, see pp. 15, 123, 135, 137, 177, 183, 199, 217.

3. Jocelin de Furness, *The Life and Acts of Saint Patrick, the Archbishop, Primate and Apostle of Ireland,* ed. J. C. O'Haloran (Philadelphia: Atkinson and Alexander, 1823), chaps. 6 and 7; see also chaps. 62, 80, 79, 81, 82, 144, 145, 185.

4. Ibid., chap. 80.

5. Ibid.

6. Ibid., chap. 181.

7. Roger of Wendover, *Flowers of History, Comprising the History of England from the Descent of the Saxons to A.D. 1235,* formerly Ascribed to Matthew Paris, ed. and trans. J. A. Giles (London: Henry G. Bohn, 1869), pp. 156–57.

8. "The Vision of Gunthelm and Other Visions Attributed to Peter the Venerable," ed. Giles Constable, *Revue Bénédictine* 76 (1956): 93–114.

9. "The Vision of Thurkill, Probably by Ralph of Coggeshall," ed. H. L. D. Ward, *Journal of the British Archaeological Society* 31 (1875): 432.

10. Furness, *Life,* chaps. 1, 169, 181.

11. Ibid., chap. 145.

12. Ibid., chap. 20.

13. "Lebar Brecc Homily on S. Patrick," p. 475.

14. Furness, *Life,* chap. 24.

15. Bernard of Clairvaux, *The Life and Death of Saint Malachy the Irishman,* trans. Robert T. Meyer (Kalamazoo: Cistercian Publications, 1978), p. 33.

16. *The Vision of Tnugdal,* trans. Jean-Michel Picard (Dublin: Four Courts Press, 1989), p. 111; Bernard, *Life and Death of Saint Malachy,* pp. 15, 33.

17. Gerald of Wales, *Expugnatio Hibernica,* ed. A. B. Scott and F. X. Martin (Dublin: Royal Irish Academy, 1978), p. 37. Gerald contrasts the brutality of the Irish

with the relatively civilized military practices of the French: "there [in France] knights are taken prisoner, here they are beheaded; there they are ransomed, here they are butchered" (p. 247).

18. Ibid., p. 67.

19. William of Newburgh, *Historia rerum anglicarum,* in *Chronicles of the Reigns of Stephen, Henry II and Richard I,* 2.26, ed. Richard Howlett, 4 vols., Rolls Series (London, 1884–89), 1:165–66.

20. Cited Robert Bartlett, *England under the Norman and Angevin Kings, 1075–1225* (Oxford: Clarendon Press, 2000), p. 101.

21. Gerald, *Expugnatio,* p. 233.

22. The coincidence of the legend of Saint Patrick and the Anglo-Norman miracle, though little commented on by historians of medieval Ireland, is something that Shane Leslie observed without elaboration very early on; see *Saint Patrick's Purgatory: A Record from History and Literature* (London: Burns Oats and Washbourne, 1932), p. xvi.

23. Marie Therese Flanagan, *Irish Society, Anglo-Norman Settlers, Angevin Kingship* (Oxford: Clarendon Press, 1989), pp. 57–58.

24. Flanagan suggests that in the course of the quarrel between the daughter of Henry I, Matilda, and her husband Geoffrey of Anjou, on the one hand, and his nephew Stephen, on the other, the Angevins might have recruited in Ireland (ibid., p. 69).

25. "Si la requist mult souent / De fin amur couertement. / E la dame li ad mande / Par vn messager prue / Que tut freit sa uolunte" ("Thus he besought her very often / For her true love covertly. / And the lady sent him word / By a secret messenger / That she would do all his will"). *Conquête d'Irlande: Song of Dermot and the Earl,* ed. Goddard Henry Orpen (Oxford: Clarendon Press, 1892), v. 54.

26. For a founding and lucid account of these extraordinarily complicated events which I have ruthlessly simplified, see Goddard Henry Orpen, *Ireland under the Normans, 1169–1216* (Oxford: Clarendon Press, 1968), 1:142ff.

27. A. J. Otway-Ruthven, *A History of Medieval Ireland* (London: Ernest Benn, 1968), p. 42.

28. John of Salisbury, *Metalogicon,* ed. Clemens C. Webb (Oxford: Clarendon Press, 1929), book 4, chap. 42; Orpen, *Ireland,* 1:295; Flanagan, *Irish Society,* p. 52.

29. Orpen, *Ireland,* 1:302.

30. Otway-Ruthven, *History of Medieval Ireland,* pp. 48–49. For a succinct discussion of Henry II in Ireland, see also W. L. Warren, *Henry II* (Berkeley: University of California Press, 1973), pp. 187–206; see also Bartlett, *England under the Norman and Angevin Kings,* pp. 85ff.

31. Gerald, *Expugnatio,* pp. 93, 95, 96.

32. Ibid., p. 97.

33. Cited Flanagan, *Irish Society,* p. 246; see also p. 229; Bartlett, *England,* p. 89; Otway-Ruthven, *History of Medieval Ireland,* p. 50.

34. On the abortive invasion of 1185, see the somewhat biased account of Gerald of Wales, who actually accompanied John (*Expugnatio,* p. 229); also Bartlett, *England,* pp. 88–90; Flanagan, *Irish Society,* pp. 263–65; Orpen, *Ireland,* 2:32, 93, 96, 105.

35. Ian Short, "Patrons and Polyglots: French Literature in Twelfth-Century

England," *Anglo-Norman Studies* 14 (1991): 240; *Conquête*, v. 671. The estimation of 300 Welsh might be an exaggeration. Otway-Ruthven claims there were only 100 (*Medieval Ireland*, p. 44); see also Orpen, *Ireland*, 1:162.

36. See Otway-Ruthven, *History of Medieval Ireland*, pp. 102–4; Orpen, *Ireland*, 1:110–13; Flanagan, *Irish Society*, pp. 175, 197; H. G. Richardson and G. O. Sayles, *The Administration of Ireland, 1172–1377* (Dublin: Stationery Office, 1963), p. 9.

37. Furness, *Life*, chap. 173.

38. Richard Fitz Nigel, *Dialogus de Scaccario: The Course of the Exchequer*, trans. Charles Johnson (Oxford: Clarendon Press, 1983), p. 63.

39. Bartlett, *England*, p. 98.

40. Stephen Greenblatt, *Hamlet in Purgatory* (Princeton: Princeton University Press, 2001), p. 74.

41. See my *Medieval French Literature and Law* (Berkeley: University of California Press, 1977), pp. 189–202.

42. Leslie, *Saint Patrick's Purgatory*, p. 6.

43. Ranulf Higden, *Polychronicon*, trans. John de Trevisa, chap. 35, cited ibid., p. 16.

44. See my *Medieval French Literature and Law*, pp. 111, 124, 128

45. C. H. Haskins, *Norman Institutions* (Cambridge: Harvard University Press, 1918), pp. 38, 60, 277.

46. *Très Ancien Coutumier de Normandie*, in *Coutumiers de Normandie*, ed. E.-J. Tardif (Rouen: Cagniard, 1881), p. 24.

47. Haskins, *Norman Institutions*, p. 239.

48. Otway-Ruthven, *History of Medieval Ireland*, p. 116.

49. Cited Orpen, *Ireland*, 2:129.

50. Otway-Ruthven, *History of Medieval Ireland*, p. 185.

51. Flanagan, *Irish Society*, pp. 237–38.

52. Gerald, *Expugnatio*, pp. 251, 253.

53. See Flanagan, *Irish Society*, pp. 7, 52, 54; J. F. O'Doherty, "Rome and the Anglo-Norman Invasion of Ireland," *Irish Ecclesiastical Record* 42 (1933): 131–45; Otway-Ruthven, *History of Medieval Ireland*, pp. 38–39.

54. I am aware, of course, that there is also a move away from monastic organization and toward centralization of church hierarchy in twelfth-century Ireland; see Warren, *Henry II*, pp. 189–90. I am also aware of the fact that the Cistercians were not the only order favored in Ireland by the Normans, under whose rule a considerable number of Benedictine, Augustinian, Victorine, and Arrosian houses were also founded; see Otway-Ruthven, *History of Medieval Ireland*, pp. 121, 127.

55. Flanagan, *Irish Society*, p. 71.

56. Bernard of Clairvaux, *Life and Death of Saint Malachy*, p. 22.

57. Flanagan, *Irish Society*, p. 103.

58. Orpen, *Ireland*, 1:260.

59. Ibid., 1:276–77.

60. Gerald, *Expugnatio*, p. 97.

61. See Seán Duffy, "The First Ulster Plantation: John de Courcy and the Men of

Cumbria," in *Colony and Frontier in Medieval Ireland,* ed. T. B. Barry, Robin Frame, and Katharine Simms (London: Hambledon Press, 1995), pp. 8–9.

62. Jacques Le Goff, *La naissance du Purgatoire* (Paris: Gallimard, 1981), p. 229.

63. See Claude Carozzi, *Le voyage de l'âme dans l'au-delà d'après la littérature latine (Ve–XIIe siècle)* (Rome: Ecole Française de Rome, 1994), p. 499.

64. Leslie, *Saint Patrick's Purgatory,* p. xvi.

65. See Carol Zaleski, *Otherworld Journeys: Accounts of Near-Death Experience in Medieval and Modern Times* (New York: Oxford University Press, 1987), p. 78.

66. See Hugh Shields, "The French Accounts," in Michael Haren and Yolande de Pontfarcy, *The Medieval Pilgrimage to St Patrick's Purgatory: Lough Derg and the European Tradition* (Enniskillen: Clogher Historical Society, 1988), p. 83.

67. Otway-Ruthven, *History of Medieval Ireland,* pp. 35–36.

68. See Flanagan, *Irish Society,* p. 131; Richardson and Sayles, *Administration of Ireland,* pp. 8–15; Warren, *Henry II,* p. 200.

69. Hugh de Lacy, 1172–73; Richard de Clare, earl of Pembroke, 1173–76; Raymond le Gros, 1176; William fitz Audelin, 1176; High de Lacy, 1177–81; John de Lacy, constable of Chester, 1181; Richard of the Peak, 1181; Hugh de Lacy 1181/82–1184; Philip of Worcester, 1184; John, lord of Ireland, 1185; John de Courcy, 1185–92(?).

70. *Rotuli litterarum clausarum in turri Londinensi asservati,* ed. Thomas D. Hardy, 2 vols. (London: G. Eyre and A. Spottiswoode, 1833–44), 1:497. See Bartlett, *England,* p. 88; Otway-Ruthven, *History of Medieval Ireland,* pp. 102, 144, 188.

71. Richardson and Sayles, *Administration of Ireland,* pp. 21, 24.

72. Ibid., p. 44.

73. Otway-Ruthven, *History of Medieval Ireland,* p. 190.

74. In fact, the "Vision of Thurkill" does contain an actual theater in which each sin is acted out before spectators. "Vision of Thurkill," pp. 433–34.

75. In previous visions the distinction is made between hell, whose torments are eternal, and another space whose torments are limited; see *The Letters of Saint Boniface,* trans. Ephraim Emerton (New York: Columbia University Press, 2000), p. 6; Bede, *Ecclesiastical History of the English People,* ed. Bertram Colgrave and R. A. B. Mynors (Oxford: Clarendon Press, 1969), p. 495; *Vision of Tnugdal,* p. 139.

76. See Joseph J. Duggan, "The Experience of Time as a Fundamental Element in the Stock of Knowledge in Medieval Society," in *Grundriss der romanischen Literaturen des Mittelalters* (Heidelberg: Winter, 1987), 11/1:127–34; Jacques Le Goff, "Temps de l'Église et temps du marchand," in *Pour un autre Moyen Age* (Paris: Gallimard, 1977), pp. 46–65.

77. This is a version of Purgatory that will culminate, of course, in the Dantean *contrapasso* according to which life on this earth is a preparation of the self for a relation to the self after the death of the self; see Carozzi, *Voyage,* p. 583.

78. Augustine, *The City of God,* trans. Marcus Dods (New York: Modern Library, 1950), p. 795.

79. Gregory the Great, *Dialogues* (Paris: Editions du Cerf, 1980), 3:189, 194, 185.

80. Carozzi, *Voyage,* p. 92–93.

81. See also vv. 1459, 1759.

82. Thomas Wright, *St. Patrick's Purgatory: An Essay on the Legends of Purgatory, Hell, and Paradise Current during the Middle Ages* (New York: New World Press, 1844), p. 9.

83. Bernard of Clairvaux, *Life and Death of Saint Malachy*, p. 28.

84. Roger of Wendover, *Flowers of History*, p. 154.

85. "Vision of Thurkill," p. 428.

86. Cited Le Goff, *Naissance*, p. 301.

87. *Vision of Tnugdal*, p. 112.

88. Ibid., p. 113.

89. Roger of Wendover, *Flowers of History*, pp. 159, 158.

90. "Vision of Thurkill," pp. 428, 432, 435, 436.

91. Le Goff, *Naissance*, p. 295.

92. See John Noonan, *The Scholastic Analysis of Usury* (Cambridge: Harvard University Press, 1957), pp. 56–57.

93. See R. H. Bloch, *Medieval French Literature and Law*, pp. 108–61.

94. "Vision of Thurkill," p. 434.

95. *Vision of Tnugdal*, pp. 127–28.

96. Zaleski, *Otherworld Journeys*, p. 39; see also Carol Zaleski, "St. Patrick's Purgatory: Pilgrimage Motifs in a Medieval Otherworld Journey," *Journal of the History of Ideas* 46 (1985): 480. Carozzi has suggested a link between Purgatory and the *wergeld*, a suggestion that, in fact, runs counter to my argument about the individualization of legal responsibility under the forms of justice that accompanied state formation (*Voyage*, p. 193).

97. Alan E. Bernstein, *The Formation of Hell: Death and Retribution in the Ancient and Early Christian Worlds* (Ithaca: Cornell University Press, 1993), p. 33.

98. "If death were a release from everything, it would be a boon for the wicked, because by dying they would be released not only from the body but also from their own wickedness together with the soul." "Phaedo," in *Collected Dialogues of Plato*, ed. Edith Hamilton and Huntington Cairns (New York: Pantheon Books, 1961), p. 89.

99. Le Goff, *Naissance*, pp. 15, 285; for a masterful general treatment of the question of life after death in early Christianity and the High Middle Ages, see Carolyn Bynum, *The Resurrection of the Body in Western Christianity, 200–1336* (New York: Columbia University Press, 1995).

100. A satiric version of this motif is to be found in the fabliau "St Peire et le jongleur."

101. "Vus i veïstes les tormenz/as chaitis ki furent dedenz;/tels en a greignurs, tels menurs,/solunc les uevres des plusurs:/cil ki plus pechierent el munt/greignurs tormenz iluec avrunt" ("You witnessed the torments/Of the wretches dwelling there;/Some suffered greatly, some less so,/According to their works./Those who sinned most in the world/Will have greater torments in purgatory" [v. 1731]).

102. See Marc Bloch, *Feudal Society* (Chicago: University of Chicago Press, 1966), 1:125; R. H. Bloch, *Medieval French Literature and Law*, pp. 68–69; Ferdinand Lot and Robert Fawtier, *Les institutions du moyen âge* (Paris: Presses Universitaires de France, 1958), 2:426–31.

103. *Très Ancien Coutumier,* p. 49; "The duke cannot make peace with a murderer until he has been reconciled with the relatives of the man he has killed" (p. 27).

104. Br. Laws, vol. 2, p. 226, l. 13, and p. 224, ll. 8 and 9. See Orpen, *Ireland,* 1:120–22.

105. Br. Laws, vol. 3, p. 68, ll. 12–14, and vol. 4, p. 248, l. 25. Cited, Orpen, *Ireland,* 1:122.

106. Orpen, *Ireland,* 1:123.

107. R. H. Bloch, *Medieval French Literature and Law,* p. 228–29.

108. Fitz Nigel, *Dialogus de Scaccario,* p. 75.

109. See J.-C. Payen, *Le motif du repentir dans la littérature française médiévale* (Geneva: Droz, 1968), pp. 1–93.

110. Le Goff, *Naissance,* p. 15.

111. See Colin Morris, *The Discovery of the Individual* (New York: Harper, 1972), pp. 65–70.

112. John of Salisbury, *Policraticus,* ed. Clemens C. Webb (Oxford: Oxford University Press, 1909), 1:19.

113. Carozzi, *Voyage,* pp. 635–36; Le Goff, *Naissance,* p. 290.

114. Abelard, *A Dialogue of a Philosopher with a Jew and a Christian,* trans. Pierre J. Payer (Toronto: Pontifical Institute of Mediaeval Studies, 1979), p. 152. For a discussion of the psychologizing of Purgatory, see Carozzi, *Voyage,* pp. 544–49.

115. Le Goff, *Naissance,* p. 390.

Index